...le as low as possible

...f engine 25¼ above ground.

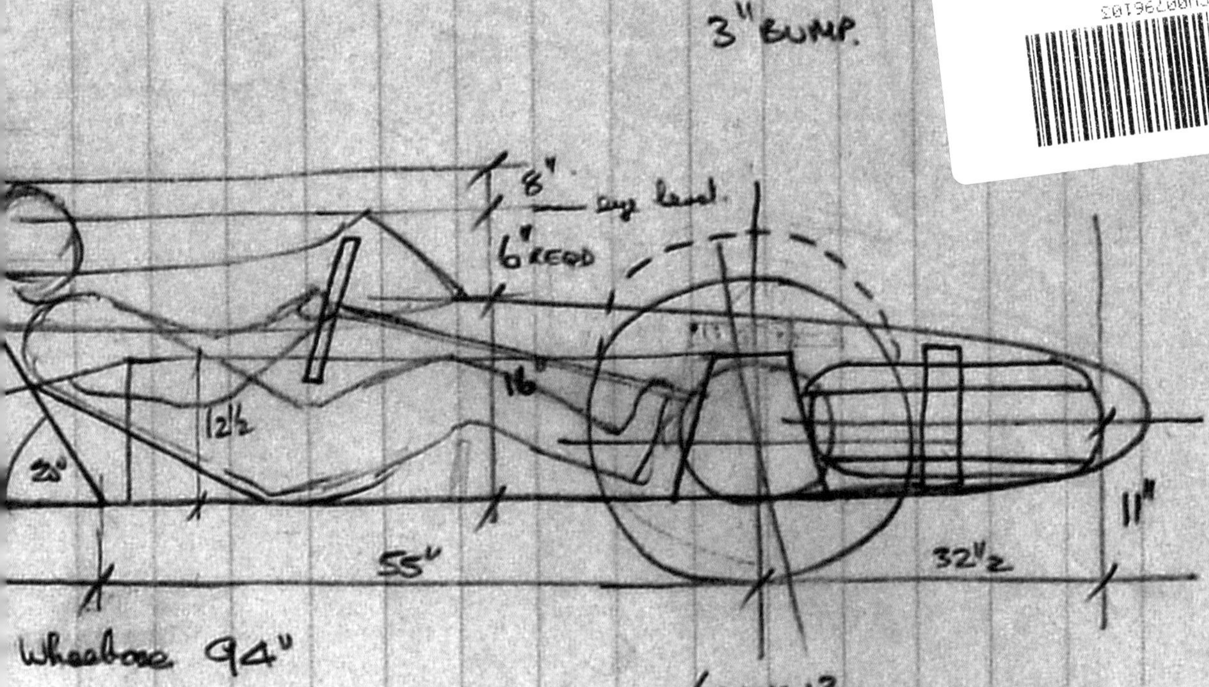

3" BUMP.

8"
6" REQD

eye level.

16

28°

12½

11"

55"   32½"

Wheelbase 94"

600 x 13
DIAM   25"
WIDTH   9"
TREAD   6"
TRACK   53"

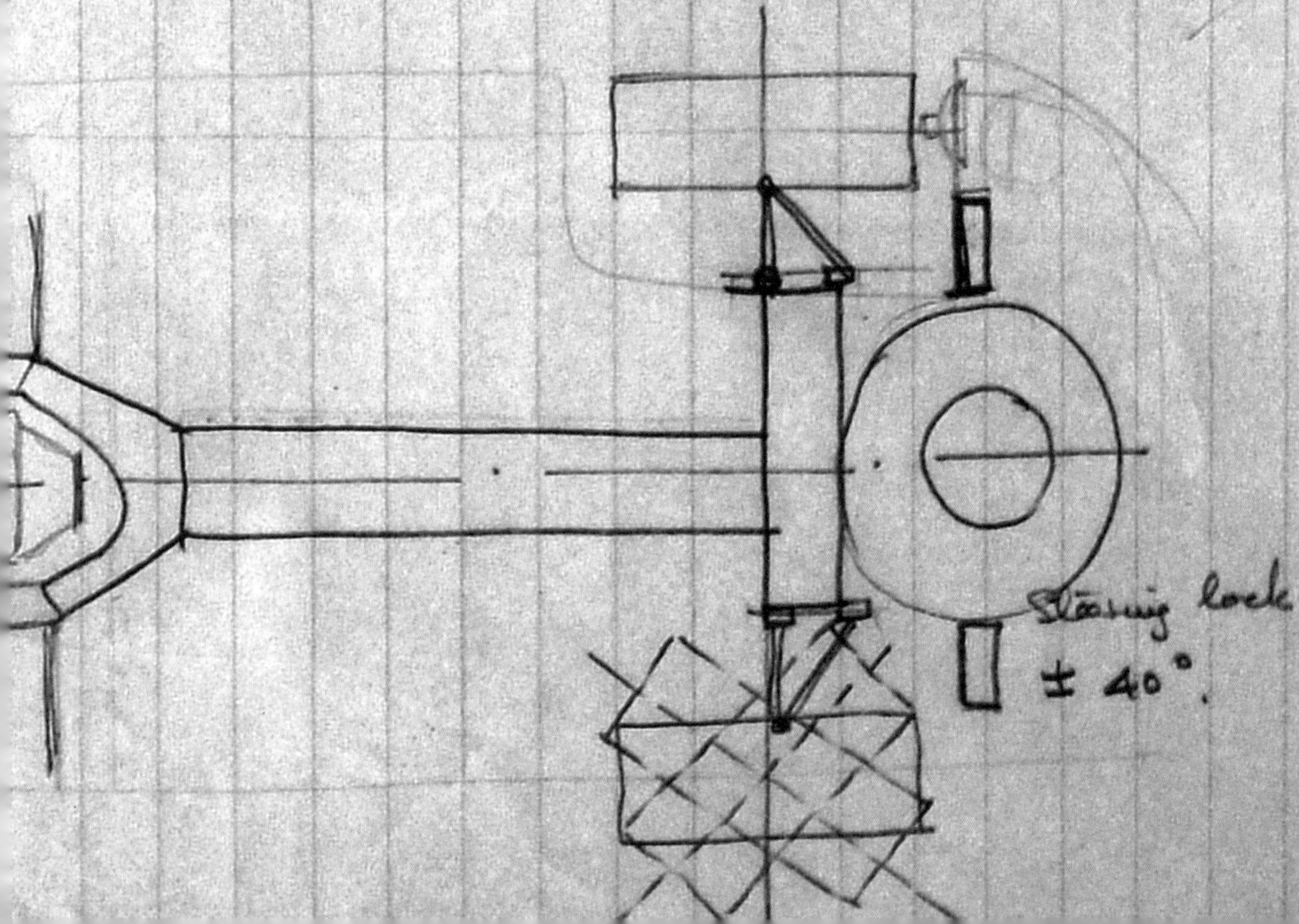

Steering lock
± 40°.

INSIDE THE INNOVATOR

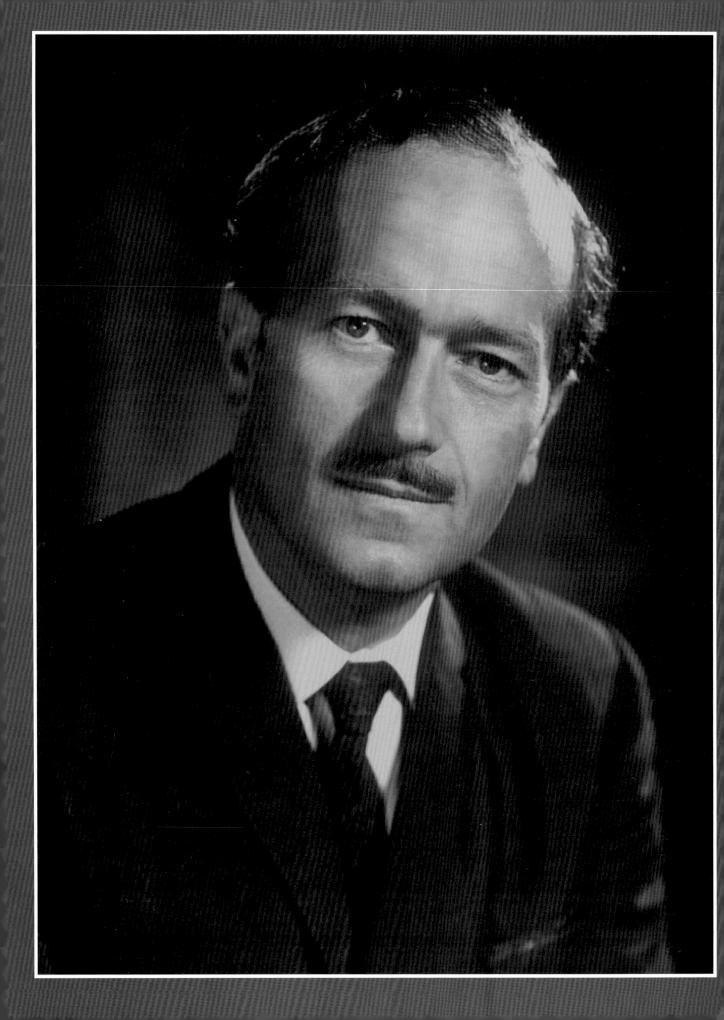

INSIDE THE INNOVATOR

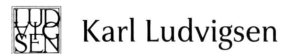

Karl Ludvigsen

Haynes Publishing

For two friends who helped,
Mario Andretti and Emerson Fittipaldi,
and the memory of Jim Clark

First published in May 2010
Reprinted October 2010 and February 2012

A catalogue record for this book is available from the
British Library

ISBN 978 1 84425 413 2

Library of Congress control no. 2010921619

Published by Haynes Publishing,
Sparkford, Yeovil, Somerset BA22 7JJ, UK
Tel: 01963 442030 Fax: 01963 440001
Int. tel: +44 1963 442030 Int. fax: +44 1963 440001
E-mail: sales@haynes.co.uk
Website: www.haynes.co.uk

Haynes North America Inc.
861 Lawrence Drive, Newbury Park,
California 91320, USA

Designed by James Robertson

Printed in the USA

CONTENTS

FOREWORD
by Emerson Fittipaldi

I am very honoured to be invited by my friend Karl Ludvigsen to write the foreword for his book about Colin Chapman. Karl's in-depth review of Colin's amazing achievements brings back the most vivid memories for me.

In my opinion Colin was one of the most important people in the history of motor racing. I had the privilege of not only starting my career in Formula 1 on his team, but also working with him for four years, when I won

my first races in Formula 1, and my first World Championship in 1972.

I remember how nervous I was when Colin asked me to come to the Lotus headquarters near Norwich and meet with him. After all, this was the man for whom some of my idols — Jim Clark, Graham Hill, and Jochen Rindt — had raced. By then Lotus was already a leading team in Formula 1, having won three Championships and also the Indy 500, in both cases with revolutionary cars and strategies.

That day in May of 1970 my legs were shaking throughout our conversation. When Colin told me that he wanted me to drive for his Formula 1 team, it was one of the most exhilarating feelings of my whole life. I'd arrived in England less than a year earlier and I had only raced in Formula 3, with Lotus cars, so it was amazing to be invited to race for one of the top teams in Formula 1.

I can safely say that Colin was one of the most important people in my career. He was a 'maestro' who taught me many things about developing a car and getting it in top competitive shape. I learned so much with him and am very privileged to have had that opportunity.

Colin was a real genius in building and developing racing cars — a brilliant and restless innovator. At a time when much of the effort to increase performance was focused on engine design, Colin was one of the first to give attention to aerodynamics, body structure and materials. This brought so many innovations to motor

Belying his youth, Emerson Fittipaldi soon established a reputation as a thinking, learning racing driver. This was right up Colin Chapman's street.

racing that it's hard to imagine what the sport would have been like without him.

Colin was extremely competitive. He had an unbreakable spirit. There was nothing he couldn't overcome. He was also very tense and focused at work. Despite all that, he took me in as a member of his family. I fondly recall spending time with him, Hazel and their kids at their farm.

By the time I joined Team Lotus, Colin had a great cadre in Peter Warr as team manager, Dick Scammell as team co-ordinator and Eddie Dennis, my mechanic. They were finishing the cycle of the Lotus 49, which had been very successful, and were developing the Lotus 72. It had many revolutionary features for its time, like the wedge shape, the inboard front brakes, the torsion-bar suspension. It turned out to be the best racing car that I ever drove.

Despite all his knowledge Colin was also a great listener. On so many race weekends when the car wasn't handling well on Friday, we'd go out to dinner — just the two of us — to talk about the performance of the car. He'd grill me with questions about how the car handled on each curve and each part of the circuit.

After dinner he went back to the garage. He knew exactly what needed to be done to the car. Back then I was very concerned about my communication skills, because I was still learning English, but he obviously understood everything I said because by Saturday morning the car would be handling great.

So it went, race after race. He would bring fresh changes to the car and improve it further. Needless to say, the Lotus 72 had a very long and successful life for a Formula 1 car, but the 72 that was racing in 1973 was very different to the one from 1970.

Many people took Colin for a cold or detached person. In fact he was the opposite — a very warm and caring person. The loss of Jim Clark, Mike Spence and then Jochen Rindt had a great impact on him. He told me that after they died he made a promise to himself not to be so close to his drivers in the future, but we still had a fantastic relationship.

His tense and competitive spirit were present in all aspects of his life. When we were invited to open the London Auto Show in 1972, we were supposed to fly from the Lotus headquarters to London. The weather was miserable with no visibility, but Colin was determined to get there on time so we flew anyway — with him piloting the plane, of course.

When we got to the airport in London, he told the driver who met us to move aside and took the wheel, racing like a pro through horrible London traffic. I still

Pictured in 1971, Fittipaldi was struggling with unsuitable tyres on his 72. Effort invested then came good with a World Championship in 1972.

remember him driving on the wrong side of the street in Knightsbridge, flashing the car's lights at the startled drivers who were driving on the right side! It was one of the scariest and — in hindsight — funniest moments of my life. Needless to say, we got there on time.

God bless you Colin!

At Watkins Glen in 1970 Fittipaldi had strict instructions to beat Ferrari-mounted Jacky Ickx to preserve Jochen Rindt's World Championship. He obliged, winning the race as well.

INTRODUCTION

How do you get to grips with the work of a legendary engineer and innovator? That was my aim. I wanted to understand how Colin Chapman went about his tasks, how he coped with the technical challenges he faced and how he interacted with people inside and outside his businesses. Of course I wasn't the first to address such topics so I had to find a way to do it that would enlighten me and you as well.

My first approach was chronological, following the Chapman career year by year through its ups, downs, ups and more ups. It was the proven formula of Chapman biographers Jabby Crombac and Mike Lawrence. But I couldn't convince myself that it was revelatory. At various times Colin would move forward in some disciplines, stall in others and fall back in more. It didn't seem to suit an engineering agenda.

The book only took wing when I adopted a thematic approach. This allowed me to follow Colin Chapman through specific disciplines to see how he coped with them through the years, how his thinking evolved – or didn't – with time and experience. I found this adventure enlightening and hope you will too.

The only drawback is that you'll have to do any needed cross-referencing between, say, suspensions and aerodynamics. However, I hope you'll find this easy enough as you become familiar with the main phases of Chapman's activity. To assist a timeline of the Chapman career is provided (page 13). Those phases have their

Pictured by Ove Nielsen late in his illustrious career, Colin Chapman had a lot on his mind. Above all he was searching for the next step forward in racing-car design.

own overlaps as well, such as the incredible 1960s when he was active in Formula 1 plus lesser formulas, sports-racing and Indianapolis, all at the same time.

In these pages I've tried to let Chapman speak for himself whenever possible. This has its risks. An entire industry is dedicated to revisionist analysis of the utterances of Chairman Chapman. Some see him as a veritable Baron Munchausen, a legendary spinner of tall tales, who deliberately and blithely falsified history. He's accused of arrogating all credit to himself at the expense of his hard-working assistants.

There's evidence for this. His early published accounts omitted many allies and conflated facts and events. Keith Duckworth recalled a Chapman who gave journalists different stories about problems with his cars, seemingly for the mental exercise it afforded. One designer was shunted aside after he revealed too much in print about the inner workings of Lotus Grand-Prix-car design.

In the early days of Lotus people worked for Chapman for the sheer challenge and excitement of it. They didn't fret about not being mentioned. 'I didn't mind that Colin got the credit,' said engineer Gilbert 'Mac' McIntosh about his behind-the-scenes activity, 'because Colin needed the credibility. He was the front man for us all.'

Having reflected on their Chapman years, however, many participants are stepping forward to tell their stories. It has been my responsibility to reconcile their testimony with Chapman's own accounts where they involve engineering innovation. In this effort I can only be sure that I've failed. I hope that those involved will credit me with having made a good-faith effort to follow the threads of Lotus design evolution. Needless to say, any errors of fact and interpretation are down to the author alone.

I was gratified to discover the extent to which Colin Chapman is quotable on his own work. Stripped of their ambiguities, his 1954 writings have value. For public consumption he wrote about the design of his Formula 2 Twelve, in defence of light racing cars, on his change to rear engines, on the features of the 77 and on his disappointments with the 88. Interviews with photojournalist David Phipps in 1960 and 1967 are useful in spite of – or because of – Phipps's closeness to the Lotus effort.

Early visits to Hornsey by the staff of *Motor Sport* convey something of the excitement of life at Lotus. In 1958 I interviewed Colin at Monza about the design of the Sixteen and his new transaxle for an article in *Sports Cars Illustrated*. In 1966, first year of the new 3.0-litre Formula 1, Graham Gauld interviewed Chapman as did Philip Turner and Charles Bulmer for *Motor*. Sports and technical editors respectively, Turner and Bulmer produced pure gold from their intelligent and extensive questioning. Fortunately they did the same again in 1969.

The knowledgeable Gordon Wilkins interviewed Chapman in 1963 and John Ezard did so in 1969. Interviews of value in the 1970s were those of Ray Hutton in 1972, Jeremy Walton in 1976 and, at a crucial juncture and to great effect, Peter Windsor in 1979. In 1972 I visited Hethel to see the launch of the 907 engine's production. Near the end of the 1978 season I shadowed both Chapman and Mario Andretti closely for a profile of the Italian-American racer.

Many others have written and spoken about their involvement with Colin Chapman. Their works are referenced in the Bibliography and also in the text where relevant. Several authors deserve special credit. Former Lotus engineer Peter Ross not only wrote the invaluable *Lotus – The Early Years*, putting straight many of the contradictions of the Hornsey and pre-Hornsey era, but also edits *Historic Lotus*, the journal of the Historic Lotus Register. I have adopted Peter's Lotus model-numbering conventions for this book.

Most valuable have been first-person accounts by people like Peter Ross who worked closely with Colin Chapman. In the first rank are books by Andrew Ferguson, Robin Read, Tony Rudd and Peter Wright. All have great worth as testimony from the cutting edges of Lotus history. Also of importance are the works of Doug Nye, Michael Oliver, Anthony Pritchard and John Tipler. For a splendid overview of Chapman's life and work we are grateful to the much-missed Gerard 'Jabby' Crombac for his biography, published in 1986.

Jabby's book drew criticism for its omission of the DeLorean saga which cast a shadow over the end of Colin Chapman's career. No similar reproach can be levelled at Mike Lawrence, who deals with the DeLorean topic in detail. I make some references to DeLorean but have found little value in going into that story in a book which is concerned with Chapman's engineering manners and methods.[1] Since the DeLorean car was an extrapolation of known Lotus design methods, largely carried out by the chief's lieutenants, I saw no need to expand on it in these pages.

Anyone writing about Chapman must face the fact that they could interview an almost infinite number of people about him and never get around to writing a word. My choice of interviewees focused on two Mikes. One was Mike Costin, who worked closely with Chapman at both Lotus and Cosworth. His frank and often funny take on Colin was invaluable. The other was Mike Warner, a recommendation and introduction of my friend Nic Portway. This Mike provided a business perspective that was unique and incisive. I owe warm thanks to both.

Another Mike, Mike Kimberley, did his best to assist before his recent retirement as CEO of Lotus, as did quality chief Andy Pleavin, but Hethel's cupboards were bare. Mike gave me a pithy panorama of his former chief, however. Nearby, in the erstwhile quarters of Team Lotus, Classic Team Lotus thrives today. There since 1991 Colin's son Clive has been looking after the team's own racing Lotuses and those of clients with the help of such experienced people as mechanic Bob Dance and designer Martin Ogilvie. Clive kindly reviewed the page proofs and made many helpful suggestions.

Fortunately some Team Lotus archives survive in Classic Team's premises. I'm very grateful to Clive for letting me see them and make copies for research. They gave fresh insights into many aspects of the Chapman approach to both business and engineering – disciplines uniquely combined in the Guv'nor. Many thanks are owed to Clive and his team for their generous assistance.

I pestered many others in my search for Chapman information. Bill Bradshaw of prop-liners.com found

---

1   Perhaps some personal recollections are allowable. When I had lunch with John DeLorean at London's Connaught Hotel in 1980 he told me that his discussions with Chapman about design of the DMC-12 had led to the idea that the Lotus companies might be folded into the growing DeLorean empire. As they explored this in depth, however, a snag arose. 'The level of financial disclosure that the SEC required for such a deal,' said John, 'would have meant Chapman going directly to jail.'
   Former Corvette chief engineer Zora Arkus-Duntov was a consultant to DeLorean on the DMC-12 project. In a communication to me at the time he was scathing about Hethel's contribution, saying, 'Lotus engineering is the worst.' The company hadn't yet mastered the level of design that was needed to build cars at a rate an order of magnitude faster than it was used to.

While shadowing Andretti and Chapman for a 1977 magazine profile, the author took photos at Watkins Glen. In the rabble of press men and hangers-on he is wearing a flat cap near the centre.

pictures of the Convair CV240 airliner that clearly show its 'wobbly-web' wheels. ZF's Claudia Mangold and Janine Vogler searched out information on that company's transaxles and personnel while Grahame Walter provided information on his wind-tunnel tests and copies of early Lotus test reports. Alec Osborn not only gave information about the BRM 'wing-car' project but also loaned rare images of the wind-tunnel model. Charles Helps and Graham Haley identified an unknown driver in a key photograph.

Long-time friend Bill Milliken vividly pictured some Chapman incidents. Charles Bulmer, an early Chapman friend and advisor, provided valuable insights. Peter Wright and Peter Ross took time to respond to specific questions. Duncan Rabagliati kindly supplied a scan of the cutaway of the Rhiando Trimax, which he owns and races. On my team Gil Pearson transcribed texts and interviews while Mike Holland carried out periodical research in the Ludvigsen Library to find Chapman references.

I want to express my deepest thanks to all whose remarks, researches and writings have contributed to this work. I hope and trust that they consider that they are adequately and accurately quoted and credited. In some instances I have sub-edited quotations for brevity and clarity without affecting their meaning.

I'm deeply indebted to Mark Hughes, Steve Rendle, James Robertson and the rest of the team at Sparkford for their efforts in this book's design and production. I much appreciate the keen and knowledgeable backing that they've given to its concept and realisation through several twists and turns.

Throughout the 'Chapman project' my wife Annette was warmly supportive, as she has been throughout our 25 years together. Without her generous and loving assistance, coping with the demands of the Ludvigsen Library and a car-obsessed husband, none of my book projects would have come to fruition. Thank you very much, Annette.

What would Colin Chapman think of this book's review of his designs and activities? 'He had a drive to improve,' said son Clive, 'so much so that he didn't like looking back.' Too bad, Colin, I say. We enjoy looking back – and learning. You've given us a lot to think about.

Karl Ludvigsen
Hawkedon
Suffolk
December 2009

COLIN CHAPMAN TIMELINE

1928

Anthony Colin Bruce Chapman is born on 19 May in Richmond, Surrey.

1944

The 16-year-old Chapman meets his future wife Hazel Williams at a dance in Hornsey, North London, where his father owns the Railway Hotel.

1945

Chapman enters University College to study engineering. After he crashes his motorbike his parents buy him a Morris 8 tourer.

1947

Flying solo with University Air Squadron begins Chapman's lifetime passion for aviation. His spare-time career as second-hand car dealer collapses when the basic petrol ration is withdrawn in October.

1948

Chapman completes first Lotus trials special in Hazel's father's lock-up garage and graduates with BSc (Eng) as structural engineer.

1949

While serving with the RAF, Chapman builds second trials car during his leave.

Colin Chapman's Lotus Mark VI opened a new world of racing to enthusiasts in Britain and abroad. Bob Hicks raced his to third place in the third race at Brands Hatch on 11 April 1955.

1950

Chapman drives his Lotus to victory in marque's first race, a five-lap scratch event at Silverstone, beating Dudley Gahagan's Type 35 Bugatti. Chapman joins British Aluminium as salesman.

1951

Lotus Mark III, built in Allen brothers' workshop in Wood Green, is unbeatable in 750 Formula racing.

1952

Demand for replicas of Mark III inspires setting up of Lotus Engineering Company on 1 January and move to stable behind Railway Hotel. Business partner Michael Allen works full time while Chapman and Nigel Allen work whenever they are not at their day jobs, including weekends. First Mark VI is built and raced. Lotus Engineering becomes limited-liability company on 25 September.

1953

Mike Costin joins Lotus to work same hours as Chapman. Production of Mark VI begins; Lotus wins seven of nine 1172 Formula races. Chapman family and Hazel Williams buy out Allen's interest in Lotus Engineering.

1954

Peter Gammon wins 14 races out of 17 with his Mark VI. Debut of streamlined Mark VIII in British Empire Trophy at Oulton Park. First international race by Lotus sees VIII finish fourth in Eifelrennen at Nürburgring. Chapman in Mark VIII beats Porsche to win sports-car race at British

GP meeting. Chapman marries Hazel and resigns from British Aluminium.

1955

Chapman and Mike Costin start working full-time for Lotus. Mark X created to carry 2-litre Bristol six. Mark IX, designed to carry promising new 1.1-litre Coventry-Climax FWA four, enters production and races successfully.

1956

Pathbreaking Lotus Eleven introduced. Chapman designs new space-frame for F1 Vanwall and joins Vanwall team for French GP at Reims. Crashes in practice, aborting a promising GP career. Chapman awarded Ferodo Gold Trophy. His first child, Jane, is born.

1957

Chapman greatly improves Grand Prix BRM suspension. With 750cc Climax engine, Eleven wins Index of Performance at Le Mans. First Lotus single-seater, Twelve F.2 car, makes its debut, as do Lotus Seven and Elite.

1958

First F1 race for Lotus at Monaco and first points won when Lotus 12 finishes fourth in Belgian GP. New low-line F1 Sixteen and sports-racing Fifteen introduced. Second daughter Sarah is born. Season's F1 points: 3.

1959

Strut-type front suspension proves a failure on new Seventeen for 1.1-litre class, which Lotus leaves at the season's end. Expansion to produce Elite road car prompts move to new factory in Cheshunt. Season's F1 points: 5.

1960

Chapman considers mid-engined Eighteen his first pure F1 design. Cosworth-Ford-powered Lotus 18 dominates Formula Junior. Stirling Moss wins Lotus's first F1 victory driving Rob Walker Eighteen in Monaco GP. Begins eleven straight seasons in which a Lotus will win a Grand Prix every year. Season's F1 points: 34.

1961

Formula Junior 20 is first Lotus to have new 'laid-back' driving position. Formula 1 21 introduced with inboard front springing. Innes Ireland wins first championship Grand Prix for Team Lotus at Watkins Glen, only to be dropped from team. Season's F1 points: 32.

1962

Introduction of space-frame F1 24 followed by radical 'monocoque' 25. Launch of new Ford 105E/109E-based twin-cam Lotus engine, used in new Elan. Jim Clark's twin-cam-engined Lotus 23 dominates 1,000km race at Nürburgring until fractured exhaust fills cockpit with fumes. Clive Chapman born. Clark leads Lotus Grand Prix team. Season's F1 points: 37.

1963

First Lotus entry with 29 in Indianapolis 500 sees Jim Clark placing second. Wins USAC race at Milwaukee. Clark becomes world drivers' champion and Lotus wins manufacturers' championship. Lotus Cortina launched. Season's F1 points: 58.

1964

Shunned by Ford for its Le Mans programme, Chapman envisages retaliation with Type 30 family of mid-engined backbone-frame cars. Ford V8-engined Lotus 30 sports-racer is not a success. Season's F1 points: 40.

1965

Jim Clark wins second world championship with Lotus-Climax and wins Indianapolis 500 with Lotus-Ford. Lotus is champion constructor. BARC award gold medals to Chapman and Clark for Indy victory. Chapman persuades Ford to invest £100,000 in development of new F1 Cosworth engine, the DFV. Season's F1 points: 56.

1966

Lotus begins move to new factory on ex-USAF airfield at Hethel, Norfolk. Mid-engined Lotus Europa introduced. New 38 and 42F raced at Indy. Clark wins US Grand Prix with BRM-powered 43, using engine as rear structure. Season's F1 points: 21.

1967

Move to Hethel completed. Graham Hill rejoins Lotus. New Ford V8-engined Lotus 49 dominates F1 racing in sheer speed from its first appearance in Dutch GP at Zandvoort but failures give makes' championship to consistent Brabham. Season's F1 points: 50

1968

Chapman becomes millionaire at 40 when 48 per cent of Lotus is floated on Stock Exchange. Elan +2 introduced. Radical four-wheel-drive 56 with turbine power amazes Indy with new wedge shape and almost wins. Gold Leaf Team Lotus is first team to run under new rules allowing cars to carry sponsors' livery. Jim Clark dies in F2 race at Hockenheim. Graham Hill wins world championship and Lotus wins manufacturers' title. Season's F1 points: 62.

1969

Newly created Group Lotus takes over as holding company for subsidiaries including Lotus Cars and Lotus Components. Collapses of huge wings on Lotus 49B contribute to their banning. Hub failures keep four-wheel-drive turbo-Ford 64 from qualifying at Indy. Grand Prix 4x4 63 proves ineffectual. Season's F1 points: 47.

1970

Radical wedge-shaped 72 with side radiators introduced. Posthumous world title for Jochen Rindt (Lotus-Ford). Lotus wins manufacturers' championship with six victories from 13 races. Season's F1 points: 59.

1971

Chapman moves into marine field with personal acquisition of Moonraker Boats. Problems with new tyres blunt 72's attack. Diversions with turbine-powered 56B for Grand Prix racing erode Lotus competitiveness. First season since entering F1 that Lotus scores no wins. Season's F1 points: 21.

1972

New Jensen-Healey sports car uses Lotus engine. Emerson Fittipaldi wins world championship with 72 and Lotus win manufacturers' title. Season's F1 points: 61.

1973

Caterham Cars take over manufacturing rights to Seven. Robbing points from each other, Fittipaldi and Peterson finish 2–3 in F1 drivers' championship and take Lotus to manufacturers' championship. Season's F1 points: 92.

1974

Lotus type 907 16-valve twin-cam four-cylinder engine announced for new Elite, first of new upmarket car range to be introduced. New Grand Prix 76, launched with automatic clutch, proves a disappointment. In updated 72 Ronnie Peterson scores three wins. Season's F1 points: 42.

1975

Eclat 2+2 introduced. Team Lotus reverts to updated 72, scoring no wins and plummeting to seventh in makes standings. Chapman returns from holiday with fresh thoughts on Formula 1 cars and demands new research. Season's F1 points: 9.

1976

Mid-engined Esprit, with Giugiaro styling, launched. Chapman's father Stan dies in road accident. 'Adjustable' 77 F1 car introduced and Mario Andretti joins Team Lotus, winning last race of the season. Season's F1 points: 29.

1977

Colin Chapman moves office to Ketteringham Hall base of Team Lotus. Ground effect comes to F1 with introduction of Lotus 78. Season's F1 points: 62.

1978

Lotus agrees to engineer DeLorean road car. Mario Andretti wins F1 world championship with Lotus 79. Lotus wins manufacturers' championship. Season's F1 points: 86.

1979

Lotus signs joint marketing pact in US market with Rolls-Royce. Extreme ground-effect Lotus 80 introduced but is a step too far. No F1 victories for Lotus. Season's F1 points: 39.

1980

Chapman turns attention to light-aircraft developments including microlights and aero engines. Lotus 81 introduced as interim F1 design that gives modest results with best placing second at Brazil for Elio de Angelis. Experiments conducted with 'twin-chassis' 86. Nigel Mansell joins team. Season's F1 points: 14.

1981

Conclusion of DeLorean project. To Chapman's extreme disappointment 'twin-chassis' Lotus 88 Grand Prix car is banned by FISA. Like interim conventional 87, it pioneers carbon-fibre for frame tub. Best placing is Mansell's third in Belgium. Season's F1 points: 22.

1982

US marketing partnership with Rolls-Royce ends. F1 91, evolved from 87, enjoys modest success with a win for Elio de Angelis in Austria – Chapman's last victory. After returning from December FISA meeting in Paris, Colin Chapman dies on 16 December of massive heart attack. Season's F1 points: 30.

Chapter 1

CONCEIVING CONCEPTS

He wasn't a detail designer and never had any ideas of limits and fits. He never seemed to take the disciplines of detail design on board. But Colin was certainly the most brilliant conceptual engineer that I've known.

Keith Duckworth

In 1948 conceptual thinking was far from the immediate concerns of Anthony Colin Bruce Chapman. At the age of 20 he was hard at work in a Muswell Hill garage where an innocent 1929 Austin Seven was being transformed into a sporty special for that peculiarly British sport, mud-plugging trials over sodden hilly countryside. Work with friends in the lock-up of his future wife's parents had to be shared with studies towards his civil engineering degree, which he received that year from University College, London University.

The son of a hotel owner in North London's Hornsey, Colin Chapman exploited his early interest in cars by trading in used autos as a sideline to his studies in the years after the war. Shared with Colin Dare, a fellow student, this profitable trading came to a screeching halt in October of 1947 when used-car prices collapsed after the basic petrol ration was withdrawn. Liquidated at a loss, Chapman's final stock consisted of the Austin which he was fitting with the angular radiator surround that won its 'Rolls-Royce Austin' nickname.

The car-trading lark aroused young Chapman's critical faculties, he recalled in 1954: 'My first vehicle had been a

Thoughtful as always, Colin Chapman kept his grey matter buzzing with ideas for new car concepts, even on race weekends.

three-wheeler of a make which happily is no longer produced. I kept it for slightly less than 29 hours because in driving home after buying it I was so appalled at the way it handled that the next day I decided on a re-sale. This came off. Someone who was perhaps less critical than I took it away and left me £10 the richer. It seemed such easy money that I bought and sold a few more semi-derelict machines after that. As motor cars they were all right but they were all found wanting as far as I was concerned. I wanted to enjoy my motoring so gradually the idea of a Chapman "special" grew and grew.'

Penury prompted early manifestation of one of Colin Chapman's conceptual mantras, related early colleague and Lotus historian Peter Ross: 'What set Colin apart from other contemporary racing-car designers was his very practical approach. This was in part dictated by his almost total lack of working capital. Whilst other companies could afford to start with a blank sheet of paper, Colin's first thought was, "What existing part can be used or what existing part can I adapt to do what I want?" For example the outer half-shaft of the [1954 Mark VIII] back axle was made from an Austin A90 Atlantic half-shaft.'

Continued Ross, 'Colin used his charm and enthusiasm to persuade large companies like Hardy-Spicer to send him dimensioned drawings of virtually every part they currently made for the British car industry. In most cases

Above: *A proclivity for sourcing from car makers' parts bins led to Ford components for the bumper and windscreen of the Lotus Elan +2. This a 1970 US model.*

these could be used without alteration or – with a small amount of machining – could be adapted. Where this was not possible most companies would have had a forging made or would have had something turned out of a solid block of metal.' Knowing this only too well, Chapman had the guile and persuasiveness to get these companies to supply the raw forgings from which he could machine the parts he needed.

'Instead of using space which he did not have – and engaging staff – to make these things himself,' added Peter Ross, Chapman 'built up a relationship with many small engineering companies who would make patterns, castings and machine parts, whose expertise was such that detailed instructions on fits and tolerances were not needed. We would supply the bearings and they would ensure the right type of fit.'

Left: *A popular offering, the Lotus Seven cleverly exploited the frame of the Eleven with cycle wings and a simple specification to produce 'a cheap kit car for the boys'.*

This ideally suited the Chapman style, which was conceptual rather than detailed. 'He never had any ideas of limits and fits,' said engine wizard Keith Duckworth, who worked both with and for Chapman. 'For mechanical fits, lots of things require clearances to be about right to work and you've got to make bits to within reasonable limits to make certain the greatest and biggest fits and differences will still operate.'

'He was a magpie,' recalled former Lotus engineer Ron Hickman. Colin Chapman never shook his passion for exploiting existing components where they were available from the motor industry and where they suited – or could be made to suit – his requirements. For example, said Hickman, the Elan +2 was designed around the windscreen of Ford's Consul Classic Capri, whose glistening chromed surround appealed to his boss. Bumpers too were adapted, often influencing the shape of a Lotus. The +2's nose had to be widened five inches to take the bumper from the Ford Anglia.

For better or worse – often the latter – this proclivity was a frequent source of criticism from the motoring press. They took delight in cataloguing the mass-produced sources of switches, latches, vents, handles and other components inside and outside Lotus production cars. Nor were the components always the best available. With Lotus unable to commit to volume purchases and often operating on a financial knife edge, suppliers wouldn't give it priority for quality.

Nevertheless Mike Warner, who tackled quality in the 1960s, defended the inherent robustness of Lotus's bought-in parts: 'A lot of the faults that came across with Lotus were of the assembly-design aspect rather than the actual structural make-up of the car, the castings and so forth. If you look at the competition side of the Elans, for example, they really got hammered and thrashed and a lot of them used standard components.'

Instead faults were introduced at the assembly stage, especially electrical. 'We allowed the electrics to be developed on the line by the electrical fitters that were fitting the harnesses, fitting the lights,' Warner recalled. 'We never actually had a competent electrical engineer go through and look at all the various loadings on the circuitry and design it.' Nor did Lotus have effective inspection of incoming goods, added Warner: 'We didn't have a standards room. We never had what I would call the correct facilities for doing our own inspection. So I had to do it at the premises of the suppliers using other people's equipment.'

A big-picture man, Colin Chapman left issues like

One of the world's most iconic sports cars, the Seven was introduced in 1957 to general acclaim. It continues in production at Caterham Cars.

The Seven was ideal for track as well as road as Chris. Davis showed, pedalling his Series 2 example at Brands Hatch in the early 1960s. .He was still competing in 732NKR 50 years later.

Caught in an earnest pose in 1969, Mike Warner was already working on a new version of the Seven to replace the money-losing Series 3.

these in the hands of others. 'Colin was *totally* uninterested in a car five minutes after it had been launched,' recalled sales chief Graham Arnold. 'He was a great man for proving that something could be done, but that was that. He would have the baby but someone else had to rock the cradle and change the nappies.'

Chapman's first series-production Lotus was the Mark VI, introduced in 1952 and offered in kit form from 1953 to 1955. This raw front-cycle-winged Lotus most often had side-valve Ford power. Some 100 were made before production was stopped at the end of 1955 to give way to envelope-bodied sports-racing cars and preparation of the Elite.

For better or worse the Mark VI established Lotus as a maker of uncompromising sports cars for the rabid enthusiast. That Lotus had abandoned this market was bemoaned in 1957 by Colin's wife Hazel at a Sunday lunch at their home, Gothic Cottage at Monken Hadley in Barnet, Hertfordshire north of London. Lotus no longer made 'a cheap kit car like the VI for "the boys",' she complained to Chapman and colleague Gilbert 'Mac' McIntosh. The men were nominated to do the washing-up after Hazel's lunchtime cooking, but they spotted a way out.

'Hazel was intrigued,' recalled McIntosh, 'and Colin could see she had her toes dug in so he proposed that in return for doing the washing up herself we could have a look at the idea.' This was to base a car on the Eleven chassis without all the costly aerodynamic bodywork made by Williams & Pritchard.

'By tea time we had done a weight check,' said McIntosh, 'cost estimate, quick performance check, done a few sketches of bodywork and the idea looked good – so good we got out of washing up tea and got on with the suspension calcs and drawings. We had finished by midnight. Colin ordered the springs on Monday, moved an Eleven chassis to the panel beaters and the Seven was running by the following weekend,'

Thus reborn was a concept that had been established at the very start of the Lotus legend, an enduring concept that many still associated with Lotus long after the company itself stopped making Sevens. It was anything but comfortable, road-testers agreed, but compensated with rewarding performance. 'When driving the Lotus Seven in reasonably traffic-free conditions,' said *The Autocar* in 1957, 'one soon forgets minor discomforts in the exhilaration of its performance and the manner of its achievement.' And this with a humble Ford Prefect engine and three-speed gearbox!

Many improvements, including flared front wings, marked the Series 2 or 'Super' Seven of 1960. 'With all

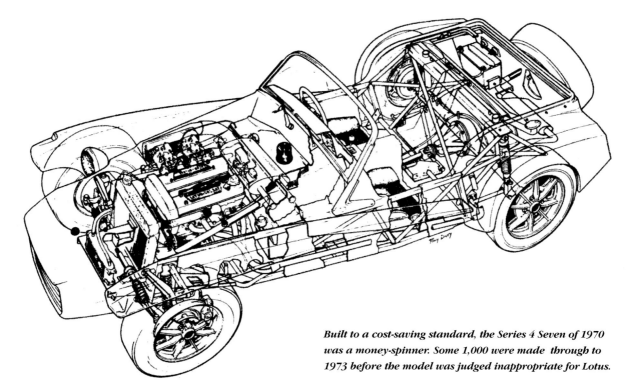

Built to a cost-saving standard, the Series 4 Seven of 1970 was a money-spinner. Some 1,000 were made through to 1973 before the model was judged inappropriate for Lotus.

its discomforts,' said *Road & Track* in 1962, 'the Lotus Super Seven was one of the most inviting cars ever to fall into our collective hands. It is the very embodiment of that "thinly disguised racing car" people are always talking about and, while it has serious shortcomings for day-in, day-out transportation, few cars offer as much excitement and fun. Actually the Super Seven should be classified as a racing car, pure and simple, and the fact that it can also be driven on the street is just an incidental advantage, not its primary function. Only on a race track can the car be driven as it should be.'

In 1968 the Seven moved on to a Series 3 version. This delighted enthusiasts but not Lotus bookkeepers, who reported losses of £150 per car. Nevertheless the Seven concept was so powerful that it deserved a rescue. This was engineered by Mike Warner, then in charge of Lotus Components, without reference to Chapman. He worked with engineer Peter Lucas to create a new Seven that took advantage of the new facilities that had been installed to build the Europa and Elan.

The Series 4 Seven had an all-in-one glass fibre body that dropped over a frame of mixed tubes and sheet. With by far the best passenger protection of any Seven it was seen as effete by many compared to the older model, now being sold in kit form by Caterham Cars. However, it had the advantage of being profitable: 'We ended up making about two hundred and thirty quid profit on every car,' Mike Warner recalled.

The Series 4's creation was a surprise to Colin Chapman. He first saw it in a directors' presentation of

new models near the control tower at the Hethel aerodrome where Lotus was based. Warner opened the hangar doors to reveal three versions of the Series 4. 'When Colin got really mad and excited', said Warner, 'he'd drop into North London patois, which was a bit Cockney-ish. Hazel and the wives were standing there and he said, "'ere, Hazel, he's made a bloody new car with my badge on! I'm not having a bloody badge on the front of a car that I haven't seen and tried!"'

Warner was in the doghouse big time. 'One day I drove in in my Series 4,' he said, 'which had a hard top, little sliding windows. Colin just arrived and pulled in alongside me. I expected to see what I saw, which was a Chapman glower, which is where the hooded eyes come over. "Well," he said, "I hear it's selling. I might as well try the bloody thing. Come on, let's go." Off we went round the track. He was really hammering the car. He rattled off about ten points, six of which we were already working on; he'd picked them up immediately. When we got back in he cocked his head in that way of his and looked around and said "Yes, mm, okay". Off he went. And that was it.' A new Seven passed muster.

The Seven's demise at Hethel came in 1972. With its new production models Lotus was aiming more upmarket; the crude Seven's face didn't fit. Said Chapman, 'A small-car manufacturer cannot get into the very cheap market without vast volume and vast tooling costs. This isn't really the sector we should be competing in. We are specialist car manufacturers and should be filling relatively small sectors of the market which are not

covered by the mass-producing car manufacturers.' Although the latter description clearly included the Seven or something like it, *Le Patron* decided not to tackle it. The Series 4 run-out was handled by Caterham, which thereafter concentrated on the rortier Series 3 version.

While the Seven made its own way in the marketplace Colin Chapman was concentrating on his next steps up the rungs of the motor-racing ladder. This was with sports-racers at first, following the hyper-aerodynamic Mark VIII of 1954 with the more practical but also envelope-bodied Mark IX of 1955. A significant difference between the two was the positioning of the fuel tank. While the earlier car had a conventional rear-mounted tank, the Mark IX had its tankage alongside the passenger seat or in the scuttle on cars intended for the road.

As presented at the time, this change reflected the use of a lighter Coventry Climax engine in the new car instead of its predecessor's cast-iron MG unit, calling for a lighter rear end to balance a lighter front. In fact, however, Chapman was in the thrall of the concept of tankage near the centre of gravity where it least affects handling as petrol is consumed.

His next racing models, the sports Eleven and single-seat Twelve of 1956, had the same feature. Of the Twelve Chapman wrote as follows: 'Fuel comes from a 12-gallon scuttle tank mounted amidships over the driver's legs in the usual Lotus practice of minimising the handling changes which take place as the fuel level drops. With only this tank in the car the weight distribution is 53 per cent on rear wheels and 47 per cent on the front. An [additional] 10-gallon tank can be mounted in the tail, which if used can give a 60/40 weight distribution.'

With this concept Chapman aligned himself with

Mike Warner wasn't the only Lotus man to get the 'hooded eyes' treatment from Colin Chapman. This gave a hint of what that felt like.

When the Mark IX was created for 1955, Chapman was dedicated to placement of the fuel centrally to minimise handling changes as the supply was consumed. [LAT]

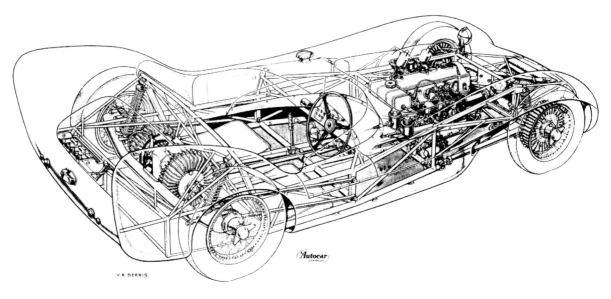

V R BERRIS

Ferdinand Porsche, who used similar tank positions for similar reasons on his racing Austro Daimlers and Mercedes-Benzes of the 1920s as well as his rear-engined Auto Unions. In opposition in the 1950s were Rudi Uhlenhaut of Mercedes-Benz and the engineers of Ferrari and Maserati, who accepted the likelihood of changing handling to get the greater rear-wheel grip of a tail-heavy car. For his Grand Prix W196 in 1955 Uhlenhaut devised a mid-race control the driver could use to reset his suspension to suit the lightening fuel load.

Challenged to find room for 55 gallons of alcohol fuel in his design for the 1956–57 Formula 1 Vanwall, Chapman compromised. He allocated 35 gallons to a tail tank and fitted two 10-gallon tanks alongside the driver. Rather than keeping and enlarging the latter when petrol was adopted for 1958 and races were shortened to 200 instead of 300 miles, Vanwall preferred to rely on the tail tank alone. It may not be coincidental that Rudi Uhlenhaut was advising Vanwall on various matters.

These were the natal years of the Lotus Elite, which was also intended to carry its fuel amidships. Taking advantage of otherwise-unused volumes in the front wings behind the wheels, fuel tanks were created by boxing in the glass fibre and then spraying the interior with a rubber compound to create an integral tank. Outfitting one tank on the passenger side would give an eight-gallon capacity while both sides could be exploited for racing.

In the event it proved impossible to effect a good seal for the built-in tank. Fuel was carried in a tail tank instead. For racing the wing volumes could be used, but with aluminium inserts. When the Lotus Sixteen succeeded the Twelve in 1958, for Formulas 1 and 2, it had a large tank in the rear. Then the rear-engined Eighteen of 1960 carried its fuel in perhaps the least likely location, high above the driver's legs in the nose. Later Lotuses were broadly opportunistic in their petrol stowage, up to and including the sports-racing 30 with a fuel cell in its central backbone frame.

Introduction of the Eighteen marked a sharp change in direction for Colin Chapman. He stepped well back from everything he'd done to date in order to make a completely fresh start with a new concept whose engine was rear-mounted. With impeccable timing in the Eighteen he produced a new car which uniquely achieved the feat of being suitable for three Formula categories: Junior, 2 and 1. And only slight tweaking was needed to adapt it to a world-beating sports-racer, the Nineteen.

Here was a brilliant manifestation of Chapman's conceptual competence. He gave credit for his ability to think a problem through from first principles to 'a professor at London University – Vaughan, I think his name was – who was very fond of putting the theory forward. Far too many people are prepared to take what has already been established and improve on it or make small changes. Whereas I much prefer to go right back to square one and try to assess what the basic reason is for doing anything and find the most basic, straightforward and simple way of doing it.' He did this triumphantly with the Eighteen.

The Sixteen of 1958 marked a sea change in Chapman thinking with its fuel and oil tanks in the extreme rear, held by the popular bungee cords.

A damaged Eighteen revealed the location of its fuel tankage, above the driver's legs in the most unusual location ever chosen for a racing car by Chapman.

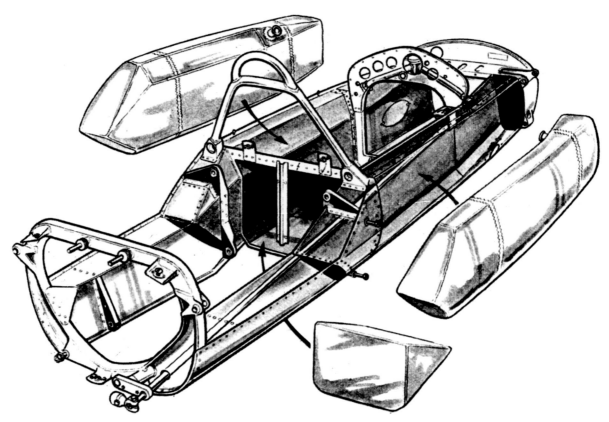

For his Formula 1 25 of 1962 Chapman placed the fuel in bags in the monocoque's side members and behind the driver's seat.

At the time Chapman explained how he went about designing a new car: 'First of all you select tyre sizes, bearing in mind the potential speed and weight of the car. Then you decide on wheelbase and track and draw in the wheels. In the case of a rear-engined car, you draw in the power unit and gearbox, the driver, the radiator and all the other bits and pieces, and then put in the chassis to connect them all up. Alternatively it's a matter of locating all the mounting brackets and joining them together with tubes.'

That his all-new concept was mid-engined was obviously a move in the direction pioneered by Cooper. Some were surprised that it took the observant Chapman so long to follow the Cooper lead. 'Colin Chapman used to tell me that the engine *had* to be in front,' recalled Jack Brabham. Former Lotus man Robin Read felt that the influence of aerodynamicist Frank Costin was strong. Costin, with whom Chapman had worked on the Vanwall, thought the front-engined layout had merit. Read mentioned other reasons for Chapman's reluctance:

'The reason why Colin took so long to follow the Cooper example was that he genuinely felt distaste for

the way in which engineering was done at Surbiton – Chapman had a healthy contempt for the chassis designs of Cooper – coupled with a modest jealousy of the way in which John Cooper was Leonard Lee's favourite and always got the first and best Climax engines. However, when the maligned Cooper started to win world championships, Colin knew the game was up.' Another harbinger was a rear-engined prototype shown by BRM at 1959's Italian GP.

'Having overcome this massive psychological barrier,' Read continued, 'and having braced himself for the inevitable taunt that he had finally copied the arch-rival Cooper, Chapman set to work. He then designed the Eighteen extremely quickly in the winter of 1959 and with a sense of relief. This car immediately demonstrated in its Junior, F2 and F1 forms that the Chapman genius was alive and well. Incidentally, too, he paved the way to a veritable transformation of Lotus's fortunes.'

Colin Chapman was pragmatic about his change of direction: 'We have reached the stage where we have decided in view of the size and facilities of the firm, and our numerous other commitments, to go for a basic, simple and easily maintained design rather than a technically superior but more complicated one. The rear-engine layout offers several advantages for a Formula 1 car – low frontal area, a low centre of gravity (with no propeller shaft problems) and minimum power loss through the transmission. The chief disadvantage of such a car is that it has a low polar moment of inertia.'

Chapman didn't create his new concept in complete isolation. 'At the end of 1959,' wrote Innes Ireland, 'Colin Chapman asked if I would prefer to drive a different type of car to the 2½-litre front-engined car with which we had battled throughout the year. What he had in mind was the first of the rear-engined Lotuses, for which he had made advanced designs. Personally I always preferred the front-engined car because – so long as it kept motoring – I had got it mastered. It handled well, it went quickly and, let's face it, any car looks right with the engine in front.

'I expressed the opinion that the front-engined car could be made into a good one if it was redesigned and properly built.' Ireland added, 'but came to the conclusion, albeit reluctantly, that having the engine in the back end was going to be the thing.' Ireland drove the first F1 Eighteen in its debut on 6 February 1960 in Argentina, where it showed excellent speed before ultimately finishing sixth with steering and gearbox maladies. In mid-April at Goodwood it won, easily having the legs of all its rivals including the Cooper of Moss, whose fastest race lap a second quicker than his qualifying time showed he'd been under pressure.

Strategically the early introduction in Argentina of the latest Lotus misfired badly in a season whose next championship race was almost four months later at the end of May, because it gave Cooper enough time to ready a robust counter-attack with its low-line Type 53. Chapman would learn from this experience when, in the late 1970s, he had another breakthrough with his first ground-effect car.

Colin Chapman wasn't put off his stride by Cooper's quick counter-attack. On the contrary. He was on a conceptual roll that took him into 1961 at warp speed. 'I think of them in the bath,' said Chapman about his creative inspirations, 'and also in the wee small hours of the morning, lying in bed. Everything seems to be so much clearer then, doesn't it? I need about five-and-a-half to six hours' sleep a night, and when I'm thinking about something I usually spend an hour or so just lying there, mulling it over. You chew it all over, over and over again, looking at it from different viewpoints, assuming something is static and moving all the other variables around and then all of a sudden you say, "Hey! Why didn't I think of that before?"'

'His most annoying characteristic was that he was almost always right,' testified racing-team manager Peter Warr. When Chapman came in with one of his brainwaves 'you'd think, "He's really gone off his rocker this time. I'm going to have it out with him." And nine times out of ten the bugger would turn out to be right. But when he did get it wrong he made some big ones.'

One that was undeniably right, for 1961, was steeply inclining the driver's seat to achieve a striking reduction in frontal area. This was a completely natural and indeed inevitable concomitant of the adoption of the rear engine, since there was no longer an engine to block the driver's view. With the Sixteen Chapman had attained what in retrospect would be viewed as the ultimate in frontal-area reduction of a front-engined Grand Prix car. Now, with no engine in the way, Chapman saw that even further shrinkage was possible. He was the first to twig this inviting potential of the mid-engined layout.

It's tempting to speculate whether Chapman, with

Pictured in the Formula Junior trim in which it was first revealed, 1960's Eighteen marked Colin Chapman's acknowledgement that a rear engine was the way to go. [LAT]

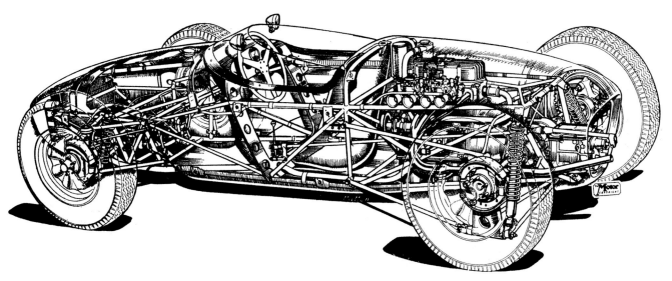

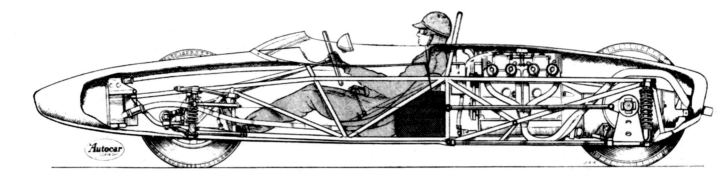

With no engine in the way, Chapman was quick to reduce frontal area by sloping the driver 50 degrees from vertical in 1961's Formula Junior 20. [LAT]

his RAF experience and interest in aviation, weighed the idea of a driver in the prone position. The Wright brothers used it for their first Flyer and the German flight research establishment tested it extensively in the 1940s, again with the aim of frontal-area reduction. Many of his ideas came from aviation, as he explained:

'It really gets down to what making progress in any engineering field is all about. I think that progress comes,

The steep recline of seats in the post-1961 Lotuses was at first unnatural to drivers including Jim Clark, here preparing to tackle the hilly Watkins Glen circuit.

to a large extent, from a cross-pollination of ideas from other engineering fields and not just through having a blinkered approach to your own discipline. I like reading a lot on subjects other than racing. In fact, I think I get my ideas because I take in subconsciously a tremendous amount of information and design philosophies from other fields. You've got to have a pretty general sort of knowledge. That's why I'm very interested in aviation and why I read all the aviation magazines.' In this instance, however Chapman must have concluded that the prone driver of a racing car wouldn't have welcomed having his head so close to the accident.

Until this Colin Chapman breakthrough racing-car designers had been content with a conventional seated position, gently reclined according to taste. Colin himself had hitherto set 20 degrees from the vertical as the rake

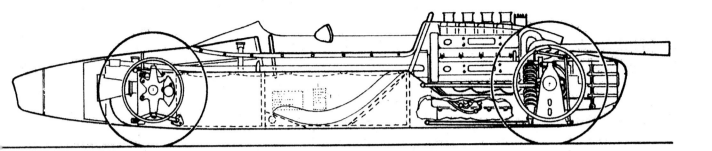

to be maintained. In Chapman's first new-concept design, his Formula Junior 20 of 1961, the seat squab sloped back at 50 degrees to the vertical. A concomitant was a steering wheel reduced in diameter to 13 inches to fit into the shrinking space between the driver's legs and the windscreen. The result, in the 20, was 30 per cent less frontal area than in the Eighteen – a vast reduction in a low-powered car for which this was instantly useful.

Trying a 20 at Brands Hatch J.W. Anstice Brown of *The Motor* found that 'one lies in the car rather than sits, tucks one's feet under the anti-roll bar and finds the pedals. Sitting so low in the car gives the circuit a different appearance than it would have in a normal touring car and the driver is very conscious of being surrounded by the road whilst quite small undulations in the track appear as hills.' John Bolster of *Autosport*

Seat inclination in 1962's Lotus 25 was 55 degrees from the vertical, demanding a distinctly laid-back attitude on the driver's part.

remarked that 'the driving position was quite new to me as although I have previously been recumbent in a car, it was perfectly stationary at the time.'

The Formula 1 Lotus 21 of 1961 and its successor the 24 of 1962 had seat-back angles akin to that of the 20. 'The first time we tested the car at Goodwood,' wrote Jim Clark of the 21, 'I remember having great difficulty adjusting myself to that position. The front wheels

His comments in the text about the strains imposed by steep seat inclination are well supported by this 1965 image of Jim Clark at the wheel of the Lotus 33.

seemed much higher than eye level and the fact that my weight, more than ever before, was distributed up my back, meant that the theory of driving by the seat of one's pants had to be extended.'

In the semi-monocoque 25 of mid-1962 the seat-squab slope was even steeper at 55 degrees and the steering wheel even smaller at 12 inches. 'This initially caused Jim Clark some concern,' reported David Phipps, 'as he was unable to see the road close to the front of the car and also had less warning of impending rear-end breakaway.'

In the 25, said Clark, 'this lying-down position, though not completely new to me, was somewhat more accentuated than it had been in either the Lotus 21 or 24. I required some time to become accustomed to it. It was a great benefit for the designers from an aerodynamic point of view, but at first it held some difficulties for the driver. For example the worm's eye view of the track which this position gave meant reorienting oneself with the features of the track to

A drawing from 3 October 1963 shows Colin Chapman's initial layout of the sports-racing car envisaged as a member of his Type 30 scheme for a new family of racing and road cars.

which one had been accustomed. But once I had mastered the new position I wondered how I had ever driven a racing car any other way.'

Jim Clark cited two limitations to the degree of seat recline allowable in a racing car: 'One is that the driver's shoulders must be high enough to allow his arms to move freely without his legs and the rest of his body getting in the way. The second is the tremendous muscular strain which comes from having to keep your chin jammed down on to your chest in order to see where you are going. On a long race this position, combined with the heavy g forces which come into play at high speeds, is likely to cause a very stiff neck.' Ultimately in fact g forces were destined to prevail in demanding greater neck strength from Grand Prix drivers.

Although he realised that he imposed new demands on his team drivers and customers alike with his supine seating, Colin Chapman was unapologetic. 'We never make our cars any bigger than they need to be,' he said at the time. 'But in our Lotus 25 single-seater, for example, there is more space than in some of its competitors. When there was a discussion about minimum interior dimensions, the Lotus was the only one that fully conformed.'

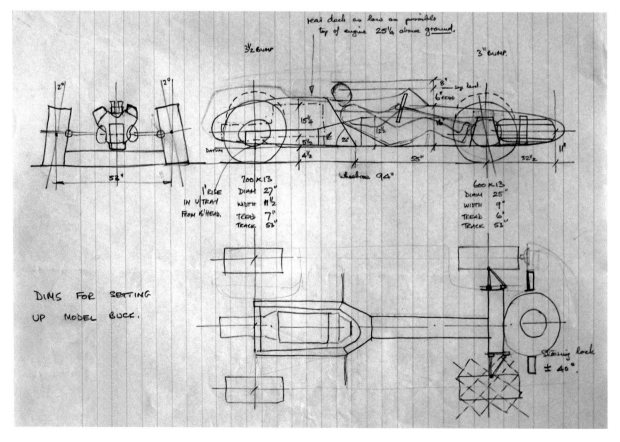

Another Chapman concept of the early 1960s had its origins in negotiations with Ford. When in 1963 his Lotus was already involved with the Blue Oval in racing projects in Britain and America, Ford decided to tackle Le Mans as well. As an ally in this endeavour, wrote Ford racing historian Leo Levine, 'the most obvious choice was Chapman.' Colin thought so too, said designer Len Terry: 'He called a big meeting of the staff and told them he was sure he would get it; he thought he would because of the Indianapolis tie-up with Ford and because of his previous experience.'

'It should have been no contest,' continued Levine, 'but there were things militating against Chapman. There was the question of how well he would take direction, whether or not he and [Carroll] Shelby would rub egos, whether the capacity of his plant was such that it could absorb the Ford GT along with the other things under development – and just how much publicity Chapman would seek.' But Ford knew it would be working with a brilliant designer, especially when it saw the ultra-low coupé concept that Lotus proposed, rendered by designer Ron Hickman.

Ford decided to go to Le Mans with Eric Broadley, an upstart newcomer whose Lolas had been annoyingly competitive with Lotuses. Fortuitously for Broadley, earlier in 1963 he'd shown a mid-engined Ford-powered GT coupé that illustrated his credentials for the job. Chapman – who during Ford's tour of his facilities had offered to sell them to the American company – didn't take the decision well. 'Colin was so mad when he found out,' said Len Terry, that 'he wanted to prove to Ford and the world that he was a better designer than Eric Broadley.'

'Colin got very miffed about that,' recalled Mike Warner. 'I remember the whole place having to be tarted up for the big Ford visit. When Ford's team and Harley Copp came over, they thought – and correctly at the time – that Broadley's outfit at Lola would represent a better base from which they could be more influential over the final design than Lotus would. Chapman had a lot of plates in the air on bamboo poles then.'

*Below: **Foreseen in the Type 30 project was the GT coupé that Lotus offered to Ford as a Le Mans contender, an ultra-low conception with nostril radiator-air inlets.***

*Bottom: **As the Lotus 30 was actually constructed for racing in 1964, the ultra-reclined driver concept was retained, as were 13-inch wheels that compromised braking.***

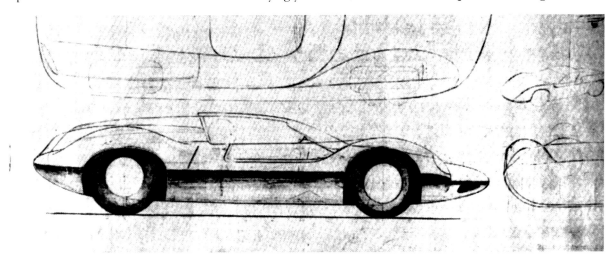

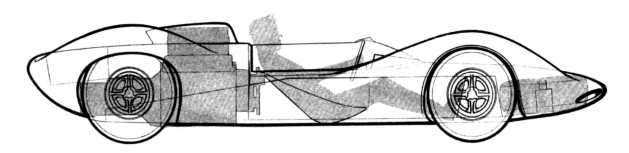

True to Chapman's vision of October 1963, Jim Clark was well laid back at the wheel of 1964's Lotus 30 in search of the lowest possible aerodynamic drag.

The result was a new Chapman concept, a *grand projet*, to rival the way the Eighteen had spawned a new Lotus range. A new type number, 30, covered a project that would spawn a family of related road and racing cars. At its heart was a new sports-racing car, 'the first of five projected variants,' said Len Terry. The car that became known as the Type 30 was created on the rebound from Ford's rejection of Lotus as a Le Mans partner, Mike Warner said: 'He didn't like that very much so he commissioned the 30, saying, "This is what *we* can do." It had to be done very, very quickly because he wanted it yesterday.'

Number two in the planned range 'was basically the same car,' said Terry, 'but with a 1.6-litre Lotus-Ford Twin Cam engine. Numbers three and four were going to be closed, road-going coupé versions of one and two. Number five was going to be a racing version of number four. Number four eventually became the Europa and after that the Esprit. This was all planned from the outset.'

The version that first appeared, the sports-racing 30 with its 4.7-litre Ford V8, showed the direction that Chapman planned to take. Following the lead of his single-seaters, it was extremely low thanks to its steeply reclined driver. He was determined to use this same principle for a range of road and racing two-seaters, thereby stealing a low-frontal-area march on his rivals.

Features of the Type 30 that were intended to benefit the four other variants fatally compromised the sports-racer, first shown in January of 1964. One was its 13-inch road wheels, fine for smaller-engined cars but enclosing brakes that weren't up to the job. Another was a one-piece glass fibre body, a splendid idea for volume production that made trackside access for maintenance and adjustment a nightmare. Yet another was a steel backbone-type frame like that of the Elan introduced in 1962, whose stiffness was of the wet-noodle variety when pitched against the torque of a 350-horsepower Ford V8. Only the 1966 Europa emerged with honour from this flawed concept.

Creation of the Elan's backbone frame – a novel concept at the time – illustrated another aspect of Colin Chapman's conceptual fertility. The Elan traced its origins to a project to create a 2+2 successor to the original Elite, still with monocoque glass fibre the planned structural concept. Before the structure was ready the engineers in Ron Hickman's research and development department needed a rough and ready body with which to try out the engine and suspension. An off-the-shelf British Falcon glass fibre shell was bought to cover the test mule.

'Brian Lough and a couple of his engineers lashed up a test bed in the R&D section to run the twin-cam on,' recalled Mike Warner. 'It was a Y-shaped test bed, embracing the engine, with a beam coming through to the tail to give it rigidity while it was being tested. That was it. Chapman saw that and, as only Chapman could – full credit where credit's due – saw it and immediately

recognised the potential.' Instead of a pure glass fibre structure the open Elan would have a steel backbone frame inspired by a test chassis that pointed the way.

Here was a valuable Chapman talent, said Mike Costin: 'He was brilliant at having a quick look at anything that was put to him and then work at it – that was the new concept.' Colleague Graham Arnold put it differently: 'Colin just needed a starting point. He needed to see the efforts of others before he knew just what he wanted. He would look over the shoulder of a designer and make incredibly apposite suggestions, or come up with elegant solutions to some knotty problem aired in conference.'

Arnold gave a relevant example: 'One year he arrived at our motor show stand at Earl's Court the day before

Although a commercial failure, the original Elite was a striking concept with its unitised glass-fibre body/frame that introduced Lotus to the mainstream road-car market.

press day. The stand was finished but the cars were still out on the public walkway. "Why aren't the cars on the stand?" he snarled, ignoring the fact that, having somehow obtained union cards, we had built it ourselves overnight during a stand fitters' strike. "I didn't put the cars on, Colin, because wherever I put them, you move them," I said. "Yes, but I won't know where they should

As the Elite's successor the Elan of 1962 had a backbone frame shared conceptually with the 30 and establishing a format for future Chapman road cars.

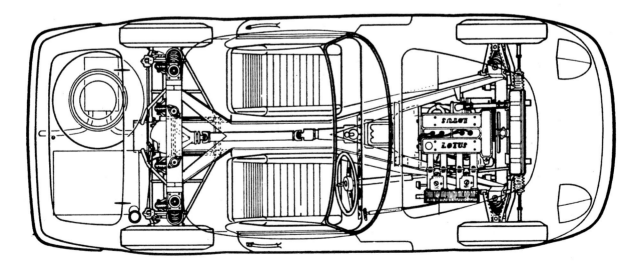

be until you have put them in the wrong places," he replied, breaking into one of his disarming smiles.'

A similar starting point had been the seed from which the original Lotus Elite grew. The idea of a roadgoing Lotus surfaced early as Chapman explained in 1954: 'I have been encouraged by the acceptance of the Lotus, of which already more than 100 Mark VI replicas have been or are being assembled privately. At the same time I do hope to branch out with another project. We intend to offer a complete sports car in open and in coupé form, giving a very high performance. This is my answer to the sporting motorist who has not the time or the inclination to "roll his own".'

The result was the Lotus Elite, whose unique unit chassis/body is discussed in Chapter 5. It took the concept of a glass-fibre automobile structure to its limit of feasibility. 'The one deserved criticism of the Elite we never fully cured was the vibration and noise,' admitted Peter Kirwan-Taylor, a key contributor to its styling, 'but as I look at the Elite today, especially in the round as opposed to photographs, it still seems a satisfactory solution to the objectives we set ourselves technically and aesthetically.'

It might be said of the Elite that it was *too* successful aesthetically, for it looked like a soigné grand tourer but behaved like a sports-racing car with all the disadvantages for road use that that implied. In fact few cars in all the history of the motor car have suffered a greater disparity between their appearance and their behaviour. Its commercial goose was well cooked by the introduction,

Pictured in the Series 4 version introduced in March of 1968, the Elan succeeded in being both smaller and lighter than its Elite predecessor.

only a year after Elite deliveries began, of the Jaguar E-Type – a sports car of similar price that looked exactly like what it did and vice versa.

Ron Hickman was quoted as saying that 'where the Elite was 60% beautiful and 40% practical, the Elan was to reverse that apportionment.' Conceptually as well the Elan was strikingly small – shorter, narrower, lower and lighter than the Elite. 'The Elan is a very compact car,' reported *Motor Sport*, 'and one realises this when it is necessary to step down into it from a high kerb, the ensuing wriggling and puffing not helping to endear the car to tall or stout people. Other traffic seems completely oblivious to the tiny projectile, as other drivers carry on with their overtaking manoeuvres even when the Elan is alongside and the passenger is knocking on their bodywork!' Its compactness gave the Elan immense agility and allowed it to outperform other cars of far more power – a Chapman hallmark.

The mid-engined Europa of 1966 followed in the same idiom but with the frame's Y-shape reversed to suit its rear-mounted power train. Here was the sole survivor of the range that Chapman had hoped to launch with the Type 30 family concept. Laughably low at only 43 inches tall, at its introduction the Europa shared the supine seating of Chapman's racing cars. Less radical seating was installed in the early 1970s to broaden the appeal of the model its creator called 'a Kings Road type of car – glorious impracticality.'

In the early 1970s Colin Chapman calculatedly moved his Lotus product range upmarket with the consequences for the Seven already described. 'As a company with a sporting image,' Chapman told Ray Hutton in 1972, 'we should always have a model in our

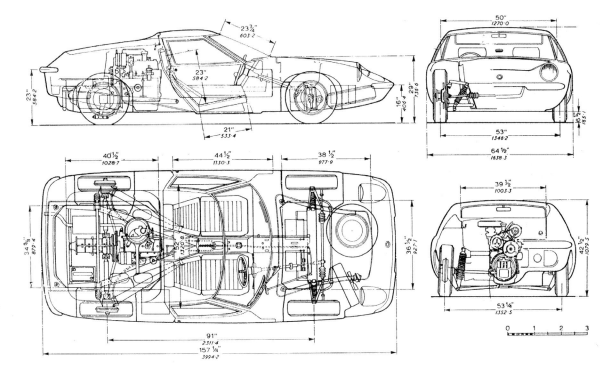

range of a more advanced sporting nature such as a mid-engined two-seater, but not to the exclusion of more conventional designs. Our current range – a front-engined two-seater, a front-engined four-seater and a mid-engined two-seater – is the sort of line we will continue with.' This remained the case through the rest of Chapman's life.

Hutton wondered if this foreshadowed a 'softening' of the cars in future. Would automatic transmissions be offered for instance? 'Yes,' came the reply. 'Our objective is to produce a very comfortable high-performance car. Anything that makes the environment of the car easy, more pleasant, like automatic transmission, power steering, standard air conditioning etc will be incorporated into future Lotuses.' Here was a striking new vision of the concept of the Lotus road-car range. It traced its origins to the success of the Elan +2 of 1967, a coupé whose good looks ideally complemented its fine road manners albeit with power that was 'adequate more than sensational.'

If this sounds like the new range was conceived to appeal more to the American market that would be misleading. In fact when the USA began its safety and then emissions campaigns Chapman became wary of that fickle market. Around 1970, said senior engineer Tony Rudd, the boss 'did not want us to get too dependent on the States as a car market – at that time it was the largest market for us – as we all felt that it would result in us building cars suitable only for American use. He wanted

Clearly another offshoot of 1963's Type 30 family concept, the Type 46 or Lotus Europa was only 42½ inches high with its rear engine and sloped seating.

to keep building cars that would appeal in Europe.' Here was, at best, a misunderstanding of America's standards and desires for specialist sports cars.

In his range of the 1970s Colin Chapman realised a concept for their fabrication that he'd nurtured since the 1960s. In 1969 he said, 'If you could have a mould and lead a hose up to it and squirt something in a hole and there was a complete motorcar…it can be stressed, in fact it can be coloured so you don't have to paint it. This is what I would like to see Lotus do on a commercial scale in a production car. And we will be doing it within the next 10 years.'

In 1976 Colin Chapman was awarded a patent on a process that did very nearly what he envisaged. Typically he had immersed himself in such technology as existed in composite materials to replace the crude glass fibre methods used hitherto. 'It was such a messy unscientific business,' he said, 'all buckets and brushes. I decided I wanted to turn it into a normal industrial process and part of that scheme was to go ahead with a low-pressure injection-moulding process. A factor that helped a lot was the availability of polyurethane paints which can withstand the heat and stress of being in the mould and provide a good finish.'

Introduced in 1966, initially for export only, the Europa offered enthusiasts a mid-engined Lotus that mirrored the glamour of the company's racing cars.

Using Lotus's Vacuum-Assisted Resin Injection (VARI) process, Chapman's road cars were made henceforth in top and bottom halves. Each of these was formed by VARI in matching male and female moulds that were drawn together by vacuum, a benign force that allowed the moulds themselves to be of light and inexpensive construction. Chapman's vision and enterprise were such

Illustrations from Chapman's patent show the VARI system's progression from the upper state to the lower, in which vacuum has drawn the moulds together and distributed the resin throughout the glass-fibre part.

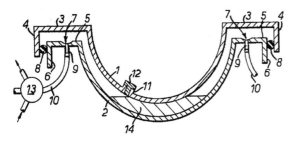

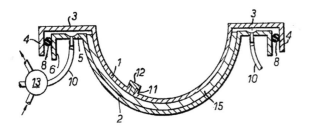

that he'd marched into a completely new and unrelated field to establish novel and valuable technology to be used in his own works and profitably licensed to DeLorean.

The 1970s also witnessed new racing-car concepts from the Colin Chapman grey matter. It was no secret that these were implemented by talented engineer-designers who brought their own skills to Chapman's projects. 'In the days of the Types 77, 78 and 79,' recalled Martin Ogilvie, 'I worked alongside Geoff Aldridge and Mike Cook, with Tony Rudd, Peter Wright and Colin Chapman, who were a sort of think tank. It was people like Ralph Bellamy, myself and Geoff Aldridge who did the actual bits and pieces, so it's difficult to actually identify who did what. There was quite a divide as to what came out of the think tank and came to us, which we had to draw.'

'You spent a fair bit of time playing around, ultimately trying to get at what Chapman wanted,' said Geoff Aldridge. 'I never saw him do a proper drawing at a drawing board. I know he was well capable of it because I've seen his stuff. But we'd get sketches on cigarette packets, or whatever, and then lay it out as best we could. And then of course he'd come in and have a look and say, "No, that wasn't quite what I wanted." It was a sort of to-and-fro situation until we ended up with something that he was happy with.'

'He wasn't one to have design meetings,' added Martin Ogilvie. 'He would breeze into the drawing office and go around the drawing boards having a look, offering a bit of advice here and there, and then back out again. It was immensely frustrating because you could be beavering away for hours or days and he would come in and within ten seconds spot the obvious mistake. He loved to do that, to come in and show that he was right on top of it – which he was in those days. He was very good at leading you to find your own way around the problem. He would present you with a problem saying, "I want this feature. Design me a car that incorporates it."'

Personal chemistry played a role as well of course, added Ogilvie: 'When I joined in 1973 Ralph Bellamy had just started, having been at McLaren and after a short stint at Brabham. He did the Type 76 Lotus, which wasn't a huge success – Chapman said it was a Type 72 with a hundred more mistakes. Ralph was a super guy but very conservative. He wasn't dynamic enough for Chapman's liking and they didn't get on at all well, so it wasn't long after the Type 76 came out that Chapman

Opposite: Introduced for the 1976 season, the Lotus 77 brought a new concept of complete variability to GP racing with the aim of adapting the chassis to each circuit.

Designed into the 1976 Lotus 77 were provisions to alter its wheelbase by up to ten inches and its front and rear track by nine and four inches respectively.

Made by Len Terry early in the 1976 season, modifications to the Lotus 77 included repositioning of its brakes inside the wheels to help keep the front tyres up to temperature.

felt he couldn't really work with him any longer and found an alternative role for him.' Bellamy moved to a successful career at Lotus Components.

At a time when he was searching for a new approach to racing-car design Chapman produced a new concept for 1976 that verged on an experimental test-bed exposed to the full glare of racing in Formula 1. 'We feel that motor racing is becoming more and more competitive as each year goes by,' said Chapman in explaining the Type 77's design. 'The circuits have different characteristics; some are fast, some are slow; some are twisty, some have open bends; some are smooth, some are bumpy; and so on, so that different configurations of racing cars do better on certain circuits. For instance, McLarens, because of their very wide track, might be ideal on some circuits, while the Brabhams, being very narrow and with a short wheelbase, would do better on others, and the Shadows, with their softer suspension, would be good somewhere else.'

To cope with these circuit variations, added Colin Chapman, in the 77 he was producing a car that could be much more adaptable than hitherto:

It was obvious that to optimise the design of a car to suit all circuits was becoming much more difficult. Although we have all been capable of making minor adjustments and changes to things like springs and roll bars, dampers and so on at each circuit we go to, it has not been possible up to now to change the basic configuration of the racing car to suit each particular circuit's requirements better. This car therefore is an attempt to produce what could be described as a 'variable-geometry racing car' in that the major dimensions are adjustable.

For instance, we can alter the front track very easily by moving the whole of the suspension system out on the very simple sub-frame. We can carry a number of these sub-frames in our transporter and it is only a matter of an hour or so to alter the track over the quite large variation of nine inches. It is also very easy to change the rear track. In fact, this is achieved simply by swapping over the rear wheels, which varies the track by four inches. We can alter the wheelbase by up to ten inches because there are five inches of adjustment at both the front and the rear, and so we can have either a long- or a short-wheelbase car. At the same time, depending upon how it is set up, it is possible to change the location of the centre of gravity, a fairly major adjustment which normally cannot easily be effected once any particular design of racing car exists.

So the basic concept of the Lotus 77, apart from trying to produce a light, strong and efficient racing car, is to attempt to effect quite large geometry changes very easily. This is not to say that we will go to a circuit and immediately start altering the car, although that could be done quickly. The idea is that if we are going to a circuit where we know that a long-wheelbase car would probably perform best, we will set it up in the workshop as a long-wheelbase car. If we felt that a wide track would be beneficial for a particular circuit, then we will set up the car in that form. Then, if we found we were mistaken, we could very easily and very quickly change it.

The new concept's detail design was carried out by Geoff Aldridge for the monocoque and Martin Ogilvie for the suspension.

Knowingly or not, Colin Chapman was following the initiative of his much-admired Mercedes-Benz. For the 1955 season, which introduced a greater variety of circuits, including several slower ones such as Monaco and Aintree, Mercedes introduced two shorter-wheelbase versions of its W196. Throughout 1955 it used three different wheelbase lengths in search of the right balance of handling and weight to suit each circuit.

'Before the 77 was unveiled,' wrote Doug Nye, 'it was realised that to test all possible combinations of geometry, track, wheelbase and weight distribution – plus all the peripheral variables involving wings, springs, dampers, brake balances etc – might take something like two years' daily running without entering a single race.'[1] When Ronnie Peterson tested the 77 at Paul Ricard in November of 1975 the best set-up for that circuit seemed to be a wide track and long wheelbase.

For the first race of 1976 on the wildly sinuous Interlagos track in Brazil the 77s were built to minimum dimensions of both track and wheelbase. Mario Andretti said that his 'handles like a go-kart. I just can't get any precision with it.' Ignominiously the Lotus team-mates crashed into each other early in the race, Peterson leaving the team thereafter while Andretti persevered to win the season's wet final race in Japan driving a much-improved 77.

'In the beginning of the season the 77 was a disaster,' agreed observer Emerson Fittipaldi. 'During the race in Africa I was passing Nilsson and it was a joke to see the Lotus. It was terrible, understeering into the corners

---

1   Obviously a gift to pre-race evaluation of the optimum set-up of such a versatile car for each circuit would have been the use of the computer simulations that were commonplace by the end of the 20th Century. These were still in the future – albeit not all that far.

and oversteering out of them. Then Tony Southgate joined the team. They lengthened the wheelbase, widened the track in front and reinforced all the suspension points. By the end of the season it was very quick but still quite inconsistent. It wasn't easy to keep it at 99 per cent effort all the time.'

'Chapman was a driver's dream,' said Andretti, whose persistence helped morph the 77 into the successful 78, 'because when he was motivated you *knew* that he was trying to give you that advantage, somewhere. Colin's mind was going 24 hours a day. He was always thinking, always probing, always asking questions. The man was in a category of his own. In his day, when there was room to make huge improvements, he was the one who would think totally out of the box.'

Chapman could be volatile in reaction to initiatives by his designers. 'If someone else had an idea he'd listen,' said Peter Warr, 'and sometimes it would suddenly become his idea. But more often he'd look at it from a completely different angle and he'd say, "Why don't we take it a step further, why don't we do this?" And you'd think, "Bloody hell, he's done it again!" His genius was to be able to take an idea, refine it, adapt it, think it through from a different direction and say, "I can use this in a racing-car application." Then he'd engineer it so it worked how he wanted it to work.'

Ultimately Colin Chapman's compulsive quest for new concepts would prove more a failing than a strength. 'He would never allow for compromise,' said Martin Ogilvie, 'and would always find the "unfair advantage". Whether it was downforce, sticky Goodyear tyres or Nicholson engines, it would take precedence over everything else.' Fatally an attractive novelty would often prevail over the improvement of an existing concept that had shown great potential.

A factor as well, from the mid-1960s onwards, was Chapman's employment of first-rank 'name' designers to pen his racing cars. While this freed him to spend more time on his other enterprises, it also led to discontinuities in design. This was pointed out by Brabham designer Ron Tauranac, who said, 'Unless there's a change in the regulations, if you have to make a new car each year it's an admission that you cocked up last year's car. In that

During 1976 Tony Southgate joined Lotus to help turn the 'go-kart' 77 into a raceable Grand Prix car, as pictured by Ove Nielssen at Monaco driven by Gunnar Nilsson.

respect my philosophy was different to Lotus, but part of that I think was that Lotus employed designers, and the designers felt they had to come up with new cars all the time.' In fairness to Chapman, cars like the 25, 49 and 72 had impressive longevity thanks to advanced initial concepts. But towards the end of the 1970s both the cars and the designers were changing almost yearly – not always for the better.

In a 1968 musing to John Bolster, Chapman indicated that he was cognisant of the risks inherent in his go-for-broke philosophy. 'I was tremendously impressed by Colin Chapman's absolute certainty that there is vast scope for future development in Grand Prix car design,' said Bolster. 'He insists that so far we have scratched the surface but admits, rather ruefully perhaps, that innovation may bring unreliability while other people may reap the benefit later on.' Nothing could have described better the rocky saga of Colin's pioneering exploitation of under-body downforce a decade later.

Colin Chapman's innovation of ground effect in his 78 and 79 was a sensational step forward, taking Mario Andretti to the drivers' championship in 1978. To Mario, however, who could hear rivets popping under the stresses of downthrust, the 79's design seemed under-developed. 'Chapman wanted the smallest possible chassis so that he could have maximum ground-effect down the sides,' said Geoff Aldridge. 'To give more

Seen in the hands of Gunnar Nilsson in his home Swedish GP in 1976, the 'adjustable' 77 served as a test bed for many of the features that contributed to the 78's success.

room for the aerodynamics down the sides it had to have a slim chassis, and we knew it needed to be as stiff as possible. There was a contradiction here because you can't necessarily have small things very stiff. While the 78 chassis had two skins, the 79 was in fact single-skinned, with just one skin down the side.'

'The irony was that the 79 really wasn't very well developed,' recalled team engineer Nigel Bennett, 'but Chapman said, "Don't worry, my boy, we've got this great new idea coming along." In fact we'd have done better developing the 79, as Williams showed with their very successful FW07, which was an improved 79. Chapman wasn't very interested in development. He would find the current situation totally boring. It was new ideas that kept him going, trying to stay ahead.'

His new idea this time was the 80, which had curved front-to-rear skirts that doubled the downforce but defied all efforts to make them work consistently. 'Chapman saw the 80 as the next step,' said Geoff Aldridge. 'I think they should have developed the 79. If Lotus had done that, they'd probably still have had a winning car. But that wasn't Chapman's philosophy.'

No, it certainly wasn't.

Chapter 2

ENGINE ENTERPRISE

Colin really didn't know anything about engines. I sometimes think he knew less than me. Whenever he sketched a car he would draw it very exactly, but at the back he would just draw an oblong box and write 'ENGINE' on it.

Walter Hayes

Two engine-related factors provided the driving force for many of Colin Chapman's innovations. The first, the factor that drove his earliest achievements, was his lack of competitive engines. Buyers of his Mark VI fitted such available units as MG J4, MG TC, Ford Consul and Ford 1172. Chapman was on safe ground when competing in the Austin Seven-based 750 Club and 1172 series which mandated basically similar engines – though that too would spur his creativity. But when Colin wanted to move up to unlimited international classes for 1.1- and 1.5-litre cars Britain's cupboards were little better than bare.

In 1954, when Chapman's ambition was to beat the Porsche Spyders on the Nürburgring, he had nothing like the exotic four-cam engines of the German cars. 'A 1½-litre engine built-up of TC MG and Morris "10" components was chosen as the power unit' for his Mark VIII, he related. Problems were initially experienced with misfiring. This was traced to oiled plugs from a lubrication leak. After this was stanched the hybrid four worked reliably'.

Running in his racing engines 'was very scientific,'

Arriving in 1967, Ford's Cosworth-built DFV V8 was staunchly behind both Chapman and Clark and would power all subsequent GP Lotuses – save for a lone turbine – during Chapman's life.

said colleague 'Mac' McIntosh. 'Colin had a plot of rpm against compression pressure. You checked the pressure on all four pots, took the lowest, read off the appropriate rpm and then tried to run as near that as possible for the next 100-odd miles. The idea was to get a light load and high rpm. As Colin said, if you are rubbing down with sandpaper you don't rub slowly with high load for a good finish!' Even with the savviest break-in, however, an engine from the Nuffield Motors parts bins was a far cry from the pure-bred twin-cam racing engines of the likes of Osca and Stanguellini, not to mention Porsche and Borgward.

Thus disadvantaged, Chapman had no choice but to advance the boundaries of structures, suspensions and aerodynamics as exemplified by his spectacular Mark VIII of 1954. Lotus customers fitted Connaught, Lea-Francis, BMW and Bristol engines as well as MG-derived units to their Mark VIIIs. Bristol's six took the cars into the 2.0-litre class, for which Chapman chanced his hand with an appeal to Tony Vandervell, whose first single-seated Vanwall Special of 1954 had a 2.0-litre four before it was uprated to the GP capacity limit of 2.5 litres. Vandervell spurned the chance to sell 2.0-litre versions to the then-little-known Lotus outfit.

Once good racing engines became available from British sources like Coventry Climax and Cosworth, a second

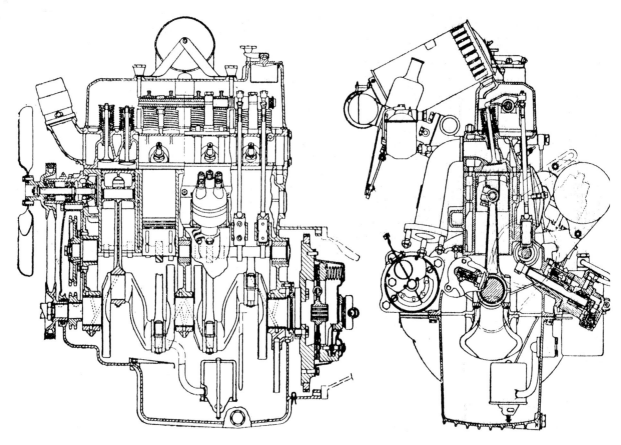

With its pushrod-operated overhead valves, the rugged
engine of the MG TC, Type XPEG in Nuffield jargon,
powered early Lotuses including the Mark VIII.

Shown as the deLuxe Saloon of 1934, the versatile Austin
Seven provided the raw material for cars competing in
750 Formula races.

driving factor came into play in Chapman's thinking
about power units, namely, how to beat someone else
using the same engine. The first such competitor was the
eponymous motor company of Charles and John Cooper,
father and son. 'Cooper and ourselves have such an
intense personal rivalry,' said Chapman in 1960, 'that we
tend to outstrip the others in our own little efforts. But
we don't worry a bit about using the same engine. We
spend all our time on chassis design. It would put the cat
among the pigeons if either of us bought a dynamometer
and started playing with the engines too.'

Almost 20 years later Colin Chapman pledged
allegiance to the same combative spirit in a conversation
with Peter Windsor. 'Being of a naturally competitive sort
of nature,' he said, 'I like to beat other people, preferably
using the same equipment as them. I think there's much
more satisfaction in beating other Cosworth-engined cars
because you've all got the same power unit and so
therefore you must have a better chassis or driver.

'I don't think I'd want to get involved with engines,'
Chapman continued. 'I'm not an engine man, really. Mr
Ferrari himself was an engine man; Carlo Chiti is an
engine man; Tony Vandervell was an engine man, but I
am a chassis man, loosely speaking. And I think that
good engine men don't necessarily make good chassis

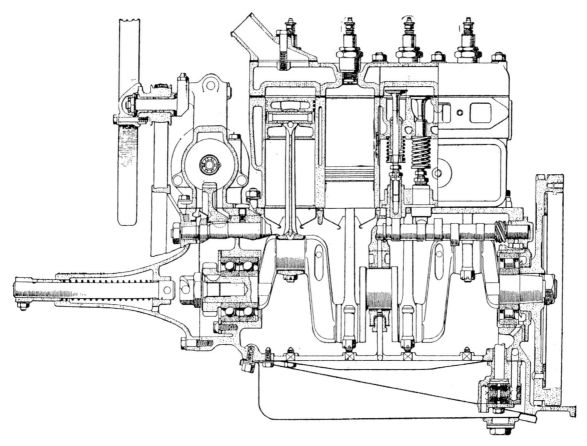

Thanks to its robust bottom end with ball front and roller rear main bearings – here with a late-1930s centre plain bearing – the Austin Seven four could withstand both tuning and racing.

men, and vice versa. Engine men tend to feel that the way to win races is to get more power from the engine. That's what they understand, what they like doing. I'd rather have a nice, reliable, standard engine just like everybody else and try to build a better chassis.'

Here was the essence of the second factor that ruled the Chapman approach to auto engineering. Both factors in combination – conditioning as a consequence of his early engine deprivation and competitiveness against others using similar engines – were powerful forces propelling the Chapman spirit of adventure in every other aspect of the design of cars for road and track.

Colin's first challenge to compete against others with similar engines came in the 750 Formula for Austin Seven-powered cars, for which he built his Mark III in 1951. Chapman explained his approach to the ground rules of the category: 'The Austin Seven, like most production four-cylinder side-valve engines, has inlet ports "siamesed" on cylinders one and two and again on three and four. "Siamesing" is the joining together of two cylinder inlets so that both are fed from one port.

'Under racing conditions that system is not efficient,' Chapman continued, 'because the ingoing charge of

fuel/air mixture to the inner cylinders (2 and 3) of each pair is robbed by its neighbour as each induction stroke takes place. The valve on No 4 opens before the inlet on No 3 is shut and likewise No 2 inlet is shutting as No 1 is opening on a 1, 3, 4, 2 firing order. This is an important factor at high engine speeds because it prevents complete filling of the inner pair of cylinders.

'No other competitor seemed to be paying much attention to this subject,' added Chapman, 'but I gave it a great deal of thought. It wasn't until I was enjoying a Christmas party in 1950 that the solution to this problem suddenly struck me. I seem to get my best design ideas after Christmas parties, probably because I have time to sit back and think. Anyway, the idea was to "de-siamese" the inlet ports.' The idea had occurred previously to Australian enthusiast Ron Ufindell, who passed it under heavy persuasion to Derek Jolly. Jolly's successful Austin engine and person arrived in Britain early in 1951, but by then Colin and the Allen brothers had begun their onerous modification of the block to make two inlet ports into four.

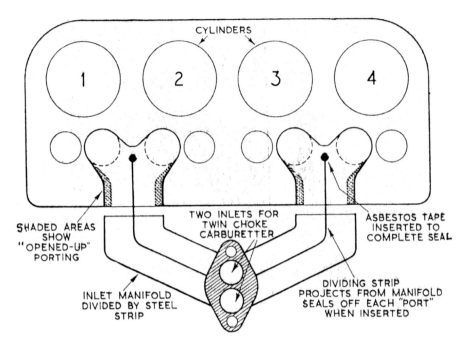

CYLINDERS

1 2 3 4

SHADED AREAS
SHOW
"OPENED-UP"
PORTING

TWO INLETS FOR
TWIN CHOKE
CARBURETTER

ASBESTOS TAPE
INSERTED TO
COMPLETE SEAL

INLET MANIFOLD
DIVIDED BY STEEL
STRIP

DIVIDING STRIP
PROJECTS FROM MANIFOLD
SEALS OFF EACH "PORT"
WHEN INSERTED

This illustration shows a method of 'de-siamesing' the inlet ports of the Austin Seven four that was used when Chapman's Mark III was sold after its 1951 season. In fact for 1951 the cylinder block of this side-valve engine was modified by the Allen brothers by onerous and exacting grinding and brazing to create four individual inlet ports. The special inlet manifold, much less contorted than the one shown, had four matching branches that were cleverly disguised to mislead the scutineers.

Feeding the modified four, said Chapman, was a twin-choke downdraft Ford V8 carburettor: 'Each of the chokes mated with its corresponding port in the top flange of the manifold, providing in effect a twin-carburettor induction system. The modification permitted a clean alternate "pull" on each induction stroke which reduced the "changes of direction" inevitable with an ordinary two-port system with only one carburettor. This resulted in a worthwhile power increase and for the season that I raced the car, no other 750 Formula car could beat it.'

Here was at least a passing acquaintance with the fundamentals of engine design on Chapman's part. As in every other aspect of his work he had absorbed the principles elucidated by an expert. Sir Harry Ricardo's great work on engine design, first published in 1923, was his source in this instance.

In his book's chapter on mechanical design Ricardo took a strong line against compromise in engineering, saying that 'Fewness of parts too often denotes excess of compromise. All design must necessarily be based on compromise, and it is upon the soundness of judgement by which the compromise is arrived at that the success of an engine ultimately depends.'

Colin's other early contribution to racing-engine design was his modification of the tappets of a Ford 1172 engine. Though the series rules required a standard Ford camshaft, they made no mention of the tappets – a loophole that Chapman exploited for his Mark VI in 1953. Being flat-faced, the standard tappets seemed to offer no option for earlier valve opening and later closing to

improve performance. Chapman differed. He devised an arched extension to the tappet face that would give that very benefit. The tappets had to be keyed to the block to prevent the slightest rotation.

Devising the radical tappet was one thing, making eight of them that would work another. 'How the bloody hell could we put those tappets in?' asked the then Lotus technical boss Mike Costin rhetorically. 'I designed and made all the tooling to generate that shape and then started the laborious work of grinding the form. When they were nearly finished we had them case hardened and then ground the circular bit that goes up into the block. Then I finished round the actual form again. I mean a labour of love. When I'd finished I'd most likely spent 100 hours making those tappets. In the end we never even checked them again. It is astonishing that they did not seize up or scuff. They lasted the whole season.'

The modified tappets were a well-kept speed secret that contributed to Mike Costin's successes in the Lotus works Mark VI. 'I remember being allowed to drive the car up Muswell Hill,' recalled Peter Ross, 'and being amazed at the way the engine would rev. It seemed to have power over a much wider range…but none of us could understand why.' The Mark VI and its engine were sold to French journalist Gerard 'Jabby' Crombac, who although appreciating their unfair advantage experienced some trouble with the special tappets.

Meanwhile famously at Coventry Climax in Britain's Midlands a new engine was developed by Wally Hassan and Harry Mundy, engineers whose handiwork included

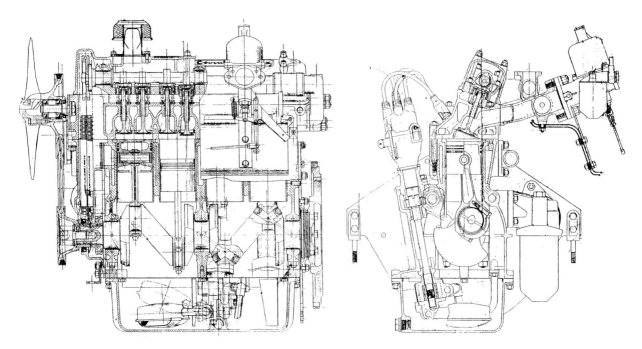

Jaguar's twin-cam six. War in Korea prompted Britain's government to issue a specification for a new portable fire pump that required twice the capacity of its predecessors from a unit weighing half as much. It would need an exceptionally efficient engine. Hassan and Mundy schemed it with aluminium block and head, five main bearings and wedge-type chambers fed by

Compact and light with its aluminium block and head, the overhead-cam Coventry Climax FWA four had what it took to power Kieft, Lotus and Cooper sports cars.

Here with twin Weber carburettors in a Lotus Eleven, the Climax FWA began its career with two 1½-inch SU carburettors and producing 71bhp at 6,000rpm.

inclined valves from a single chain-driven cam through inverted-cup tappets like those of their Jaguar six.

When this FW – for featherweight – engine of 1,020cc first ran it handsomely exceeded its design target of 30bhp at 3,500rpm. Coventry Climax proudly displayed the finished pump set on its stand in the marine section of the 1953 motor show, where it was spotted by John Cooper, Colin Chapman and Cyril Kieft. Their plea that its engine be adapted to auto racing was agreed to by Climax chief Leonard Lee, provided it didn't interfere with other work at the Widdrington Road factory. 'Thus the FW became the FWA,' wrote Wally Hassan, 'with new bore, pistons, steel crank, twin carburettors plus revised valves and porting and was ready to race within months.'

Although Kieft was the first to race the FWA, at Le Mans in 1954, Lotus and Cooper most famously and successfully exploited it, Chapman in his Mark IX and Eleven and Cooper in his 'Bobtail' mid-engined T39. 'When I was first approached by Colin Chapman – who was only then starting up in motor racing – I had never met him,' said Climax's Wally Hassan, 'or even heard of him, and when I asked Harry Mundy about him he could only say that he had read the name in magazines and

that he had started making a few kit cars. We got to know each other much better in the next few years!'

Here was Chapman's introduction to the art and science of racing against rivals using exactly the same engine, for 'in the main,' wrote Hassan, 'we did a good job of building production-line racing engines which all produced, within a very little, the same power curves, and kept everyone happy. This also meant that providing an engine was kept in good condition, victory or defeat in any race was almost certainly due to the quality of the driving or the virtues of the rest of the car.'

This of course did not debar an effort on Colin's part to make some of his engines more equal than others. Wally Hassan gave an example:

Colin Chapman, who was always sharp as a razor but charming with it, sent back an engine for test before he fitted it to a Lotus for a particular sports-car race in Britain. We asked him what he had done to it to make it worth re-testing and when he said, 'Nothing at all,' quite cheerfully, we had no hesitation in giving it the full treatment. The result, which I think we anticipated, was that

With all-aluminium construction and an integral transaxle the Renault 16's 1.5-litre four was ideal, in a tuned version, to power the mid-engined Lotus Europa.

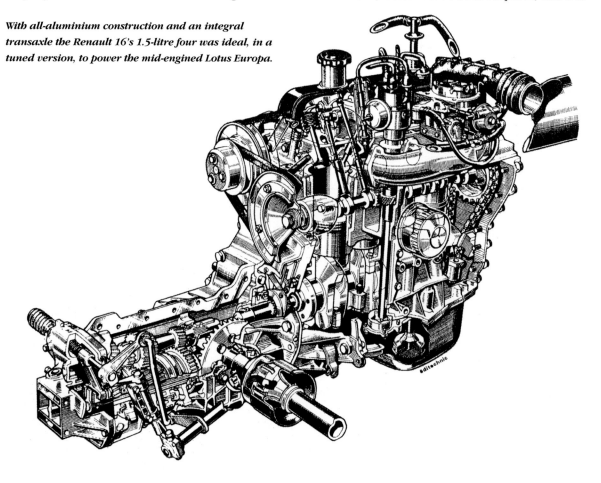

the engine blew up on the test bed, and when it was stripped we found (as we had suspected) that among other things the compression ratio had been pushed up a long way. On this occasion we felt that we had to make a stand over the deception, so we sent Colin's engine back in its blown-up state and let him know that his ploys had been rumbled. Then I got on the phone to his big rival, John Cooper, and asked him if he would like to try an experimental unit we were developing – for the same race that weekend! I'm happy to say that we proved our point by [Roy] Salvadori winning that race. After that we had to introduce a further stage of tune, so as to maintain our policy of fair do's for everyone!

The FWA's first class win came in 1954's Tourist Trophy at Dundrod, appropriately enough in a Kieft although Lotus was already racing one. By the end of 1955 Coventry Climax had produced 125 such engines, in their Stage 2 version delivering 83bhp at 6,800rpm from 1,097cc. Competing in 98 events they scored 69 firsts, 50 seconds and 41 thirds in Cooper, Lotus and Lola chassis. In 1,460cc FWB format they gave access to the 1.5-litre category and 1957's new Formula 2.

Early development problems with the FWB, with both bore and stroke increased, were highlighted in the report produced after two Elevens thus equipped raced in the British Empire Trophy at Oulton Park on 14 April 1956, driven by Chapman and Mike Hawthorn. 'The SU carburettor dampers started falling to pieces in practice,' it related, 'and each car got through two sets in the practice and the race. SUs reckon that this is due to excessive engine vibration and not the design of their dampers. We are inclined to believe this as another failure was a complete fracture of No 1 inlet manifold on Mr Chapman's car, which we also put down to engine vibration, although this may have been aggravated by the air bell touching on one of the chassis members.'

For the ambitious Colin Chapman the return to car-engine production by Coventry Climax was a godsend. Between the wars a veritable who's who of British road-car makers relied on Climax power, among them AJS, Clyno, Crouch, Triumph, Crossley, Horstman, Marendaz, Swift and Vale. A twin-cam four was supplied to Lagonda for its Rapier. Morgan was one of the last customers, racing at Le Mans with Climax engines. Immediately after the war the founder's son, Leonard Lee, took the family-owned business into the new field of fork-lift trucks to fill the gap left by collapsing military orders for fire pumps.

'He is a very persuasive fellow,' said Wally Hassan of

Cast integrally with the head, the long inlet passages of the Lotus Twin Cam four sloped steeply downwards to give the best possible flow through its inlet valves.

As designed by Harry Mundy and detailed by Richard Ansdale, the Lotus 'LF' twin-cam head on a Ford 105E block had valves inclined at 27 degrees from the vertical.

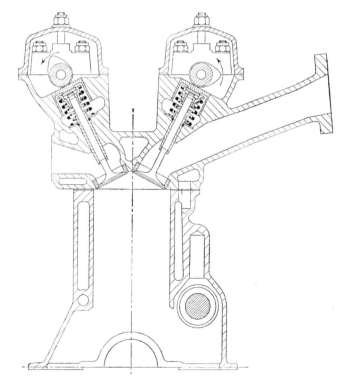

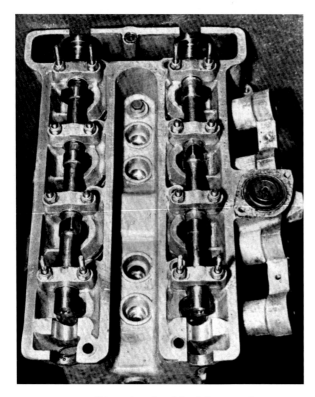

An experimental Twin Cam head had shorter inlet pipes to suit different types of induction equipment and camshafts with lobes for the rearmost cylinder that were overhung, unsupported at the extreme rear.

After a handful of 1.5-litre Twin Cams were made the final design had 1,558cc and five main bearings thanks to Ford's bigger-bore 116E cylinder block.

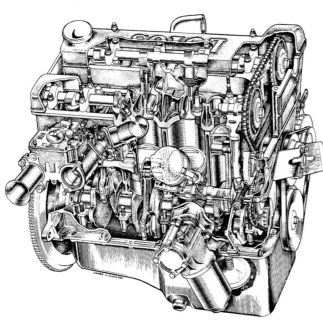

Chapman, who 'managed to convince Coventry Climax that a special "productionised" version of the FWA should be built to power his Elite, and guaranteed that at least a thousand would be sold. This engine was the FWE (E for Elite, of course) and was a combination of FWA and FWB in that we used the FWB's block and cylinder bore allied to the FWA stroke.' How the cash-strapped Chapman could have 'guaranteed' the purchase of 1,000 engines is a mystery, although an answer could be the City role that was played behind the scenes by the Elite's stylist, Peter Kirwan-Taylor.

Climax's road-proving of the hybrid four was in an MG Magnette ZA saloon, which with its 100mph top speed startled not a few fellow road users. The unit was ideal for the ultra-light Elite, weighing only 215 pounds. But among its drawbacks were high oil consumption, need for frequent overhauls and heavy periodic vibration unless the engine and clutch were well balanced. These faults tended to be overlooked by Climax, whose main aim during production of the FWE to 1963 was cost reduction rather than product improvement.

In 1966, three years after the run-out of the Elite, Colin Chapman sourced another complete engine from an outside supplier. When he opened his 22 January 1965 issue of *Autocar*, Chapman found a full description of Renault's new front-drive 16, complete with a cutaway drawing of its 1,470cc all-aluminium four. Five days later he wrote to Jabby Crombac to ask for help in contacting Renault to negotiate the purchase of a possible 500 units a year complete with matching four-speed transaxle.

Through Renault's PR chief Bob Sicot, Crombac made arrangements for clandestine meetings with the French company's engineering head Yves Georges and its commercial personnel. The upshot was exclusive production for Lotus of a hopped-up version of the Renault four to propel Chapman's new mid-engined Europa. In spite of its plebeian pushrod valve gear it was as useful as the overhead-cam Climax with 82bhp at 6,000rpm while weighing only 200 pounds. The Renault unit continued to power the Europa into 1971.

Replacing the French engine in the Europa was the first dedicated Lotus engine, known internally as the 'LF' to acknowledge its Ford foundations. Its conception dated from the late 1950s when Graham Hill and Steve Sanville were running the small shop at Lotus in which engines and gearboxes were tweaked as necessary. Marketed in the name of racing driver Raymond Mays, a special cylinder head had been developed for Ford's Consul engine. Chapman had one of these in his personal Consul which 'gave a great deal

of power.' This led to thoughts of a dedicated Lotus engine based on a standard unit.

Colin's motivation was his vision of a grander place in the world of cars for Lotus. 'Chapman had set his aspirations on Porsche,' recalled Mike Warner, 'at the centre of excellence of engineering. He realised that until Lotus created its own engine it was never going to be recognised fully as a member of the automotive world. Chapman had that vision.' From 1958 he and Steve Sanville were kicking around ideas for modified versions of standard engines that might be well suited to sports and competition cars.

How was this to be done? The procedure used reflected one of the two ways Chapman went about design, Mike Warner felt:

There were two sides to Chapman in the engineering sense. One was the in-depth Chapman who would get down and really go through the first principles of the engineering and come up with a completely new design concept – albeit influenced by another concept, it doesn't matter. The other side was the Chapman who would say, 'We want an engine, but we need a different head on it. Ford are coming out, I know, with a five-bearing-crank bottom end. Who's around?' And someone would say, 'Oh that's what this guy Harry Mundy does. He worked with Wally Hassan and

From 1971 the Twin Cam was installed in the Type 74 Europa, producing 105bhp at 5,500rpm and driving through a Renault transaxle.

he's a pretty good guy.' 'Well, get him in and have a chat to him. Let's see what we can do.' And that would be it. Chapman would water-ski over it and Mundy was left to get on with it. Working with Steve Sanville, they came up with a concept. And that's how the twin-cam evolved.

In fact as Warner well knew the first test engines of late 1961 were built on blocks with three-bearing bottom ends, which weren't up to the job. 'Jimmy Clark had one fitted in one of the very first Elans,' Warner recalled, 'and he got through three engines in six months.' Chapman may well have been aware that a five-bearing version was in the offing, for when it was announced for Ford's new 1500 model in May of 1962 he, 'Steve Sanville and John Standen (chief buyer) lost no time in visiting Ford at Aveley,' wrote Twin-Cam historian Miles Wilkins, 'and returning with a 1500 block in the boot of their car.'

Then technical editor of *Autocar*, Harry Mundy did indeed pen the new cylinder head's basic layout in return for a flat fee rather than the royalty arrangement proffered as an alternative by Chapman. Had he chosen a royalty of, say, £1 per engine he would have done well from a unit of which some 34,000 are thought to have

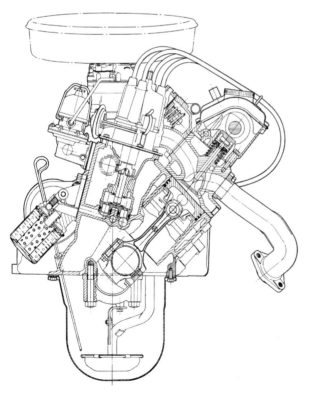

With twin Stromberg carburetion to meet American emissions rules, the Big Valve Twin Cam won out over bought-in engines to power the Elan +2, here in 1971.

been made. Lest Mundy be thought a dupe, however, his decision must be set against Lotus's perennially precarious finances and the unreliability of its books, from which both cars and engines were often 'lost' – this being a euphemism for their appropriation for the benefit of others, especially directors.

Although Mundy's first proposal was a single-overhead-cam head not unlike the Climax FWA, Chapman asked for twin cams instead – a decision that assured the engine's long career. Detailed production drawings of the new head were the work of Vienna-born Richard Ansdale, based in Britain since 1935 and a former Coventry Climax designer. Although working as a freelance Ansdale asked very little for the work, Wilkins reported: 'I enjoyed doing it, out of friendship to Colin, and I wanted the project to succeed.' No better

Obviously conceived as half a future V8, Vauxhall's Victor four of 1968 was the right size and shape to serve as a test bed for Lotus's own new engine, the LV range.

description could be given of the motivations that attracted so many talented engineers and others to work for the mercurial Chapman.

Colin Chapman's links with Ford improved in 1962 when Walter Hayes joined the company's British arm as director of public affairs. As a Fleet Street newspaper editor Hayes had earlier asked Chapman 'to write a new type of motoring column' for him. Thus the new 1,558cc engine had careers not only in the Elan, from 1962, but also in the Lotus-Cortina from 1963. The latter, a Lotus-built Cortina with a twin-cam engine, was the outcome of a typical dinner with Chapman at which, Hayes said, 'he would have nine or ten ideas to discuss; he wanted to work on them all at once.'

Although Chapman did indeed 'water-ski' over the new engine's many teething troubles, dealt with manfully and successfully by his team, he came to the party when key decisions had to be made. On a visit to William Mills at Wednesbury, the foundry struggling with the head castings, Mike Warner noticed what looked like brown paint on the heads Mills was casting for Jaguar. He discovered that the heads were being given a vacuum-infused sealing of Bakelite plastic that filled blow holes and kept casting sand from creeping out and acting as a powerful abrasive.

'I went back,' said Warner, 'and put this to Steve Sanville, the engine guy. "We can't go with that extra cost," was his reaction, so I went to see finance chief Fred Bushell and said, "If you look at what we're paying out in warranty cost because the sand particles are getting into the tappet sleeves and hour-glassing them…" Fred said, "Well, I'll have a word with Colin." And Colin overruled Steve Sanville and we had it put in. Of course Steve and I didn't get on very well after that.'

Starting in 1963, when the larger and heavier Elan +2 was being readied for its 1967 launch, Chapman and company weighed the use of other engines to give it Lotus-level performance. Through 1965 the units considered included a Lancia V4, Daimler V8, Triumph 2000 six, Ford V4 and V6, Cortina 1600 and even the Rover V8. Ultimately however the choice fell on the Twin-Cam. Chapman himself vetoed the idea of a complete bought-in engine for this prestige model, saying, 'I don't think it would be in keeping with the Lotus image to use one of the relatively large mass-produced engines which are available at the present time.'

In the heavier Elan +2 the Twin-Cam gave performance described as 'adequate more than sensational' by *Motor Sport*. When in October 1970

Colin Chapman asked engineering director Tony Rudd for ideas to improve sales of the +2, Rudd suggested more power and was told to get on with it. This was the birth of the fabled 'Big Valve' version of the engine, which Rudd knew well from 1965 and onward when his former employer, BRM, was making the racing versions. Subtle changes to its inlet passages included inlet valves a scant 0.036 inch larger whose contribution to the jump from 105 to 126 bhp was nominal.

By 1967 Lotus was increasingly taking over the production of the Twin-Cam head. 'We are actually machining the engine components ourselves at this stage,' Chapman told David Phipps, adding that 'we shall soon be doing the final assembly, and a new engine test house with five dynamometers that we are building at the present time should come into operation about March or April next year. In about a year's time we will be making our own cylinder blocks, and so on until we're making our own engine complete.' The production of blocks would in fact have to await the arrival of a new design that would 'be developed from our existing facilities over the next few years until it is a 100 per cent Lotus engine built 100 per cent by ourselves.'

The work of former Jaguar man Ron Burr, the Type 907 engine had a capacity of 1,973cc with main-bearing diameter of 2.5 inches and 2.0-inch rod journals.

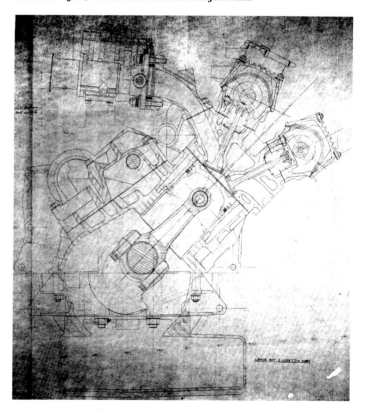

Aeroplane and Motor Aluminium Castings Ltd used its low-pressure process to cast the 907's head, block and main-bearing girdle of LM 25 WP aluminium alloy.

Although not the work of *Le Patron* himself, that new design which surfaced in 1972 has every right to be seen as a more Chapmanesque creation than its Twin-Cam predecessor. That was the view of Mike Warner, who said, 'The first real engine concept that Chapman came up

The Lotus 907 four had four valves per cylinder, symmetrically inclined at an included angle of 38 degrees. Inlet valves were 1⁵/₁₆-inch and exhausts 1³/₁₆-inch.

with, Chapman the designer, was the slant-four. This was started under Ron Burr, whom he got in from Jaguar. Ron, a really nice guy, a Midlands engineer, designed the slant-four working very close with Chapman. That slant-four, also conceived as a V8 – which was held back basically by economics – was the birth of the real Lotus engines.'

'The main reason that we went for our own engine,' Colin Chapman told Ray Hutton, 'was that we needed a high-performance two-litre and at the time Ford were not making – and had not in prospect – a suitable basis on which we could continue making a Lotus-Ford engine as we did with the Twin Cam. The overhead-camshaft Ford engine did not have the right stroke-to-bore ratio to produce the sort of high performance engine we wanted to make.' This was a reference to Ford's 'Pinto' four with its nearly-square dimensions of 90.8 x 87.9mm.

As a first step Chapman asked leading engine-building companies to prepare suggested designs for his consideration. BRM, for example, proposed a 120-degree V6, a design it had considered in the 1950s for the 2.5-litre Grand Prix rules. By the autumn of 1967, however, Lotus decided that its future needs would best be met by an aluminium in-line four inclined at 45 degrees to the left, with a twin-cam cylinder head and four valves per cylinder. Chapman and Ron Burr prepared a preliminary layout of such an engine in 2.0-litre size.

Then the Lotus engineers took a tour of the London Motor Show in October of 1967. On the stand of Vauxhall, a General Motors subsidiary, they were surprised to find that the new Victor had an engine arranged and

Lotus 907 cams were driven by a Powergrip cogged-rubber belt 1 inch wide with a $^{3}/_{8}$-inch pitch, its tension maintained by an idler pulley adjusted by an eccentric cam.

dimensioned much like the one they were planning, though of cast iron and with only one camshaft overhead. Chapman and Burr decided to save development time and money by using the Vauxhall block and bottom end as a slave unit to accelerate the realisation of their own engine. With oversquare dimensions of 95.3 x 69.2mm this was much more to their liking.

Ron Burr rewrote his cylinder head to suit it to the 4¼-inch bore spacing of the Vauxhall. This was closer than Burr had originally envisaged because his design had wet cylinder liners in an aluminium block instead of the Vauxhall's all-iron block. Next some cylinder heads were made to give them a baptism of fire in racing on the Vauxhall block. Known as the Type 904 Lotus engine, this first roared into life in September 1968. Fuel-injected versions were installed in two Type 62 cars, the racing version of the Europa. They validated the ideas of Chapman and Burr by scoring seven wins in 19 starts in 11 races.

In June of 1969 one of these engines was built up as a touring unit with Weber carburettors. After 51 hours on the dynamometer it covered 14,000 miles on the road in a Vauxhall Viva GT, giving results that were used to confirm the final engine design. This power unit, the Type 905, was the last of the test engines to use the Vauxhall cylinder block. During 1969 the sand-cast-aluminium components for the prototype Type 907 engines were machined and assembled. Test-running the first of eleven prototypes began in December of 1969. Two years later, early in 1972, its die-cast counterpart was entering the first stages of production.

Although Lotus internal codes used 'LV' for the new engine range, Colin Chapman was at pains to 'kill the idea that the 907 is a development of the Vauxhall engine. It is an entirely fresh design which was done before the Vauxhall engine became known to us. At that stage we were becoming concerned about the cost of building and developing prototypes. As a cost-saving measure we put our four-valves-per-cylinder head on a production bottom

Introduced in the new Lotus Elite in 1974 and a year later in the Eclat, the 907 four produced 162bhp at 6,200rpm breathing through twin Dell'Orto carburettors.

end to see how well it worked. Vauxhall introduced their slant-four with exactly the same stroke and bore as our own and almost the same cylinder centres – so we used that. But the present 907 owes nothing to Vauxhall. Their crankshaft is the only part that would fit. We will be making every part ourselves.'

The new Hethel-built Lotus four was first used in the Jensen-Healey from 1972 in 140-horsepower form with twin Zenith-Stromberg carburettors.

Former Lotus sales chief Graham Arnold took credit for eavesdropping on a train-borne conference over the use of a BMW engine in a new sports car to discover that Californian Kjell Qvale was planning to back the project, whereupon he suggested that the 907 might ideally suit the car that became the Jensen-Healey. Such a sale, a striking reversal of fortune with Lotus the supplier rather than the buyer of engines, would go a long way towards paying for the $1,250,000 worth of new machine tools needed to produce the 907. Chapman agreed the deal on the condition that the engines were sold to Jensen without warranty. Qvale was sanguine about this, saying, 'The warranty Lotus was going to give us wasn't worth anything anyway.'

Tony Rudd arrived from BRM just in time to tackle the commissioning of the engine-production tools. They were numerically controlled Marwin machines which, although versatile and aerospace-proven, were judged by many production men to be highly experimental for series production. 'The thing turned into a nightmare,' Rudd ruefully remembered. 'We discovered that the machine tools were voltage-sensitive, so they were not operating correctly half the time they were working on reduced current.' As well, Rudd found, 'these tools work beautifully when fully warmed up, holding tolerances precisely, but while they are warming up all sorts of cock-ups on dimensions and machining occur!'

Although the early 907 engines had problems with lack of oil drainage from the camshafts, vibration and insufficient torque, Jensen-Healey backer Qvale remembered 'a pretty good engine' whose main fault was a tendency to jump a few teeth on its cam-drive belt on a frosty morning, causing heavy damage. This was blamed on insufficient wrapping of the belt around the cam sprockets. Problems like these were gradually tackled as the engine moved into Lotus models, starting with the Elite in 1974 and expanding to power the entire range. In turbocharged form it gave the Esprit performance to match its looks. When the Jensen-Healey stopped production in the early 1980s the four was supplied to Chrysler UK to power the Talbot Sunbeam Lotus.

Times and finances never caught up with Colin Chapman's vision of a V8 version of the 907. It was built in 4-litre racing form as the Type 908 and as a road-car engine as the 909. The eight too had a Vauxhall heritage, for the GM sister had been planning an eight-cylinder version of its slant four. This had been part of chief engineer John Alden's ambitious range of front-drive Vauxhalls, on the design of which BRM had consulted during Tony Rudd's years there.

The Lotus eight used the 907's cylinder heads on a

new crankcase designed by Brian Bayliss assisted by Tom Brindley. 'Brian kept telling me he had no experience whatsoever of designing for die-casting,' Tony Rudd recalled, 'but his V8 crankcase was a work of art – lighter than the four-cylinder crankcase.' This contributed to an engine weight of some 375 pounds.

Chapman missed few opportunities to find backing for his V8. In mid-1968 he pointed out to Ford's racing executives that it could easily be enlarged to the Indy limit of 4.2 litres, at which it would produce 500 horsepower on petrol or 600 on methanol. 'Colin confirmed that Lotus could commence production of such an engine immediately,' wrote Andrew Ferguson, 'promising that a sufficient number for Indianapolis 1969 could be produced and race-tested with time to spare. Moreover, Colin continued, if Ford America provided the development costs of $100,000, plus a further $100,000 to cover the cost of the first five

An early stage of the 907's evolution was the LV220 of 1969, using the new head on a Vauxhall block to give 220bhp at 8,000rpm, powering a racing version of the Europa.

engines, they could be called Fords. Further examples, he said, could be supplied for $17,500 each.'

Here was a chance to build a pure-bred Lotus racing engine. The initiative was thwarted, however, by Ford's decision to reduce its existing V8 to 2.6 litres to compete in turbocharged form. Lotus professed indifference to its failure to muster funding for the big V8 for either racing or its road cars. 'We first ran a V8 in the form of a Rover-engined Europa,' recalled Mike Kimberley, referring to a 1968 project publicly attributed to industry supplier GKN. 'In our experience the car contradicted our basic search for a balance between the factors that go to make up a high-performance road car. The handling balance was affected and the fuel consumption was poor.'

Seen in the 1969 BOAC 500 at Brands Hatch, the Type 62 version of the Europa scored seven wins from 19 starts in 11 races with its fuel-injected LV220 four.

Nevertheless in 1976 Chapman still had hopes for his in-house V8 as a road-car engine. 'If you study our model numbers,' he told Jeremy Walton, 'you will find that there are three more obvious numbers to insert. Those will be the V8 versions of the existing cars – which will probably go through minor production facelifts, but they will be substantially the same car.[1]

'We designed the V8 as a 4-litre before the fuel crisis,' Colin added. 'It'll be all right though in a couple of years' time. We will be able to do it then. Right at the moment we do not have the resources to put the bigger engine into production.' Doing so, he said, would cost around £1 million, which he hoped an improving market would generate. It would probably have fuel injection, he added, 'because a carburettor layout will not give us the sort of fuel distribution we need.'

Having been frustrated in his plan to install a V8 in his cars, Colin Chapman subsequently professed

wariness of big engines. 'We're looking for high performance with very low fuel consumption,' he told Peter Windsor in 1979, 'or for low tyre wear and low brake consumption, and if we can achieve any of these things obviously we are better off than with something heavier, more powerful and thirstier.

'I think that if you design a car right,' Chapman continued, 'you can get the performance out of it that you need without using a lot of power. If you drive an Esprit or an Eclat *hard*, there aren't many opportunities on the road to use more power than they've got. And they've only got 2-litre engines. What do you want four litres for?' As a philosophy it was commendable – as long as it bore some relationship to the desires of buyers.[2]

Chapman entertained an earlier flirtation with a V8 in 1966 in partnership with a fellow creative entrepreneur. This was Alejandro de Tomaso, Argentinian resident in Modena and a prolific creator of fascinating prototypes. Having seen a de Tomaso-modified American Ford V8 in

---

1 The relevant type numbers are 83, 84 and 85.

2 Expectations for the 4-litre V8 didn't expire. In 1984 the Giugiaro-styled Lotus Etna was shown, powered by the eight, said to be producing 330bhp at 6,500rpm and weighing 415 pounds in road-equipped form. Assigned the M300 type number by Lotus, it was a dream car that failed to become reality. In 1996 Lotus introduced a 3.5-litre V8 engine for its Esprit in twin-turbocharged format, destined to be produced through to 2003.

1965, Colin Chapman commissioned an all-aluminium version. The resulting 5,512cc eight kept pushrod valve gear instead of the customer's preferred overhead cams and had bowl-in-piston combustion chambers. Design features were stronger pistons and connecting rods and six cylinder-head studs around each bore instead of four.

Credited with 500bhp, the Type 868 was a promising candidate to power a sports-racing Lotus. With the Type 30 and its successor the 40 being phased out, Chapman planned to install the engine in a new car using a tubular space frame with the suspension components that had been created for the Type 41 Formula 2 car. He told Andrew Ferguson that Frank Costin would be designing 'a negative-lift body from the word go' to suit it and that he hoped to start testing it after the Indianapolis rush was over. Sidelined in favour of other projects, however, this failed to reach fruition.[3] The 868 V8 remained another exhibit in de Tomaso's panoply of prototypes.

Colin Chapman had more than enough engine talent at his disposal in the UK. In pole position after Harry Mundy was the fast-thinking, slow-talking and witheringly acerbic

Chapman hoped to interest Ford in a racing version of his 908/909 V8, a 4.0-litre unit using 907-type cylinder heads on a new aluminium block.

Keith Duckworth. For one year, starting in the autumn of 1957, Keith worked at Lotus as a transmission development engineer. 'Colin was an impossible person to deal with,' he told Graham Robson, 'but he and I had a relationship which was extremely good. While I worked there I lost engineering arguments that I should have won because he marshalled his thoughts and his facts so much quicker than I could, so I would find myself agreeing to something that is wrong.

Duckworth hit it off with Chapman's principal lieutenant, Mike Costin. The pair set up Cosworth Engineering in September of 1958, though it remained a one-man band – with some help – for three years before Costin was released from his Lotus service contract. Thus Mike was still at Lotus when, in 1959, it was time to choose an engine for the Formula Junior Lotus Eighteen. 'I was somewhat instrumental in getting the Cosworth engine used,' Mike Costin related, referring to the new short-stroke 105E Ford four that Duckworth had tuned for racing.

---

3   This project did not progress far enough to warrant issuance of a type number.

In the post-Chapman era the Type 909 V8 was mooted as power for the Lotus Etna, Giugiaro-styled and first shown at Birmingham late in 1984 and then at Geneva.

The rival unit was BMC's four tuned by Speedwell, where former Lotus mechanic/driver Graham Hill had been a director since 1957 with founders John Sprinzel and George Hulbert. Still a driver for Lotus, Hill was keen to see Speedwell's engine adopted. 'I have it in mind that we made two Eighteen prototypes, one with each engine,' Mike Costin said. 'We took them testing and even with Graham driving, the Speedwell wasn't any quicker than the Cosworth Ford.' The latter's selection was not only a bonus to the Eighteen's performance but also a bonanza for Cosworth, which supplied 125 engines in the Eighteen's first year plus others to such rivals as Elva and Gemini.

Albeit successful in its own sphere, Cosworth was a minor player through the 1950s and early 1960s in the British racing-engine world. The *grande fromage* was Coventry Climax, which had raised its game. In for a penny, in for a pound, Climax produced an all-new twin-cam 1.5-litre racing engine for the Formula 2 that opened for business in 1957. Dubbed the FPF for 'Fire Pump Four', it was a happy engine from the start with a feisty 148 horsepower.

Both Cooper and Lotus had urged the FPF's creation. Looking the first engines over, Colin Chapman contributed to a significant change. The water pump was mounted too high, he told Wally Hassan. If the cooling system were to lose water, he pointed out, the supply to the pump would soon be air instead of water. Placing it lower would minimise this risk. Its location was lowered accordingly.

Lotus made good on its commitment to the FPF in 1957 with its Twelve, Colin Chapman's first single-seater. Looking ahead to 1958, Chapman envisaged a new family of sports and racing cars that would use the FPF in a novel way. 'It was evident at once,' he related, 'that a flat or near-flat engine position would be a big step forward both for our sports cars and for our new Formula 1 project. Gets the centre of gravity down of course, allows a smoother shape and in the case of the single-seater would put the driver much nearer the ground. The chaps at Indy have been happy with it and Mercedes didn't have such bad luck either, so we were pretty enthusiastic about the idea.'

Steeply sloped engines were indeed in vogue at the time. A straw in the wind had been a radical Cummins diesel racer of 1952, for which Frank Kurtis designed a chassis that sloped its big six-cylinder engine to a near-horizontal 85 degrees. This was food for thought for George Salih, a technician at Meyer & Drake, maker of the four-cylinder 4.2-litre Offenhauser four that dominated at Indianapolis. For the 1957 running of the 500-mile race Salih readied a car with its engine inclined at 72 degrees to the right – the first 'lay-down' Offy.

Salih and machinist Al Long fashioned a new dry sump on the low side of the crankcase, needing six tries to get it right. Drainage from the lower exhaust camshaft was improved and new inlet ram pipes curved to keep the throttle bodies horizontal. Quin Epperly collaborated with Salih on the chassis design, which exploited the lay-down engine with an ultra-low bonnet. In its debut Indy outing in 1957 the resulting Belond Special won at record speed. This car, which won again in 1958, was the subject of a cutaway drawing and description in *The Motor* of 23 July 1958.

A slope to the left was the approach adopted in 1952 by Mercedes-Benz to get the overhead-cam six under the low bonnet of its racing 300SL. The angle was 50 degrees, to which three degrees were added in the Grand Prix W196 of 1954–55. The sports-racing 300SLR of 1955 had the more extreme slope of 57 degrees. The in-line eight-cylinder racing engines were designed from scratch to operate at these angles, which drew the approbation of Colin Chapman.

'Naturally our first move was to pay a call on Climax' after he had this idea, said Chapman. 'They couldn't see any reason why their FPF four should mind being flopped over at 62 degrees to the right, so we plunged ahead and designed all our 1958 equipment around this premise.' One reason why the Climax boffins were sanguine about this idea was that the FPF's cylinder head had been derived from the right-hand bank of a stillborn racing V8, so in theory it was already accustomed to being sloped at 45 degrees in that direction.

There's every indication that Chapman implemented a back-door approach to the Widdrington Road premises of Coventry Climax to achieve the 'unfair advantage' of a sloped FPF. In his memoirs Wally Hassan derided Chapman's initiative, saying huffily that 'we were not consulted about this at first, and if we had been we would not have approved.'

Though such disdain implied a complete lack of co-operation, Chapman was explicit in telling the author that 'reports from bench testing at Climax showed the "flat" engine to be consistently down on output about twelve horsepower from the usual vertical set-up. We were assured that this was just a matter of getting a few details worked out and that there was no reason why the engines shouldn't produce full power in due time.' Much like the lay-down Offy, the inclined Climax had curved manifolds from its inlet ports to horizontal Weber or SU carburettors.

'The first to be completed were the new Fifteen sports cars,' Colin Chapman related. 'These went like blazes in short events at home, but we were being plagued by unusually high oil temperatures – as high as 120°C in some cases.' But with the reassurance given by the reports from Climax mentioned above, 'we went ahead on the construction of "flat" chassis for the GP cars.

'The reports from Climax were still discouraging, though, when it came time to build the Le Mans cars,' Chapman continued, 'so to be on the safe side we tilted the twin-cam engines back 17 degrees to the left. This necessitated a small hood bulge for the exhaust cam box but allowed much straighter intake piping – one of the points where we felt power was being lost. Well, that two-litre car astonished everybody including us at

Power in the range of 330–360bhp was suggested for the V8 in the Lotus Etna. Drive was to be either through a CVT or conventional five-speed transaxle.

Le Mans, and inspired us to do some very quick work on one of the single-seaters. These cars were just about finished by now, since we were aiming to have them ready to race at Reims just two weeks after Le Mans.

A pact between Colin Chapman and Alejandro de Tomaso created the Type 868 V8 of 5.5 litres to power a new sports-racing car using the F2 Type 41's suspension.

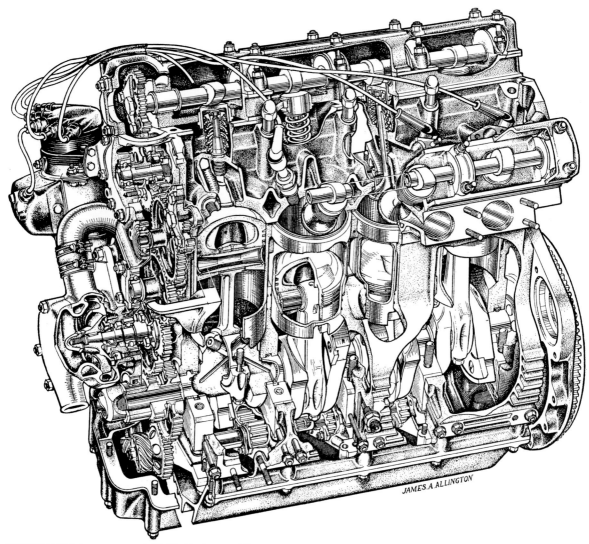

JAMES.A.ALLINGTON

Arrival of the pure-bred racing Coventry Climax FPF four in 1957 offered new horizons to Lotus and its British rivals, first for F2 and then for F1.

'We pulled the engine from the 1.5-litre car and cut away all the brackets for the "flat" mounting,' Chapman added. 'Then we swung it back into the frame and fudged about until we had it at about the proper left-hand tilt, angling it a bit so we could get the drive to the gearbox. With a drive shaft jury-rigged in place we then asked the drivers to try it and see if they thought they could drive the thing with their left knee high in the air over the shaft. When they said "yes" we welded in a few tubes here and there to keep the engine from falling

As used in the Lotus Twelve in 1957 – here in 1958's Monaco Grand Prix – the Climax FPF was vertical, fed by special twin-throat SU carburettors. The water pump was still high, later to be lowered at Chapman's recommendation.

out and there we had our upright mounting.

'In spite of being a half-litre down on the other, this revised car went so well that our drivers were literally fighting over it,' related Chapman. 'This did it as far as we were concerned. Before Silverstone a rather neater conversion had been made on the other car and we were out of the flat-engine business. And all this time, in the course of some fifty runs on the bench, Climax had been unable to come up with any conclusive evidence as to the exact reason for the power loss. We think it's a combination of loss of ram effect in the curved intake piping with excessive fluid pumping losses in the sump, but that shouldn't be so hard to solve, should it?'

Curved inlet piping could have been the culprit. Mike Costin thought so, saying that 'the inlet port still went in there and you had to bend the port round to get at it. Now you won't ever see a Cosworth engine with a bent port, because you've got to go straight down to that inlet valve. A bent inlet costs a lot of horsepower. Whether the horsepower you lose is compensated by a slightly smaller frontal area I don't know.' Nevertheless the 1954 Mercedes-Benz W196 had curved inlet ram pipes, changed to straight pipes in 1955 only to get better performance correlation between the test bed and the car.

The high oil temperatures experienced in the Fifteen did seem to indicate problems with oil circulation and scavenging, problems which as Chapman suggested were not insoluble. But while Coventry Climax was prepared to push the boat out for Cooper it was less amenable to extra development work for Lotus. In retrospect it's evident that both gave up on the idea prematurely. The mutual failure of Lotus and Climax to crack the challenge of a lay-down FPF stands as a lost opportunity for both.[4]

Colin Chapman and bank angles of the FPF figured in bizarre experiments in the middle of the 1960 season, the last of the 2.5-litre Formula 1 era. Having given up his controversial Sixteen and adopted the rear engine, Chapman was at odds to understand why – according to his drivers – his Eighteen couldn't match the Coopers in straight-line speed. Noting that his rivals sloped their FPFs at 20 degrees to the vertical so that their carburettors were inside the bodywork, Chapman built a new Eighteen of the same configuration for the fast Belgian Grand Prix at Spa.

For his Belond Special, winner at Indy on its first appearance in 1957, George Salih successfully inclined a 4.2-litre Meyer & Drake four at 72 degrees to the right.

Meanwhile Cooper too was worried about its top-speed performance against the Lotuses. Thinking that the speed of the Eighteen indicated that it might not need its inclination of the FPF and the associated modification of the sump, Cooper built a straight-up version of its low-line GP car. Both raced their respective test cars during the summer, Lotus at Spa, Reims and the British GP. After results that were inconclusive both reverted thereafter to their normal layouts.

That Chapman's Lotus wasn't in the best books of Coventry Climax was evident from allocations of the company's new 1.5-litre V8 in 1961. The first went to Cooper for double world champion Jack Brabham and the other to Rob Walker's private stable whose driver was Stirling Moss, the

---

4 The ghost of Chapman may have smiled on observing the Grand Prix efforts of Brabham and engine supplier BMW in 1986–87. To steal a march on his rivals designer Gordon Murray proposed that the turbocharged BMW four be sloped at 72 degrees to the left, allowing an ultra-low driving position to improve the rear wing's effectiveness. Though BMW's Paul Rosche made a good fist of the engine, transaxle and other problems blunted their challenge. These 'flat-iron' Brabhams marked the end of BMW's Formula 1 participation in the turbo era.

As initially installed in the new Lotus Fifteen sports-racer of 1958, the Climax FPF was inclined at 62 degrees to the right, its inlet ducts being curved to suit.

man who had first won championship GP races for Lotus-Climax in 1960. Not until the 1962 season did Lotus receive its three FWMV engines for a two-car team.

Like its rivals Lotus had to work out the best positioning on its chassis for the bulky 'bomb' that housed the pressure pump of the Lucas fuel-injection system. 'First of all the bomb was mounted at the very tail,' Chapman explained. 'We thought the fuel would run to it more easily in the rear position, the plumbing

was easier and there was a mounting position for it but it got too hot and we were suffering from all sorts of vaporisation troubles. We then moved it to a side location and that really didn't solve the problem so we finally decided we would put it in the coolest place where there was any space – at the front – and we've kept it at the front ever since.'

Supplying racing engines to Colin Chapman was no walk in the park. This was illustrated by an incident when the FWMV V8 was converted to fuel injection for 1963. Climax historian Des Hammill wrote that Chapman 'thought there wasn't enough air getting into the latest fuel-injected engine. Chapman claimed that the air was being deflected over the head of the driver and wasn't being inducted by the engine. Coventry Climax engineers said this was not happening and, to convince him, fitted a Bowden cable and control lever to the five-position adjustment plate so the driver could alter the fuel content (rich or lean) when the car was going. It made no noticeable difference, clearly proving that the mixture was correct and that the engine was getting the air it needed to function.'

Chapman's ability to get into trouble with his engine suppliers was exemplified by an incident at the 1963 German GP when Jim Clark's Lotus-Climax was misfiring from the first lap to second place at the finish. 'It was a faulty sparking plug,' said Colin, 'a trouble which he had had right from the fall of the flag and which steadily got worse. Racing plugs were in very short supply and by the Nürburgring we were down to running on reconditioned plugs.'

The steep rightwards inclination of its FPF four superbly suited the architecture of the new Fifteen and was initially adopted as well for the all-new Formula 1 Lotus Sixteen. [LAT]

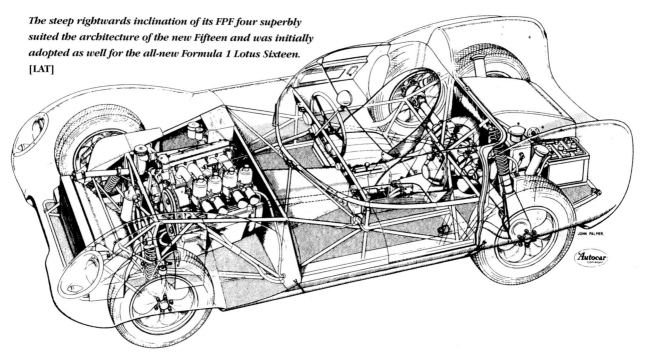

After early running of the inclined engines in the Fifteen proved problematic, they and the Sixteens, shown, were revised with the four angled at 17 degrees to the left.

To this both Climax and plug supplier Champion took vigorous exception. Inspection of the plug from the offending cylinder showed that it was shorted out by grit from the process used by Champion to clean sparking plugs. The cleaned plugs had been returned to Lotus for use in testing with no thought that they'd be chanced in a race. 'How many bloody times do we have to tell you to only ever use new spark plugs for a race?' was the reproof to Chapman by Harry Spears of Climax, said Des Hammill. Thereafter Champion stopped returning cleaned plugs to the Grand Prix teams.

Reciprocally, Chapman explained, changes in the Climax V8 kept Lotus on the hop: 'They gradually introduced bigger piston clearances and reduced ring tension which increased blow-by and pressurised the crankcase. As there was no breather we started to blow oil out and cam-cover gaskets kept blowing too. So they put in much bigger scavenge pumps to maintain crankcase depression and this gave us terrible oil aeration. We finally went to a centrifuge-type air/oil separator in the top of the oil tank which worked very well.'

'Engine mountings we had to change for structural reasons,' added Chapman about the eight's installation in the 25. 'No two engines seem to be the same size and with rigid mountings we were putting pre-loads into the mounting points. So now only two points fix the fore-and-aft location and the other six have fore-and-aft compliance but not lateral compliance, because the engine contributes a lot to the torsional stiffness of the rear end.'

Starting in 1964 Climax produced a 32-valve version of the FWMV, one of which was released to Lotus in 1965. 'When we first used the four-valve engine,' said Chapman, 'Jim Clark felt it was quicker for one reason only – it carburetted better – but they never did get much power out of it. We had a two-valve engine which Mike Spence used most of the season which has always been within one or two horsepower of it. Every time Climax got an increase on the four-valve they could go

back and get it on the two-valve for the same reason. Toward the end of the season Jimmy wasn't sure it even carburetted better and he could almost always jump into Mike's car and go quicker. I would say Mike had the quicker car most of 1965.'

An important early evolution of the Climax V8 was the creation by engineer Gray Ross of the 'bundle of snakes' exhaust manifolding that gave evenly spaced exhaust pulses with the 90-degree sequence of rod journals used on the early crankshafts. Simpler manifolding was adopted with the use of a 180-degree or 'flat' crankshaft.

The flat crank showed no power increase on the test bed, said Colin Chapman, but 'there may have been some installed difference because the engine was breathing less hot air with the low exhaust system. We feel this is an incidental advantage for the low individual exhaust systems used on the flat-crank engines. The pipes come out, down and away so far from the

Coventry Climax engineer Gray Ross conceived the 'bundle of snakes' exhaust that gave equal exhaust spacing, improving scavenging to boost the FWMV's power.

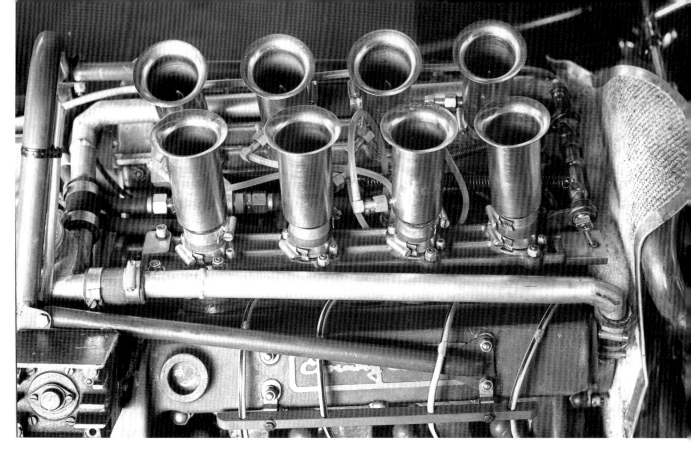

Above: Seen at Spa in 1963, Lucas fuel injection for the Climax FWMV V8 eliminated the problem of cutting out under lateral g forces that afflicted Weber carburettors.

Below: Pictured in the Lotus 29 test mule, the 4.2-litre racing version of Ford's Fairlane V8 had Weber carburettors and individual exhaust stacks at first.

carburettor intakes that there's no possibility of hot air getting into them.'

The exhaust system created by Gray Ross for the 90-degree-crank V8 came in handy when Lotus allied with Ford to attack the 500-mile race at Indianapolis. In 1963 Chapman rang Ross to say that 'he wanted to try the crossover exhaust system on the small-block Ford engine instead of the eight "stack" pipes that the Americans were currently using,' wrote Des Hammill. 'Gray supplied the details of the design and, some time later, the exhaust system was made and tried out on one of these engines. The Ford engineers got back to Colin Chapman telling him how successful it had been. Colin, in turn, rang Ross to tell him the incredibly good news that the engine's maximum power had increased by 63bhp!'

As usual with any project Chapman was taking more than a casual interest in the engines Ford supplied for the Indy effort. The target that he set Ford for its engines in 1963 was 350bhp as Dan Gurney – a partner in the effort – explained: 'We came up with this figure because I knew last year with Mickey Thompson's car I'd had about 330bhp at best and even during the race, when I'd had considerably less than that, we still weren't completely out of the picture. I figured the Lotus would be better, too, and we wanted to have a realistic power figure.'

SUGGESTED ENGINE SPEC

Bearing in mind the type of car that this engine is to be used in and the inherent advantages this incurs over the more normal Indianapolis machinery then the emphasis on the engine design is to be on reliability for light weight on gasoline rather than maximum possible power from a heavy engine using high consumption rate fuels, tyres etc.

In view of this then LOTUS CARS would like to suggest the following are the requirements for a power unit to fulfil the above conditions and prove capable of winning the race in 1963:-

1. Light weight: (a) Aluminium block and heads.
   (b) All other non-structural components such as pan, timing cover, water & oil pumps etc, inlet manifolds, etc in magnesium.
   (c) Lightweight steel crankshaft.
   (d) Lightest possible flywheel to carry clutch – maybe aluminium with steel facing.
   (e) Target weight for complete power unit 350lb [less if possible].

2. Reliability: (a) Con-rods forged from special material in standard dies.
   (b) Dry sump oil system [pan depth 6¾"].
   (c) Forged pistons very highly desirable.
   (d) Weber* carburettors tested against fuel injection.
   * Downdraft as used on 4.5 litre Maserati V8.

3. Power: (a) Highest obtainable from pushrod configuration. Suggest 350bhp at 7,000rpm, max permissible rpm 7,500.
   (b) Largest practicable bore in light alloy block [say 3.76 x 2.87].
   (c) 'Cross-over' exhaust system for better middle power range.
   (d) If carburettors used, then use small enough bodies & chokes to give good part throttle response and not necessarily the size required for absolute full throttle max power.
   (e) Lotus would like to supply a camshaft for test based on their English Ford cams.

4. Installation: (a) No accessories down either side of cyl block which extend out sideways more than the side face of the block itself.
   (b) Water pump etc to be held as close as possible to the front face of engine to keep overall length to the minimum. Inlet to pump to be on the left hand side and horizontal.
   (c) Additional lugs cast on magnesium pan to assist in locating gearbox/clutch bell housing.

Colin Chapman's complete want list for the engine, as presented to Ford, is shown as a sidebar opposite.

'Ford could make the engine but didn't know how to build the chassis,' said Chapman. 'We said we would supply three cars and race two if they would build an engine specifically for the race. They made a wonderful engine based on the Ford Fairlane of 4.2 litres. In its normal specification the block is cast iron and weighs 140 pounds but for us they agreed to make it in light alloy. If we had just reproduced the existing shape it would have weighed 50 pounds; we got them to make it stronger and put an extra 20 pounds of alloy into it, giving us a 70-pound block. It produces 350bhp and is the only engine I know which gives more than one horsepower per pound.' The engines Ford provided for Chapman's Type 30 sports-racer lacked the advantage of this aluminium block.

The Indy project's philosophy in 1963 was to benefit from a light car and excellent fuel economy, Chapman added: 'Most Indianapolis cars do about 2½ miles per gallon. Ours gives 7½–8.' Ford elected to carry out its high-performance engine development in-house, a decision which was looking ill-advised less than three months before the race when high-speed tests at its Arizona proving ground produced several failures. The first, a broken rocker arm and bent pushrod, came after only four laps at 4,500rpm. Another V8 was shut down after 'evidence of misfiring and roughness.' More failures followed.

'It would appear that adequate performance exists to achieve the race times required,' Chapman reported to Ford, 'and what is now required is absolute reliability.' With this looking elusive, Chapman and his partner Dan Gurney had a crisis of confidence. 'We don't want to go with you,' they told Ford. 'You've got major problems.' They asked that the engines be built in California instead, probably by the respected Traco outfit. With a last-minute push and improved valve gear Ford managed to avoid such embarrassing outsourcing.

Meanwhile back in the Old World a new Grand Prix Formula 1 was taking shape. In late November of 1963 the FIA invited representatives of the racing teams to a meeting in Paris to give their views on the new rules to take effect from 1966 onwards. Talking among themselves beforehand, the team chiefs agreed they'd like a 2-litre limit. 'We agreed that whatever we asked for,' said BRM's Tony Rudd, 'the FIA would reduce. Someone said, "Let's ask for three litres. They will cut that down as they always do. They cannot make it 2.5 – as we'd just had such a formula – so they will give us two litres."

'We all agreed the tactics,' Rudd continued, 'and that Colin should do the talking. There was a long rambling

Technology transfer from Formula 1 gave a huge boost to the Indy Lotus programme with Ford's adoption of the 'bundle of snakes' exhaust system that suited a 90-degree crankshaft.

introduction, then the FIA president asked: "What would you gentlemen like?" Colin said, "Three litres." The president looked round his colleagues, nodded and said, "Done. Thank you for your time, gentlemen." That was that. We filed out, absolutely thunderstruck.' Wally Hassan's immediate reaction was that he'd be unable to get funding for a 3-litre Climax engine.

Relative engine performances on methanol and petrol were evaluated during the 1963 Indy effort to help reach the conclusion that petrol's better fuel economy made it the right strategic choice.

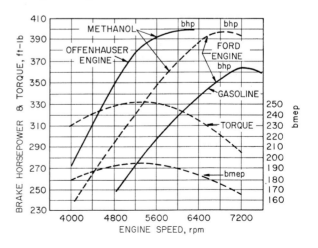

Above: *Driving a sister car to Dan Gurney's 29, shown, Jim Clark came 19 seconds from winning at Indianapolis in 1963 after Ford overcame its V8's teething troubles.*

Below: *Still using an aluminium version of its Fairlane block, Ford introduced this four-cam 32-valve version of its V8 for Indy racing in 1964.*

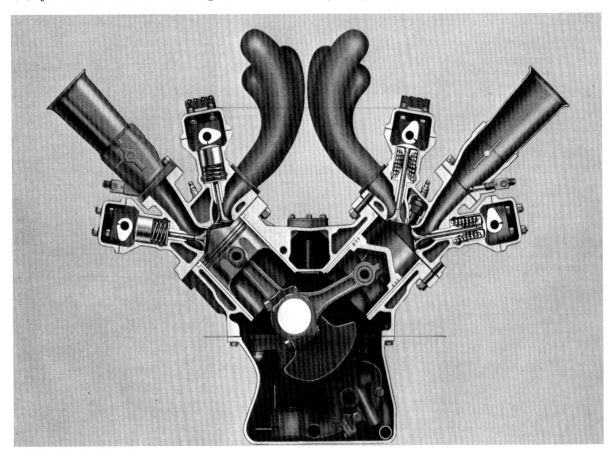

In fact the 1966 Formula 1 included a remarkable provision that allowed supercharged 1.5-litre engines as well. Soon after its announcement Colin Chapman called the new Formula 1 'a logical development. It gives us the chance of running with 1,500cc engines during the next two seasons and fitting superchargers on them for 1966. I think that the sort of power band which we will get from a supercharged 1½-litre engine will call for some rather exotic type of transmission which will fully utilise it.'

Asked whether he foresaw power outputs as high as that of the fabled supercharged BRM V16 of the early 1950s, Chapman said, 'I don't think, initially at any rate, that we shall get as much as 580bhp but I think it is possible to think in terms of 500bhp fairly early on. But we will have a much better torque curve than was apparent with the old V16 BRM engine. It depends, of course, on the type of blower. If you use some type of positive-displacement supercharger you will get an improvement throughout the entire speed range.'

Neither Climax nor Chapman was a stranger to supercharging. For a 1957 record attempt in the 1.1-litre class, Climax produced an FWA four equipped with a Roots-type blower that it normally used for a two-stroke marine diesel. Delivering 124bhp, it propelled a special

Eleven to five speed records at Monza. Its average over 50 kilometres was an impressive 145.5mph. Later a private owner boosted a single-cam Climax using a vane-type Shorrock supercharger, fitting it in an uprated Seven.

Thus signs seemed set fair for the creation of a supercharged 1.5-litre engine for Chapman's use. The technology of the day would have excluded turbo-supercharging; although introduced for road cars in the early 1960s this was still in its infancy. Nor would turbocharging have produced the kind of power and torque curves that Chapman – as he mentioned above – knew were required. The V16 BRM's centrifugal blower would have been disqualified for the same reason. Only a Roots- or vane-type supercharger would have been suitable, probably with multiple stages for efficiency and an intercooler since petrol was the mandated fuel.

Widdrington Road wasn't short of the required technology. In setting out his plans for the 1964 season Colin Chapman wrote to his designers, 'There will be an entirely new 1½ litre engine available from Coventry

Lotus adopted Ford's four-cam V8 for Indianapolis from 1964, installing it in that year's 34 and from 1965 in the 38, with which Jim Clark won the 500-mile race.

Climax about the end of July and this will necessitate the construction of a special, much modified, car which will be designated Type 25/3. More details of these requirements will be given under the relevant Project Spec but in the meantime design and manufacturing capacity must be reserved to enable a vehicle to be produced in time to meet the promised engine delivery.'

This was a reference to a new engine that Climax was producing to meet the V8 and flat-12 challenge from Ferrari, where John Surtees was revitalising the red cars' attack. Although the chassis was duly prepared, the engine wasn't ready for it in either 1964 or 1965. It was a 32-valve flat-16, the FWMW, whose many development challenges kept it from reaching race-readiness while the 1½-litre formula was in force.

Looking ahead to the blown option offered by the new Formula 1 Peter Windsor-Smith, the flat-16's designer, urged that the FWMW be completed so that it could be supercharged to take part in Grand Prix proceedings

from 1966. 'Coventry Climax did look into this,' wrote Des Hammill, 'and contracted [consulting engineer] H. R. Godfrey to do a feasibility study on it. The company even claimed that the turbocharged [*sic*] engine would theoretically produce 450bhp if it was intercooled.' The associated cost would have been substantial.

The alternative, for which Colin Chapman pressed Climax, was to boost the existing FWMV V8. The eight had always been regarded as somewhat over-designed and not a high revver; this would have been advantageous in a new role as a supercharged engine. When Wally Hassan demurred, Chapman offered to carry out the supercharging at Lotus if Climax would co-operate.

Hassan had other ideas. Early in 1965 he was about to turn 60. Involved as he was in work on Jaguar's new V12, he realised that he couldn't also keep watch on an ambitious new racing-engine programme. At his recommendation Climax decided in February of 1965 to cease developing new racing engines. Its sole concession to the persuasive Colin Chapman was to provide Lotus with two 1,974 cc V8s to tide it over in 1966 and '67 until it had proper 3-litre engines. These also came in handy for racing in the Tasman Series.

During much of 1966, however, Lotus was already competing with a pukka 3-litre racing engine. In *Motor* this was described as 'the most sophisticated and the most complicated Grand Prix engine of all time…designed to produce over 400bhp in its first season, over 500bhp by the end of the new GP Formula and stressed for 600bhp at 13,500rpm.' This was BRM's Type 75, composed of two flat-eight 1.5-litre engines geared together.

BRM's readiness to make this engine available to a bitter on-track rival was owed to a wave of commercialism that was then sweeping the racing activities of its proprietor Rubery Owen. In 1965, when BRM was selling both V8 F1 engines and four-cylinder F2 units, it had come close to breaking even on racing. This gave Rubery Owen the idea that they might actually be able to make money at it. Colin Chapman struck a deal to lease the H16 engines from BRM until his other arrangements came to fruition.

To suit the engine Chapman and chief designer Maurice Phillippe prepared their Type 43. Like BRM's own car this used the bulky engine as the rear of the chassis, introducing this technology to Lotus. 'We delivered an engine and gearbox to Lotus,' recalled Tony

As a stopgap in 1966 Chapman leased BRM's Type 75, a heavy 3-litre H16 that struggled with both power and reliability. An Indy version was attempted as well.

Rudd, then still at BRM, 'which nearly destroyed the small van they sent to fetch it. They were absolutely thunderstruck by its weight. The engine weighed 555 pounds plus 118 pounds of gearbox and clutch.'

Only late in the 1966 season was the Lotus-BRM raceable. Taken along by BRM as a spare to the US Grand Prix at Watkins Glen was a heavily salvaged H16 with metal plates and patches of Araldite holding its crankcase together. Giving some 375bhp, this engine was rushed into service for Jim Clark's Type 43 at the last minute under BRM's lease agreement with Lotus. It survived to win the Grand Prix – the only victory ever achieved by the H16.

Rashly, even greedily, BRM's July 1965 agreement with Lotus also called for the supply of an alcohol-fuelled 4.2-litre version of the H16 for a 1966 Indianapolis effort sponsored by Andy Granatelli's STP Corporation. It was to be installed in a Type 42 version of the Grand Prix car. When Tony Rudd baulked at this more than doubling of

Driving the Type 43, designed to be BRM-powered, Jim Clark had a lucky win at Watkins Glen in 1966 when leaders Bandini and then Brabham both retired.

his workload a meeting was called at Rubery Owen's Darlaston offices, its chief Sir Alfred Owen in the chair.

'Colin played all his cards superbly,' recalled Rudd, 'stroked every one of Sir Alfred's pressure points – the little man doing it for Britain against the might of America – and got everything he wanted! Many years later Fred [Bushell] told me that Sir Alfred must have been convinced he had a world-beating engine if Colin Chapman wanted it so badly, which is why he agreed to make the 4.2-litre for Colin.'

Neither in 1966 nor in 1967, its potential last gasp, was the big H16 ready for Indy. With similar shortcomings to the 3-litre version plus others that were even more severe, it was run eventually to 10,000rpm on a mixture of gasoline with 40 per cent methanol. Rough and harsh,

In the earliest days of Cosworth's Ford-branded V8 Mike Costin, right, ministered to the DFV's needs on the Northampton company's test bed.

COLIN CHAPMAN

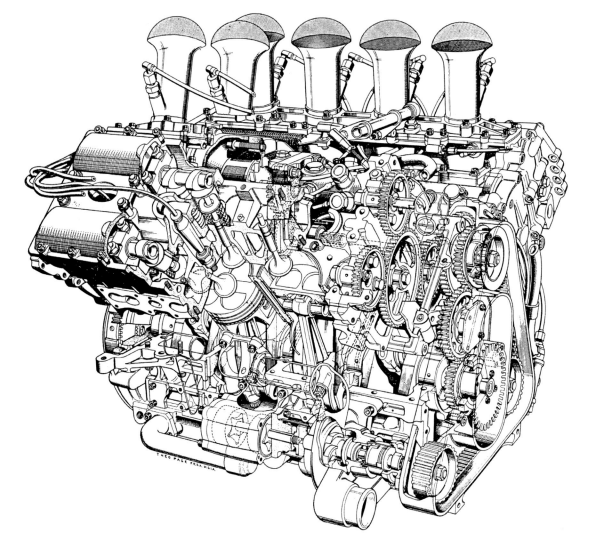

Key features of Keith Duckworth's DFV V8 design were its flat crankshaft, Gerotor-type oil pumps and narrow vee-inclined angle in four-valve chambers.

the 4.2-litre H16 kept breaking pieces which were strengthened sufficiently for it to record a maximum power reading of 585bhp. Recalled an engineer who saw it in action: 'It is probably the most awesome, almost terrifying engine I have experienced running on a test bed.'

Attached to a Lotus Type 42 chassis, BRM's Indy engine lasted for only five laps of Snetterton before it tore up the centre gear and bearings of the gear set that joined its two crankshafts. In later Mark 2 form the 4.2-litre engine – still very rough-running – gave no more than 530bhp and continued to devour its output gear train. Seeming to defy ready solution of its problems, the big engine was shelved. In 1966 and '67 Chapman had to fall back on Ford's four-cam V8 for his Indy efforts. In the latter year he raced one Type 42 chassis adapted to the Ford engine.

On 4 June 1967, amidst the sand dunes of the Dutch coastline, Colin Chapman's permanent solution to his engine problem scored the debut victory for which it is justly celebrated. Bolted to the new 49 chassis was the V8 conceived by Keith Duckworth and Mike Costin. To

Chapman's eternal credit it was his idea to approach these former Lotus engineers to ask whether they were prepared to build a 3-litre Formula 1 engine and, if so, how much they thought it would cost.

'It was in 1965 that Colin came along,' recalled Keith Duckworth, 'and asked, "Do you want to have a go at a Formula 1 engine and how much do you think you need to design and develop it?" In our great scientific costings of that era, I asked my co-directors – Mike Costin, Bill Brown and Ben Rood – how did £100,000 sound? Yes, we should be able to do it for that. So Colin said he'd try and see whether he could raise £100,000 from somewhere.'

Esso, which backed Lotus, wasn't interested. David Brown, owner of Aston Martin and Lagonda, was almost too interested, demanding too much control for his investment. BMC was off limits, linked as it was with John Cooper and the Mini. An early contact at Ford was dismissive but during a later approach public affairs

chief Walter Hayes was open to the idea. He had to convince others, among them newly arrived engineering chief at Ford of Europe, Harley Copp. It was up to Chapman to convince Copp, saying, 'Look, you're missing out on the best investment you've ever made. For £100,000 you can't go wrong!'

There was also the little matter of what sort of engine it should be. With 12s and 16s being built it seemed that the new Formula 1 was moving in an exotic direction. Was Duckworth heading the same way? He recalled the conversation with Chapman: 'The argument had been, with Colin and me, "Do you think you can make a 12 down to weight and get the fuel in the right place? With 200-mile races, is that possible?" Doesn't look possible. Right, we can make an eight down to it' – to the minimum weight of 500 kilograms. 'If they'd said 550 kilograms then I'd have changed it to 12 possibly. You've got to look at the whole picture.'

'Of course I'm tremendously grateful to Ford for funding this Formula 1 racing engine,' said Colin Chapman two years later. 'When Coventry Climax packed up racing, we were at our wit's end to know where to go for a power unit. At that time Len Crossland – now Sir Leonard Crossland – and Walter Hayes and Harley Copp, three of the Ford directors, were prevailed upon to fund an engine to be developed by Cosworth. If it hadn't been for their doing it, I don't know where British racing would be today.'

A Chapman refinement contributed to the success of the Lotus-Ford package. An early challenge for Jim Clark and Graham Hill had been a sharp surge in power that was hostile to subtle control. Suffering a flat spot around 5,000rpm, the V8 would then surge from 6,500rpm onwards so suddenly that Clark likened it to a second engine cutting in. To give more progressive response Chapman designed a new throttle linkage which Maurice Phillippe detailed.

Such was the form of the 49-DFV, leading every race in the rest of 1967 and winning four, that Ford's Walter Hayes 'began to think that we might destroy the sport. I realised that we had to widen the market for the DFV engine so that other teams could have access to it. At dinner one evening before the German GP I said to Colin Chapman, "You know, if we don't make this engine available to everyone else we'll kill the whole thing because there's no reason why anyone else will ever win". He said something like, "Oh, well, what a pity,"

Bolted to the back of the Lotus 49's monocoque, the Ford DFV enjoyed simple low-placed exhaust manifolding thanks to its flat or 180-degree crankshaft.

After its release to other teams in 1968, the Cosworth-built Ford V8 remained the engine of choice for Formula 1 Lotuses throughout the 1982 season and part of '83.

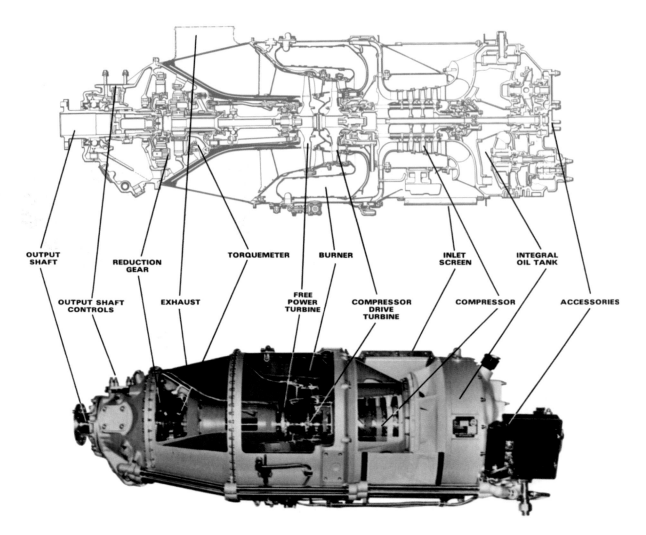

| OUTPUT SHAFT | REDUCTION GEAR | TORQUEMETER | BURNER | INLET SCREEN | INTEGRAL OIL TANK |

OUTPUT SHAFT CONTROLS   EXHAUST   FREE POWER TURBINE   COMPRESSOR DRIVE TURBINE   COMPRESSOR   ACCESSORIES

*A cutaway and drawing reveal the secrets of Pratt &
Whitney's versatile ST6 gas turbine, first used at
Indianapolis by the STP-Paxton team in 1967.*

*With its output shaft pointing forwards, to the right, the
ST6 gas turbine nestled in the rear of the four-wheel-drive
Type 56 Lotus built to compete at Indy in 1968.*

and we agreed. No argument, no histrionics, nothing. In
later years I used to wonder about that – was he so
supremely confident in his ability?' Answer: yes, he was,
as the future would testify.

Although Matra and McLaren gained the V8 in 1968,
it was Graham Hill's Lotus-mounted world championship
that year after the grievous loss of Jim Clark in a Formula
2 crash at Hockenheim. In all with the Ford DFV Lotus
would win four championships for drivers and five for
constructors through the rest of the Chapman era.
Albeit often exploited by others, Colin's innovations
were decisive in maintaining the DFV's competitiveness
against Ferrari's relentless attacks.

A might-have-been season was 1977, when Lotus
failed to convert the immense promise of the new 78
into either championship. Its efforts were undermined
by a spate of four straight engine failures in the second
half of the season followed by a fifth for good measure.
This was the result of a Chapman decision, in the view
of Ralph Bellamy: 'Not content with having

aerodynamically the best car on the track, he had to go off and do a deal to get development engines. But development engines blow up. Races were lost due to engine failure when the car should really have won every race once the skirts were fixed.'

What Bellamy didn't know was that Chapman was only responding to the demands of his star driver. 'In the first few races with the car,' said Mario Andretti, 'I don't think we had the best engines, which didn't help. I started making a lot of noise in that area and I think I probably stimulated the engine-development programme somewhat. As it turned out, of course, that was both good and bad.' At one point, said the driver, 'it seemed like all I had to do was look at a Cosworth engine and it blew up.'[5]

That the DFVs in question were to some degree experimental contributed to their fragility. As well, said

Maurice Phillippe's aviation experience helped him devise the best mounts in the 56 for the P&W gas turbine, which expanded notably in all dimensions when hot.

Tony Rudd, 'we found that when Andretti eased off on instructions from his pit, he reduced rpm to a speed which coincided with a camshaft resonance that overstressed the valve springs, just as Cosworth hit a minor valve-spring problem.'[6]

Engines were indirectly to blame for the disastrous season of 1971, when no Lotus won a Grand Prix, the first shut-out season since Lotus began taking Formula 1 seriously. 'I have always referred to 1971 as "the year of the turbine",' wrote Elizabeth Hayward, the *nom de plume* of Priscilla Phipps, who was timer and scorer for

5   The problem was severe enough for Mario to be tempted by an offer to drive for Ferrari in 1978. He weighed its attractions seriously but stayed with Lotus when Chapman matched Ferrari's financial terms.

6   This was analogous to a problem that Stirling Moss had with his private Maserati 250F in the 1954 season. To conserve his engine he drove it at reduced peak revs, which kept it more often in a speed range that excited damaging resonance in its valve gear.

Seen at Brands Hatch in 1971, Emerson Fittipaldi devoted much of that year to Chapman's effort to make the turbine-powered Lotus 56B competitive in F1 racing.

Team Lotus. 'Frankly I held the opinion that Colin jeopardised his prestige and the morale of the team by persevering with an idea that was fabulous in theory and just didn't work in practice.'

Colin Chapman's unique and unprecedented attempt to make a gas turbine power a Grand Prix car unquestionably undermined his team's 1971 world-championship effort. But declaring himself 'hooked on turbine power,' he was fascinated by its potential. 'Running a gas turbine car is very exciting,' he said. 'It is entirely different from any other racing car, and what's more there are no engine worries. All we have to do to the engine is to check the oil level now and then, which means that we can concentrate on developing the rest of the motor car.' In this important respect the turbine was Chapman's dream engine.

Advantageously chief designer Maurice Phillippe knew his way around turbines. 'A turbine is a very thin stainless-steel stove pipe,' he said. 'Shafts and gears are mounted internally and, in some ways, they are very fragile. When cold,' Phillippe said of the Pratt & Whitney turbine used by Lotus, 'the engine was about 40 inches long but when it was running hot it was 40 and five-

sixteenth inches long! It expanded a tremendous amount, not only in length but also in diameter.

'We adopted a version of the 3-2-1 mounting,' Phillippe explained. 'One mounting had three planes of restraint, up and down, lateral and fore and aft. The next mounting had only two planes of restraint and so on. That way the engine structure could expand in width and grow in length.' In Formula 1 races the turbine-powered 56B Lotus was driven by Reine Wisell, Dave Walker and Emerson Fittipaldi.

'We spent from the end of 1970 to the end of 1971 testing that car,' Fittipaldi said. 'That was bad for the Formula 1 programme.' It was also risky, he added: 'Five times the suspension broke while I was driving that car.' The tests and races in this period were conducted with the aim of showing enough potential to influence engine builder Pratt & Whitney to take the project more seriously. To its credit P&W took only a week to repair a damaged engine at its Canada base and return it to Europe.

Fittipaldi gave the Lotus turbine its Formula 1 debut in the Race of Champions at Brands in March 1971. Its 56B chassis was based on the wedge-shaped four-wheel-drive Lotus 56 that almost won the Indianapolis 500 in 1968. The compressor stages of its turbine were modified by Pratt & Whitney to meet the FIA's regulations for such engines. Although he qualified

COLIN CHAPMAN

respectably, Emerson never figured in the race, the kerosene-laden racer 'bottoming all round the circuit,' said Doug Nye, 'showering sparks as it graunched and ground over the bumps.' One of Emmo's five suspension failures retired it.

Suspension breakage stopped Fittipaldi's turbine in another non-championship race, this one at Silverstone in May. Emerson was deeply disappointed with his second-lap exit in the first heat after having qualified the whooshing racer on the front row, an onlooker saying that 'he seemed to cope with the turbo lag pretty well, and the sheets of flame exiting just behind his head on the entry to Stowe left us, and the marshals, pretty impressed.' Repaired for the second heat, Fittipaldi's turbo-car scythed through the field from the back row to finish third – but was nowhere on aggregate for the International Trophy after his aborted first heat.

Technically oriented as he was, Emerson had a love-hate relationship with the Lotus turbine. 'It was a very difficult car to drive,' he said, 'very, very difficult. We knew we would have to do a lot of development on that car to make it competitive. It never gave good results.' It had two last chances in 1971, one of them in a championship Grand Prix at Monza. With hot weather not suiting the turbine Emerson struggled, finishing eighth a lap behind. Its final outing was in a September *Formule Libre* race at Hockenheim, where Fittipaldi started from the front row, set fastest lap and finished second in a mixed field.

'The turbine still lacked the throttle response a driver requires for car control on a twisty circuit and it also lacked engine braking,' said Lotus engineer Peter Wright. 'The brakes suffered further when the drivers discovered that to maintain the gas-generator rpm for a better response they had to enter a corner under braking with the throttle open. The problems were too great to overcome at that time.' Among his many engine adventures, however, none would surpass Chapman's quixotic effort to tackle road racing with a turbine.

Other problems of throttle response loomed in the future a decade hence when GP competitors rediscovered the neglected potential of the 1.5-litre supercharged alternative lurking in the rules. Though he stayed loyal to the Ford-Cosworth V8 through 1982, Chapman was aware of the need to go turbo in 1983. But he wasn't wild about the idea.

'With unrestricted boost pressure it has turned into a money game which serves no real purpose,' Chapman told Alan Henry. 'I don't see anything clever in simply developing power by throwing unrestricted amounts of fuel at an engine. It's not producing any result that we can pass on to road-car development. It's simply a case of how much money you are prepared to spend. I will join the turbo ranks in 1983 but I don't *want* to. I am doing it because I *have* to for the team to have a chance of remaining competitive.'

One option Chapman explored was a liaison with Germany's Zakspeed, where Erich Zakowski's team had developed turbocharged fours derived from 16-valve Cosworth engines that performed well in Germany's Group 5 championship. To Zakowski's disappointment Chapman instead snapped up an offer from Paris to use Renault's turbocharged V6. Renault was on the rebound, having been turned down by Williams and Tyrrell. Though Lotus's recent record had been patchy at best, 'their past reputation was sufficient to guarantee that an association with them could be a great help to Renault,' said the French company's racing manager.

Renault could only have been deeply disappointed to learn of Colin Chapman's death before the 1983 season opened, but to its credit it continued to supply engines. And contrary to Chapman's assertion the technology of turbocharging did became useful for Lotus road cars, in fact in 1980 finally endowing the Esprit with performance that matched its looks. Thus was the loop closed between Lotus engines for road and track under the demanding guidance of Colin Chapman.

Entered by 'Worldwide Racing' to avoid attracting the attentions of Italian authorities to Team Lotus, the 56B turbocar competed in 1971's Grand Prix at Monza.

Chapter 3

TRANSMISSION TOPICS

That bloke – that bloody bloke –
just when I'd got my hands on our
first profit all the costs came in for
that bloody gearbox!

Fred Bushell

Not unlike the bumblebee, which flies even though theoretically it can't, the racing-car gearbox is physically incapable of coping with the loads imposed upon it. That was the view of veteran Mike Hewland, who designed more such transmissions than most of us have had hot breakfasts. What Mike meant was that not engine torque but tyre traction determines the maximum load on the gearbox of a light and powerful racing car. He also meant that the application of accumulated know-how has more to do with drive-line success than abstruse theoretical analysis.

Not that the practical and outspoken Hewland had garnered much respect from Colin Chapman. Designer Martin Ogilvie referred to 'Chapman's antipathy to Mike Hewland. Whether they crossed swords at an earlier time I don't know. At any rate, Chapman didn't have much regard for him.' 'Chapman didn't like me and I didn't like him,' said Hewland. 'He said I was a "bloody blacksmith" or something. I didn't care. I rather admire blacksmiths!'

Early Lotus cars for the lesser formulas used Hewland transaxles. For these, felt Mike Costin, a rigorous running-in programme was essential: 'In those days,

Colin Chapman believed in building light and bolstering the parts that broke. He was destined never to grasp that this mindset didn't work with racing-car transmissions.

with early Hewland gearboxes the oil just went like silver paint because it was knocking off all the edges from the dog ring and gear dogs. So in practice I said to the driver, "Do one lap and then come back into the pits." We then changed the gearbox oil and did whatever else that was necessary and the driver did one more lap. The same oil that was full of very hard pieces of steel also lubricated the bearings on the pinion. We repeated this until all the rough bits had dropped off and the oil was clear.'

Whether for these or other reasons Colin Chapman dedicated much of his career to designing or buying alternatives to Hewland's offerings. His earliest transmissions paid tribute to the efforts of MG in making four-speed boxes with good sporting ratios. Behind his 1.1-litre Climax engines he used MG J2 transmissions, rebuilt and fitted with aluminium instead of iron bell housings. Later the TC gearbox was useful.

For his production cars Chapman was eclectic in his choice of gearing. The first Elite used BMC B-series gears in an aluminium housing while BMC Maxi gears were found in Lotus housings in some 1970s front-engined models. Bought-in Ford and Getrag transmissions figured as well. An ingenious import for the Esprit was the five-speed transaxle made by Citroën for the Merak produced by its then-subsidiary Maserati. Later this was replaced by a Renault transaxle like that in the DeLorean.

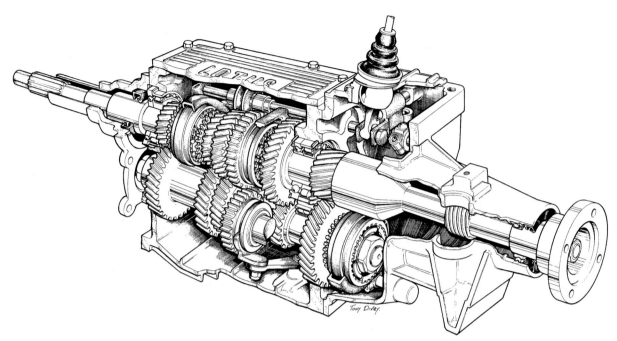

The nearest Lotus came to its own transmission for road cars was this five-speed unit built around an Austin Maxi gear set as fitted to the Elite from 1974.

Citroën transaxles figured in the mid-engined racing cars made by Lotus arch-rival Cooper in the 1950s. In 1959 Cooper designed its own five-speed transaxle, introduced in 1960 in its low-line Type 53. By then Colin Chapman had not only designed and built his own transaxles but also produced them in three varieties for various purposes.

The catalyst for the thinking that produced the new Lotus transaxle was the design of the single-seater Twelve for Formula 2 racing starting in 1957. Nothing would have prevented the Twelve from having its gearbox in unit with the engine driving a rear differential through a step-down gear train to allow a low driving position; in fact the first raceable Twelve was built just this way. But Chapman was keen to shift the gearbox mass to the rear to give the chassis the high polar moment of inertia that he felt was desirable.

Exploring ideas for a transaxle design, Chapman huddled with Harry Mundy, designer of the twin-cam Climax engine and then technical editor of *Autocar*. They soon concentrated their thoughts on a layout that would pack five all-indirect gear pairs back to back for the ultimate in both lightness and compactness. This would probably mean that they'd have to be selected in sequence, not skipping a gear, but this was seen as no disadvantage for a competition car.

Conferring also with Richard Ansdale, who would later assist with the Twin-Cam's head design, they considered how they might engage the gears. This had to be done on the input shaft, finding some means to lock the driving gear of the desired pair to the shaft. To their credit they considered several ways of doing this. One not on their agenda was the pawl engagement used in the Diamant transmission that Ferdinand Porsche installed in his Maja of 1907. This turned out to be an Achilles heel of his first-ever petrol-car design.

Porsche's engineers returned to the theme 40 years later with their design of the transaxle for Project 360, the mid-engined Grand Prix Cisitalia. It made the first use of Leopold Schmid's ring-type synchromesh to select five ratios sequentially. Although elegant, the design wasn't amenable to quick or easy ratio changes – an attribute important to Chapman.

They looked at several other solutions. One, the work of former Aston Martin engineer Claude Hill, used a plunger to push six cams outward to engage the desired gear. Not dissimilar was another, used by Germany's Goggomobil, which engaged with balls instead of cams. Their final choice was a design originated by British innovator Archie Butterworth. This moved the input shaft itself from gear to gear, engaging internal dogs with a ring of external dogs.

In fact the creative Butterworth had already built a sprint car using an all-indirect transmission to this design mounted behind its Steyr V8 engine. First appearing in 1948, the AJB Special proved its merits with course records in both sprints and hill climbs.

hill climbs. Among the ideas that Butterworth implemented for choosing gears in his box was a two-pedal system – one for upshifts and one for downshifts. Intrigued by the system, Colin Chapman negotiated with Butterworth for the rights to use it but no agreement was reached.

Strikingly similar to the AJB Special's design, the Lotus gearbox layout executed in detail by Richard Ansdale suggested confidence on its creators' part that Butterworth wouldn't sue for infringement. Its five gear sets were packed in cheek-by-jowl, the gears fixed by splines to the upper secondary or output shaft but free to rotate around the lower input or primary shaft. The latter was a long, hollow sleeve carrying a ring of dogs – staggered to assist selection – which were engaged with internal dogs on the desired primary gear by sliding the sleeve to the proper point.

Though the transmission's designers pointed proudly to the fact that its five gears took up only 3⅝ inches of longitudinal space, this compactness would turn out to be a weak point of its design. 'The gears are so designed that with only one additional pair of gears,' said Chapman, 'it is possible to get six different top-gear ratios and a comprehensive selection of intermediate ratios.' The latter included a suite of 22 different gears to get ratios that were ideal for each circuit. In the first design, for the Twelve, gears had to be changed by dismantling the front of the box. Positioning the gears at the rear was ruled out because a de Dion axle was part of the Twelve's original design.

'The pairs of gears always had a total of 44 teeth between them,' said racing mechanic Peter Bryant. 'Even if you had to change the ratios in a hurry, it was almost impossible to mismatch a gear set. If one gear had 20 teeth, its mate had 24. If one gear had 18 teeth, its mate had 26. I thought whoever had designed that feature was a genius. It meant, of course, that all the teeth had to be the same size, so first gear was as strong as top gear.'

The elegant result was a phenomenally compact transaxle that weighed only 49 pounds. Its shaft centres were spread as far apart as was practical, 3.9 inches, while the drive from the secondary shaft to the differential was by a hypoid bevel set, giving a total downward offset of 5 inches for low driver seating. All versions of the unit had five forward speeds plus reverse. To scavenge and circulate its lubricant a two-chamber pump was skew-gear-driven from its input shaft.

Initial servicing responsibility for the new Lotus transaxle fell to Graham Hill. He had his hands full because the crown wheel and pinion wouldn't last more than 50 miles. Chapman suspected the hypoid gearing's

In 1907 Ferdinand Porsche chose this Diamant transmission for his first petrol-powered car, the Maja. Its four gear pairs were in constant engagement with an extra ring and pinion providing reverse.

inherent friction, while worries about rigidity of the magnesium housing were allayed by tests that showed it to be adequately stiff.

Assigned the job of sorting the transmission that was becoming known as the Lotus 'queerbox' – attributable to Innes Ireland – Keith Duckworth looked into its lubrication. 'You couldn't blame the oil, really,' recalled Mike Costin. 'Castrol made us a special oil that was better than anything else. But none of them survived

The shaft in front showed how the Diamant transmission's gears were engaged by a pawl that popped up inside the desired ratio. This proved unreliable.

until Keith made a shroud that went round the back of the crown wheel and put in a jet that went into the closing side. And that was the end of the overheating, which was the basic problem.'

The transmission's reluctance to shift consistently was another challenge for Duckworth. Between every gear there was a neutral, which the box found all too often. Downshifts were a particular bugbear, especially when the driver was expecting some help with braking. The first driver control had a quadrant with a notch for each ratio. 'It meant going through every gear up and down the gearbox,' said driver Cliff Allison. 'I'd graduated from gearboxes with a positive-stop gearchange in 500cc racing so I found changing gear on this Lotus box not too bad at all.'

By 'positive-stop' was meant a gear lever that needed a simple push one way to go up a gear and the other way to go down a cog, much more secure for the driver than a quadrant. The Lotus system was an improvement from the fertile mind of Keith Duckworth. 'All kinds of people had tried to design a positive stop,' said Keith. 'I kept saying this wouldn't work and that wouldn't work, so eventually Chapman said I should design the stops myself. There needed to be a pawl and mechanisms. It required incredibly precise positioning and accurate detents.' Replacing the notched quadrant, the driver now had a lever that he pulled back to upshift one gear and pushed forward to go down one ratio.

Within the lower shaft of the 1947–48 Grand Prix Cisitalia's transaxle, designed by Porsche, ratios were engaged by a sliding dog flanked by two synchronising rings.

Duckworth's success impressed a man who was not easily impressed, Mike Costin: 'The first thing that really made me a Keith fan was that he did all the drawings for the positive-stop change and all the bits as well. He came and demonstrated it to me – click, click, click and the rod moves. It worked first time, straight off the drawing board. Everything was fine. And I thought, well, that's bloody reasonable for a young man like that.'

Even with these improvements the 'queerbox' was delicate. The problem was that the dogs on the gears and especially on the hard-worked selector shaft were getting their corners knocked off by shifts. 'You are effectively trying to balance two slippery drums on top of the radii,' Duckworth explained to Graham Robson. 'If you don't manage it, and the gear selects to ten-thousandths of an inch off the right position, it just squeezes out like a pip, into neutral.

'What we really needed to do was to lengthen the gears by about a tenth of an inch,' Keith continued. 'Then it would take a lot longer until the dogs were radiused. We would still have a bit of parallel portion in the middle and we could rely on it staying in gear. You'd have needed a new casing, but Colin was making a new casing anyway because he'd decided to lay the gearbox down on its side and angle the engine for the next model, the Lotus Sixteen.'

'We can't afford to do that,' was Chapman's response, 'because we've got quite a few sets of gears. It would mean making new gears and we can't afford that, so we've got to make do with what we've got.' Finance chief Fred Bushell's concerns about cost – expressed at the beginning of this chapter – seemed to be striking

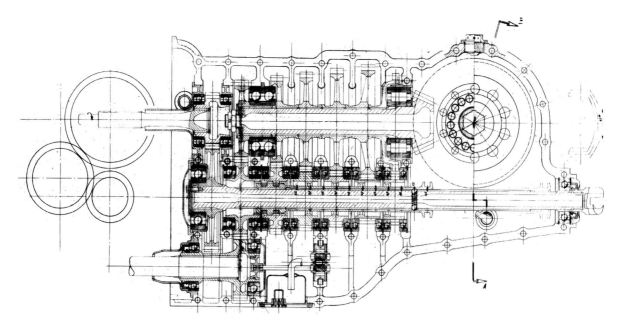

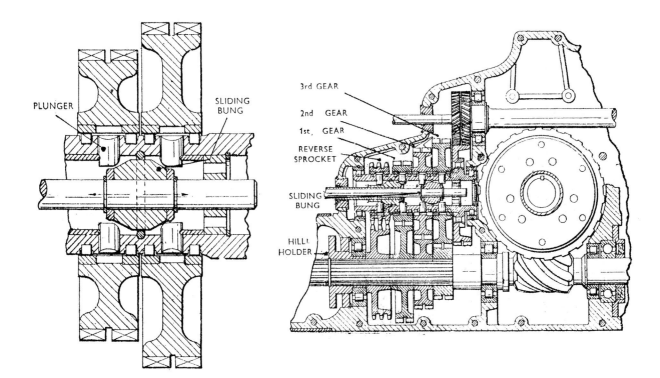

PLUNGER

SLIDING
BUNG

3rd GEAR

2nd GEAR

1st, GEAR

REVERSE
SPROCKET

SLIDING
BUNG

HILL
HOLDER

home with *le patron*. His decision triggered the departure of Keith Duckworth, who told the Lotus chief that 'I'm not prepared to waste my life developing something that will never work.' Only by fitting a fresh selector shaft for every race was the 'queerbox' made reasonably serviceable.

The Lotus Type Sixteen's transaxle was a new design to achieve maximum lateral offset so that the propeller shaft could go to the left of the low-seated driver. Neatly the box was laid on its side. The spiral-bevel pinion stayed on the left of the crown wheel, which itself was moved as far to the left as possible within the final-drive case. The result was an impressive displacement leftwards of 8 inches from the car centreline to the input shaft.

This was the transaxle that shared cockpit space with a very warm driver in the claustrophobic Lotus Sixteen, as raced in Formula 1 in 1958 and '59. 'I used to wonder what would happen if the universal joint broke on the back of the bell housing,' recalled mechanic Peter Bryant. 'Spinning at 6,500rpm, the drive shaft would probably have chopped off the driver's leg or even his private parts – not a nice thought. I recall taking great pains to ensure that the drive-shaft axis did not line up perfectly with the centre of the crankshaft. If it did, the needle bearings in the universal joint wouldn't rotate and would eventually cause the box to fail.'

One later owner of a Lotus Sixteen considered that

Claude Hill's transmission design, created in the 1940s for a Ferguson prototype, engaged its three gears and reverse by plungers pushed outward by a sliding bung.

he sat next to 'an unreliable piece of Chapman minimalism which would produce a bang like a shot gun, next to his left buttock, every time the drive dog fired itself out of the gear with which it was supposed to be engaged.' He fitted a conventional gearbox instead, a step taken by many racers of these cars in historic events until rulemakers disallowed Sixteens competing without their proper transaxles.

A third 'queerbox' variation designed for sports-car use appeared in 1959. A new housing put the gears behind the axle centre for the first time. There was hypoid gearing again, but this time offset above the output shafts with the input shaft entering two inches below them. This transmission was the most compact variation, with its twin-pump circulation system bathing five forward gear sets and reverse. Giving easy accessibility to its ratios by removing its rear cover, this was made in only one example, a 15 that raced at Le Mans in 1959. It retired with a typical failure: jumping out of gear and disabling its 2.5-litre FPF four.

This transaxle was the bridge to the unit used in the mid-engined Eighteen single-seater and 19 sports-racer, Chapman's first departures from the front-engined concept. 'When this gearbox was introduced,' related

Stirling Moss, 'the driver just jerked the gear lever back to change up and forward to change down'. Operation was not unlike that of the early Cooper 500s' – with which Moss was both familiar and successful. 'In the Eighteens a migratory lever was used, clicking fore and aft against two ratchets. It took some getting used to. It was typically Lotus – very fast but very fragile.'

Like other private teams running the Eighteen Moss's Walker stable looked for alternatives. 'I only used that gearbox three times in 1960,' Stirling recalled, 'Monaco, Zandvoort and Spa. Then we put the Colotti gearbox in.' At Monaco it held together for a dramatic win against the might of Ferrari. At the BRP team Tony Robinson decided 'it had to be replaced. You would select a gear and then the box decided which one it would select – a terrible thing.' It too went to Italian Colotti transaxles after a flirtation with Mike Hewland's early units which themselves were prone to pop out of gear.

Nor were teams running the sports 19, also with the 2.5-litre FPF Climax, sanguine about their 'queerboxes'. 'The Achilles heel of that car,' said Dan Gurney's

Designed and built by innovator Archie Butterworth for his 1948 sprint special, this all-indirect five-speed gearbox was a direct predecessor of the Lotus transmission introduced in 1957.

mechanic Bill Fowler, 'was the Lotus transmission. Those things were nowhere near strong enough. They had a very small ring and pinion from some little British automobile and Chapman designed the transaxle around it. We had gearbox failures, just one after the other. Other than that it would have won a lot more races than it did.'

Racing mechanic Peter Bryant agreed, though not on the source of the final-drive gears. 'Originally from a standard Volvo rear axle,' he said, 'the pinion couldn't really handle the torque of a race engine during hard acceleration and often sheared off one of the pinion teeth. The broken tooth would then fall into the shifter mechanism and stop it working properly. That was how you could tell the pinion gear was broken.'

One might have expected a developed version of the Lotus transaxle to come on line in 1961, when engine size was reduced from 2.5 to 1.5 litres. Early in the season it seemed that the 'queerbox' would have a stay of execution, but in April the well-informed Harry Mundy wrote in *The Autocar* that a new transmission would 'replace the Lotus-designed unit which proved unreliable throughout last season and was responsible for the team's failure in so many races.' Coy about its maker, Mundy referred only to its 'German origin'.

'German origin' could also have been attributed to much of the troubled Lotus transaxle. That country's

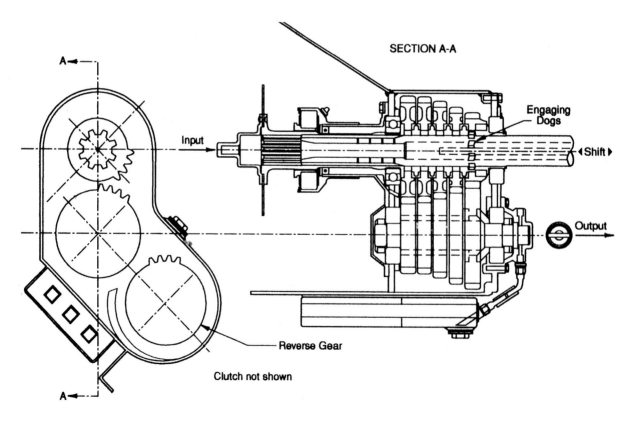

SECTION A-A

Input

Engaging Dogs

◄Shift►

Output

Reverse Gear

Clutch not shown

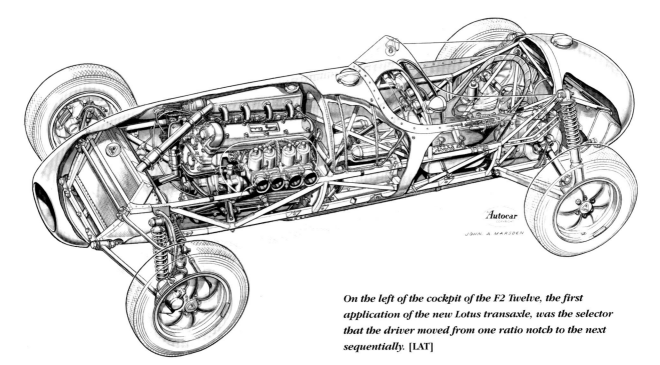

On the left of the cockpit of the F2 Twelve, the first application of the new Lotus transaxle, was the selector that the driver moved from one ratio notch to the next sequentially. **[LAT]**

Zahnradfabrik Friedrichshafen AG – better known as ZF – built the first boxes for the Twelve and continued to supply gears and components for British-assembled units. The proud and capable company on the shores of Lake Constance, founded by Count von Zeppelin to create propulsion mechanisms for his airships, subsequently expanded as a versatile supplier of drive systems for land, sea and air. It was well known both to Chapman and to his advisors Mundy and Ansdale.

On one of his visits to Friedrichshafen Colin Chapman, alert as usual, noticed a small transaxle in ZF's experimental department. He was told that the four-speed all-synchromesh unit, ZF's 4 DS-10, was destined for a small front-drive German commercial vehicle. It was being readied for production in 1961.[1] But the aluminium-cased gearbox seemed to have potential for a rear-engined racing car. Chapman negotiated successfully with ZF to obtain exclusive use of its transaxle for racing.

To meet the needs of Lotus the ZF engineers had to produce an extensively revised version of their transaxle. In the production version the input shaft was above the differential, which would have placed the engine much too high. The ZF men inverted their design so that the shaft from the clutch entered at the bottom, ideal for racing-car use. This required a completely new housing. Initially the transmission was built both as a four-speed, using the initial gear pattern but with racing ratios, and as a five-speed which required a longer case for the rear

of the unit to contain the added-on bottom gear. Unusually for a racing gearbox the synchromesh system was retained.

The new transaxle came on stream in May of 1961 at the Monaco GP in the equally new Lotus 21 behind the Mark II version of the Climax FPF. There, related Innes Ireland, Chapman 'was experimenting with two types of ZF box, a four-speed and a five-speed. They took a little getting used to. For one thing, instead of being on the left, as I had been accustomed to having it on my Formula 1 car, the gear lever was on the right. For another, the actual gear shift was back to front from the normal gear positions. Instead of having first gear on the forward left-hand side of the gate it was on the right-hand side at the back – exactly opposite to what you might expect to find on an ordinary car. And the five-speed box was just a bit more complicated because you had this extra gear tucked in there somewhere.

'Now, this was all right so long as you weren't trying to do anything in a hurry,' Ireland continued. 'But at Monaco you are always in a hurry to change gear. This circuit really was not the best place to try out the new boxes, but we had no alternative. It was fine as long as you were thinking what you were doing, but when you are racing or practising you should not have to think about things like changing gear. It should be entirely automatic.'

This was a prelude to a heavy crash in the Monte Carlo tunnel caused by mis-selection of second instead of fourth when accelerating. Innes had switched to the five-speed ZF after trying the four-speed earlier and been caught out by its unfamiliar gate, a consequence of the unit's use in a vehicle for which it hadn't been

---

1   The original transaxle remained in production until 1980. In all ZF produced almost 450,000 of them.

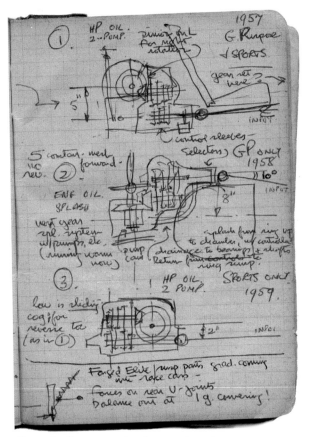

Shown in Chapman's sketches – with author's annotations – are (1) the Twelve's transaxle, (2) plan view of the version for the Sixteen and (3) the unit used in the Fifteen and later adapted to the mid-engined Eighteen and Nineteen.

A gearing chart for the 'queerbox' showed how well its gear pairs – all but the last one adding up to 77 teeth – allowed mixing and matching to get the right ratios.

designed. Thanks to the ZF's synchromesh a gear change went right through that a dog-clutch box might have kicked out. With the 21 running late in 1961, time for preliminary testing – always a luxury in the early days of Lotus – had been in short supply. ZF soon sorted the shift pattern to provide a more conventional layout.

Light and well-engineered, the new transaxle naturally continued to use ZF's cam-type limited-slip differential as it had already been supplying for the 'queerbox'. 'It's the only box in the business with synchromesh,' said Colin Chapman. 'When you get clutch trouble you can actually smack the gears through without the clutch with no bother at all. It doesn't improve the synchro of course.' The unit's main disadvantage was that its housing and bearings were so designed that changing its internal ratios was a job for the workshop, not for the field. This meant taking complete extra boxes to races to have a choice of final-drive ratios.

'We used the original ten ZF gearboxes in 1961, '62 and '63,' Chapman related. 'We ran into lubrication trouble at Monza in 1962. The real cause of it was not having a gate so that the synchro cones weren't properly located between gears – they were actually touching and going blue and the whole box ran red-hot. We didn't know this and we were using a molybdenum disulphide additive as a palliative. But at Monza we got the wrong grade and put in three times too much – the rollers started skidding instead of rolling and packed up.'

In 1963, Chapman explained, 'the ZFs are in their third season. They were getting a little worn and we had been unable to get replacements. We only had ten initially and now we are down to four usable ones, which have been built up from bits from the batch.' As well, related Jim

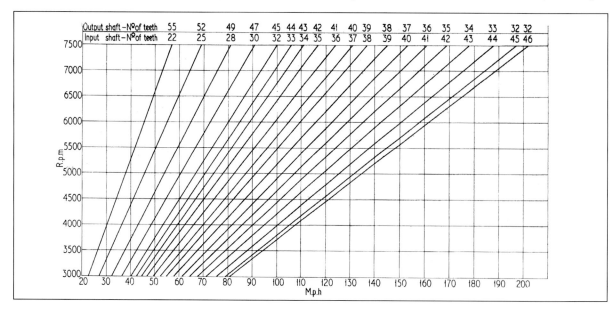

A plan view of the transaxle for the GP Sixteen showed the tricks used to get maximum offset for the input shaft from the centreline and, at top, the ratcheting gear selection created by Keith Duckworth.

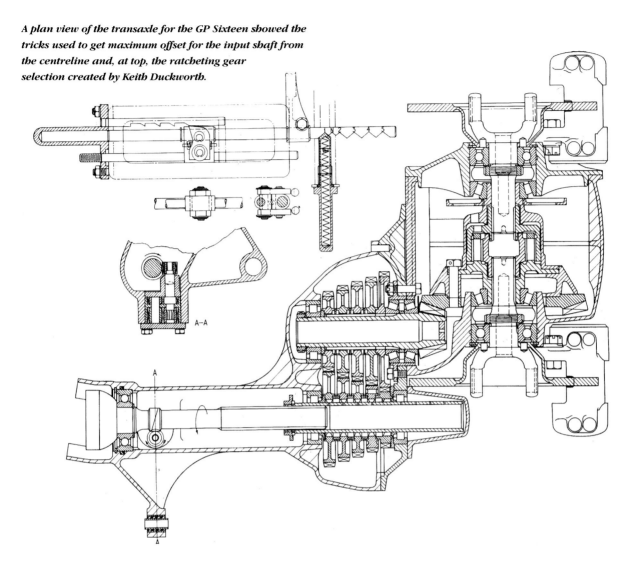

A–A

Clark, 'here we were in 1963 feeding upwards of 9,700rpm through a box that had been designed for a maximum of 7,500rpm.' These circumstances triggered a search for alternatives, which were tested in Trevor Taylor's car in races and Clark's in practice.

Chapman: 'During the year we tried a Type 32 Colotti box and later a Type 34B. In 1962 we tested a Type 34. We have also tried a Hewland box – at Monza, where a bearing seized in practice and at Oulton Park where the crown wheel and pinion broke. We haven't yet found a gearbox which approaches the reliability of the ZF.' Jim Clark's 25 had a ZF gearbox throughout his championship season of 1963, retiring from transmission trouble only once at Monaco as a result of linkage problems. ZF's 5 DS-10 transaxle was used in the Type 33 as well as the 21, 24 and 25.

Not mentioned by Colin Chapman was a development he kept under wraps, hoping for a paradigm-changing breakthrough. This was a fully automatic five-speed transaxle conceived exclusively for Lotus by inventor Howard Hobbs. Resident in the UK since 1931, Hobbs was 'a fruit farmer from Australia,' said his son David, who 'from a very early age started making mechanical things.' After the war Hobbs surfaced as the inventor of the Mecha-Matic automatic transmission, so named to highlight its all-mechnical operation, omitting an energy-robbing torque converter or hydraulic coupling.

During the 1950s Hobbs gained funding for further development of his patented automatic at his Leamington Spa base. Westinghouse became a partner, supporting the transmission's offering by Borgward in 1961 – just before that company went belly-up. The Mecha-Matic attracted the attention of British Ford, which in 1963 approved its installation by dealers. Scuppering this, however, was Ford's offering of an optional Borg-Warner automatic.

Flying the flag for the Mecha-Matic was young David Hobbs, who started racing in 1959 at the age of 20. His first car was an MGA-powered Morris Oxford with – of course – a Hobbs transmission. In 1960 he graduated to a Jaguar XK140, showing that the gearbox could cope with bigger engines. The 1961 season found him in a Lotus Elite, the property of the Hobbs development company. Over two seasons he scored 15 wins in 18 starts with the Mecha-Matic Elite. 'I had the power-sustained shift,' Hobbs told John Heimann, 'and as I went up though the gears I could keep my foot flat on the gas. Braking it was very good too, because you just jumped on the brakes and then, at the appropriate moment, slipped it into the next gear and it picked up sweet as a nut.'

Here, thought Colin Chapman, was a transmission with Formula 1 potential. Its freedom from power loss – apart from its hydraulic pumps to provide actuation – meant that it wouldn't rob too many horses from the puny 1½-litre Grand Prix engines. Howard Hobbs, enthusiastic about the idea of flaunting his design's potential in such a public arena, designed a special five-speed Mecha-Matic transaxle to suit the Lotus 25.

Above: *As installed in the 1958–59 Sixteen the 'Queerbox' was fronted by a rectangular case that housed its gear-selection mechanism, a sheet of asbestos pretending to reduce the heat reaching the driver.*

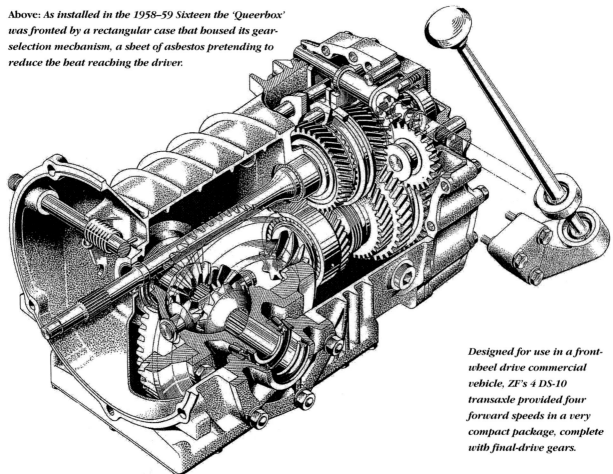

Designed for use in a front-wheel drive commercial vehicle, ZF's 4 DS-10 transaxle provided four forward speeds in a very compact package, complete with final-drive gears.

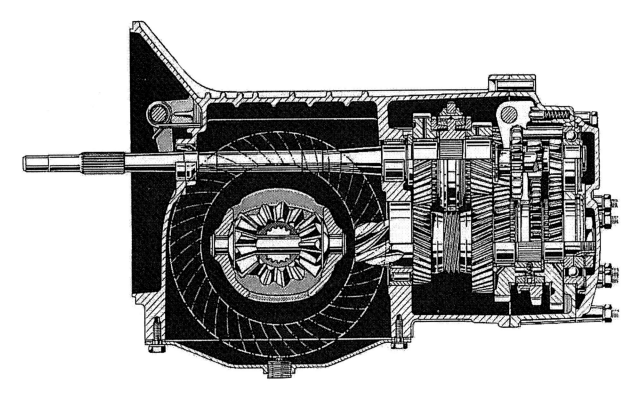

But the slamming of commercial doors against Hobbs in the early 1960s left him unable to fund the F1 box further, while Lotus had its own preoccupations.[2]

An upsurge of support for Lotus after its first championship year of 1963 did bring the benefit of a new suite of improved ZF transaxles, said Chapman: 'We prevailed upon them to make a new batch for '64 with a much stronger first gear, a better lubrication system, the differential and output shafts beefed up and the gate inside the box. The gate used to be on the lever but the gearboxes have now been redesigned for an internal gate. This eliminates the enormous difficulties of adjusting the linkage which we used to have.'

The ZFs continued to serve Lotus in the 1965 season, bringing Jim Clark's second championship, and were still used with enlarged Climax V8s in 1966 and early 1967. In these years Lotus raced its 43 with the BRM H16, in whose transaxle Colin Chapman had been the first to spot a monumental cock-up. Its outboard clutch was so configured that its heaviest mass, including the starter ring gear, had to be speeded up or slowed down during shifts instead of the much lighter clutch discs alone. This meant slow shifts and heavy damage to gearbox dog clutches. BRM had to revise it completely.

Synchromesh was provided for all four speeds of the ZF 4 DS-10 transaxle, whose input shaft from the clutch passed above the transaxle.

Next came the decision about a transaxle for the Ford-powered 49. Chapman had lost his ZF exclusivity. The German company produced an uprated unit, the 5 DS-12, suitable for the new 3.0-litre engines.[3] This was the box of choice for Cooper, married with its Maserati V12, and for McLaren, paired with its Indy-based Ford V8. For his new Repco-powered car Jack Brabham went with 'blacksmith' Hewland, as did Dan Gurney with his Eagle. What would Chapman choose for the new Cosworth-built Ford?

Cos and Worth of Cosworth urged the use of a Hewland, feeling that its ease of intermediate-ratio adjustability would allow better adaptation of their V8 to the circuits to make the most of its peaky power curve. With the ZF it was Lotus practice to take at least two extra transaxles to the track with each car, offering higher and lower final-drive ratios than the one pre-installed. Subtle changes were made by varying the diameters of the rear tyres. Would this be good enough to match the best of the 3.0-litre competition in 1967?

---

2 Some sources suggest that such a Hobbs transmission was built and tested in a Lotus 25. This is categorically denied by Bob Dance, Team Lotus mechanic who was active in those years.

3 The 5 DS-12 was also used on the Formula 2 48 and the 62, the sports-racing version of the Europa. For the Type 30, the Type 32B Tasman car and the Types 34, 38 and 42 Indy cars the 5 DS-20 was developed. This soon became ubiquitous among makers of mid-engined sports cars.

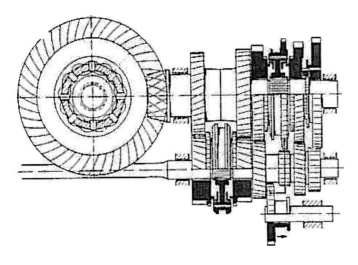

To suit the needs of Lotus, ZF inverted its transaxle to place its input shaft at the bottom and added a low ratio, for five in all, at the extreme rear.

Balancing his antipathy to Hewland with his satisfaction with the ZF's durability, Chapman decided in favour of the German transaxle. To his annoyance, however, durability became a problem. Suddenly crown wheels and pinions began to self-destruct, especially on

As seen on the Lotus 33 of 1965, the ZF 5 DS-10 transaxle was a professionally engineered unit that offered impressive reliability.

tracks where the lower gears got a workout. Immediately after a disastrous race on the short Bugatti Circuit at Le Mans, Chapman and Duckworth flew to Friedrichshafen to address the problem.

The source of the failures was deflection of the housing flanking the crown wheel, said Chapman: 'Gearbox casings are usually designed by gear designers and gear designers are usually the world's worst structural engineers for some reason. They can turn out some marvellous gears and then put them in flimsy boxes which bend and pant and twist. We had to make up new side casings first in steel, and then in aluminium; new lids first in aluminium and then in magnesium and so on to hold it all together and then it lasted out the season.' 'ZF did a very good job,' said Duckworth, 'and put long bolts through it and strapped big heavy side plates on.'

Nevertheless the transmission's limitations became more and more onerous. This was especially the case after Graham Hill joined Lotus in 1967. 'Graham likes altering and adjusting everything,' Chapman explained. 'Whereas previously we had a gearbox where we just changed the final-drive ratio for the circuit and all the intermediates were fixed relative to this, by the end of 1967 we had intermediate second gears and intermediate third gears. Then we got two different sorts of differentials – 40 per cent and 60 per cent locking differentials – and then we got the variable top gear he wanted. You could only build this box up in the workshop, so to cover all

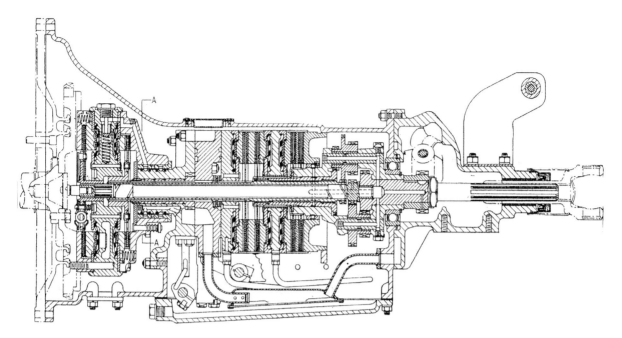

these permutations we were going to have to take about 50 gearboxes to race meetings.

'So the short answer,' Chapman continued, 'was to forget all about this gearbox and go to one which you could chop and change around. So we put the Hewland box in.' His obsession with weight was such that he asked for a special combination of the large differential of the DG box with the lighter gear pack of the FT series, the result being a unique FG transaxle for Lotus.

This was not the end of the line, however, as Chapman related: 'The whole transmission system was then quite reliable until we put a wing on and got some tyres with an even better rubber compound. The two together were raising the slipping torque at the rear wheels considerably and putting that much more load on the transmission. The transmission is always designed on the slipping torque of the rear wheels rather than on the maximum torque available from the engine, so everything started to go.' The answer was to fit the full DG transaxle late in 1968, accepting its weight penalty.

Stickier tyres combined with increased downforce played hob with other parts of the drive train, Colin Chapman told Charles Bulmer and Philip Turner: 'By this time we'd designed a rear suspension which relied on constant-velocity joints because we'd got quite short drive shafts and a lot of suspension movement. This meant that the angularity of the joints went beyond anything that you could reasonably get from a Hooke joint. At Monaco we used the small constant-velocity joints and we had no trouble at all. When we went for the airfoil we started to break the joints. First of all we broke the inboard joint, then we broke the outboard

Seen in a version like that installed in a racing Elite by David Hobbs, the Hobbs Mecha-Matic transmission used mechanical clutches under hydraulic control to change its planetary ratios.

The choice of a transaxle for the Lotus 49 fell on ZF's uprated 5 DS-12 in spite of the need to take alternate units to the track because the boxes weren't suited to changes in the field.

joint and then we broke the shaft between them. We decided that the whole lot had to be beefed up.'

Action did not necessarily follow decision, said a frustrated Chapman: 'Due to a chapter of accidents – so typical of the British component industry – it took three months to get new joints made. In the interim we used bigger and bigger Hooke joints and all this did was make the half-shaft shorter and shorter and stiffer and stiffer, so we were ending up with no torsional relief in the drive line anywhere.

'The Hewland box compounded this,' Chapman added, 'because, unlike the ZF, it didn't have such a long internal quill shaft. There was no room to get rubber couplings in so we were just building a stiffer and stiffer drive line and it was breaking. Now we've got the joints we need and we've got a long quill shaft of the right diameter giving about six degrees wind-up at maximum

torque. Of course we'd lost four races with various sorts of drive-line failure before this was achieved.'

The original small universal joints that had failed were of the same size that had worked perfectly on the turbine-powered Type 56 at Indianapolis in 1968. Its four-wheel drive was seen as the coming thing in Formula 1, a forecast that seemed reinforced by the Lotus struggles with two-wheel drive during 1968. In fact before the 3-litre rules took effect Colin Chapman said he thought it had 'a number of advantages – essential advantages.' In 1965 he speculated as follows about the need to drive all four wheels:

'I very much doubt whether the type of power that we are going to get with these new engines will be successfully utilised in the conventional type of chassis we know today. By that I mean a rear-engined car driving the rear wheels only and with the driver in front of the engine steering the front wheels and so on. We are going to end up with some sort of four-wheel drive, possibly with automatic transmission, other forms of

As visible on this Type 49 in Canada in 1967, the side plates of the ZF box were strengthened during the season by casting them in steel.

For higher-torque applications such as the Lotus 30, ZF developed the stronger 5 DS-20 transaxle. This example was pictured at Classic Team Lotus.

The ZF transaxle's lack of flexibility in the field led ultimately to the use of Mike Hewland's transaxles from 1968. They were light, simple and easily variable.

multi-step gear ratios and there will be significant changes in the chassis. The new cars, if anything, may be less spectacular than the current breed of cars. Nowadays one still uses the tail-out drift technique which can be spectacular, whereas four-wheel-drive cars will do nothing of the sort. They will just drive round the corners.'

That's exactly what the Lotuses did at Indy, taking the fast turns with huge competence. 'We've never found it possible to spin all four wheels on the starting line,' said Chapman of the 56. 'Even with the fantastic torque of that turbine where we were getting maximum torque at zero rpm we didn't spin the wheels – we just went. A little bit of black dust but no wheelspin. In fact you've got no idea really of the acceleration of that car because the noise wasn't there with it nor the gear changes.'

The turbine-powered Type 56 needed no change-speed gear because the gas-generator section of its Pratt & Whitney gas turbine could run at a steady speed, delivering its hot-gas output to a power turbine whose speed varied because it was geared to the wheels. It could easily be accelerated from rest to running speed by the engine's gas generator. The output turbine's 40,000-odd rpm was reduced to between 6,000 and 7,000rpm by a gear train built into the engine.

This output now had to be delivered to the front and rear pairs of wheels by shafts along the left side of the Type 56. How was the power to get from the engine to these shafts? This was solved by Ferguson Research, British experts in four-wheel-drive systems, whose Derek

Gardner designed the drive unit. Inside a magnesium housing Gardner specified an American Morse Hi-Vo chain three inches wide. This was a sophisticated multi-link chain that Morse had been actively promoting for automobile use through racing applications, for some of which it met the development costs.[4]

After 1968's 500-mile race the STP-sponsored Lotus turbines competed in some road races in the USAC series. One was at Mosport in Canada, where Graham Hill drove a turbine, setting fastest time in practice before damaging the car after hitting a patch of oil. He

---

4 American racer and car builder Ray Heppenstall had been discussing a drive train for his turbine-powered Howmet sports-racing cars with Morse Chain, who referred him to Ferguson Research, with whom they had worked on other projects. 'The young engineer assigned to my project was Derek Gardner,' said Heppenstall, recently relating a visit to Ferguson in England. 'Unbeknownst to me, Derek was in the process of designing a transmission for Colin Chapman to go in the Lotus turbine-powered Formula 1 car. Derek and I sat at a conference table and I sketched out my preconceived ideas of how my transmission might be designed. The problem with coupling a shiftable transmission to a turbine is that the turbine is turning so many rpm that you can't cut it loose long enough to go through neutral. My vision was to take two planetary gear sets as used in automatic transmissions and couple them together with a chain supplied by Morse. With the choice of one or the other planetary gear sets you have a two-speed transmission. My sketches and thoughts were greeted with great animosity by Derek. Later I found out why. Just the night before he had been in a meeting with Chapman and gotten the okay to proceed with his transmission design, which was very complex, very large and very heavy. The gearbox I had described you could almost hold in the palm of your hand and would weigh less than 30 pounds. To his everlasting credit, he tore up his own designs, started afresh and turned my thoughts into hardware for Colin Chapman. Our programme, of course, ended before the transmission was completed. I got no credit and to this day that haunts me.' Heppenstall's narrative is difficult to reconcile with the facts, because the Indy-specification Type 56 drive train did not use a shiftable planetary gear train as described by Heppenstall. Nevertheless such a drive train may well have been schemed for the car's 56B Formula 1 version but not built or not raced.

For the first Indianapolis campaign of 1963 the Lotus 29 was fitted with Italian Colotti transaxles as also used with the Ford V8 in the early GT40s.

reported back that its four-wheel drive was 'fabulous'. This was a strong vote in favour of an all-wheel-drive Grand Prix Lotus. So was the 56's artistic success at Indianapolis. 'We had all the sophisticated and complicated lumps of stuff laid in,' Chapman told Doug Nye, 'and since we had the bits we thought, okay, we'll have a go.

'At the time tyres were relatively lousy,' Chapman continued. 'We didn't have much download and we had a problem handling three-litre power, so putting it down through all four wheels seemed to be the way to go.' His intention, he said, had been to build a four-wheel-drive Grand Prix car at the earliest opportunity, but he had opted instead for a straightforward chassis to carry the new Ford DFV V8 so that all attention could be focused on the engine's teething troubles: 'We were having such bothers with keeping the car running that if we'd had anything really experimental in the way of a chassis, we would never have raced at all.'

In 1968, Colin Chapman added, 'when we could really have taken advantage of four-wheel drive, we ran out of time. We built the Indy cars and the whole turbine thing was so new to us that it took us all our design capacity to come up with the answers to that. We didn't really get going until October and we had the Indy cars running in March – it was a hell of a programme. This meant that we didn't get time to build the Formula 1 car we wanted to build.'

For his Type 63, the work in detail of Maurice Phillippe, Colin Chapman used a Hewland change-gear set at the car's centre, driven by a DFV reversed so that its drive emerged at the front. ZF made the centre differential as well as the front and rear drive units with spiral-bevel crown wheels and pinions. Taking advantage of the availability of drive shafts front and rear, all the brakes were mounted inboard. As in the Indy turbine cars the drive line ran down the left side of the chassis. Initially the centre differential's front/rear split of drive torque was similar to that of the Indy cars at 40%/60%.

Although Ferguson Research had developed sophisticated spin-limiting differentials for four-wheel drive, Chapman eschewed these for the 63. 'I'd rather it was entirely under the control of the driver than of a free-wheel device that's going to lock itself in and out,' he explained. 'I feel that a racing driver has got to be in charge of what's going on in the motor car. It's no good finding that if a wheel spins the next thing is that it suddenly stops spinning and then it unlocks itself and starts spinning again – you just can't have this on a race track. Anyway, I don't think wheels *do* spin on a race track. If you think about it, you can't possibly have the situation where the Ferguson system is necessary on the race track.'

For the 1969 season Chapman's principal driving cadre included Graham Hill, now a Lotus veteran, and feisty newcomer Jochen Rindt. Rindt had been keen on the introduction of a 4x4 Lotus; in fact it was a strong incentive for the Austrian to join the Gold Leaf team. But when he was presented with the actual article Rindt had second thoughts. Nor did it help that in tests at Lotus's Hethel airport circuit the 63 lost a wheel and broke a front drive shaft, depriving it of braking.

To the credit of its creators, once its teething troubles were sorted the complex 63 worked well mechanically from the word go. But it was bog slow. Everywhere it was a few seconds off the pace of the 49B, no matter what was tried. From the original torque split less and less was sent to the front wheels. Technically minded John Miles was brought in to drive it on the theory that

a driver new to Formula 1 might unlock its secret. In five outings he qualified well back and finished only once, a tenth place at Silverstone.

The 63 had its appeal, Miles reported: 'It gave a wonderfully soft and stable ride – the sort of stability that gave enormous confidence turning in under power and taking flat-out brows – the faster the corner was the nicer the car felt. It was basically a stable understeerer and so was at home on fast, sweeping corners.'

Against this, Miles related, 'the extent to which the driver can steer the car, by balancing one end against the other, is sacrificed. It handled like an early Audi quattro: once you were committed to a line, that was it. You had to be very precise. The fact that the aces did not go any quicker after three or four laps is a reflection of the car needing so little driving – its limits were mechanically pre-set.'

Graham Hill practised the 63 but never raced it, while Rindt drove it to a stolid second place half a minute in arrears in a non-championship race at Oulton Park. 'Once you've settled on entering the corner,' said Rindt, 'you've got to have it right because there is nothing you can do with the car. If you have got it wrong, you know

All precedents at Indianapolis were set aside in 1968 by the appearance of the radical four-wheel-drive Lotus 56, this car of Joe Leonard starting from pole and leading until its turbine failed nine laps from the finish.

The 1968 Lotus 56 of Art Pollard revealed the remarkably short shafts, with constant-velocity universal joints, that took the drive to its front wheels.

a long time before you go off the road that you are going to go off because you can't actually do anything with it!' This validated John Miles's description and his suggestion that 'perhaps the essence of the problem was that a *real driver* could not affect its performance.

'The aces often used to jump in to qualify in case of race-day rain,' Miles added, 'the one hope for salvation.' Ever since Stirling Moss won a partially rainy race at Oulton Park in 1961 driving a Ferguson-Climax, wet-road traction was seen as the ultimate advantage of the four-by-four racer. Thus Mario Andretti rubbed his gloves in eager anticipation when the clouds burst during practice at Watkins Glen. Instead, to his dismay he found that 'the car was diabolical in the wet!' In a result that was seen as the final nail in the coffin of the four-wheel-drive Grand Prix car, it was just as much off the pace in the wet as in the dry.

'I'd driven the 63 in the wet at Snetterton,' John Miles

Derek Gardner of Ferguson Research holds the Morse Hy-Vo chain and case that took the drive from the 56's turbine to a fore-and-aft shaft on the left side of the chassis.

attested. 'It was awful. As soon as you opened the throttle it spun. Plus there was so much inertia in the transmission that lifting the throttle provided only a delayed effect. That long wheelbase was ponderous, slow to react. You were a passenger. Chapman's attempt to make it more like a rear-wheel-drive car by increasing the rear axle's drive load didn't make sense on a car with tyres close to equal size front and rear.' Late in the 1969 season only 18 per cent of the DFV's torque was going to the 63's front wheels.

In the Lotus 63's defence, with nine appearances and a podium place it was by far the best of the bunch of 4x4 GP cars that raced in 1969. Matra's effort raced only three times, McLaren's only once and Cosworth's not at all. Against it must be reckoned the awesome expenditure of time, effort and money that the 63 represented for such a poor result. As team mechanic Bob Dance said, 'We slowly found out that two-wheel drive was as quick as four-wheel drive with half the problems.' Better tyres and wing-induced downforce were providing all the drive traction that Formula 1 cars needed.

Dating from the 63's 1969 season was another drive-train idea that Colin Chapman wanted to try. 'I've seen job lists from as far back as 1969 saying "Fit electric clutch",' said engineer Ralph Bellamy, whose job it turned out to be to make good this commitment in the design of the all-new 76 for the 1974 season. Semi-automatic clutches had been prominent on the motoring landscape since the 1950s, most often in embodiments that released the clutch automatically when the gear lever was touched. Examples were Porsche's Sportomatic and Renault's Ferlec.

Another pioneer in this field was Automotive Products, whose Manumatic used a vacuum servo to operate the clutch in response to electric signals from the gear lever and throttle. From its introduction in 1952 AP continued to be active in this field through its Borg & Beck arm, a supplier of racing clutches, so it was to them that Chapman and Bellamy turned to get an 'electric clutch'.

In fact only the triggering was electric, from a button on the gear lever, with clutch operation being hydraulic with 800psi pressure from a pump driven by the starter motor. To make the motor perform both functions it was controlled by relays which rotated it in

Andy Granatelli, whose STP Corporation sponsored the Lotus 56s at Indianapolis in 1968, took a close interest in changes being made in the Speedway's pit lane.

either direction, to choice. In the usual rotation it started the engine while in reverse it drove the pump, which pressurised the clutch-release system and its accumulator.

The rationale for the system was chiefly to free the driver's left foot to operate the brakes, giving him greater control over the car. The lesson came from Lotus's experiences in Indiana, Chapman explained: 'We learned at Indy the only quick way was to honk into corners on the power and the brakes at the same time to minimise pitch change, then come off the brake and leave the corner smoothly under power. On faster road circuits you sometimes have to just dab the brakes to check the car – and that unsettles it. If our drivers could left-foot brake with the power still on they could damp out pitch. The nose wouldn't fall. Then by rolling off the brakes away they'd go.'

Ronnie Peterson tested an early version in a Lotus 72 in 1973. 'He was impressed enough to want to carry on with it,' said Ralph Bellamy. 'Obviously it appealed to him because he's an ex-kartist. He was therefore used to two-pedal control. There was never any doubt in Ronnie's mind that that was what he wanted and it became inevitable when he got together with Chapman.'

In the footwell were four pedals. Initially the alignment had the clutch pedal at the far left, for starting only, and the throttle on the right. Between them were two brake pedals, either one operating the full system. After pre-season testing this was changed to swap the clutch and the left-hand brake pedal so the latter was all the way to the left. To help Jacky Ickx acclimatise to the system his road-going Elan +2 was converted to the AP set-up.

Like four-wheel drive, the automatic clutch and left-foot braking appealed more in theory than in practice. Ickx never used it in racing while Ronnie's only race outing with the four-pedal array – but with the clutch actuation removed – was in the debut of the 76 in the third race of 1974 at Kyalami. Problems in practice included engine stalling when the push-button short-circuited and failure of the hard-working starter motor. In the race Peterson's throttle stuck on the first lap and he punted Ickx, who managed to continue but later retired. Thereafter the 76's other problems were so overwhelming that the AP system was never reinstated.

Mario Andretti, here, was the only driver able to get competitive speed from the 1969 Lotus-STP Indy 500 entry, the four-wheel-drive 64. All three cars were withdrawn after a rear hub broke in practice.

Thus an opportunity was lost to provide – a quarter-century ahead of time – the two-pedal control that was to become the norm in the Formula 1 of the 21st Century. A worry at the time had been the punishment the brakes would get. 'It gives the brakes a helluva caning,' said Ralph Bellamy after tests of the system. This was further aggravated by experimental use of a freewheel, expressly to relieve the drive line of unpredictable engine drag while braking. In those pre-carbon/carbon days this could have been risky, even though the Lotuses of this era were deliberately over-braked to take advantage of left-foot braking. Nevertheless this stood as a visionary idea to the credit of Chapman, who stated, 'Two-pedal control simply offers a quicker way of driving.' He was right.

By 1977 the 76 and its successor the 77 were forgotten and the first full ground-effect Lotus, the 78, was strutting its stuff. Since 1976 Chapman enjoyed the services of Mario Andretti, at 36 still at the peak of his considerable powers. Adept at finding advantages, Andretti was the ideal driver for Lotus at this time, an important ally to the creative Chapman. And he had an idea about improving the 78.

From his USAC campaigns Mario was well aware of the traction advantage gained from locking the differential, giving the equivalent of a solid axle that allowed no differentiated rotation of the drive wheels. The only problem was that a locked drive tended to force the car to go in a straight line. It didn't like turning. 'Most Formula 1 cars would just understeer themselves into oblivion' with a locked diff, Andretti said, 'but the 78's front end stuck down so well that it worked. The car was not too easy to drive like that, but it was worth it on some courses.'

The first use of the solid drive was in 1977 at Jarama in Spain, where Andretti's 78 had the legs of all its rivals. Soon competitors were muttering about the lack of a differential, thinking it the secret of the 78's speed. No one in the John Player Special team did anything to disabuse them of this notion, which acted as a cover for their exploitation of underbody ground effects. The locked rear was a useful addition to the Lotus armoury of speed secrets.

In fact in some races the Lotus 'wing cars' used the 'locker' differential developed in the United States by Pete Weismann. Specified for use instead of the ZF differential on circuits with two or more corners taken at less than 80mph, it used caged rollers under spring control to provide effective wheelspin limitation. Andretti was aware of its merits, having used one in his successful 1965 quest for the USAC championship. The

Weismann was on a list of 'next new car requirements' drawn up by Colin Chapman on 3 March 1976, along with '6 speed gearbox'. A six-speed Hewland was raced by Gunnar Nilsson in the 78 but Andretti baulked, saying, 'I'd had this five-speed pattern imprinted on my hand for 20 years and wasn't about to change.'

Meanwhile Chapman was on a campaign to rid his cars of the despised Hewlands. A major complaint was the mass of heavy gears and engagement dogs that extended from the back of the chassis. 'He didn't like the weight of all the gears hanging on the back axle,' said designer Martin Ogilvie. 'He wanted the car to have a much more compact gearbox.' In 1976 Chapman's thoughts turned again to the 'queerbox' concept that engaged the desired ratio from the inside of a stack of cogs.

'He told me about his idea to develop the original Lotus gearbox of the 'fifties,' said Tony Rudd, 'which operated by pulling a sliding dog through the gears. We

The Indy 64's chassis components had much in common with those of this four-wheel-drive 63 for Formula 1. Both had all four brakes mounted inboard.

discussed together how this might be converted into the form of a "clutchless" gearbox. I came up with the idea of having a collection of steel balls inside the shaft which were forced outwards by a cam, which then drove the gear. The loads were pretty high and I spent a considerable time working out mathematical formulas to ensure that the balls would fly out, but under centrifugal force the gears would push them back again. It was a pretty complex piece of engineering.'

Thus Tony Rudd reinvented the selection method used by Goggomobil that had been considered and rejected during development of the 'queerbox'. In the Goggo design, built for them by Germany's Getrag, four balls within the centre of each gear were pushed up to engage the ratio by a moving bobbin inside the shaft. Preliminary drawings of such a transaxle by Ralph Bellamy showed that although the gears were still outboard of the ring and pinion they were lighter and much more compact.

'Colin wanted ZF to produce it for us,' said Rudd, 'and when we were going to a race at Hockenheim we visited ZF beforehand, but they were not very keen. I was then sent to see Getrag, another possible

Among the features of the new 76 for the 1974 GP season was electro-hydraulic clutch control, favoured by former kart racer Ronnie Peterson, testing it here.

manufacturer, who smiled and showed me patents which went back many years. So they knew that the idea would work but they were not so sure that it would do so on the scale we were talking of. Nevertheless we worked on it with them for some time and in the end the gearboxes were made.'

When Bellamy moved to another project the new gearbox was taken over by Tony Rudd and designer Brian Spooner, who was told to base the unit on the elegant final drives made by ZF for the Type 56 Indy Turbines. Crown wheel and pinion had been made by Swiss firm Oerlikon, whose analysis showed that they might just be up to the DFV's near-500 horsepower. ZF made the differentials while Getrag built the gear-selection components to Lotus designs.

A refinement of the Goggomobil original was the use of twin selector bobbins. This allowed one bobbin to shuttle between second and third and the other between fourth and fifth, first being conventionally engaged. With this improvement a conventional lever

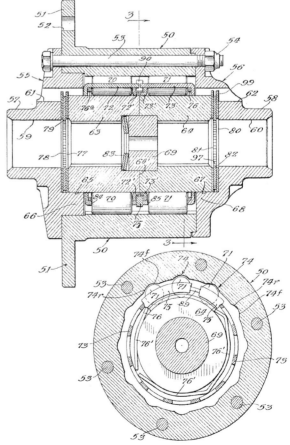

The 1964 patent shared by Pete Weismann and his father showed features of the Weismann differential, which exploited characteristics of an over-running clutch.

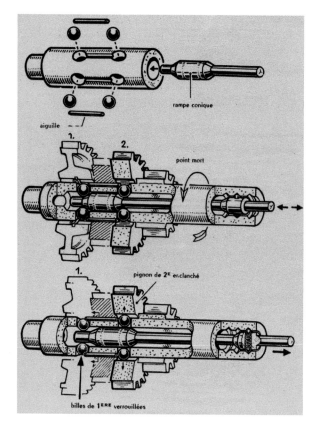

Diagrams illustrate the principle of the gear-selection system used by Getrag for special transmissions tested and raced in 1977–78 in the Lotus 78 and 79.

and gate replaced the 'queerbox' sequential shift with all its problems. Spooner's design had provision for a third bobbin to allow sixth and seventh ratios to be added.

In the metal near the end of 1977 the Lotus-Getrag transaxle was a useful 14 pounds lighter than the Hewland. Its compactness was beneficial to the cleaning up of the rear of the car that helped air escape from the ground-effect venturis. Installed in a 77, the transaxle was endurance-tested at Snetterton by Gunnar Nilsson. It suffered various problems that seemed solvable. Nilsson was happy with it. Andretti liked it too, seeing it as an advance, so it became part of the 79's specification.

In December of 1977 the first 79 was tested at Paul Ricard circuit with the Getrag gearbox. This car, which never raced, was later a test mule for the transaxle. In January Ronnie Peterson had the new box in his 78 at the Argentine GP but practice running showed flaws so he raced with the Hewland. The difference was significant as the team found when trying to adjust the suspension to suit the heavier gearbox. The story was

exactly the same with the 78s in Brazil at the end of January and South Africa in early March.

A 78 and a new 79, both with the 'Goggobox', were prepared for Silverstone's non-championship race in mid-March. 'Ronnie and I had exactly the same experience with the Getrag box,' said Mario Andretti. 'At first it felt like a real advance on the Hewland, lighter to operate and quicker. But after a few laps the thing would suddenly get stiff and imprecise, like it was starting to seize up. Still, we figured to give it a run at Silverstone to see how it would hold up in a race.'

They didn't hold up. Both failed their drive pinions after 58 laps in practice while in the race both Lotuses were out too early to give any indication. 'I really made up my mind about one thing that weekend,' Andretti related. 'We had to have a Hewland gearbox in the car. I had my doubts that the Getrag would have held up even in that short race. I was having trouble hooking fifth even on the first lap.

'We had a fabulous race car there,' Mario continued, 'but the damn gearbox was suspect and I didn't want it to detract from the development of the car. It wasn't easy to convince Colin. I could understand that. He had a lot invested in it and didn't want to just let it go. But I think he also realised it was an unnecessary risk, so he'd already started to redesign the back end to take a Hewland. The Lotus gearbox project was, let's say, suspended rather than shelved.'

Colin Chapman's personally recommended crown wheel and pinion turned out to be the transaxle's weak point. The dimensions of the Type 56's drive units were inadequate. When the new 79 next appeared, in practice for Monaco in May, it was wearing a Hewland for the first time. With the season now in full swing and the 79 showing it was no slouch even with the hated Hewland, the 'Goggobox' was indeed suspended – permanently.

Again a costly and ambitious transaxle programme had been launched with the highest hopes for the best of reasons. Again it had stumbled at the hurdle of Chapman's obsession with lightness and compactness. For a racing-car designer these were the worthiest of obsessions. But gear trains were unsuited to the Chapman technique of building light and adding strength where experience showed it to be needed. This was one lesson the inveterate innovator was unable or unwilling to learn.

Discussions over Ronnie Peterson's Lotus 79 in the pit lane included assessments of the lighter Lotus-Getrag gearbox, which was never judged reliable enough to use in a championship Grand Prix.

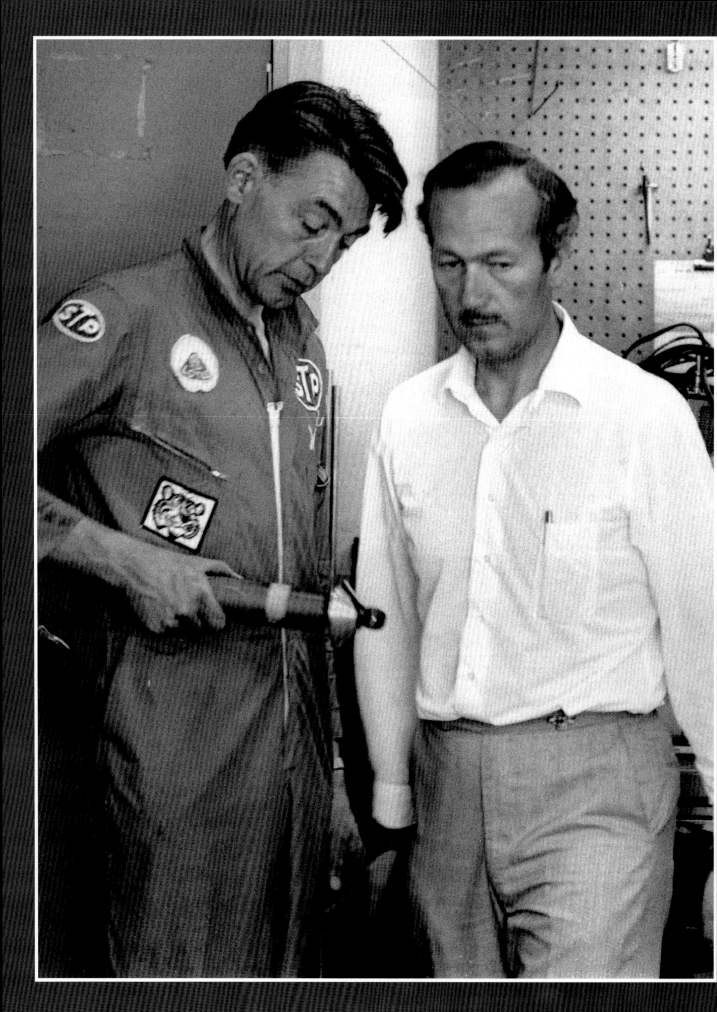

Chapter 4

SUSPENSION SAGAS

I had the privilege of driving Jimmy's Lotus 33 at Kyalami at the end of 1964. Its grip level seemed to be about twelve inches below the surface of the track and by comparison the BRM seemed as though it was on marbles. Really, the difference between the cars was as dramatic as that.

Jackie Stewart

It verges in the impossible – or at least the implausible – to envisage the creator of the world's most advanced racing cars slogging through muddy hills, meadows and ravines in his first prototypes. The uniquely British motor sport of trials demands the maximum in traction and manoeuvrability to cover as much as possible of increasingly steep and usually slippery hillsides. But this was the kind of challenge that Colin Chapman relished.

Chapman's first Austin-based special, his Lotus Mark I, was built with trials in mind although it also had to serve as his road car. This meant that it needed plenty of ground clearance, to cope with off-road tracks and hillocks, but still needed to be manageable on the road. And in Chapman's book 'manageable' meant that the Austin Seven's congenital oversteer had to be tamed.

By 'oversteer' we mean that sometimes alarming sensation of turning into a corner and finding the car turning more than you intend, its rear end coming around excessively. Through most of his career Chapman preferred cars that understeer, responding more slowly to the helm and needing more and more steering-wheel movement to hold them into a turn. Unless taken to an extreme, understeer is the inherently

At Indianapolis in 1967 Colin Chapman discussed damper tuning with chief mechanic Jim Endruweit. Few could match Chapman in suspension-tuning expertise.

safer and more confidence-inspiring handling mode, though some – Porsche drivers especially – like a car with the eager cornering that can verge on oversteer.

'Take the case of Austin Seven and oversteer,' wrote Chapman in 1954. 'That may have been all right when the original "Chummy" staggered up to 45 mph, but it wasn't all right for me who wanted a snappy "special". The reason for oversteer was obvious. The back springs sloped downwards so that as the car rolled on a corner the outside spring flattened and moved the back axle backwards, whereas the inside one did the opposite, which together helped steer the car into a corner.

'The sports models got over it,' Chapman continued, 'by having straight springs, but that lessened ground clearance and as the Austin was for trials I wanted plenty of ground clearance. The obvious solution was to turn the axle upside down, which brought the links to the top, and without any sacrifice in ground clearance I obtained the understeer I required.' With the axle housings now above rather than below the Austin's quarter-elliptic springs the latter could be flattened to reduce the steer effect while maintaining ground clearance.

Grandly Colin Chapman called this 'the obvious solution' to reducing the roll-oversteer effect of the standard Austin suspension. But how had this solution become

ROAD MANNERS OF THE MODERN CAR. 14

ROAD MANNERS OF THE MODERN CAR.

By MAURICE OLLEY*

(MEMBER).

NOTE TO PRESS.—*Reproduction of more than 10 per cent of this paper is not permitted before 4th February. Thereafter up to 75 per cent may be published. Publication must always be accompanied by acknowledgement of source, and a copy of the matter published forwarded to the Secretary of the Institution.*

INTRODUCTION.

IN the U.S. the ordinary passenger car is regarded as the most important transportation mechanism in the world. Its ability to move persons and things, rates it at least level with the merchant ship. The passenger car is important, not just because it represents in the U.S. such an enormous present volume and potential increase, but because it confers on every man the ultimate liberty of going from anywhere to anywhere at his own time and convenience. This is a freedom of movement dreamed of through the ages but never attained before.

It seems to the author that this divergence in British and American points of view finds its origin in the fact that roads and road transport preceded the motor vehicle in Britain by many centuries, whereas, as in the U.S., the car came before the roads, which were therefore built to meet its particular requirements. In the States the great inter-town distances make mechanical transportation essential, and prior to the advent of the automobile, American cities were strung like beads on the steel threads of the railroads. Only twenty-five years ago sizeable American cities were isolated in winter except by rail. In the winter of 1920-21, the author was unable to enter Detroit by road. To-day, Americans think that the internal structure of any country which is not built around the use of personal transportation is obsolete and inefficient.

As automobile engineers, whilst grudgingly admitting the present need for public transportation because the congested mediæval design of allegedly modern cities demands the crowding of people into such conveyances to take them into these rabbit warrens in the morning and extract them at night, we believe that unless the living standards of the world are to be reduced wholesale the continuation of the unsanitary conditions and personal humiliation of such conveyances is unthinkable. Cities must be opened up in texture until they can take personal transportation without overcrowding. For lack of such an opening-up process, the crowded centres of many American cities are visibly decaying, and becoming slums.

Passenger cars are the product of their surroundings, moulded by their surroundings, and in turn moulding their surroundings. This is true in small things as in great. To mention one of the small things—small roughnesses in the road cause the tyres to jump, and the jumping tyres mould the road surface into corrugations, which in turn increase the violence of the jumping. To mention one of the larger things : it is evident that long-continued official

* Vauxhall Motors, Ltd., Luton, Beds.

11

Maurice Olley's 1947 paper for the Institution of Automobile Engineers became a touchstone for Chapman's comprehension of suspension statics and dynamics.

obvious to the young engineer? Chapman, the glutton for information, had found all his prayers answered by the publication of Maurice Olley's paper, *Road Manners of the Modern Car*, by The Institution of Automobile Engineers. Presented in February of 1947, it was published in the Institution's Proceedings for 1946–47.[1]

Occupying 36 pages and enlivened by 23 drawings, most from Olley's own hand, this set out the fundamentals of vehicle handling in lucid terms that explained the behaviour of tyres and suspensions in a technical but accessible manner. Then working in the UK at Vauxhall, British-born Olley had been with General Motors in America in the 1930s when he and fellow GM engineers Bob Schilling and Ken Stonex brought analysis from experience to the previously black art of auto-suspension design.

Colin Chapman could have asked for no better 'open sesame' to the arcane world of car handling. Olley's formulas and principles guided his work into the 1950s. So did a 1950 paper by G. E. Lind-Walker on directional stability. Another paper that Colin filed for reference was an article by former Auto Union engineer Robert Eberan von Eberhorst on 'Roll Angles' published in the October 1951 issue of *Automobile Engineer*. More lead for Chapman's pencil came from respected chassis engineer David Hodkin in his paper *The Nature of Steering*, published in *Autocourse* in 1953. Documents like these, said one observer, 'provided Chapman with a starting point for much of his work which seemed to others like so much magic.'

Although the Lotus Mark I started out with a solid front axle the latter was soon split in two, the inner ends pivoted to provide a simple swing-axle independent front suspension with a transverse leaf spring. That this was a good arrangement for the trials in which the car competed, giving better adaptation to changing terrain, was already well known. Allards, which like Lotuses were first built for trials, had divided-axle suspensions before the war on the model developed by Leslie Ballamy, who marketed a conversion for Ford front axles. Noted racing drivers Whitney Straight and Richard Seaman had Ballamy's split-axle kit on their Ford Pilot V8s.

In his fourth special, his Mark IV built for a specific customer in 1952, Chapman introduced a novel feature. 'I made what I have always referred to as my "jelly-joint",' he related, 'a device which was decided upon after spending some time studying tractor front "suspension" systems. They usually consist of a springless beam axle, pivoted in the centre to allow the front wheels great freedom of movement. Tractor front wheels will "pick their way" over the roughest going, but high speed on the road is out of the question.'

The engineer's challenge was to reconcile this floppy suspension – great for the timed tests of trials – with the need for proper springing to get from one observed section to the next on the road. 'My "jelly-joint" gave "tractor" advantages for cross-country motoring and rigidity for high-speed road work,' Chapman explained. 'It was a simple affair which consisted of a front spring bracket modified to carry a pin which hung in a bracket attached to the chassis. This allowed the front axle to swing from a pivot. The whole thing could be locked solid by the simple expedient of tightening two bolts

---

1 '"Mac" McIntosh showed Colin his copy of the Maurice Olley paper,' colleague Peter Ross recalled. 'He never got it back!' Had this not occurred the paper would certainly have been brought to Colin's attention by Holland Birkett at a meeting of the 750 Motor Club. A keen student of suspension technology, Birkett 'had a sort of missionary zeal to pass this knowledge on to the 750 Club,' said Charles Bulmer.

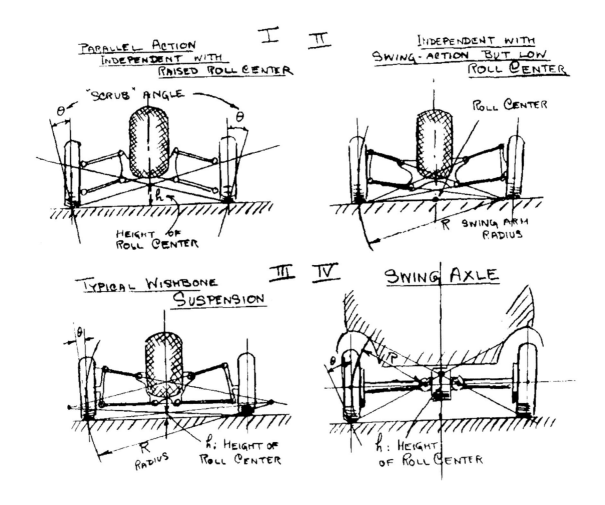

with welded-on tommy-bars in the centre of the transverse leaf spring.

'It was highly satisfactory,' said the engineer. 'As soon as the observed section was finished I would tighten up the "jelly-joint" and drive off to the next one with a perfectly good road car possessing excellent handling qualities. Naturally I had to be careful where I carried out my "tightening" and "slackening" because I wanted to keep the secret of my "jelly-joint" to myself.' In fact most of these manoeuvres were carried out by the Mark IV's owner, Mike Lawson. Although intrigued by Colin's novel solution Lawson soon replaced it with a standard Ford front axle.

Like Sydney Allard, who used the design on his sports cars until 1956, swing-axle front suspension was an early passion of Chapman's. 'It was not arranged specifically to fit in with the use of Ford axle components,' he said, 'although it was very convenient. The reason for using a swing axle is because I think that with a small, relatively low-powered car it is absolutely essential to keep your

Among Olley's lively drawings illuminating his 1947 paper were these showing roll-centre heights and effective swing-axle lengths of various suspension designs.

wheels as vertical as possible whilst corncring. As soon as your wheels start to lean out on a corner they develop camber thrust which has to be resisted by an increase in cornering force and to provide this the wheel must run at a greater slip angle.

'Now as the slip angle is increased,' Chapman elaborated, 'so does the drag, or rolling resistance, and this means that as a car with "leaning-out wheels" goes through a corner it suffers a considerable retarding force which slows it down appreciably. This effect is quite noticeable. Once or twice I have nearly been caught out when following one of these cars through a flat-out corner, as it gives the impression that the driver in front has applied his brakes although his stop lights have not come on at all.'

By 'leaning out' Chapman was referring to parallel-wishbone suspensions in which the wheels tend to

Pictured in September 1953, a Mark VI Lotus displayed
both the coil/damper combination pioneered by Chapman
and its I-section front swing axles.

Racing at Castle Combe in 1954, Peter Gammon's successful
MG-engined Mark VI showed the swing axle's ability to give
its front wheels a good purchase on the track.

slope outwards at the same angle as the car's roll in a
corner unless measures are taken to counter this. 'This
wheel "lean out" is tolerable when there is tremendous
power on tap to accelerate away from the corner,'
Chapman felt, 'but when the engine is of small capacity
and relatively low power it is imperative that "way" is
not lost through the fast corners.

'The finest way to achieve cornering with upright
wheels,' he continued, 'is with a beam front axle, but
this type of axle has several inherent defects in "shimmy"
and "tramp" when used in conjunction with currently
desirable soft suspension. A swing-axle front end will
give you an almost upright wheel angle if a low enough
roll-centre is used and it will also provide the desirable
soft ride in conjunction with ample suspension
movement.' Implementation of this philosophy included
a lowering of the half-axle pivots on the Marks VIII and
IX to about six inches above the ground.

Objections to divided-axle front suspension often
focused on the effects of forces generated gyroscopically
because the wheel went through a large angle change
with its deflection. 'The drawback of gyroscopic "kick"
must be faced,' Colin Chapman admitted. 'On a small
light car the wheels can be made sufficiently light to
make this factor unimportant but naturally as the speed
goes up the gyroscopic forces increase. I had previously
assessed the limit to be about 120mph, but decided to

incorporate this suspension on the [1954] model as I felt that its medium-speed advantages would far outweigh its disadvantages. I was subsequently pleased that I did so because the car handled perfectly, and it seems that the limit has not yet been reached. In fact 150mph should be easily possible.' That this was so was demonstrated by the contemporary Allards.

Chapman took care to have equal-length steering rods to the wheels from a pivoted central bell-crank lever which was operated by a drag link from a worm and nut steering box. According to Bill Boddy of *Motor Sport* the Mark IX's steering 'is geared like that of a "chain-gang" Frazer Nash, asking barely 1¾ turns lock-to-lock with a reasonable turning circle. The result is that in cornering the wheel is scarcely moved. It is fatal to grip the wheel tightly or the Lotus proceeds in a series of swerves, yet kick-back from the divided-axle IFS precludes letting the wheel go free, the technique over bumps being to let the rim play through one's fingers.'

Transverse-leaf front springs were used until the Mark VI of 1952, which adopted tubular dampers – from the earliest days a Chapman favourite – from Woodhead Monroe surrounded by concentric coil springs. The same form of springing was used at the rear. This was not a completely new idea. Car makers

Pushrods from the rear swing axles of the Formula 3 Erskine Staride met at a transverse coil spring which provided springing that offered no roll resistance.

Colin Chapman's rear-suspension design for the 1956 Vanwall featured a rare use by the engineer of a Watt linkage to provide lateral location for its de Dion axle tube.

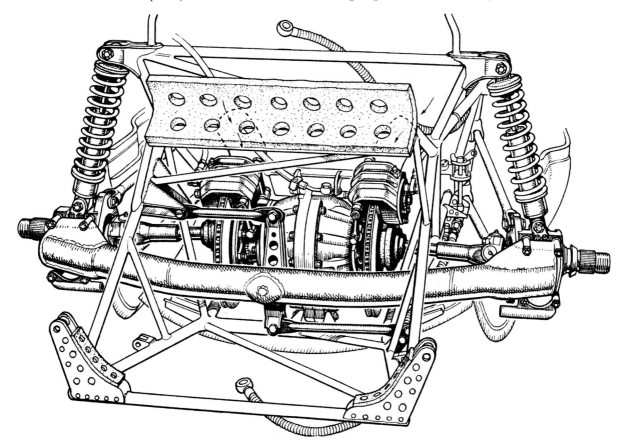

From 1957 onwards the Vanwalls also adopted Chapman's preferred coil/damper units instead of their previous transverse leaf springs.

A victory ceremony at Silverstone on 5 May 1956 included, from left, Chapman in his lucky tartan shirt, partly hidden Jim Russell, Ivor Bueb, Tony Vandervell at the microphone, Stirling Moss and Aston Martin owner David Brown.

like Fiat and Mercedes-Benz had put dampers inside coil springs, but not with the dampers accepting the spring forces.

In 1949 special-builder Geoff Richardson had explored the idea with Girling, which had been reluctant to subject its dampers to the added stress of springs. Where Richardson didn't succeed, Chapman prevailed. At the front his spring/damper unit combined both functions with utter simplicity. A drawback was that to adjust the characteristics of either element the assembly had to be dismounted and dealt with but this was a minor flaw in a scheme whose successful exploitation was to Chapman's credit. The units were steeply inclined towards the car's centreline on the Mark VIII but near-vertical on the Mark IX and the Eleven.

At the rear the first Lotus cars had live axles. For a special project in 1952, initiated as a Formula 2 car for the Clairmonte brothers, Chapman used a de Dion axle for the first time. 'This form of rear suspension was chosen mainly to keep down wheelspin,' its designer said, 'and to reduce unsprung weight. A live axle tends to lift under throttle openings, as torque reaction tends to lift one rear wheel to induce wheelspin. This is obviated with the de Dion-type axle due to the "diff" housing being bolted up solidly to the frame, the drive

being taken out to the rear wheels by two separate short drive shafts.'

Colin Chapman's near-future strategy for his Lotuses was to offer live axles in kits for road use or less-well-heeled customers and de Dion axles for works cars and competition. Some Mark VI Lotuses were de Dion-equipped. That they delivered the creator's preferred handling was confirmed by owner Mike Anthony. 'The Mark VI understeered like mad,' he recalled. 'The front-end adhesion was so poor that it was easy to initiate a four-wheel drift, even though we only had 75bhp. In my youth I suffered from the delusion that I would go round corners faster if I didn't use the brakes; I used to slow the car on tyre-scrub and steering.'

Another owner, Graham Howard, described the behaviour of his de Dion-axled Mark VI:

The car is an understeerer just to look at: negative rear camber, positive front; wider front track than rear; smaller front tyres than backs. Dynamically, it then has built-in understeer additives – the front springs are three times stiffer than the rears and while the rear suspension allows nil camber change, the front guarantees added positive as cornering forces rise.

One thing you do not do is brake with the wheels turned. Accelerate, yes, but brake no. Don't even back off unless you have rehearsed it. For all its in-built understeer, this is a car which will come round quickly under negative acceleration. On the other hand, if the dreaded understeer does get out of hand, then a quick back-off solves all that, just as long as you get on to the power again pronto.

And does it ever get its power to the ground! All that trouble and complication of the de Dion makes the car almost foolproof. On bumpy surfaces it excels and on all surfaces it makes throttle control almost incidental. I can quite understand why the little car is so fast off the line and likes tight hillclimbs so much.

The long-travel, soft suspension swallows up the bumps and asks only for a little bit more lock to maintain the desired line through corners. Actually, if it's a longish corner, the car will ask for extra lock quite a few times. The Lotus is a clever, ingenious, honest little car.

A de Dion rear was a feature of by far the most ambitious Lotus yet, the Mark VIII sports-racer of 1954. In its design Chapman was determined to achieve the ultimate in understeer, his objective being to free the

A typical Chapman Lotus de Dion rear suspension had parallel radius rods guiding each hub and a low diagonal rod, just visible, for lateral axle location.

drive wheels of cornering loads so they could focus entirely on propelling the car. This required a suspension that offered little resistance to roll.[2]

This idea was much in the wind at the time. A Formula 3 Kieft designed by Ray Martin for Stirling Moss in 1951 used this concept with great success. 'I wanted it to be stable,' Moss said of the Kieft, unlike a Cooper, 'which would begin to slide very easily. Cooper cornering tended to be a series of lock-on lock-off stabs instead of a smooth, long sweep.' Such behaviour was anathema to Chapman. The Kieft achieved zero roll resistance by joining the axles with bungee cords in tension, a method also used by Reg Bicknell for his Revis racers. The Erskine Staride for Formula 3 had a single transverse coil spring in compression to achieve the same ends.

The Lotus Mark VIII's de Dion tube was located like those of contemporary Ferraris and Maseratis by two trailing arms at each side and a central block sliding in a frame-mounted vertical channel. Springing was by a long single coil in tension – the metallic equivalent of the bungee-cord method – placed transversely under the nose of the frame-mounted differential. Bell cranks linked to the ends of the axle tugged on the spring

2   Introduction of rear suspension systems that reduced – but did not eliminate – roll resistance occurred on the Continent during the 1930s. Mercedes-Benz effected it on its 540K by linking two complex coil springs in tension to levers below its swing axles, while the Lancia Aprilia supplemented its rear torsion-bar springs with a transverse leaf spring that was pivoted at its centre to make it ineffective in roll. On the rear-engined Rover Scarab of 1931, which did not go into production, coil springs at the rear abutted against a transverse beam which was pivoted at its centre so that the springs acted in support of the car but offered no roll resistance.

His glimpse under the rear of a Goggomobil early in 1957 showed Colin Chapman this ultra-simple independent suspension, making its axles part of the linkage.

when the wheels were in jounce, supporting the car, but when the Lotus rolled they shifted the spring to one side or the other with minimal resistance.

Initially Chapman tried to modify a lever-type damper to do double duty as the bell crank, in accord

For his first rear-engined Scarab of 1932 William Stout used this swing-axle rear suspension, whose high-placed coil springs were inspired by aeroplane landing gear.

with his philosophy of minimum parts for maximum effect. 'Colin designed it,' recalled Mike Costin, 'and we all said, "That's a crazy way of doing it." "No, that's all right, that'll be all right," said Colin. Well, it failed and then we had to redesign it. Colin needed somebody to make sure that his concepts were designed to be fit for purpose. Of course then we were all amateurs working from seven in the night until three in the morning every bloody morning. We were the ones who carried the can, who re-made all the parts.' After the dampers were overloaded they had to fabricate separate bell cranks.

'The entire rolling force was resisted by the front end,' recalled Lotus engineer Peter Ross, 'which put a

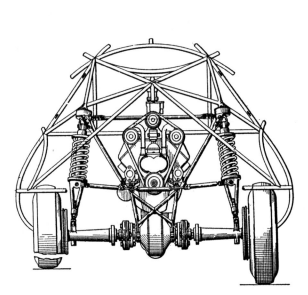
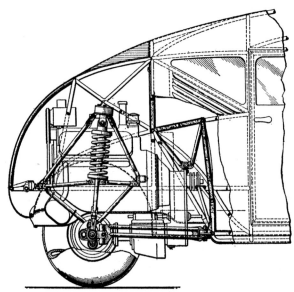

much heavier than normal load on the outside front tyre and the roll caused this wheel to run at a considerable negative camber. On the [Mark VIII] the driver had to keep enough power on the rear wheels to ensure that their tyres were loaded as much as the outer front – not easy to learn!'

Racing the Mark VIII Mike Costin recalled 'the much softer ride and the subsequent greater roll angle.' In testing it, related Tony Holder, 'I think we were cornering at much higher speeds than normal because you just didn't feel you were going that fast. Because it was so stable you went round the corners without slowing down. Driving it was absolutely neutral. It was amazing how it just went exactly where you put it. Uncanny.'

Nevertheless for his next model, the series-built Mark IX, Chapman discarded the complexity of the Mark VIII's rear suspension in favour of a de Dion tube with coil/damper units and a Panhard rod giving lateral location. To maintain balance, the spring rates at the front were increased at the same time.

While worm and nut steering was retained for the production Mark IX Lotus, the two works racing cars had rack-and-pinion steering, its rack linked at one end to a two-piece track-rod layout to suit the split front axle. The gears were proprietary but in Lotus's own magnesium housing. Brakes were magnesium as well, wide drums with radial fins on the Mercedes pattern that were intended to duct air outwards when positioned against the Borrani wheels at the front; rear brakes were inboard.

De Dion axles were still on Colin Chapman's agenda in the winter of 1955–56 when he was asked to cast an eye over a new chassis being planned by Vanwall for its 1956 Grand Prix contender. Tony Vandervell's original Vanwall of 1954 had a frame designed by Cooper's Owen Maddock around Ferrari suspension and transaxle. A mock-up of a new frame was in progress at Vanwall's

In the 1936 version of the Stout Scarab the vertical coil/ damper strut acted more directly on the end of the swing axle, controlled by a trailing radius rod.

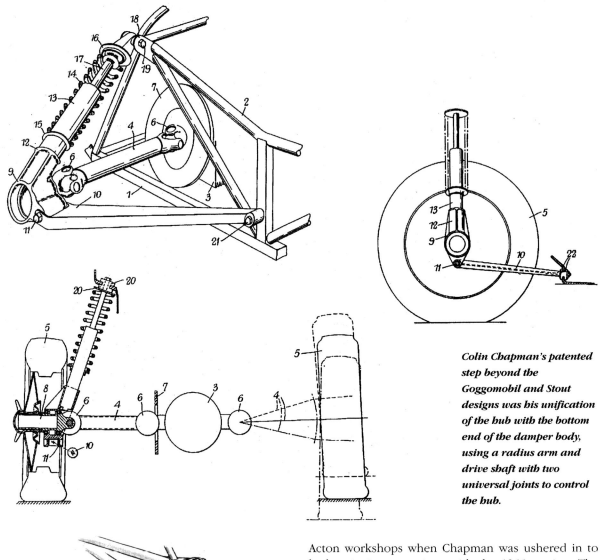

Colin Chapman's patented step beyond the Goggomobil and Stout designs was his unification of the hub with the bottom end of the damper body, using a radius arm and drive shaft with two universal joints to control the hub.

Acton workshops when Chapman was ushered in to look at it, in comparison with the 1955 version. The upshot was that Colin was commissioned to design a new frame and, where necessary, suspension.

Albeit now with tubular dampers, the Ferrari-type parallel-wishbone front suspension was kept. So was de Dion rear suspension, with the two parallel radius rods guiding each hub that Ferrari had introduced in 1950. Drawings of the Lotus Mark IX suspension served as a starting point for the Vanwall axle. Instead of sliding-block lateral control, however, or the Panhard rod used on the Mark IX, Chapman used a Watt linkage, a grouping of three interconnected links whose centre point moved vertically over a limited range. Its centre was attached to the de Dion tube and its ends to the frame.

Simple Hooke-type universal joints sufficed for the Chapman strut's axles, which acted as suspension linkages and thus needed no sliding joints.

The 1958 Lotus Sixteen's Chapman struts were steeply inclined. In 1959 the design was revised to employ a lower wishbone, requiring sliding joints in the half-shafts.

Watt linkages weren't thick on the ground at the time. Mercedes-Benz used them to locate the hubs of the rear swing axles of an experimental 1953 300SL – secretly at the time – and in the same manner for the 1954 W196 Grand Prix car. In America the creative Frank Kurtis used a Watt linkage to control the front and rear hubs of his 1954 500C Indianapolis cars. On the Vanwall it gave precise lateral axle control without the friction inevitable with sliding-block guidance.

Initially Chapman kept the transverse-leaf spring inherited from the previous Ferrari-type design but this was changed in 1957 to coil/damper assemblies. Rear-suspension jounce travel was increased to avoid suspension bottoming. Another change initiated by Colin was an increase in negative camber at the rear to three degrees to add rear grip, enhancing understeer. The result was a Vanwall that conformed to the Chapman handling ethic of the day. It demanded a special technique as Stirling Moss told Doug Nye:

'These basically understeering cars had to be driven between very precise limits and were never as forgiving, indeed delightful, in their handling characteristics as the essentially oversteering Maserati 250Fs. Sometimes one could lift an inside front wheel and I rarely found another car so sensitive to damper settings and fine tyre differences, but the change from transverse-leaf spring to coil-spring rear suspension had undoubtedly been a great leap forward.'

What was good for the goose was good for the gander, as Vanwall rival BRM decided in early 1957 when its chief designer Peter Berthon decided to ask for help from Chapman, whom he described to company chief Alfred Owen as 'a good driver and intelligent and practical engineer'. Colin also took a remarkable

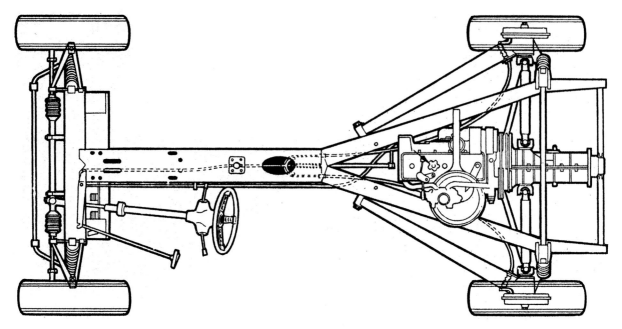

In the Lotus Europa, whose hub guidance was by long radius arms instead of the bottoms of the struts, serious conflicts arose over the disparate needs of the engine/ transmission mounts for vibration damping and lateral wheel guidance respectively.

approach to the business aspect of his consultancy, saying that he would only ask for payment if his recommended changes were successful.

In May of 1957 Chapman test-drove the four-cylinder P25 BRM both at Goodwood – which he described as 'the most difficult and demanding where roadholding is concerned' – and a fortnight later at BRM's own test circuit at Folkingham aerodrome. He was critical of too-light steering that gave inadequate feedback, understeer that for him was excessive because power couldn't be applied smoothly to initiate a four-wheel drift and suspension that had too many elements that introduced friction into the system. Springing should be stiffer, he felt, and steering quicker, using a geometry which – unlike the traditional Ackermann linkage – turned the outer wheel in a corner more than the inner one.

A major addition from Chapman's box of tricks was the use of coaxial coil/dampers. At the rear these displaced a transverse leaf while at the front they replaced the Lockheed air/oil struts that had been used on all BRMs hitherto. The latter posed a special challenge because space for the struts was limited, a challenge overcome by Chapman and Armstrong in concert. Colin warned BRM that the shorter damper could tend to overheat, which it duly did. Nor was he

entirely happy with the front-suspension geometry but he felt that modifying it was a tear-up too far. A Watt linkage again was specified to locate the de Dion tube laterally.

Chapman pressed BRM very hard to make all his recommended changes at once rather than piecemeal, saying that 'we do not have the time for research of this nature at this stage in the season.' They obliged. 'Working non-stop,' said BRM's Tony Rudd, 'we converted the first car in about 100 hours.' Afterwards, Rudd added, 'it felt totally different, just like a touring car, yet there was very little wheel movement visible.' The final touch was the installation of new friction-free ball-splined half-shafts to accommodate the altered suspension movement.

Ultimately BRM's drivers reported an improvement of four seconds around the Folkingham track with the Chapman changes. In July a BRM driven by Jean Behra won a 189-mile Grand Prix at Caen in France. Although not a championship race, this was BRM's first victory on the continent in eight years of trying. In November of 1957 Chapman confirmed the payment he was expecting for his services: a Ford Zephyr saloon with the Raymond Mays high-performance conversion – a very quick as well as practical road car which he used in coming racing seasons.

In 1956 and '57 these experiences greatly enriched the Chapman grey matter on the subject of suspensions, giving him confidence in the validity of his theories as applied to more powerful racing cars. Meanwhile he'd been taking big steps forward with his own cars, introducing the Eleven in 1956 to both acclaim and success. It retained the divided front axle but with lower pivots that added cornering power by avoiding positive camber. Following its success in the works Mark IX racers, rack-and-pinion steering was adopted.

At the rear of the Eleven Colin Chapman's idea – as in the car shown to the press in February of 1956 – was to locate its de Dion tube at three points: a high radius rod at each hub and, below the tube, a curved member that engaged a ball joint under the axle. Used in early Elevens, this suffered so many failures of the curved locator that Chapman was obliged to find a solution that was more structurally sound. He fitted parallel radius rods at each hub, for lateral location providing a tubular rod from below the right-hand hub running diagonally forward to a pivot next to the centre tunnel. It was said to be the geometric equivalent of a Panhard rod five feet long.

Initially Chapman used a very similar de Dion suspension for his Twelve single-seater of 1957. Its diagonal rod for lateral bracing ran across the frame from the right-hand hub to the left-hand side. This however was changed during development early in 1957 to a block sliding in a vertical groove attached to the back of the transmission case. Although the latter arrangement was considered for production, track tests were showing that, although made as light as possible, the mass of the de Dion tube was deleterious to both handling and traction in such a light car.

At the time Chapman set out his thoughts on the merits of alternative solutions. 'The de Dion system,' he said, 'still widely used, can have many advantages: fixed camber angle under roll; no rear-wheel steering due to suspension travel; constant height of roll centre. The disadvantages can be high unsprung weight, the need for sliding splines in the transmission system and – by way of anomaly – constant height of roll centre; this latter can have a very definite influence on cars with variable weight distribution, that is those with fuel tanks at the rear, which for real efficiency demand a self-compensating suspension system.' Eric Broadley pinpointed the Lotus Eleven's de Dion rear as a weak point when he designed his Mark 1 Lola in 1958, giving it an independent rear suspension that used the drive shafts as stressed members.

Clues to a solution presented themselves to Chapman at a meeting of the 750 Motor Club in London early in 1956. One of the members brought a new German import, the tiny T300 Goggomobil. At the front its suspension was on established Lotus lines, a divided axle. The drive from the gearbox attached to its rear engine was by exposed half shafts, swinging from inboard universal joints. At the hubs simple bearings,

Parallel-wishbone front suspension came to Lotus in the 1957 Formula 2 Twelve, which used the anti-roll bar as part of its upper wishbones.

In its 1958 design the Formula 1/2 Lotus Sixteen had front wishbones that made use of the anti-roll bar as in its Twelve predecessor and brake calipers placed forward.

Revised front suspension for the Sixteen in 1959 placed the anti-roll bar at the rear of the upper wishbones and shifted the brake calipers to the rear.

The 'wobbly-web' magnesium wheel, first used on the Lotus Twelve in 1957, is seen here as a spare for a Lotus Seventeen at Le Mans in 1959.

attached to trailing radius rods, carried the shafts. Combined coil/damper units handled the springing.

'Chapman's fertile imagination,' wrote Robin Read, 'easily made the necessary forward leap in developing the Goggo example to his pressing need on the Formula 2 car.' An important benefit, already present in the de Dion version, was the Twelve's inboard brakes. Their positioning meant that the rear suspension was free of brake torque so only had to cope with fore-and-aft as well as cornering thrust. In the Goggomobil the radius rods accepted braking torque.

Brakes had been outboard in a noteworthy predecessor. This was the rear suspension designed by William Bushnell Stout for his rear-engined Scarabs of 1932 to 1936. In adopting this design the prolific American engineer was inspired by his aviation work, saying that 'the airplane landing gear is the easiest type of running gear for comfort yet devised,' pointing out that 'an airplane in landing may have to negotiate a ploughed field and yet not bounce the passengers.' Stout fitted combined coil/damper struts above rear swing axles, using trailing radius rods to take brake and drive forces.

Soon to become known as the 'Chapman strut', the system Colin conceived for his Twelve used the half-shaft as a suspension member. Unlike the Goggo and Scarab designs the half-shaft had two universal joints, for it was not a traditional swing axle. Each hub had three locating members, corresponding to the three axes in which a wheel must be positioned. Vertical movement was controlled by a concentric coil spring and tubular damper angled inwards and rigidly attached to a robust hub carrier.

Driving and braking forces were applied to the chassis through a radius arm running forward and inward to the frame. The arm was pivoted to the hub, the axis of this pivot being transverse. Adjusting the anchor position of the radius rod set the rear-wheel toe-in. The Chapman strut's marriage of this type of location with its sliding pillar provided a roll centre between hub level and the ground.

This suspension had several advantages, not least its elimination of the need for some means of allowing the half-shaft to change its length. As Chapman had learned in his work with Vanwall and his own de Dion axles, this could be a bugbear because any 'stiction' in this area, especially under power, could stop the suspension from working. As well, the fact that the suspension's roll centre and negative camber were not fixed met Chapman's criterion of a 'self-compensating suspension system' in which negative camber rose to give added cornering grip with an increase in weight at the rear.

This, he said, was important in a racing car carrying its fuel at the rear – something he initially avoided but accepted with his Sixteen of 1958.

At rest the half-shafts were under tension. As cornering forces increase the heavily loaded outside wheel tended to compress the half-shaft. Depending on the angle of the spring pillar these opposing forces cancelled out at high cornering loads, at one lateral g if the pillar were at a 45-degree angle. Residual lateral loads were accepted by the shafts and bearings of the differential housing, which had to be configured to cope.

The design was not without its development challenges. Racing an early Twelve, Cliff Allison 'suddenly noticed the wheel had got closer to me. The rear wheel and half-shaft had spiralled. It had wound up and just pulled itself in. The trouble was that the half-shaft was made of mild steel. In fact it was made from exhaust

Roy Fedden designed 'wobbly-web' wheels for his air-cooled Cosmos light car of 1919. It was considered for production by Bristol but not progressed.

Above: *A 'wobbly-web' design was used for the wheels of the Convair CV240, introduced in 1948 as a pressurised successor to the DC-3. Some 571 were produced.*

Below: *The 'wobbly-web' wheel's distinctive design soon became an identifying feature of Lotus cars. Only progressively smaller-diameter tyres sealed its fate.*

tubing and just twisted like a stick of Blackpool rock.' As well the angled strut was vulnerable to the unpredictable 'stiction' that Chapman deplored.

Offering the ultimate in lightness and simplicity, the Chapman strut was ideal for a racing car whose differential or transaxle could be fixed firmly to the frame. This was vital, for any lateral freedom of motion would affect the location of the half-shafts and thus the suspension, degrading its precision. In a road car such as the Elite, in which the strut was soon to be used, this placed constraints on the amount of rubber that could be used in the differential's mounts to suppress the transmission of noise and vibration into the body.

This was still a problem in later Lotus road-car suspensions that used the half-shafts as part of the linkage. The challenge was heightened in the Europa, whose rear-mounted engine and transaxle needed rubber mounting to suppress vibration into the frame and body. 'If they were soft enough to absorb engine vibrations,' said Tony Rudd, the engine's mounts 'were far too soft to maintain the suspension geometry and there was excessive camber change under cornering loads. On the other hand, if they were made stiff enough for good roadholding most of the engine vibrations were transmitted into the car.' For the Europa sandwich-type mounts were adopted that allowed vertical or rolling motion of the power unit but were resistant to lateral forces.

Goggo-inspired or not, the Chapman strut was a striking innovation to its creator's credit. That he realised this was shown by his patenting of it in several countries. The original submission in Britain was made on 13 June 1957. The hub carrier proudly bore the cast-in legend PATENT PENDING.

In 1959, however, Colin Chapman abandoned the purity of his original design in search of better performance for his Formula 1 Sixteen. Below each half-axle he installed a reversed wishbone, braced to the rear, to control the hub. With the strut guiding the wheel vertically, this required use of the hated sliding splines in the half-shaft. Between splines and struts this was a 'stiction'-susceptible suspension. For its rear-engined GP car, first raced in 1960, BRM adopted a similar layout to which it brought the advantage of extremely costly but efficient ball-splined shafts.

Not counting the Mark VII or Clairmonte Special, described later in this chapter, in 1957 the S2 version of the Eleven and the Twelve were the first Lotuses to have parallel-wishbone front suspension. 'I realised that the high-speed potential of the F2 car would produce a further increase in gyroscopic loading if the

swing axle were retained,' Chapman explained, 'and as I feel that the limit must nearly have been reached I decided to adopt a fairly conventional wishbone layout. We now have double wishbone location with the front member of the top wishbone doubling up as an anti-roll bar; the springing and damping still being effected by one direct-acting unit. The designer of the proprietary king-pin assembly is quite happy about its suitability for its new role.'

The bottom wishbone was a simple open tubular vee, rubber-bushed to the frame at two points and connected to the stub-axle forging by a double threaded trunnion, fitted because the lower wishbone, assisted by the angled coil spring/damper, supported the weight of the car. At the top was a single arm, ball-jointed to the stub axle upright and braced by the trailing end of the anti-roll bar. The same suspension was adopted for the Elite, which first ran in 1958.

In 1959 at Le Mans, where their front-suspension failings would be least evident, two Lotus 17s competed but retired with overheating of their 745cc engines.

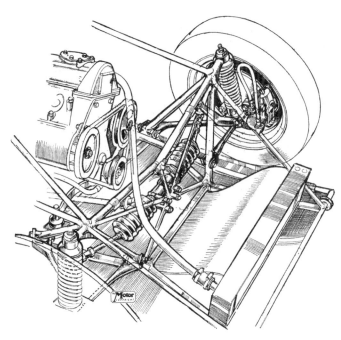

The 1959 Lotus Seventeen's front suspension comprised lower wishbones and short spring/damper struts providing both steering and upper guidance for the wheel hubs. [LAT]

Chapman's new suspensions for 1960 were displayed at Goodwood by a Formula 2 Lotus Eighteen, where it met its front-engined predecessor the Twelve.

Chapman could have confidence in this use of the anti-roll bar, which was a less-stressed version of the layout introduced on British Fords in 1950 by Earle MacPherson, bracing the bottoms of the struts named after him. In fact modified lower-arm forgings from the Ford 100E were used initially for the upper Lotus arms until the company had bespoke forgings. While with its rubber bushings the suspension was suitable for the Elite and the Sevens, it would be insufficiently rigid to have a long lifetime on Colin's racing cars.

Like the Chapman strut, the anti-roll bar doubling as one leg of a wishbone exemplified this engineer's obsession with making few parts do the work of many. Late in his career when he was presented with a listing of Lotus design principles Colin marked this one out as especially important. Tony Rudd recalled 'good-humoured arguments' with Chapman over design features of his Lotuses, such as the single bolt attaching the top mount of the rear suspension of the 25 where on his comparable BRM, said Rudd, 'I had not compromised, but I had 25 pieces where he had five.'

In this obsession there was a certain irony. One of the engineering texts for which Colin Chapman had great respect was *The High-Speed Internal Combustion Engine* by Sir Harry Ricardo, his bible for engine design. In it Ricardo went out of his way to be critical of those who would oversimplify. 'While it is obvious that the number of parts should be kept down to the minimum compatible with efficiency and mechanical correctness,'

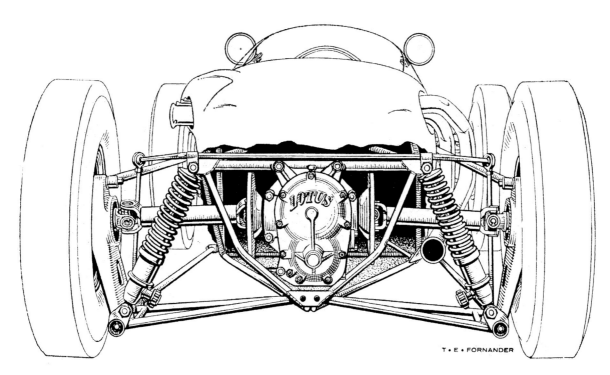

Tom Fornander's drawing of a 'queerbox'-equipped Eighteen illustrates its high-placed anti-roll bar operated by long links from its lower wishbones.

he wrote, 'this can easily be overdone. The craving to make one single member perform several distinct functions is often very difficult to resist, but it should be firmly controlled. Fewness of parts too often denotes excess of compromise.' Memorably Ricardo concluded with this vivid admonition: 'It is far better to use 500 parts if need be, to comply with the laws of sound mechanics, than to defy them with a single part.'

Throughout his 35 years of engineering of transport vehicles Colin Chapman would not only ignore this counsel but also train new generations of engineers who would consider his blending together of components to be the Holy Grail of design. Although the expression 'simplicate and add more lightness' is often attributed to Chapman, as a Chapter 6 sidebar explains it was in fact the mantra of William Stout, creator of the Ford Trimotor aeroplane and the Scarab cars of the 1930s with their strut-type suspensions.

Referring to aviation engineering, Bill Stout wrote that 'the greatest study is made to make each part do the work of two or three things to save weight, simplify cost and add strength.' Thus Stout's 'simplication' can well be taken as one of Chapman's guiding principles – sometimes for worse and often for better.

In positioning the calipers of the Twelve's disc brakes Colin Chapman broke with convention. Usually calipers were placed at the rear of wheel-mounted discs. With this layout the retarding force at the disc edge was countered by a downward reaction of the wheel against the spindle – opposite the usual wheel-bearing loading. The objective was to relieve the wheel bearings under braking conditions instead of overloading them.

When he tried this rearward placement on his Twelve Chapman found that its brakes suffered a front-wheel chatter under heavy retardation. This was traced to small but still noticeable play in the front-wheel bearings. When the brakes were applied the spindle was pulled up to the top. Then car weight would tug it down again, setting up a cyclic vibration.

Chapman's solution was to shift the calipers to a near-frontal position, causing bearing loadings which were unidirectional. 'We have fitted a heavier-than-standard spindle which permits a wider bearing spacing in the wheel hub,' he explained. 'This, in its turn, enables the wheel bearings to deal with the slight increase of load brought about by the fitting of the disc brake calipers ahead of the king pin, in order to assist in cooling.' This last was a by-product of the change, not its main motivation. In 1959 Chapman would move the calipers to the rear again to make room for a new steering linkage ahead of the suspension.

Brake cooling was an issue with the new wheels that Chapman introduced for his Formula 2 Twelve. 'I was not worried about front-brake cooling' with new solid wheels, said the designer, 'because with a non-

Doing without an anti-roll bar, the rear suspension of a Formula Junior Eighteen showed the design's use of its half-shafts as upper suspension members.

That concerns were expressed about possible conflict with the ground with a flat or absent wheel was evident from a look at the rear suspension of an F1 Eighteen.

enveloping body there is no shortage of cooling air behind the wheel. On the Lotus this is further improved by the convolutions of the new wheel which create air turbulence around the brake disc.'

The convolutions referred to earned the new wheel the 'wobbly-web' nickname. Its designer was 'Mac' McIntosh, who was happy to be the back-room boy in this as in other instances. 'The wheel was my baby, start to finish,' he told Mike Lawrence. 'I didn't mind that Colin got the credit because Colin needed the credibility. He was the front man for us all.'

'This peculiar design,' Chapman explained, 'was chosen as the lightest and strongest possible type of wheel since unsprung weight represents a major problem with cars as light as this, and I also felt that the time had come to discard the heavy conventional knock-off wire wheel.' Feasible because the car was planned for the shorter races that characterised Formula 2, this feature played into the hands of Lotus in 1958 when minimum GP race distances were shortened from 500 kilometres or three hours to 300 kilometres or two hours. In 1958 Vanwall began using similar wheels albeit with knock-off hubs for the rear wheels

'In order to keep weight down the web of the wheel should be as thin as possible,' Chapman explained, 'consistent with strength and for ease of manufacture the foundry likes uniform thickness. In order to satisfy these two requirements and yet obtain the required variation in bending strength throughout the wheel a solution is to use the "wobbly-web" principle. With this the peripheral distance at various radii from the hub is kept approximately constant which results in quite deep folds near the hub where great strength is required. These fade out to quite shallow waves at the rim where loads are less.' At the base of each of six folds was an attachment stud.

In the modern era Colin Chapman's realisation of the wobbly-web wheel, cast in magnesium by Stones of Charlton, was unique. But it was pre-dated 38 years by the wheels of the Cosmos light car, introduced in October of 1919. The Cosmos was the work of Straker Squire chief engineer Roy Fedden, already famed for this aeronautical engineering. In 1948 another embodiment appeared on the Convair CV240, a new airliner introduced to take the place of the DC3 in the post-war world. His wide reading and interest in aviation ensured that Chapman was aware of its features.

Low unsprung weight wasn't Colin's only interest in magnesium wheels. 'Coopers had used magnesium wheels for years,' Mike Costin recalled, 'and Charlie Cooper used to reckon he made more money making

Competing in Goodwood's 1960 Easter Meeting, Alan Stacey showed the pace of Lotus's Eighteen. For best performance it demanded high precision from its driver.

and selling wheels than he did on the rest of the car.[3] That sort of thing would light up Colin's eyes. He was the best plagiariser in the world!' Both Cooper and Lotus were plagiarising Ettore Bugatti, who introduced cast-aluminium wheels on his Type 35 in 1924. In one fell swoop Bugatti freed himself from the cost of bought-in wheels while creating a major money-spinner in the sale of spares and replacements.

Into 1959 Colin Chapman spread his new wheels to all racing Lotuses together with his eponymous rear struts. With a new model, the sports-racing Seventeen to compete in the 1.1-litre class with Climax power, he fitted struts at the front as well. 'Colin panicked a bit when he saw how quick we were,' said Lola creator Eric Broadley, 'and rushed out the Seventeen to replace the Eleven. I thought, oh dear, this is going to be a problem. But he'd gone overboard, made one of his rare mistakes. That was a bit lucky for us, to be honest.'

Colin's designer Len Terry had expressed reservations: 'I told Chapman that he couldn't use suspension like that at the front because the struts were so short. I

thought that the car would suffer from "stiction" and I was proved right. Even at normal driving speeds the front would lock solid under braking and turn-in.' While strut suspension was by now commonplace on road cars, their struts were very much longer so their damper shafts weren't susceptible to cocking in their guides. The Seventeen's failure ended Lotus's challenge in the 1,100cc class and launched a new career for Len Terry, who left Lotus to design a successful parallel-wishbone conversion kit for the Seventeens.

In 1960, the year in which he introduced his first mid-engined cars, Colin Chapman set out his philosophy of suspension design. 'The first thing is to decide on the required roll centre,' he said, 'bearing in mind the conflicting interests of roadholding and ride, and then design a linkage to give it. Then, after deciding on the virtual swing-arm length – the factor which governs camber change – the suspension can be drawn in.

'The type of suspension used is not important as long as it fulfils a number of basic requirements,' Chapman continued. 'These are minimum unsprung weight, minimum change of roll-centre height, correct camber change, minimum angularity of the drive shafts and elimination of sliding splines [in the half-shafts]. Another essential is to select the correct spring rate,

3   In fact broken and discarded Cooper wheels that had been returned to the foundry to be melted down to make new wheels played an important part in the design of the 'wobbly-web'. At the foundry, 'Mac' McIntosh related, Chapman was allowed to 'take the odd thing from the stores, in other words, the wheels which had failed. That was gold-dust. The way we worked was to look at things which had failed and work back from there. That is what we wanted more than anything else. Colin, a very happy man indeed, loaded his car with Cooper's rejects. We had everything that had gone wrong with their wheels and that is precisely what we needed.'

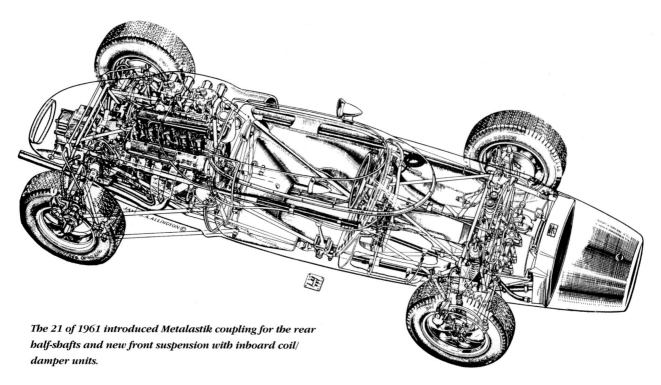

The 21 of 1961 introduced Metalastik coupling for the rear half-shafts and new front suspension with inboard coil/damper units.

which in effect means deciding on the softest possible spring, one which will give maximum bump absorption with reasonable wheel travel – that is, without increasing ground clearance from a minimum of four inches for the sprung mass of the car.'

These principles were applied to the design of the Lotus Eighteen of 1960, Colin Chapman's first mid-engined racing car. At the time he said that 'anti-roll bars are needed to obtain the required handling characteristics, but are not necessarily an essential

For the Maserati 4CLT/48 of 1948 Alberto Massimino penned a front suspension that placed its coil springs inboard, operated by levers from the upper wishbones.

feature of suspension design'. This would have been of interest to BRM designer Peter Berthon, who on seeing the new Eighteen said, 'There must be something dreadfully wrong with it. It's got a roll bar each end.' He was addressing colleague Tony Rudd, who 'did not make myself very popular by saying that I wished our car was as far wrong as the Lotus.'

With his Eighteen Chapman eschewed use of the anti-roll bar as part of the front suspension and fitted a full wishbone at the top, something he'd tried on the Sixteens at the end of 1959. 'This is for increased rigidity,' he explained. 'While the other layout is perfectly satisfactory on all our other cars, the speeds encountered in Formula 1 racing, and the severe braking required, call for extreme rigidity. The new suspension has achieved this.' A separate anti-roll bar was fitted – to the confusion of Berthon – and a nylon bush replaced the screw-threaded trunnion at the bottom of the Standard-Triumph upright.

Lacking enough height at the rear of the Eighteen to fit his patented struts, Chapman installed a much-improved suspension. It reverted to use of the half-shaft as part of the linkage, now serving as the upper member of what he called his 'double-transverse-link suspension'. 'In practice,' Colin explained, 'the fore and aft members are only radius arms and the suspension geometry is dependent on the transverse links; the upper one is the drive shaft and the lower one controls camber/angle and toe-in.' In this there was general similarity not only to Lola designs but also to an experimental suspension that Chapman had seen at BRM in 1957.

Most controversial to observers was the way the Eighteen's cast hub carriers reached down to a couple of inches off the ground in order to accommodate the coil/damper units. Chapman brooked no compromise in the length and positioning of these units, resulting in the extreme dimensions of the uprights. Aware as he was of the loss of effectiveness of overheated dampers, he preserved in this way the fullest possible hydraulic capacity at the rear where overheating was most likely.

First to experience the benefits of the new design was Innes Ireland. 'I found immediately that one needed a completely new technique to drive it,' he wrote, 'and this took a bit of time to get used to.' In his first races with the new car, Ireland added, 'I could get round the corners and out of the corners more quickly, and that is where motor races are won.'

The need for a new technique was striking to those who had been racing the tail-happy Coopers. 'With the Coopers you could push on,' said Roy Salvadori, 'drift it. But with the Lotus you had to be very precise, very correct. It didn't like being drifted through the corners like we wanted to do.' Stirling Moss agreed, saying that 'the Eighteen was not forgiving and was harder to drive than the Cooper. You had to keep it operating within a very tight envelope. If you could maintain it within those limits its ultimate braking, cornering and traction were all superior to the Cooper's.'

Former motorcycle-racing champion John Surtees was quick in the Eighteen in 1960. 'I think the F1 Lotus Eighteen was much more of a motorcyclist's car,' he said, 'less forgiving than the Cooper perhaps but extremely efficient at high limits. You had to be precise with that car. That was an important factor. You needed to be very correct and economical.'

Similar sentiments were expressed by Frank Matich who raced a sister to the Eighteen, the sports-racing Nineteen. 'I suppose it oversteers generally,' Matich related, 'but the degree of oversteer can be varied acutely by the amount of power you put on the road. Its great advantage over other cars is the way it enters and leaves corners. But it always has to be launched under braking, because the way you brake it for a corner controls the whole corner, including how you come out of it. This is where it begins and ends.' With these cars a new precision in the exploitation of racing tyres was introduced to the sport.

Another consideration with the latest Lotus was its adjustability. During 1959 Lotus had introduced adjustable Armstrong dampers and screw-adjustable abutments for the coil springs to allow tailoring of ride height and weight balance. Both features were on the

Seen after its conversion to a sports car, the F2 Clairmonte Special of 1952 had a Chapman-designed chassis with inboard-mounted coils and dampers.

Eighteen, which added even more ability to vary the angles of both front and rear wheels.

'It was difficult to adjust,' testified Stirling Moss, 'and there were so many things on it that could be adjusted. This made it a difficult car to work with in some ways. Eventually I tended to limit work on the Lotus so that starting with the same tyre pressure front and rear I could get a little more oversteer or understeer by changing pressures. Then we refined this by altering the damper settings. I seldom changed the anti-roll bars.' One change that Moss's Rob Walker team did make was for the sake of safety: a fresh set of half-shafts for each major race.

In his new 21 for the 1961 season of 1.5-litre racing Colin Chapman was freed from dependency on the half-shafts as a suspension link by a new rubber coupling developed by Metalastik. Used at the inboard ends of the shafts, the coupling had enough flexibility to accommodate moderate changes in shaft length. Single upper links replaced the shafts in the rear suspension, adding yet another option for adjustability. This set a pattern for racing Lotus rear suspensions that endured until the turbine-powered 56 of 1968.

On the 21 the Metalastik couplings were relieved of braking torques by moving the discs outboard. 'You can't use them inboard with the very flexible rubber couplings we have in the drive shafts,' Chapman said. 'We had to reinforce these couplings anyway to stop

For the Clairmonte Special's upper wishbones Chapman specified boxed members whose ends embraced the pivots of the coil/damper units.

As fitted to the Lotus 25 the new Lotus front suspension used oval-section fabricated-steel upper wishbones that were ball-jointed to the uprights.

them tearing.' Problems with them meant their replacement by sliding splines during 1961 until they were reliable. Inboard discs were tried again in the 24 for 1962, said Chapman, 'but we kept getting oil on them from the gearbox. It had molybdenum disulphide in it at that time and one sniff of moly and they stop working altogether.' The brakes remained outboard.

More striking at the front of the 21 was Chapman's use of a new suspension that was revolutionary. Each upper wishbone was configured as a rocker arm, operating a coil/damper unit mounted vertically inside the bodywork. Descriptions at the time suggested that the rocker arm pivoted around a frame tube, but a moment's thought will show the impracticability of this. Its pivot was carried between trunnions above a tube. The outboard element of the rocker was fully enclosed to reduce its aerodynamic drag to a minimum.

Though lower drag was an important advantage of the new design, especially with the low-powered engines of the new 1.5-litre Formula 1, it had other benefits. The ratio between the rocker's lengths on the

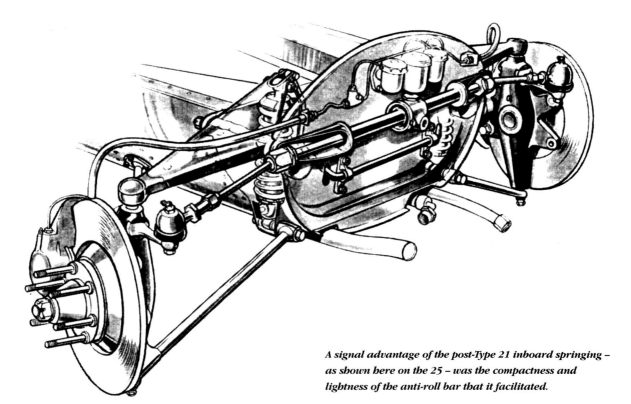

two sides of the pivot could be adjusted to determine the forces dealt with by the coil/damper unit. The positioning of the latter in relation to the angle of the rocker's inboard arm could be varied to give rising-rate springing as was later provided in the 49. Mounted inboard and operated by the inner ends of the rockers, the anti-roll bar could be much smaller and lighter.

Originated in 1948 by Albert Massimino, his similar design for the Maserati 4CLT/48 had forged rockers operating inboard coil springs through height-adjustment screws and rotary dampers through links and levers. Colin Chapman's first use of the concept had been in 1952 for what was planned as a Formula 2 car for Clive Clairmonte. Its rockers were boxed fabrications that had to be cocked upwards at their inboard ends to make room for the lengthy coil/damper units. The opportunity to fit an inboard anti-roll bar wasn't exploited.

Conceptual drawings suggest that the option of inboard springs was explored when the Twelve was being schemed. Responding to the need for low drag, some Formula 3 cars used the idea. As well, wrote Robin Read, 'in 1959 I built a Dante 1172 Formula car with that feature and a year or so later in discussion with Mike Costin claimed advantages for a layout dating back at least to the Maserati 4CLT/48 of 1948. Mike dismissed the idea as of no interest.' However, the idea matured in the Chapman grey matter and it was ready for prime time in the 21 of 1961.

At the time not everyone saw merit in following Colin's lead. One hold-out was Brabham designer Ron Tauranac, who complained that 'inboard suspension took up room at the front where the car is narrow and where the driver's feet have to go.' He considered it a more complicated design that demanded more set-up time.

Also implemented with the 21 was front-suspension geometry that resisted nose dive when braking. This required the axes of the lower wishbones to angle upwards towards the rear. Converging wishbone axes had the effect of creating a lever arm, acting towards a virtual pivot at the rear, that lifted the nose under braking. Introduced in the 1950s by Chevrolet, the concept was already well-known in the world of road cars.

Chapman had explored anti-dive in his Sixteen in 1959, inclining the axes of its upper wishbones downwards towards the rear. The sensation it produced was disliked by Innes Ireland. When on braking the nose didn't dip in the normal way it reminded him of all-too-many occasions on which the brakes had failed. It produced a sensation that was counter-intuitive. Nevertheless anti-dive, which offered the opportunity to stabilise the chassis and run close to the ground, would continue to be part of the Chapman suspension armoury.

Above: *Chapman took care to cool the now-enclosed dampers of models with inboard springing. He also provided generous steering lock to help drivers catch rear-end slides.*

Below and opposite: *The steeper slope of the 49's upper front wishbones reflected Chapman's latest thinking, which was to shorten the suspension's virtual swing-axle length to delay the onset of positive camber by the outside wheel in a turn.*

At the rear of the chassis anti-squat was sometimes applied in Chapman's designs to keep the platform stable. With the low-powered GP cars of the 1.5-litre Formula 1, however, this was scarcely a problem. In fact, wrote Doug Nye, 'in 25/33 days pro-squat rear suspension had once been adopted to improve traction.' A subtle enhancement, this could have contributed to the excellent traction that Jackie Stewart remarked upon at the beginning of this chapter.

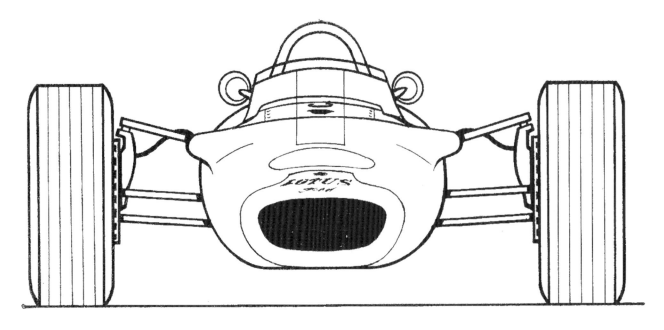

Another innovation, Armstrong's GT7 damper, was introduced in 1962. Its hydraulic cylinder was at the upper or sprung end of the mountings instead of at the lower or unsprung end. This was a small but useful contribution to the reduction of unsprung weight. With these changes the pattern was set for Lotus racing suspension design through to 1965, the end of the 1.5-litre Formula 1.

'The front suspension hasn't changed basically,' said Colin Chapman of that period in retrospect. 'The position of the stub-axle pins in the magnesium king posts [introduced in the 24/25] has been altered to accommodate different-diameter wheels without losing ground clearance or altering the steering geometry, the steering arms have twice gone up in size and there have been a number of design changes to ball joints. When we went to 13-inch wheels the steering felt too low-geared so we put in a higher-geared rack and pinion.

'The front suspension has changed mainly to increase the track and to decrease the leverage over the inboard spring/damper unit,' Chapman told Philip Turner and Charles Bulmer of *Motor*. 'We get a considerably rising rate on bump because of the angle between the inboard arm and the damper – nearly 50 per cent increase on full bump. We've also gradually reduced the virtual swing-axle length of the front suspension. We started off at twice the track and we've come down to 1.1 [times the track] in about three changes. This allows us a larger roll angle before the outer wheels change over from negative to positive camber. We don't change the front roll bar any more. We fix its size at the beginning of the season and just alter the rear one.'

At the time Chapman was keen to provide a generous steering lock, up to 45 degrees and more. 'I have a theory about this,' Colin explained. 'The degree of recoverability is in direct proportion to the lock angle. Ideally, if you had 90 degrees and put the car broadside you could still get it back if you were quick enough. But if you have 20 degrees lock, then when the car gets past the 20-degree drift angle you can't catch it. And there's a classic example. A picture of Jimmy going down the straight in South Africa sideways on and the lock is like a London taxi. He wound it right round and waited; at the psychological moment he caught it. In any other car he might have lost it.'

Suspension at the rear, said Chapman of the 25 and its successor the 33, 'has changed a lot in mechanical detail but otherwise the changes have been similar to the front – an increase in track and a shortening of the virtual swing-arm length. The main trouble has been with the top transverse link because we couldn't stop it wearing out. We started off with a rubber bush. Then we used Rose joints which kept going oval and finally we finished up with a Fabroid joint which is very satisfactory. It's an American joint which is ptfe-impregnated and has a fair amount of pre-load. We use as many as we can afford – they cost about 20 dollars each in the States. We've also played about quite a bit with the radius arms to alter roll-steer characteristics. We have them longer now and mounted as far inboard as possible so that we have very little roll steer.'

Chapman's rivals in these years felt that he had best mastered the marriage of soft springing with good wheel control, considered at the time to be the secret

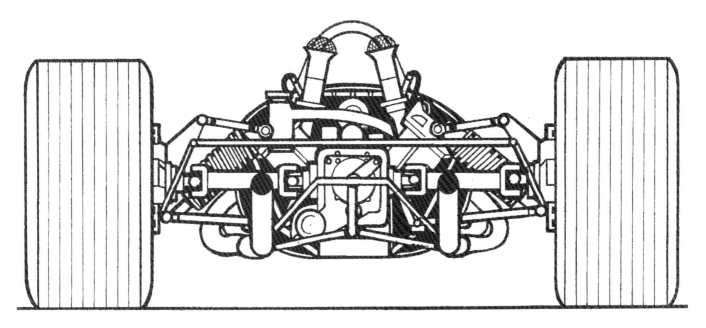

of high cornering power. However, said Colin, from 1962 to 1965 spring rates became 'considerably harder. We started off with a periodicity of about 72 cycles per minute front, 75 rear and now it's about 100 front, 110 rear with driver and half-full tanks. So the spring rates have just about doubled. This makes it possible to reduce the ground clearance without crashing through on the rough spots. The damper settings have gone up too until we can't get them any stiffer without going to the next size up – for which there isn't room.'

One of the most dramatic developments of the period was the increase in tyre widths, demanding wider wheels. 'Rim width seemed to go up about half-an-inch every two months,' Chapman related, 'and now it's eight inches at the front and nine-and-a-half inches at the back. We started with the 15-inch "wobbly-web" discs but when we introduced the type 33 at the beginning of 1964 with 13-inch wheels and the rims got wider and wider to suit the tyres and the car went faster, the brakes were starting to go on the knockings. There wasn't any airflow through the wheel so we went to a six-stud, six-spoke cast-magnesium wheel designed

This view of the new 49-Ford for 1967 emphasised the width of its rear tyres, on deep-cone magnesium wheels, during a decade that saw rapid advances in racing-tyre design. [LAT]

from the start to take an alternative knock-off hub. We changed to knock-offs when Dunlop produced different tyres for wet and dry roads which we couldn't use in the wrong conditions – they are only half a pound a wheel heavier.'

Chapman added that the change in tyres had a big impact on the suspension settings. 'We used to run three degrees negative camber at the rear with the old 15-inch tyres but now our normal setting is about one degree negative and we can't go to more than two degrees or we're just running on the corners of the tyre. Even this is only possible because there is a radius on the tread profile which in turn means that we're not getting the full benefit of the tread width.'

'On the Lotus 25 you can virtually tune the chassis as you would tune the engine,' testified Jim Clark, 'so that for Monaco you give yourself more camber to the front to make the front grip and the tail wash out on the tight corners. For Spa of course you have it the other way round.' In addition to such subtle camber changes the main adjustments made on the cars were tyre pressures and the size of the rear anti-roll bar.

In essence the same suspension concepts were carried over to the BRM-engined 43 and the DFV-powered 49 of 1967. Colin Chapman's philosophy was that he would be focusing on efforts to get these new 3-litre engines running properly so he wanted

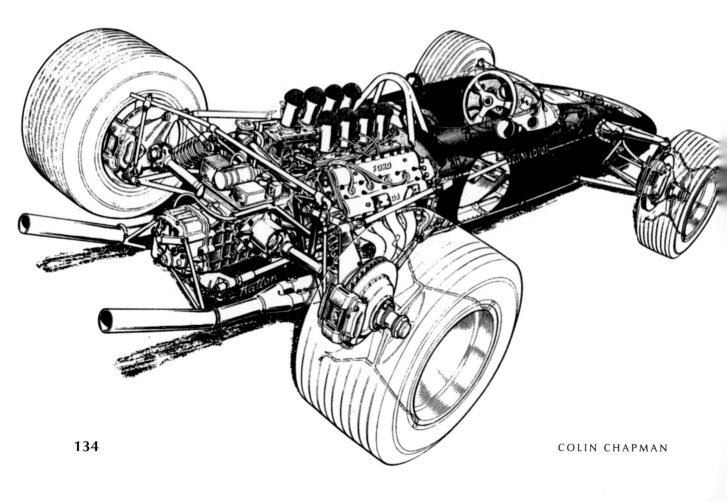

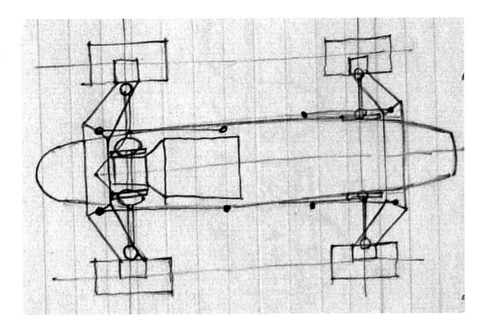

A mid-1960s Chapman musing for Indianapolis racing was this layout with inboard brakes and large-diameter titanium solid-axle tubes at both front and rear.

straightforward cars that wouldn't demand too much development attention. With Maurice Phillippe heading design the new cars had similar suspensions to their predecessors albeit with higher placement of the front wishbones in relation to the wheels and, in the 49, uprights that allowed the brake discs to be exposed to the breeze.

Brake anti-dive geometry was a feature of the 49 from the start but when in early 1968 the 49B was built it was removed. 'We've experimented quite a lot,' Chapman said, 'and every time we've gone to anti-dive we always seem to have introduced some sort of instability under braking. Maybe it's just the caster change – you automatically get a caster change with any effective form of anti-dive.'

Cooper had been using an anti-dive system that inclined both wishbone axes downwards towards the front, creating a wedging effect, but Chapman said he didn't care for it: 'I feel that any system which makes the wheel go forward as it goes up has disadvantages. What we should be doing is building fore-and-aft compliance into the suspension so that the wheel can go back when it goes up. You'll get a better ride and a better ride will presumably mean better adhesion so it's about time we started thinking about it on racing cars.'

Heavily impacting the 49's evolution was the explosion of the size of racing tyres, fitted to Lotus's light deep-cone cast-magnesium wheels. Front-wheel widths jumped from 8 to 12 inches in 1968 while rear rims grew to 15 inches wide. At Brands Hatch in March of 1968 the new wide tyres were fitted to the original suspension. Chapman described the consequences:

'We had the wider tyres and we were still using quite high camber change and quite short virtual swing arms and, of course, the tyres were coming together and almost touching at the top on bumps down the straight – so to speak. The car was in very bad shape. This was the first time we'd gone to really wide rims and we had to go back and scrap the whole lot and start again. We did a complete redesign front and rear. In fact we changed the whole car between March and May and turned out with the new cars in Spain. That was a most impressive programme we did in about six weeks, particularly as we were involved in Indy at the same time.'

Until this overhaul created the 49B, said Chapman, 'we had been going harder and harder on suspension – or rather Graham [Hill] had – to cut down camber change which you can't afford with these very wide, flat tyres. Then we re-designed the suspension to produce the minimum amount of camber change over the normal working range and in particular virtually no camber change on droop, and found that we could go back to the softer springing which we prefer to use and which, in turn, meant that we needed more travel.' The stiffer springing was a burden for the front rocker-arm wishbones, which had to be strengthened twice.

This was a volte-face from the evolution of the 25 and 33, which had been towards shorter effective swing-axle lengths. A key change with the new 1968 design, said Chapman, was the use of shorter upper links especially at the rear. 'A short top link tends to negative rather than positive camber change on droop,' the designer explained, 'so the wheels virtually go straight

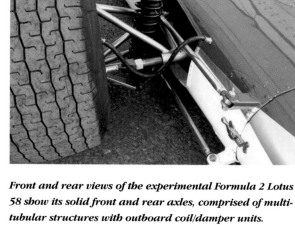

Front and rear views of the experimental Formula 2 Lotus 58 show its solid front and rear axles, comprised of multi-tubular structures with outboard coil/damper units.

down parallel. This helps braking tremendously because if these big, wide wheels develop positive camber when the back rises, the car gets uncontrollable – you just can't hold it straight in the braking area.'

The wider tyres were obviously advantageous but finding the right way to apply them was a new challenge for designers. It didn't take much of a camber angle to keep a tyre's periphery from running in full contact with the road. When that happened local overheating quickly degraded grip. Perhaps inevitably Colin Chapman's thoughts went back to the de Dion axles he'd used so successfully in his sports-racers through to the Eleven. They kept wheels and tyres parallel – or at a fixed camber angle if desired – and dead square to the tarmac.

In this was a certain irony. After his first visit to Indianapolis in 1962 Chapman had ridiculed the American 'dinosaurs' with their solid axles front and rear. He had vanquished the legendary 'roadsters' using his new-fangled all-independent suspensions. Now he too was prepared to consider this proven means of keeping the wide treads of the latest tyres flat on the ground.

Appropriately enough Colin's first thoughts focused on the use of solid axles at Indy. He sketched a version of the 29 with large-diameter axle tubes at front and rear, guided by parallel radius arms. One reference suggests that they would have been made of titanium, the new miracle metal of the 1960s. Then in 1966 Chapman began using a Type 38 Indy-car tub, the last of ten, as the basis for tests of a de Dion rear suspension. Instead of the traditional big tube this used a multi-tubular 'space frame' to join the rear hubs together. Tests during the year didn't lead to adoption of the system for later Indianapolis Lotuses.[4]

Enough positives came from the 1966 trials to warrant Chapman's planning two cars for 1968 with solid axles at front and rear. One was the Type 57, for Formula 1, and the other was the Type 58, planned to compete in Formula 2. Both were designed but only the latter was built and tested. It was the first Lotus since the Mark I of 1948 – in its initial incarnation – to be completely innocent of independent suspension.

---

4   The author considers it highly likely that Chapman would only have used such solid-axle suspension at Indianapolis if it proved decisively superior to his existing independent system. Otherwise he wouldn't have wanted to be seen as reverting to the principles he had so roundly ridiculed in the recent past.

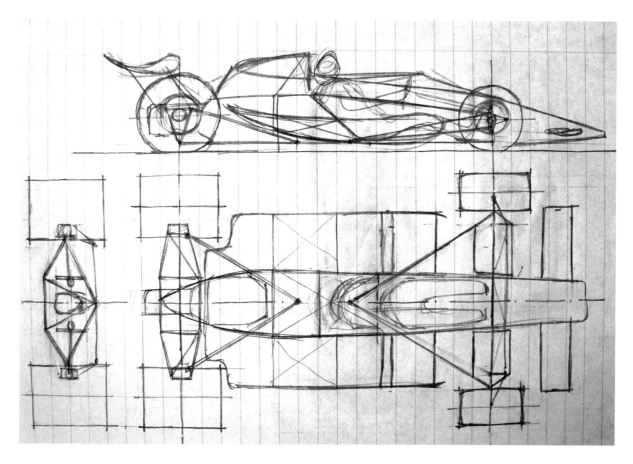

The Type 58's 'axles' were tubular-steel space frames, at the back having tubes above and below the transaxle. Both axles were guided by pairs of trailing radius rods, wide-spaced at the rear, and laterally by tubular triangles that could be either high or low to position the roll centre. Near-vertical coil/damper units were mounted outboard.

For steering Chapman adopted a method that he could have seen on some cars at Indianapolis. He built the rack-and-pinion gear into the front axle, so that it rose and fell with the axle. This assured consistent steering precision at the price of a small increase in unsprung weight – which was in any case higher than that of an all-independent suspension.

Jim Clark's testing of the wedge-shaped 58 was due to commence after he returned from the race at Hockenheim on 7 April 1968 in which he was killed. Nevertheless Chapman persevered with new number-one driver Graham Hill. 'The initial response was tremendous,' Colin related. 'We went out and ran so much quicker than we'd ever run before, the first time out, that it was unbelievable. But then we tried it on faster circuits and found that really the car was a bit too big – we were gaining on the turns but losing on maximum

Colin Chapman drew this layout for a possible 1977 Formula 1 wing car using space-frame solid axles front and rear, guided by wide-based radius-rod triangles.

speed. We rather clouded the issue by deciding to build a Formula 2 car initially simply because we had Formula 2 engines to spare.

'The thing that I was really worried about was the steering problem,' Chapman added, 'and it just hasn't appeared at all. The biggest problem is roll because we've got very low roll centres – we tried to run it without anti-roll bars but the roll was enough to use up too much of the suspension travel. We've only got about six inches of suspension travel at the front. We made a mistake there. And when Firestone changed all their tyre diameters we lost another inch because of ground clearance.'

Another worry had been behaviour on bumpy circuits, with the higher unsprung weight, but late in 1968 Chapman denied to Charles Bulmer that this was a failing: 'We've run it at Snetterton, which is as bumpy as most, and it behaved very well. We've also got a very high pitch oscillation, very high. Even though we're running fairly high spring rates, we're still getting far

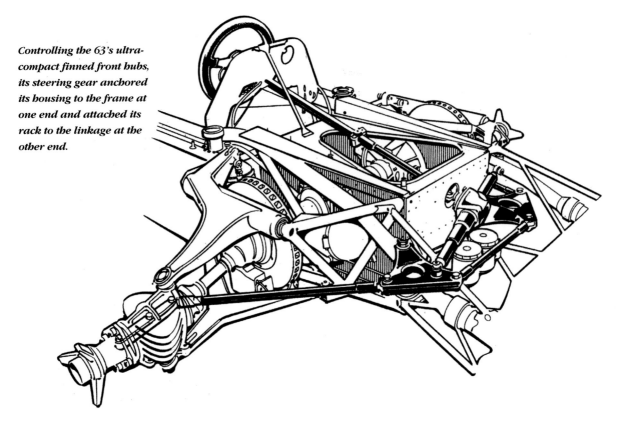

Controlling the 63's ultra-compact finned front hubs, its steering gear anchored its housing to the frame at one end and attached its rack to the linkage at the other end.

too much pitch. We're running at frequencies of about 100/105 laden which is different from a year ago – we had it all very soft then but we've still got too much roll.

'We're putting anti-roll bars on now,' Chapman added. 'We were trying to get away without them. We tried to cut the roll down by raising the roll centre. That definitely reduced the cornering power so we've now gone back to the low roll centre with roll bars. It sounds easy but in fact with the particular configuration of the car it's not very easy to put them on. It's the old, old story: we should have designed them in in the first place. So we're cobbling some on at the moment and then we'll see how it goes.'

These experiments with the 57 late in 1968 were carried out with the aim of using the chassis in the 1968–69 Tasman races, installing a 2.5-litre DFW V8. Mechanic Leo Wybrott, a New Zealander, was tasked with its preparation. 'The team's number-one driver was distinctly underwhelmed by its performance,' Wybrott told historian Michael Oliver. 'Graham drove it for quite a time. It wasn't just one or two laps to say that it was a bucket of rubbish. He did persevere with it a bit on the day.' Not enough of a positive nature was discovered to make it a candidate for Tasman racing. Thereafter, with the demands of the 4x4 Type 63 looming, the 57 was set aside.

Conceptually Colin Chapman kept faith with the idea of a revival of solid-axle suspension. In the run-up to the design of the Type 78 'wing car' for 1977 he sketched a layout that showed space-frame solid axles front and rear on the lines of the 57, but guided by long low-placed radius rods that were triangulated to central pivot points in plan view.[5] Execution of the design would have imposed heavy constraints on the car's structure. The concept was never realised in the metal.

Leo Wybrott, the Kiwi who had first test-driven the 57, performed the same service to shake down the new four-wheel-drive Formula 1 Type 63 on its debut at Hethel in mid-June of 1969. Using many of the same components, its suspension was derived from that of the Type 56 turbine cars that raced at Indy in 1968, both having four-wheel drive. Both used front and rear suspensions with inboard coil/damper units operated by the upper wishbones. To suit the vehicle packages the springs were at the extremes of the chassis in the 56 and towards the centre of the 63.

In both cars the wishbones had to be short, reaching deep into the wheels, because chassis width was taken up by differential units and inboard brakes at both front and rear. A significant aim of the inboard mounting was to reduce the amount of heat radiated into the wheels and tyres so that Firestones of a softer compound could be used reliably.

---

5 This method of guiding the axles would have looked familiar to Henry Ford, who used it on millions of automobiles.

With wheels of only 13-inch diameter this meant close-spaced wishbones for the 63 and extremely short hub carriers that were finned for heat dissipation. Steering them challenged the wit of designer Maurice Phillippe, who worked out a three-piece track rod that was driven by a steering rack anchored to the chassis at one end. A peculiarity was that the steering wheel moved in and out up to one inch as it was turned. At the rear an adjustable radius rod, to adjust toe-in, took the place of the steering linkage.

In parallel with the 63 the hard-pressed Lotus crew were building a scaled-up version, the Type 64, to carry Ford's turbocharged V8 at Indy in 1969. The two cars were closely related in design albeit structurally enhanced in the 64 to handle the Ford's 1,000 horsepower. Both cars were costly dead ends, the 63 through lack of performance and the 64 withdrawn from the 1969 '500' after Andretti's crash and failure of

the others to get up to speed. Suspension played a secondary role in the sagas of both cars apart from agreement by their drivers that their steering was notably heavy.

After all this work designing and building three complex four-wheel-drive racing cars the return to thoughts of a successor to the two-wheel-drive 49B was balm to Colin Chapman. To chief designer Phillippe he said, 'I'm going to write down a series of requirements for the new car and I'd like you to do the same.' Said Phillippe, 'That made it possible to come up with individual ideas and then discuss them together. It was a real challenge and you felt that you had to come up with good ideas.' The result was the 72, introduced in 1970.

Heavy steering was noted by the drivers of Lotus's 1969 Indy contender, the four-wheel-drive 64. None qualified so they didn't have to cope with it in the race.

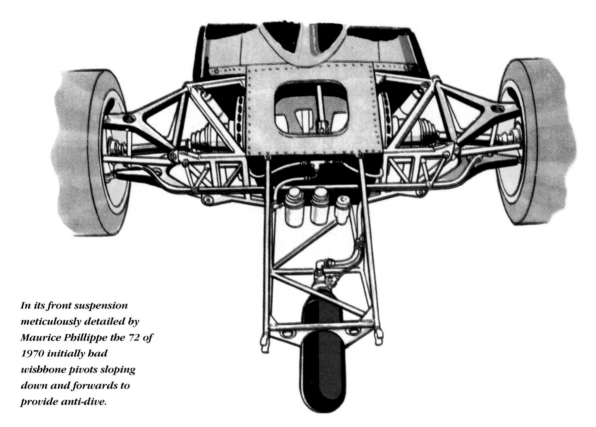

In its front suspension meticulously detailed by Maurice Phillippe the 72 of 1970 initially had wishbone pivots sloping down and forwards to provide anti-dive.

'He insisted that he wanted a rising-rate suspension,' Phillippe added. 'I wasn't convinced but he was the boss.' This was springing that became stiffer as the wheel moved upwards. Only half in jest Chapman said that he wanted such suspension to frustrate Graham Hill's tedious sorting of bump stops during training. In fact the limit to the 72's wheel travel was striking the surface of the track; skid blocks were fitted below its nose to take the impact. 'On the other hand,' said Phillippe, 'the idea of inboard front brakes came from me.' They'd been used on the four-wheel-drive Lotuses and indeed on the 1954 racing Mercedes and Lancias, but not hitherto on a two-wheel-drive Lotus.

Although conventional, the front and rear suspensions of the 72 were fabricated meticulously of high-strength steels that allowed sections so small that drivers quizzed engineers about their reliability. The magnesium rear uprights had the finning of the four-wheel-drive cars. Linkages at the rear included single upper radius rods that were inclined upwards towards the front to introduce anti-squat. The aim was to give the car a stable platform under both braking and acceleration to make best use of Firestone's latest tyres.

For front anti-dive Colin Chapman renounced his earlier objection to the method used by Cooper. He angled the axes of the upper and lower wishbones downwards towards the front at 12 degrees, which gave

100 per cent cancellation of dive under braking. Compared to his previous on-and-off efforts the 72 represented a wholesale commitment to anti-squat and anti-dive by Chapman.

The consequence of his decision was nothing less than a fiasco. It threatened to destroy the 72's career before it properly began. 'The main thing was that the car didn't really handle at all well because of the horrendous amounts of anti-dive and anti-squat it had,' John Miles told historian Michael Oliver. 'The result is that you have no braking feel because the car won't dive at all. The first thing that you know about the brakes locking is that you see smoke coming off the tyres. You don't have any sensation at all and the car is not slowing down quickly.' Here was a clear echo of Innes Ireland's objections of a decade earlier.

At the other end of the 72, added Miles, 'they found all the anti-squat on the rear was producing a lot of jacking effect. A little anti-squat can work but they put a hell of a lot on the back. It didn't actually lift the rear wheels; you just got appalling traction.' The combination of the front and rear geometries was diabolical, said team manager Peter Warr: 'What happened was, if you turned into a corner it picked up a front wheel and as you accelerated out it picked up the rear wheel.'

When the 72 went to its first races in 1970, the Spanish GP and Silverstone's International Trophy a week apart, it suffered mechanical troubles and wasn't especially fast. Chapman was deeply resistant to giving up his 'anti' features, which he defended as not the source of the car's problems. Not helping the situation was that his drivers were Jochen Rindt, not at all constructive in his criticism, and John Miles, knowledgeable but not a driver of the first rank. Based on his previous experience at BRM Tony Rudd felt the 'antis' could be unproductive, while Graham Hill agreed after test-driving a 72 at Silverstone. Reluctantly Chapman ordered the offending geometries removed.

The result was a driveable 72 for the first time. 'I think Colin was mortally wounded that it didn't really work at all,' Peter Warr told Michael Oliver. 'He therefore applied himself to the degree and level needed to produce a bloody brilliant car. And he came up with a set of modifications which just transformed the car and made it unbeatable.' It was especially wounding to Chapman that the problems were in the 72's suspension, a discipline in which he'd hitherto ruled supreme.

Another novel feature of the 72 was its use of torsion-bar springs. These offered lightness and efficiency as well as a means of providing the rising spring rate that Colin Chapman desired. Instead of the long bars that were familiar from production cars, however, Chapman used what was called a compound bar in which a bar was splined at one end to its tubular housing so that both the bar and the tube acted as spring media. The remote end of the assembly was simply guided, all the stresses being taken at the action end where the outer tube was anchored and a lever arm twisted the inner bar.

In the late 1930s compound torsion bars were used by Vauxhall in its version of Dubonnet independent front suspension. They surfaced again in 1954 for the front suspension of the Grand Prix Mercedes-Benz W196 and the following year for the 300SLR. They had the merit of compactness, needing roughly half the length of traditional bars. Serviceability was a bugbear, however. At one race, said Jochen Rindt, there were torsion-bar problems, 'but it's such a long job, torsion-bar assembly, that there was no way of finding out before the race. We wouldn't have been able to take them apart and put them together in time. It's about a three-day job to set the car up properly.'

Placed low and longitudinally, each torsion bar was twisted by a lever linked to a tubular triangle on the bottom of the upper wishbone. At static height the connecting link had high leverage, which progressively reduced with jounce to give the effect of a higher spring rate. Torsion-bar springs were used in the 'Texaco Star'

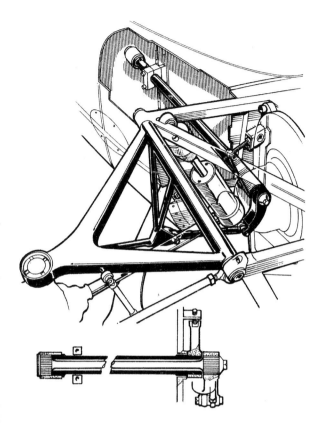

Designed to give a rising stiffness at the wheel, a link and lever from a pyramid attached to the 72's upper wishbone operated a compound torsion-bar spring.

Compound torsion bars – a bar inside a tube – were a feature of the Dubonnet-type front suspension of late-1930s Vauxhalls.

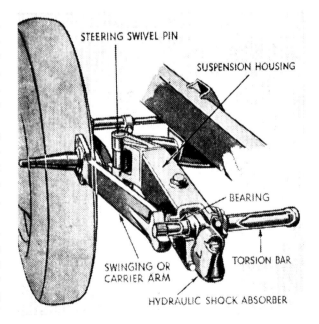

Wrapped in tape to prevent stress-raising scratches, the 1954 W196 Mercedes-Benz's compound torsion bars protruded forwards from the pivots of its lower wishbones.

Formula 2 Lotus of 1973 and the Grand Prix 76 of 1974, neither of which was successful. Chapman reverted to coil/damper units for the 77 of 1976 and remained loyal to them throughout the rest of his career. In 1989 John Barnard revived compound torsion bars for the Type 640 GP Ferrari. With a few exceptions the Italian company has been loyal to them since.

Emerson Fittipaldi was tasked with leading the Lotus team in 1971. Firestone produced new low-profile tyres for the 72 from which great things were expected. Because an engine shortage nullified Lotus's plan to test pre-season, practice in Buenos Aires for a non-championship race was Emerson's first experience of his 72 with Firestone's new rubber. He was shocked by the dodgy handling of a car that had worked so well in 1970. 'One of the few times I spun a car was in Argentina,' he told Elizabeth Hayward. 'I had never spun in Formula 2 or Formula 1 since I'd started racing, and this was the first time because I was trying too hard to drive the car quickly, and it just didn't handle.

'I went back to Lotus to speak to Maurice Phillippe about it, and I told him the car was impossible,' added Emerson. 'He wanted to know how it could be so good in 1970 and how I, as a new driver, could possibly know. I couldn't tell him why it was wrong.' That his colleagues knew something was wrong was evident, as Philip Turner wrote after the Argentine race: 'The Lotus team were terribly puzzled by the odd handling of their 72s and are now busy collecting and studying all the photographs they can lay hands on of the cars in action.'

Chapman wasn't convinced. He felt 'my bloody drivers' were at fault. 'Reine [Wisell] and I were still so new to Formula 1 racing,' said Fittipaldi, 'that Colin just didn't believe us. When we were explaining a problem to him we had a job to convince him that it was a real one and not simply our lack of experience. On top of this Colin was more interested in the turbine car. We were really lost. The first six months up to July and August we were going round in circles, chasing our tails.' A handicap was that the team was unable to test, working hand to mouth with insufficient cash.

Finally towards the end of 1971, with the turbine 56B near its retirement, Chapman started listening to his young Brazilian driver. Emerson pointed to success on his Formula 2 Lotus with Dutch Koni dampers, which Chapman adopted. He also argued for reduction of the rising-rate effect and the return of the bump rubbers

that Colin had tried so hard to eliminate, saying that it would help set up the car for the bumpy tracks on which it had been least competitive.

Made in time for the US Grand Prix of 1971, the changes brought an immediate benefit. 'Watkins Glen was very important for us,' said Fittipaldi, 'because it was there that the car started to come good. It was there that we found the limit. It became a forgiving car. Being qualified second fastest I was sure we were going the right way with the car.' He was in fact less than two-hundredths of a second slower in qualifying than the Tyrrell of pole-sitter and 1971 world champion Jackie Stewart.

'In many ways we started 1972 there,' said Emerson. For his championship 1972 season twin radius rods made an appearance at both side of the rear suspension where some anti-squat was judiciously added in concert with added grip from the latest Firestones. For 1973 Lotus was promising new cars, but the 76 didn't appear until 1974 with much the same suspension. When the 76 failed the career of the evergreen 72 was prolonged.

As described in Chapter 1, in 1976 the 77 appeared with – as a major feature – adjustability of track and wheelbase. 'It was purely a chassis test-bed,' said Chapman. 'We were definitely lost at the time,' added

In 1971's United States Grand Prix at Watkins Glen, pictured, changes to the 72 started taking effect, leading to Emerson Fittipaldi's world championship in 1972.

designer Martin Ogilvie, 'at the end of the Type 72 and the 76, just flailing around. We didn't know what to do. One week it was falling rates of suspension, then it was two millimetres of movement, the next minute it was three inches of movement.'

A novel feature of the 77 at its launch was its use of exposed frame-mounted brake calipers that also served as suspension attachments. 'This saves a lot of structure,' Chapman explained, 'and provides hard points on to which we can mount the wishbones, usually quite tricky to provide on a lightweight fabricated sheet-structured tub and, of course, the whole suspension is moveable as a unit. We can get a certain amount of wheelbase adjustment by setting the frames forwards or backwards, and we can also adjust for anti-dive characteristics, if we feel that will be beneficial, by producing a frame that rotates the whole lot by a couple of degrees.

'The same thinking is carried on at the rear,' Colin Chapman continued, 'where we again use dual calipers mounted on our special gearbox side-plates, and again carrying the track-control links into the calipers which are stiff points, easy to mount on and capable of taking

In its initial concept of 1976 the 'adjustable' Lotus 77 had its front suspension attached directly to the twin calipers of its inboard front brakes.

the load and, in fact, very adjacent to the through-bolt which goes right across the car. The normal tubular frame structures, crossbeams and such things which are required on other racing cars can therefore be done away with. This is one way of making a lighter yet at the same time stronger car, two very difficult things to do.'

Chapman's reference to the possible use of anti-dive at the front of the 77 showed that he had by no means given up on this idea. Among his 1976 ruminations about his future Grand Prix car was his thought that 'anti-dive, although in theory desirable to reduce required ground clearance, has proved enigmatic in practice and would tend to reduce the car pitch change which we probably need for our new aerodynamic system.' 'Enigmatic' was an elegant way of expressing the distaste that his drivers manifested for previous systems as on the 72. On the other hand he was open to anti-squat at the rear, finding it 'probably still desirable in order to provide more outside rear-wheel dynamic suspension travel.' He recommended an experimental trial.

At the rear the brake calipers of the Lotus 77 carried the mounts for the suspension's lateral linkage, in the Chapman tradition of making components do double duty.

Though the 77 was flagrantly problematic at launch its versatility served it well through to 1976 as a test-bed for new ideas. By the end of the 1976 season the 77 had rocker-arm front suspension with inboard coil/damper units, a quick revision carried out by Len Terry that moved the brakes outboard where they could help the tyres get up to running temperature. Chapman kept this formula and the 77's rear suspension for his high-downforce models of 1977 and '78.

Mario Andretti's arrival on the team in 1976 and his end-of-season victory in a wet Japan marked a Lotus comeback. There was no gainsaying the immense know-how that the hugely experienced Andretti brought to suspension development at Lotus. His ability to adjust tyres, springs, dampers and geometries was unmatched. 'I would go out in the car and come in again,' Andretti said, 'and tell them to adjust the springs or the damper or the track-rod end. Either go up on the right side and down on the left by, say, a quarter-turn or half a turn, and I used to drive them crazy doing that. Colin would trust my judgement because I would make a change and go quicker. I didn't want to explain, because it was my knowledge and experience that gave me that and I wasn't going to give it away.'

Andretti had to disabuse team engineers of stripping out the bizarre set-ups he sometimes imposed on his suspensions. Chapman's role was to give Mario the tools to do his job, as he said to the Italian-American at a race in 1978: 'All you seem to be doing in the pits here is playing with your spring platforms. You've got your cockpit-adjustable brake balance and your adjustable anti-roll bars, so we decided that the next thing we've got to give you is cockpit-adjustable ride height. You know, you should be able to play with the springs when you're out there on the circuit!'

Among the requirements that Colin Chapman set for his 1977 cars – see Chapter 9 sidebar – was 'FRICTIONLESS suspension links when under maximum load, front and rear'. Achieving this would ensure that no external factors affected the operation of the suspension as designed. 'A big effort was made to take all the friction out of the suspension,' Glenn Waters testified. 'If you look at the cars in detail you'll notice that all the suspension joints – the Rose joints, the bearings, or whatever – on the 78 appear to be massive. There was an attempt to have every joint as a rolling friction joint rather than a sliding friction joint.'

Colin Chapman's artistry in the conception of refined suspension components had few rivals. These were his late-1970s ideas for hub designs.

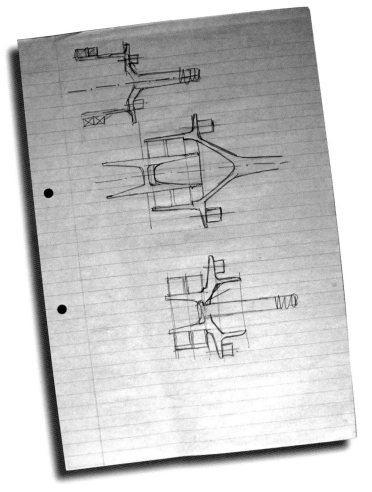

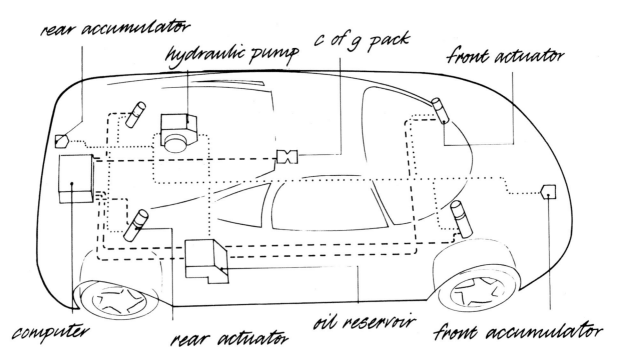

rear accumulator

hydraulic pump

c of g pack

front actuator

computer

rear actuator

oil reservoir

front accumulator

Sensors, pump, reservoir, accumulators and actuators made up the elements of Lotus Active Suspension as depicted in a generic schematic.

'We were beginning to get involved in all sorts of things which we didn't even know existed until then,' added team manager Peter Warr, 'like friction-free suspension. In fact by the end of the Type 77 era we even had a recognised procedure for boiling all Rose joints in oil for a certain length of time in order to loosen them up and so make the suspension as friction-free as possible! It was a time when, in my view, motor racing ceased to be a black art. People were now devoting themselves exclusively to the engineering side.'

By the end of the 1970s Colin Chapman had ceased being deeply concerned with suspension geometry *per se*. 'All that really matters is how wide it is, how long it is and what tyres it has got,' he said in 1978 of the new generation of Grand Prix cars. 'You only have to look at Brabham, Ferrari, Lotus and McLaren over the last few years to see that they are all turning in practice times that are very close together. So there is a fairly wide band of acceptable suspension arrangements.' Here was another hint of the thinking that allowed Colin to consider solid-axle suspensions as late as the mid-1970s.

Chapman would play a valedictory role in a breakthrough suspension concept just before his untimely death. Various outside experts had been helping Team Lotus with the conduct of tests in response to a dossier that

Chapman had produced in 1975 which challenged his colleagues to learn more about their racing car's fundamentals.[6] An example was their need for a better understanding of the grip characteristics of racing tyres in response to load. Engineer Nigel Bennett contacted various institutes as well as Goodyear to find suitable tyre-testing machines. He also conferred with Karl Kempf, who with Tyrrell had pioneered in the application of instrumentation to Grand Prix cars.

Their search for the sensors and systems needed to understand better the dynamic behaviour of a Formula 1 car led the Lotus men to control and instrumentation expert David Williams at Cranfield University. Subsequent tests 'gave us an insight into many things that were happening with the car that at that time we hadn't any idea about,' Williams related. 'For instance, with the cross-ply Goodyears they were using at the time, going down the straight 80 per cent of the torque was taken by one tyre. Tolerance in their manufacture mean that when spinning at racing speeds, the centrifugal force caused them to grow at different rates. Inevitably the larger tyre was doing most of the work and the smaller one was not developing anything like the traction it was capable of.'

David Williams assisted Lotus with instrumented studies as it found its way into the high-downforce developments of the Types 78 and 79. Problems with the ultimate development of this line, the 80, exercised the grey matter of all concerned. 'It occurred to me that

---

6   An extract from this is a sidebar in Chapter 8.

really the ground-effect car needed a suspension that would react to road inputs but not react to changes in aerodynamic downforce,' said Williams. 'The only way you could achieve that was with an irreversible suspension.' This led to the idea of a powered springing system that would rigorously control the car's position in relation to the ground.

At first Williams's suggestion of such an 'active suspension' fell on fallow ground. Lotus had its 'twin-chassis' concept to deal with this issue. When that was ruled illegal, Lotus research engineer Peter Wright decided that the Williams idea might be the way forward. He suggested to Colin Chapman that a research programme be launched to test the feasibility of an active suspension that would provide a stable platform for the exploitation of ground effect. At first the idea of going straight to a Formula 1 car was mooted, but David Williams thought this a step too far.

Finally, said Wright, 'Chapman's response to my proposal was to assign a Lotus Esprit Turbo to the project and tell me to have it running as an active-suspension car in six months. His understanding of the need to solve the aerodynamic problem and his belief that the future lay with computers – although I do not believe he really liked

them – epitomised Colin Chapman as one of the greatest motor-racing visionaries of all time.' 'Over the course of three months,' said David Williams, the test car 'went from being a total nail to something that was actually quicker than a standard Esprit.'

After driving the prototype and being driven by Elio de Angelis, said Peter Wright, Chapman 'immediately gave the go-ahead on a Formula 1 version of the system, only 12 months from his original go-ahead on the project. Another 12 months later saw the first test of the Cosworth DFV-powered 92, again at Snetterton.' They were just preparing to give the car its first run on 16 December 1982, Wright continued, when Peter Warr arrived 'to announce that Colin Chapman had died the previous night.'

The active 92 raced twice in 1983. The system was revived for the 1987 season, when Ayrton Senna scored the first win for active suspension in a 99T at Monaco. In 1993 the FIA banned the use of active suspensions from 1994 onwards. Even posthumously, Colin Chapman couldn't avoid a final tussle with racing's rulemakers.

Peter Wright, leaning on a Lotus test car, and tall Patrick Peal, two men to his left, were among the engineers at Hethel who perfected Lotus Active Suspension.

Chapter 5

STRUCTURE STORIES

No member should be subjected to compound stresses if by the provision of additional members these can be split up; for example, when a member is subjected to combined torsion and bending it is preferable, where possible, to replace it by two separate members, one designed to deal with bending alone and free from torsion, and another subject to torsion only and free from bending.

Sir Harry Ricardo

'At seventeen I went to London University,' Colin Chapman related, 'and during the following three years, between studies, I learned to fly in the University Air Squadron. This helped me when in 1948 I went into the RAF and continued my training on Harvards, because by then I had made up my mind to be a fighter pilot. This was probably the turning point in my career, because I began to read motoring publications in the Mess. I was to learn subsequently that the RAF had no real flying opportunities to offer. I got more and more interested in motoring as a sport.'

Here were the origins of two aspects of the Chapman oeuvre: his passion for cars and racing and his association with the world of aviation. Both were destined to endure throughout his career, the aviation element including microlight aircraft and engines that were maturing at the time of his death. Both also contributed to his uniquely innovative approach to the design of sports and racing cars.

'A car is but a structure,' Chapman wrote in 1954, 'as amenable as a building to stress calculation – if only one knows what stresses it must sustain and what safety

In a handful of drives for Lotus in 1963 and 1966 Pedro Rodriguez piloted Colin Chapman's 25 and 33, first of his new breed of monocoque Formula 1 cars.

factors are required. There was the "rub" because nowhere could I find the "open sesame". I haunted the Institute of Mechanical Engineers library and read everything from the most learned papers to the non-technical articles in the motoring press.'

Chapman applied his hard-won structural expertise to his first trials special of 1948, retroactively considered the Lotus Mark I. 'One thing which had stuck in my mind,' he said, 'was that other Austin Seven Specials used to lose their tails. They just dropped off. To overcome this I built up a body framework with three bulkheads and stressed the whole on aircraft principles with double-ply skin on battens of ash. These battens formed a frame which I extended aft beyond the back axle to carry a rear extension to the body which held two spare wheels.' Strength was added by omitting doors in favour of shallow cutaway sides. With the help of a welder at the workshop of his fiancée's father Colin boxed in the bottom of the Austin's U-section frame members.

An important advance in Lotus structural technology came with the Austin-powered Mark III, designed according to the rules of the 750 Motor Club for its popular series. These required the use of an Austin Seven frame, no matter how vestigial in the completed car. Initially the Mark III was powered by the two-bearing

In 1948 Hazel Williams posed at the wheel of work in progress, showing the double-ply body structure of her steady boyfriend's Austin Seven-based trials special.

version of the Austin Seven's four-cylinder engine. Its aluminium crankcase was bolted solidly to the frame to add vitally needed torsional stiffness.

This worked well, greatly improving handling, but Colin Chapman hankered after the use of the three-main-bearing engine that Austin introduced in 1936, feeling that it had greater potential. Knowing that Austin had rubber-mounted the engine to avoid twisting the crankcase Chapman did likewise, only to discover that frame bending degraded his cornering speeds through Beckett's Corner at Silverstone by five miles per hour.

A tidy job, Colin Chapman's first trials special gleamed after polishing the aluminium skins bonded to its plywood structure. Omitting doors added important stiffness.

When the three-bearing unit was solidly mounted, fast cornering was restored but the engine promptly broke its crankshaft.

'We came up with the rather clever idea of a triangulated tubular-steel frame around the engine to restore the stiffness,' said Nigel Allen, who with his brother Michael was helping build the car in the Allen family's workshop. If frame stiffness were increased the three-bearing engine could be rubber-mounted, which it clearly preferred.

'Colin didn't reckon it could be done,' Allen told Peter Ross. Fearing it would be impossible to extract the engine, he said, 'You'll never get it off! You'll never get it off!' 'He made such a fuss I told him to go home,' said Allen. 'I sat down with a length of tube and a drill. I drilled the chassis in one or two places and started with one corner and tacked it up. Then the next bit and tacked them together. I managed to get it so we could just slide the engine out. We had one tube that was removable. That put the stiffness back overnight. It made a tremendous difference; it really stiffened it up.'

In fact two removable tubes completed a triangle above the engine, pointed towards the front and based on a complex tubular structure above the clutch and gearbox. 'It is properly stressed and bolted together with high-tensile bolts,' said Bill Boddy in his report on the 'Lotus-Austin', 'so that it can be dismantled for complete engine removal, and has restored and improved upon the original [cornering] speed.' Although essentially an eyeballed palliative from the grey matter of Nigel Allen, it was the first triangulated tubular structure in a Lotus.

Chapman and the Allen brothers were to make many more demands on their local suppliers of Truewell welded-seam mild-steel tubing and cold-drawn weldless steel tube. These were the major ingredients of the frame of the Mark VI Lotus, the first model designed from scratch with an eye to series production. No surprise would have been evinced had the Mark VI's chassis been based on a ladder frame with longerons of two big tubes. This was the proven basis of many successful sports and racing cars in 1952, natal year of the Mark VI.

'Obviously the perceived wisdom of the day was to make everything along the lines of a brick shithouse,' said early Chapman ally David Kelsey, 'as a glance at any pre-war racer will indicate, and then drill holes in the bits to lighten them. This was a waste of time of course, but nobody seemed to realise that at the time. As far as I know, only Buckler and Lotus used space frames, or even made any attempt to keep the cars light from first principles. Others quickly jumped on the bandwagon when it was seen how effective the cars were, particularly the Lotus.'

'I do not believe in the "two-tube" chassis principle,' Colin Chapman affirmed, 'the type of frame which has two large-diameter steel tubes as the main frame members. Mathematically it is not as rigid as the multi-tube "space frame". The "two-tube" frame seems to me to be a waste of time because the body framework has to be built on to it, and that could so well be employed as part of the frame proper.

'My idea was to build a robust multi-tubular "body-frame" which would be rigid enough to take the suspension parts, the drive and the engine,' Colin continued. 'The suspension, engine, transmission and so on could be bolted to this basic frame. The whole should be light and made so that with easily assembled accessories it would provide a fast car for the not-too-rich enthusiast for racing and/or touring.'

In fact space frames were exploding on the scene. In the 1930s multi-tube frames were exploited by such versatile pioneers as Buckminster Fuller and William Stout. A small-tube frame was a feature of the 1946

To restore frame strength lost when the Lotus Mark III's three-bearing Austin four was mounted flexibly, Chapman colleague Nigel Allen made this multi-tubular engine-bay bracing.

Dante Giacosa's drawing of 21 August 1945 showed the multi-tube space-frame structure of Cisitalia's Fiat-powered D46 single-seat racing car.

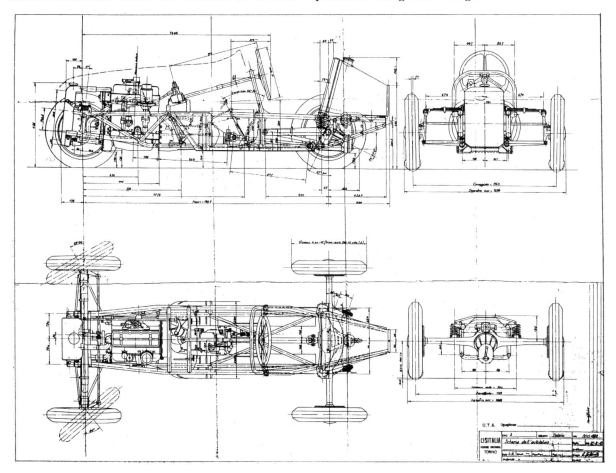

As refined by Giovanni Savonuzzi, the tubular spaceframe
of Cisitalia's D46 contributed to both lightness and
stiffness that made it highly competitive.

Cisitalia D46 racer and the sports cars that followed it.
Following the Cisitalia example, Porsche's mid-engined
Type 356 prototype of 1948 followed suit. Having

schemed a small racing car with a space frame while
working in a British military unit after the war, Rudolf
Uhlenhaut used a complex three-dimensional space
frame for his Mercedes-Benz 300SL of 1952, in parallel
with Chapman's work on the vastly simpler Mark VI.

Most likely to have influenced Chapman was the
space frame of Jaguar's XK120C sports-racer, designed

In 1947 Porsche's engineers held true to the Cisitalia
space-frame concept when they designed their Type 360
Formula 1 car for the Turin-based company. [LAT]

by Bob Knight. Described in detail in the journals in July of 1951 after the C-Type's sensational victory at Le Mans, the frame didn't escape the attention of the widely read Colin Chapman. His 'magpie' instincts recognised the suitability of a space frame for his Mark VI although without the Jaguar's elaborate bodywork. For his purposes – creating a car that enthusiasts could assemble at home – he had only to add a nose and panelling to the frame to create a sports-racer.

In Jaguar's C-Type the lower frame tubes measured 2 inches in diameter while the upper tubes were 1.5 inches, joined by 1-inch connecting tubes. Strictly speaking the differential in sizes between upper and lower tubes wasn't needed if the frame were properly stressed. In fact with the bottom tubes in tension and the upper ones in compression it would be more logical to have larger tubes at the top. Nevertheless in his Mark VI Chapman employed a not-dissimilar ratio with bottom tubes of 1.8 inches surmounted by a 1-inch upper structure. In this Bob Knight's Jaguar design may have served as a model.

Lotus historian Peter Ross offered an alternative view, writing that 'Colin probably thought that as most contemporary sports cars used two large-diameter tubes, the sight of the much smaller tubes that are all that is needed in a space frame might have come as a shock, and cause sales resistance'. While this certainly has validity it's more likely that Chapman was making haste slowly in his first space frame to be confident of having a serviceable product.

Also in 1952 Chapman honed his space-frame expertise with his design of the Formula 2 Mark VII, which ultimately surfaced in 1953 as the Clairmonte Special with its cockpit widened to compete as a sports car. Main tubes of 1.6-inch diameter were joined by 1-inch tubes in a design that sloped down to front and rear from its greatest height at the cockpit. A similar concept served as the core of the frame of the ambitious Mark VIII Lotus, which began as a wedge of the fewest tubes feasible.

In 1952, David Kelsey recalled, 'none of us, Colin included, knew very much about chassis frames at the outset, and they were essentially designed intuitively by following the strains from one tube to another in an attempt to achieve rigidity. Very likely all the tubes were stronger than they need have been and indeed we built a framework too in lighter gauges without detriment. As with most frames, the fly in the ointment is the driver, who unfortunately needs to get in the car, thus leaving a large area of virtually unsupported frame. We did toy with the concept of putting a driver in and then bolting tubes around him to maintain the integrity of the frame, like the engines in many of the cars. With the general vulnerability of racing cars to fire at that time this would not have met with the approval of most drivers.'

The application of science to structures began in 1953. During that year Colin Chapman's alliance with the Allen brothers collapsed in part because, as Nigel

An original Porsche drawing shows the tubular frame of the GP Cisitalia, which lacked the diagonal stiffening tubes used correctly in the D46.

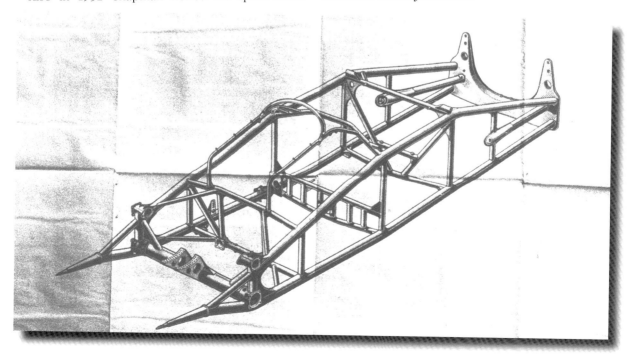

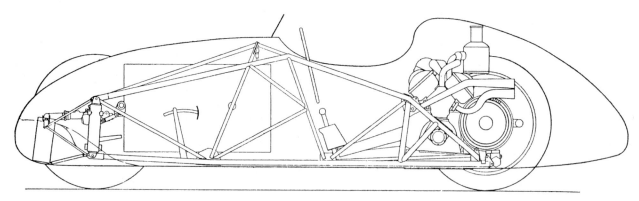

In his 1946–47 design for a 500cc Formula 3 car, Mercedes-Benz engineer Rudolf Uhlenhaut specified a deep, well-stressed multi-tubular frame.

said, 'Colin was making all the promises and we were doing all the work.' Michael withdrew his services late in 1952, so with Chapman still employed by British Aluminium some fresh blood was needed. This arrived in the shape of de Havilland aeronautical engineer and enthusiast Mike Costin.

'Peter Ross knew Colin from the 750 Motor Club,' Costin explained. 'Peter got me involved with Colin. Adam Currie was a family friend of Peter's. The two

Much as Chapman and his colleagues would do with balsa wood, Uhlenhaut finalised the space-frame for his 1952 300SL by making and testing a small-scale wire model.

families were great friends going back to long before the war. Adam bought a Ford-engined Mark IIIb from Colin and Peter was helping him with that. Colin was moaning one night at the 750 Motor Club, saying he'd bust up with the Allens and from the end of 1952 he was on his own. He said to Peter, did he know of anybody? Peter thought, well, what about Mike Costin? Colin did a deal and I started with Colin on 1st January 1953.' Like so many involved with Lotus in its early years Mike moonlighted at first. Only at the beginning of 1955 did he and Colin join Lotus full time.

Late in 1953 Chapman had drawn the nucleus of the frame he planned for his Mark VIII, the car to take on the tough international 1.5-litre class. Would it do the job? Adam Currie suggested that it be checked by Peter Ross, who worked in the stress office at de Havilland Aircraft Company. Ross not only blessed it in principle but also introduced colleague Gilbert McIntosh early in 1954. Thanks to Colin's powers of persuasion 'Mac' soon became involved in both the design and the analysis of Lotus structures. 'That was the real start of what you might call some science being brought to bear,' said Mike Costin.

'The design of all the cars from the Mark VIII to the Elite was based on aircraft practice rather than the very "hit and miss" practice of the sports-car world,' said McIntosh. 'I was horrified by the complete lack of data on loading cores for the structure, so a lot of the time on the VIII and IX was spent working back from failures to what must have been the applied loads. By the time of the Eleven we could design off the drawing board and get a light structure which didn't fail from fatigue or from unacceptable degrees of bump.

'Till we knew better,' McIntosh added, 'we stuck to the well-proven principles used on the tubular engine mountings of the Merlin in Mosquitos and Hornets as they were the nearest thing we knew to a space-frame car chassis. We stuck to cold-drawn mild-steel tubing but we had to change from the aircraft Sif-bronze welding to the car-industry fusion welding. There was always a clash of cultures between the people who had been making racing-car frames – and "knew" about the science involved – and the theory merchants from the aircraft industry. Poor old Colin had to hold the balance! I know we had opposition from the "practical" wing because Colin used to come out with comments such as, "The lads think that's a bit too fancy".' Mac's retort was that their thinking was 'agricultural.'

Growing like Topsy from the core initially conceived by Chapman, the Mark VIII frame was well short of optimum. To add stiffness some areas were enclosed by riveted-on panels while transverse aluminium 'diaphragms' were fitted at the cowl to support the aerodynamic body. While the Mark IX of 1955 had a much more rational space frame, conceived from scratch, it kept the Mark VI's needlessly weighty 1.8-inch lower frame tubes. The 'diaphragms' were gone, replaced by light tubing to support the aluminium body.

The transition to frames designed 'in the best aircraft tradition' as 'Mac' McIntosh put it, began with the Eleven. The difference was in fact profound, the new frame looking positively scanty compared to that of the Mark IX. The first two frames to this new design were used for the works Mark IXs of 1955, one magnesium-bodied with a 1.5-litre engine and the other skinned in thin-gauge aluminium to carry a 1.1-litre Climax. This was vital proving before the Eleven went into production.

'The chassis was schemed out by Colin and me on the drawing board at Gothic Cottage,' said McIntosh, referring to the Chapman residence at which the engineer usually spent his Sundays after golfing on Saturday. During the afternoon he and Colin were able to explore and evaluate some five different space-frame configurations by making balsa-wood models in small scale and checking their torsional stiffness.

The engineers' joint effort resulted in a spectacular reduction to the very optimum. The only sign of a 'diaphragm' was a curved panel at the dash to carry both the instruments and the front bodywork. Gone were the big bottom tubes, the Eleven frame's largest being 1 inch in diameter and the rest 0.75 inch. Gauges were light at 18 and 20. That the design was successful, said Bill Boddy, was shown when he had a wheel changed on a test car. 'We had visual proof of the excellence of Chapman's frame,' he wrote, 'because when a jack was raised under one side of the car the opposite front wheel rose in sympathy – rigidity *par excellence.*'

These skills were maturing when at the end of 1955 Colin Chapman was asked to visit the Vandervell workshops at Acton, west of London, to cast an eye over the new frame being mocked up for the 1956 Vanwall. 'Well, what do you think of it?' asked company chief Tony Vandervell. 'Colin was always outspoken,' wrote Denis

Characterised by a peak at its cowl, the 300SL's space-frame was first built for the 1952 sports-racing coupés and then adapted for the 1954 road car.

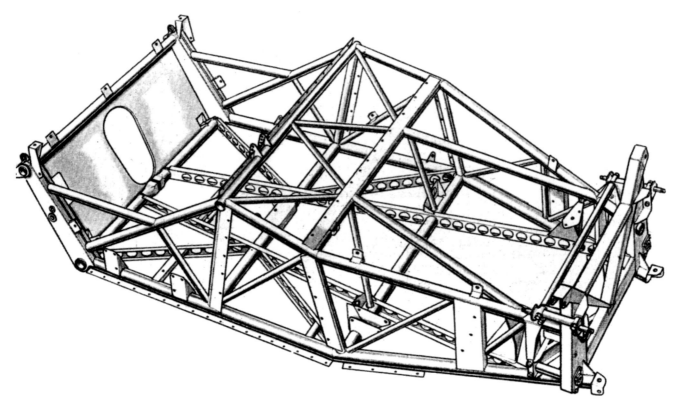

*A space-frame sample close to home for Colin Chapman
was that of the 1951 Jaguar C-Type sports-racer. Success at
Le Mans made it an attractive model for emulation.*

*Chapman's first space-frame was that of the 1952 Mark VI,
which used both square and round tubing with some bays
diagonally braced and others not.*

Jenkinson and Cyril Posthumus, 'so he said, "I wouldn't
have put that tube there," pointing at one part of the
space frame, at which the "old man" said, "Why not?"

'For a while they discussed the new Vanwall chassis
frame on the principle of "if we move that tube" and
"suppose we put one in here" and so on,' Jenkinson
and Posthumus continued, 'until Colin said, "Look, Mr
Vandervell, this is a waste of time. The whole thing is

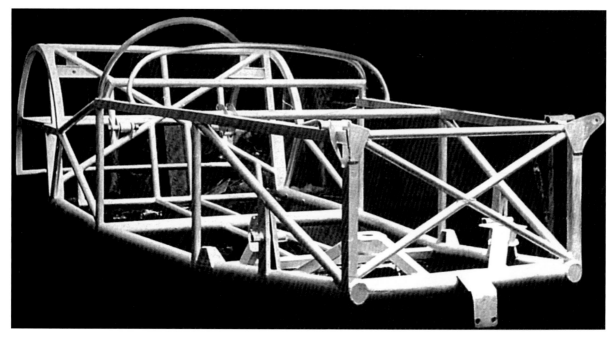

basically wrong. You should start all over again."
[Vandervell] didn't hesitate for a moment. "Right," he
said, "will you do it for me?" The resulting space frame
was vastly more efficient, providing a sound foundation
for Vanwall's Formula 1 breakthrough in 1956 and its
world manufacturers' title of 1958.

When it came time to draw the frame for the first
single-seat Lotus, 1957's Formula 2 Twelve, the
Chapman/McIntosh partnership was beautifully bedded
in. Their Gothic Cottage co-operation used the same
1-inch and 0.75-inch tubes as the Eleven and deployed
them sparingly and astutely. The Twelve initiated the
Lotus practice of using frame tubes to carry fluids, in
this instance to circulate oil between the engine and the
rear-mounted reservoir. In spite of some arguments lost
by McIntosh, who was unhappy with decisions at the
rear of the frame – and proven right by later failures –
the Twelve's was a frame of sublime elegance.

Its creators took an extra step to stiffen the Twelve's
structure as Chapman explained: 'In a racing car, due to
the fact that chassis members are disposed nearer to the
polar axis of the chassis frame, it is more difficult to obtain
the same degree of stiffness for any given weight than is
possible in a wide-framed sports car. In this respect I have
been greatly assisted in making use of the very stiff
Coventry Climax engine. I have mounted [it] rigidly in
the chassis in the form of a torque box, so that the strong
crankcase can supplement the torsional stiffness of the
chassis. This is achieved by making the rear engine plate
of 10-gauge strong [aluminium] alloy and incorporating
it as a chassis bulkhead at four attachment points, the
front engine mounts being bolted straight to the chassis
with $5/16$-inch high-tensile bolts.'

Although 'Mac' McIntosh left the Lotus world in 1957
he assisted in designing the space frame of the low-line
Sixteen. It was close kin to the Twelve's structure albeit
with a reversal of the slopes of the diagonal braces along
each side, to the front and rear of the dash. Not only in
the Sixteen but also in later frames Chapman infuriated
McIntosh and others of his advisory cadre by rejecting
the purity of the Eleven's frame with its exclusively
straight tubes. He continued to use the despised curved
tubes whose bending behaviour under stress played
hob with their welds. 'Chapman appears never to have
absorbed the importance of this,' said Peter Ross.

When the Sixteen prototype was sold the mechanic
newly tending it 'couldn't believe how thin the tube wall
was in the space frame,' quoting a dimension akin to 20
gauge. Peter Bryant 'quickly found that it needed lots of
chassis welding repairs. Where the tubes came together
with any sort of component mounting boss there were
cracked welds and cracked tubes next to the welds.

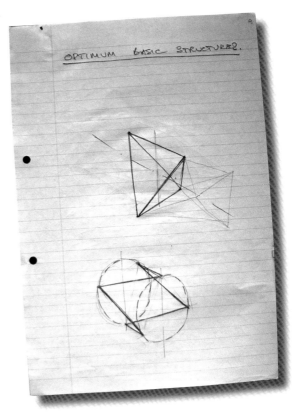

*From his Mark VIII project of 1953–54 until the end of his
career Colin Chapman remained faithful to certain basic
structures that he saw as giving optimum stiffness for
their weight.*

Many times the expansion of the frame from welding
heat had made the tube next to a weld distort and crack.
It took me two weeks to get the frame fixed.'

*Chapman and his colleagues from de Havilland were well
acquainted with the tubular structures that served in
aircraft such as the mounts that held the Merlin V12.*

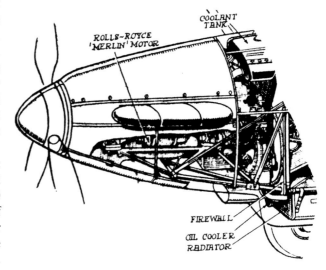

Joining Lotus for 1958 was Len Terry, a talented ex-RAF designer/draughtsman who was paid 'the princely sum of £12 a week' by Chapman. For 1959 Terry took the troubled Sixteen in hand, revising its frame and at its dash strengthening the critical cockpit area with a distinctive oval of two tubes joined by perforated panels, some of whose holes served to house instruments. Shown on page 162, this attractive concept persevered in future rear-engined Lotuses.

Tubular space frames of this pattern prevailed through to the F1 Lotus 24 of 1962. They were designed more from practical experience than from the breakthrough science of the de Havilland years. 'As far as the chassis itself is concerned,' Colin Chapman said in 1960, 'the first thing is to decide on the minimum diameter of tube – usually an inch for main frame members – and the minimum gauge which it is practicable to use from the point of view of welding (20 or 18 gauge). It is almost impossible to calculate all the stresses in a frame, but I normally work out the stresses at various points and check them on a test model.'

Though this was a far cry from the meticulous analyses conducted anew by Ross and McIntosh that transformed Lotus structures, Mike Costin continued to hold the fort for science at Lotus until he left to join Keith Duckworth at Cosworth in 1962. He and Chapman

Finely stressed tubular space-frames held both the landing gear of the 1938 Percival Q6 and the de Havilland Gipsy sixes that powered it.

evolved new designs from previous experience to create the mid-engined Eighteen, the low-line 20, 21 and 24 Formula cars and the mid-engined successor to the Eleven sports car, the successful 23 of 1962. 'Mike Costin was a brilliant designer,' said his colleague Mike Warner, 'and played a very big part in the intricacies of the Lotus 23, far more than Colin. The 23 was Mike's last design before he went full-time into Cosworth.'

From their Eighteen Chapman and Costin also developed the sports-racing Nineteen. Its frame of 16- and 18-gauge tubing used diameters of 1 inch and ¾ inch, widened through its centre section to carry two people. Thanks to lightness and the thrust of its 2.5-litre Climax four the Nineteen was unbeatable, in the hands of drivers like Stirling Moss and Dan Gurney, as long as its 'queerbox' held up.

Commissioned by Gurney to build a Nineteen to take an American Ford V8, Chapman assigned the project to Len Terry. He widened the body plug by four inches to give more room for the latest tyres and put a new frame under it. 'I didn't even refer to the Nineteen drawings,' Terry said. 'It was a completely new design – Chapman gave me *carte blanche*. I put in a much more complicated space frame. The cockpit is an unresolved rectangle and because of that most space frames will twist. If you go outside the cockpit and put some triangulation in, you finish up with a much stiffer chassis with very little extra weight.' This was the one-off Lotus 19B, which showed much speed but little reliability.

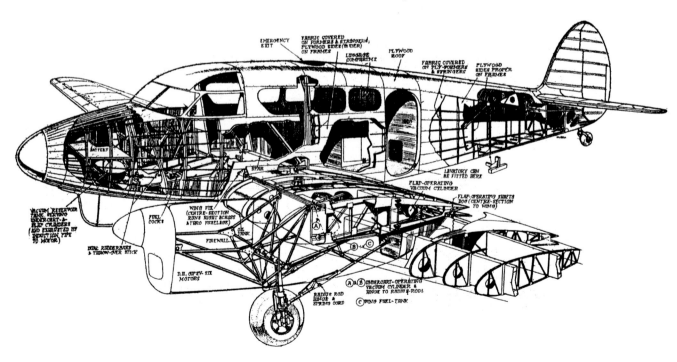

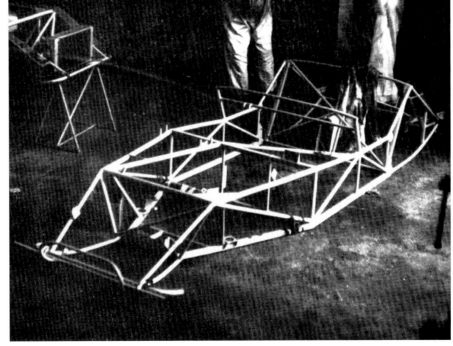

Above, left: *De Havilland's engineers were unconvinced by the space-frame of 1955's Mark IX Lotus – seen from the rear – whose lower tubes they considered needlessly large.*

Above, right: *By comparison with the Mark IX, the frame of the 1956 Eleven was impressively scanty. Viewed from the front here, it represented the absolute minimum.*

Right: *Another perspective showed the Lotus Eleven's spaceframe at the Hornsey works after essential brackets were added. It was the first properly stressed Lotus frame.*

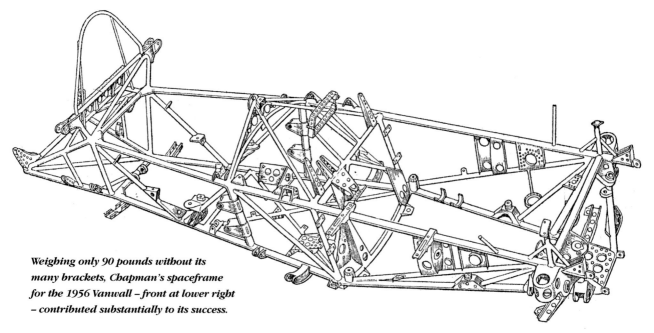

Weighing only 90 pounds without its many brackets, Chapman's spaceframe for the 1956 Vanwall – front at lower right – contributed substantially to its success.

Still moonlighting for Lotus in 1956, 'Mac' McIntosh recalled a preoccupation of the Chapman-led team. 'We wanted a bread-and-butter money-raiser to back up the Grand Prix and sports-racing cars,' he wrote. 'The problem was how to make a GT car down to a price – a poor man's Porsche.' The cost of tooling to make a conventional steel body was far too great while the bespoke Italian style of hand-hammered aluminium was

out of court as well. 'We looked at buying Ford 100E body shells,' 'Mac' added, 'which we could buy cheap, then fit our own suspension and engines – the route Lotus went with the Lotus Cortina.'

As for the views of Colin Chapman, they were that 'the ideal motor car would be one to which you could attach all the mechanical units and then drive off. The current car – the steel body – is made up of a multitude

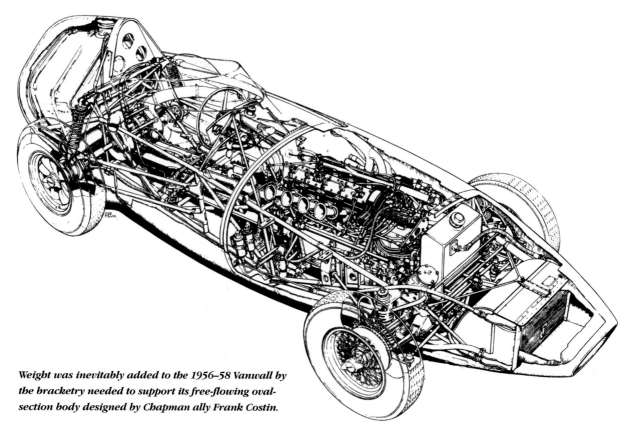

Weight was inevitably added to the 1956–58 Vanwall by the bracketry needed to support its free-flowing oval-section body designed by Chapman ally Frank Costin.

160

of little bits all welded together, which strikes me as the wrong way to do something. It is illogical to build a car, as we do now, out of steel – which rusts – and then paint it to stop it rusting.' The obvious answer was a body of glass-reinforced plastic or GRP on a simple steel frame as was used at the time by such as Turner and TVR but this lacked distinctiveness and creativity, not to mention ultimate functionality.

Meanwhile freelance designer Lawrence 'Lawrie' Bond had allied with Britain's biggest maker of caravans or trailers, Berkeley of Biggleswade, to produce a small front-drive sports car using air-cooled two-stroke engines. Bond worked with Berkeley, already vastly experienced in GRP fabrication, to make this the roadster's main material, using fabricated aluminium structures bonded into the underbody at the centre and nose to provide the additional beam and torsional strength needed by a roofless car.

Introduced in September of 1956, the cute and clever Berkeley made its debut on stand 119A of that year's Earls Court motor show. 'He was full of it,' said McIntosh of Chapman's reaction to the Berkeley, 'and we really kicked the idea round. The idea of a fibreglass chassis-body unit answered all the problems on paper but there was a helluva lot to do before we could design a car. I was okay on the structural side as far as stressed

fibreglass mouldings went because I had used them on Vampire night-fighter radomes – mark you these were different types of mouldings to the car-body mould – "bathtub" mouldings we called them.' In the new Lotus, 'Mac' added, 'I had to get round the problem of an odd-shaped box with a lot of cut-outs and no stress-calculation background from the car world. They did it all by eye and testing in those days.'

Chapman immediately aimed for the optimum, namely a complete GRP structure unsullied by metallic inserts. This was achievable, he and his colleagues felt, if a coupé instead of a roadster were the chosen configuration. The coupé's roof could add the strength that the Berkeley gained by its underbody panels. This wouldn't be easy, however, the stiffness of GRP being far less than that of steel. Colin expressed confidence, saying that 'in the early days I did a lot of work on reinforced-concrete design, studying the way the French produced very lightweight, very strong structures. This led me to use that technique in glass-fibre and reinforced-plastic design to produce the first truly structural plastic car in the Lotus Elite.'

Charles Bulmer wrote in *Motor* that the fly in this

Diagonal bracing of all its bays showed the attention given to stiffness of the F2 Lotus Twelve's space-frame by Colin Chapman and 'Mac' MacIntosh.

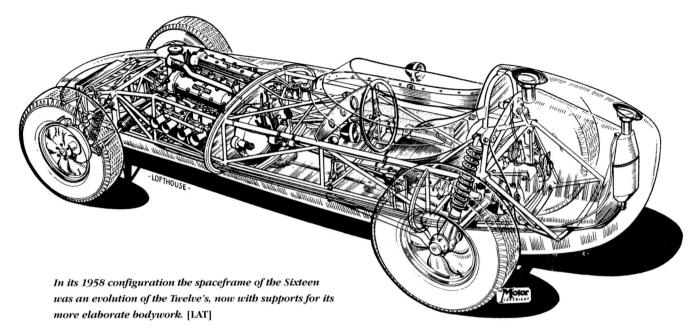

In its 1958 configuration the spaceframe of the Sixteen was an evolution of the Twelve's, now with supports for its more elaborate bodywork. [LAT]

promising ointment was the need for strength in the crucial front pillars, which had to be slender for visibility: 'Tests on a prototype showed that much of the car's overall stiffness was lost here, torsional loads causing lateral bending of these pillars whilst their fore-and-aft

Revisions to the Sixteen by Len Terry for 1959 included introduction of this stiffening hoop though the critical cockpit area, soon to be a characteristic Lotus feature.

bending permitted vertical flexing of the shell.' The solution was to bond in a tubular-steel hoop above and below the windscreen, anchoring it on vertical square pillars that solved the problem of hinging the doors. Also bonded in was a steel sub-frame at the front to carry the suspension and the front engine mounts.

The first batch of Elites saw use in competition. In these cars, continued Bulmer, 'it was soon found that the intense heat generated by the inboard [rear] disc

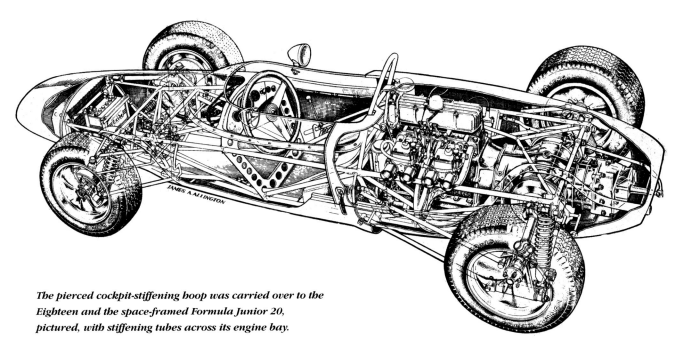

The pierced cockpit-stiffening hoop was carried over to the Eighteen and the space-framed Formula Junior 20, pictured, with stiffening tubes across its engine bay.

brakes under racing conditions caused local softening of the resin and eventual failure of the differential mounting. The trouble was later eliminated by the use of heat shields and by strengthening of this section which now has a material thickness of up to 0.7 inch compared with the average of about one-eighth of an inch, diminishing to less than one-tenth of an inch in lightly stressed areas.'

These values were the results of experiments with thicknesses both twice and half as much. The latter was nearest the skin sections of the early cars used for racing, 'resulting in a car substantially lighter than the later production versions,' wrote Robin Read. 'With hindsight it might have been better to have made prototypes suitable for crossing the Sahara rather than quickly accomplishing ten laps of Brands Hatch or even twenty-four hours of Le Mans but the Lotus reputation was founded on racing successes.'

Observing a 'shell which encloses numerous box sections and which is double-skinned throughout so that only the presentable surfaces are visible,' Charles Bulmer found it 'impossible to watch the assembly of these bodies without being greatly impressed by the structural forethought and detail planning that has gone into the design.' He judged that the Elite was 'evolved by a team of singular ingenuity and analytical ability with little regard for convention.' This was a shrewd assessment of Chapman and company at a crucial period in their exploitation of new structural ideas.

On 21 November 1957 Colin Chapman applied for a patent on the Elite structure, including its metallic inserts, which he updated in 1959. He had reason to be proud of a unique achievement in car engineering that would remain unmatched until the era of carbon-fibre sports-car structures. The travails of the manufacturing of the Elite, whose total numbered just over 1,000, are the stuff of legend. As a business venture making a Lotus version of Ford's Anglia would indeed have been a better idea. But it wouldn't have been a Lotus.

Chapter 1 related the manner in which a mild-steel backbone frame became the main structural element of the open Elan, introduced in 1962 as a successor to the Elite. Attached to the frame at 16 points, the Elan's GRP body added some 10 per cent to the vehicle's total stiffness in torsion. Type 26 in the Lotus collection, the Elan introduced a structural concept that persevered in Lotus production cars and was adapted for the DeLorean DMC-12 as well. Functionally it had much in its favour, though it offered no protection to occupants from crash invasion from the sides. Nor did the lack of durable protection from corrosion make these cars long-lived.

Although the Elan's backbone chiefly used 16-gauge steel with some components of 14 and 10 gauge, Chapman initially approved the use of lighter 20 gauge for the backbone of the sports-racing Type 30. This was soon upgraded to 16 gauge. When Colin showed the proposed scheme to his designer Len Terry, the latter was unimpressed. 'I studied it for two days and by the end I'd produced a critique covering two foolscap pages. Of all that I considered wrong with the car, the only thing he agreed to change was boxing in the rear chassis members. I told him somebody else would have to draw the car because I didn't want my name attached to it.

'With a car over five feet wide,' added Terry, 'it seemed to me silly to have a backbone chassis that was only five inches wide. To get maximum torsional stiffness you need chassis members as far apart as possible. We put the first one we built through a rudimentary torsion test and it took a permanent set at quite low loading, well under 1,000 pound-feet per degree. I also don't think that the front box gave either the upper or the lower suspension wishbones a wide enough base. This lack of stiffness accounts for the poor handling of the car.'

It also accounted for some embarrassing incidents. The first 30 was bought by Ian Walker, whose car literally collapsed at Brands Hatch, its frame failing completely. 'I did the bumpy old Zeltweg airfield circuit in Austria in the Lotus 30,' related Frank Gardner. 'It was going all over the bloody place in the closing stages but I got it home third. Back in the paddock we found that the backbone chassis had broken in two. I think the bloody doors were holding it together.' The breakage was between the backbone and the fork that embraced the engine. 'The vibration from this failure caused bloodshot eyes that were so severe they lasted for weeks,' said Gardner's team manager Jeff Uren.

This is not to gainsay the 30's potential for effectiveness. In fact its backbone was wider than Terry's 'five inches', measuring 6 inches at its top and 8.8 inches at the bottom of a depth of 10.5 inches. Its flanks continued down another 1.5 inches to create a channel in which were the oil and water pipes, brake and clutch hydraulics, the wiring harness and the throttle cable. Although handicapped by the weight of its all-iron Ford V8 and inadequate braking, the 30 did set several track records in its day.

For 1965 Chapman and development engineer John Joyce produced the 40 with a more robust frame and 15-inch wheels for better brakes while Ford delivered 5.7-litre engines that drove through Hewland gearboxes in place of the 30's ZF units. The ever-loyal Jim Clark did his best to show its paces, as he had with the 30, but without notable success. During one test he gave a ride to Denis Jenkinson, who 'commented on the vibration from the front end under heavy braking, and Jim Clark was most pleased to have corroboration of what he'd been saying earlier,' recalling Terry's criticism of the front-suspension mountings.

Welcome compensation for the 30/40's failure came from the success Lotus enjoyed with its Formula 1 Type 25, introduced at the 1962 season's first championship race at Zandvoort on 20 May. Jim Clark had the new car while Trevor Taylor had its predecessor the 24. 'We hedged our bet, as it were,' said Colin Chapman, 'in so far as the Type 24, with which we started our 1962 season, was actually a multi-tubular space-frame version of a 25. In other words, we designed the 25 first and then, just in case the monocoque didn't do what we

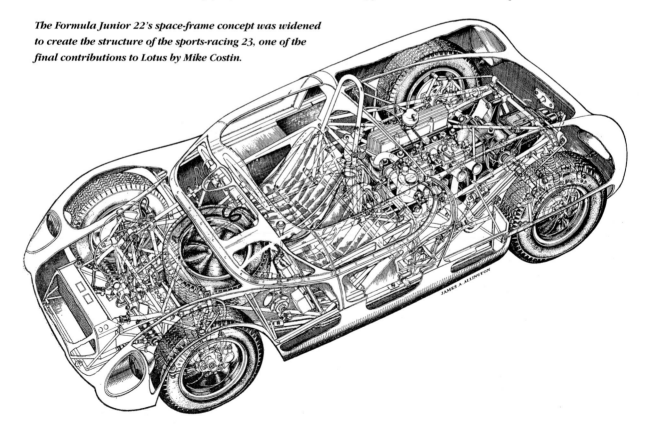

The Formula Junior 22's space-frame concept was widened to create the structure of the sports-racing 23, one of the final contributions to Lotus by Mike Costin.

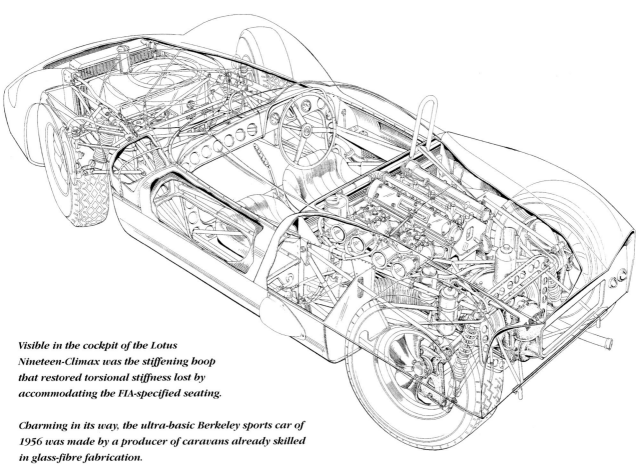

Visible in the cockpit of the Lotus Nineteen-Climax was the stiffening hoop that restored torsional stiffness lost by accommodating the FIA-specified seating.

Charming in its way, the ultra-basic Berkeley sports car of 1956 was made by a producer of caravans already skilled in glass-fibre fabrication.

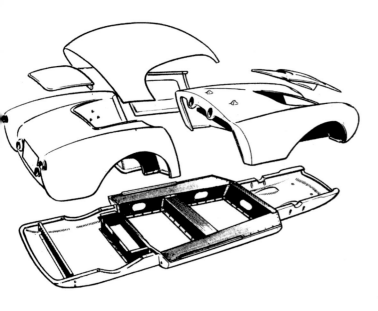

Shown are the main glass-fibre mouldings that made up a Berkeley as well as the sheet-aluminium panels that stiffened its floor pan.

Body manufacture at Berkeley was the antithesis of rational glass-fibre production. Achieving the latter was a stern test for Chapman and his colleagues and suppliers.

wanted, we took all the mechanical elements, engine, suspension, steering and so on and designed a space frame to connect them.

'The basic reason we went to the 25,' Chapman explained, 'was that one of our biggest problems in F1 racing was planning the fuel tankage. With the V8 engine we were using more fuel than with the old four-banger and it was becoming a job to get enough capacity in a small car. We thought, if we have to have huge fuel tanks down each side which in themselves could be torsionally fairly stiff, why don't we just join them to the front suspension at one end and the rear suspension at the other end and bolt the engine in the middle?' The Coventry Climax V8 was bolted at eight locations to increase frame stiffness.

Enhanced torsional stiffness was another motivation for the frame that became known as the 'monocoque', said Chapman: 'We've always assumed that 1,000 pound-feet per degree is the minimum for a bare frame. Anything under that is definitely whippy. The space frames of the 24s only gave 650–700. They used to flex and crack and fatigue and we were constantly welding the damn things up.' The new monocoque frame is well illustrated on page 24.

Fashioned of 16-gauge aluminium, Chapman added, the tubs of the first three 25s 'had a much higher torsional stiffness than our previous single seaters – about 1,500

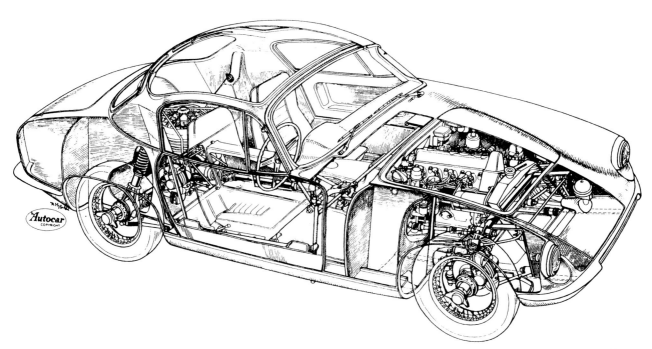

pound-feet per degree, rising to 2,400 with the engine bolted into the frame. They also showed complete freedom from any sort of tearing, cracking or working-free of rivets so we decided to try 18 gauge for R4 and we've stayed on this ever since. We also went down a gauge on all the steel bits so the weight saving was almost in proportion to metal thickness – 16 gauge is 64 thousandths, 18 gauge is 48 thousandths – 25 per cent less. The hull came down from about 80 pounds to 65 pounds and the torsional stiffness in similar proportion.'

In racing, Chapman told Gordon Wilkins, 'We have found the monocoques very much less trouble than the cars with space frames chassis. You see, there is practically no maintenance on the car's structure. We have cars running which have now done two seasons of racing and they are still as sound and firm and durable as when they were built. There is no sign of fatigue in them, no cracking – mainly, I think, because there is no flexibility in a monocoque and so less deflection than with a space frame.'

A drawback, added Colin, was cost: 'A monocoque is very much more expensive, over double the price.' Did this bring other benefits? 'You still have the same number of mechanics on the job, but having built the monocoque it is possible for them to concentrate on the finer points of preparation.' This brought rich rewards in the form of world championships for both Lotus and Jim Clark in 1963 and 1965.

Making a car's body do double duty as its structure was as old as the industry, dating from the days when bodies were carriage-derived. After a separate frame became the norm, a signal deviation was the Cornelian of 1914. Produced by

By making his Elite a coupé, with its roof adding strength, Colin Chapman reasoned that he wouldn't need the aluminium platform inserts used by Berkeley. [LAT]

As an exploded view shows, both the platform and the roof of the Elite were double-skinned, a feature of its design engineered by John Frayling.

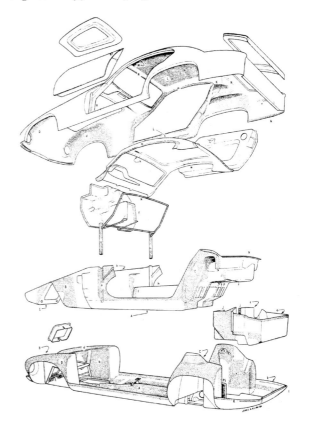

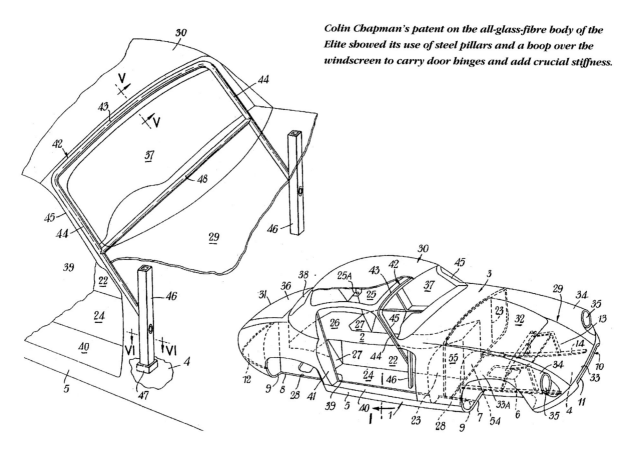

Colin Chapman's patent on the all-glass-fibre body of the Elite showed its use of steel pillars and a hoop over the windscreen to carry door hinges and add crucial stiffness.

Kalamazoo, Michigan's Blood brothers, Maurice and Clarence, the Cornelian cyclecar was designed by Maurice's son Howard, who borrowed his wife's middle name for its marque. First running late in 1913, the vee-twin-powered roadster was commercialised in 1914.

From their cyclecar the Bloods developed a fully fledged small car with the same distinctive design: a combined frame and body electrically welded of steel sheet of 20 to 24 gauge. Upper and lower transverse springs gave independent suspension at front and rear. One of these Cornelians provided the basis for a racer prepared by Swiss-born driver-mechanic Louis Chevrolet to compete at Indianapolis in 1915. By far the smallest entry with its engine of less than 2 litres, the Cornelian attracted praise for its ingenious design and plucky performance. After 180 of the 500 miles it retired with a dropped valve. As so often happens the Cornelian's advanced features weren't emulated at the time.

In 1923 an engineer whose creativity was on a similar plane to Chapman's, Frenchman Gabriel Voisin, fielded a team of cars in the French GP that used the stressed-skin construction with which Voisin was familiar from his pioneering work in aviation. 'Its body was built in aircraft style as a fuselage,' wrote Cyril Posthumus, 'with aluminium side panels pinned to ash framing with steel

reinforcement, the smooth metal undershield contributing vitally to the structure. There were no main side members in this ancestor of today's monocoque structure, yet it supported engine, transmission and springing, was extremely rigid and weighed only 84 pounds.' The advanced design was the work of André Lefebvre, who also raced one of the cars.

More than a decade later two British initiatives pointed to the potential of racing cars with integral body/frame construction. First appearing in 1939, the Lightweight Special was the creation of Alec Issigonis, a draughtsman at Rootes and later Morris, who built it with the help of his wealthy friend John 'George' Dowson. Work began in 1934 with the aim of building a really effective single-seater with an Austin Seven engine – much the same motivation as Colin Chapman's after the war.

In a manner akin to that of Voisin in 1923 Issigonis made the body's sides the principal structural members, using aircraft-type five-ply wood panels faced in 28-gauge aluminium. These were joined by a steel cross tube at the front, the firewall, seat and undershield plus the solidly mounted two-bearing engine and other components. The frame was at its deepest at the scuttle, tapering downwards towards front and rear. It was an elegant monocoque structure for the Lightweight, which competed successfully after the war.

Alec Issigonis didn't integrate the small aluminium fuel tank with the structure of his Lightweight. Neither did the technical editor of *The Motor*, Laurence Pomeroy, Jr, when late in 1938 he set out his ideas on the design from scratch of a future British Grand Prix contender. He concluded that 'it should be possible to build a racing car which is very largely an enclosed object with a stressed-skin construction in the same manner that one does the modern aeroplane. Owing to the necessity of having a hatch, as it were, through which to reach the engine and for the driver to get in and out, it would be necessary to reinforce the skin at various places with stiffeners.'

Referring to 'tests with a light-alloy model,' Pomeroy concluded that such a structure 'would be not only lighter but also more rigid than present types of German cars which have steel tubular frames with light-alloy bodies.' He decided, however, to omit both the front-end sheet metal and the rear fuel tankage from the structure 'so that their size and lines can be varied in accordance with experience gained.' Prophetically Pomeroy also proposed rack-and-pinion steering and brakes that were inboard at both front and rear.

A sports-racing car with optimised 'stressed-skin construction' as postulated by Pomeroy was designed

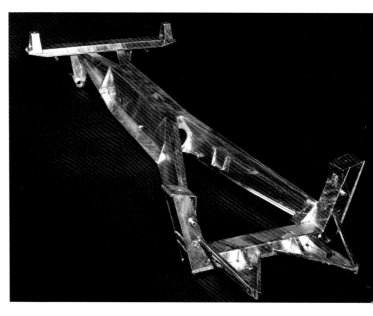

Introduced in the Elan and Europa, the backbone-frame concept was also employed for the new Elite and the Eclat, viewed here from the front in a 1980 version.

A triumph of conceptual perfection over practical rationality, the Lotus 30 of 1964 lacked the torsional rigidity to do justice to the torque of its 4.7-litre Ford V8.

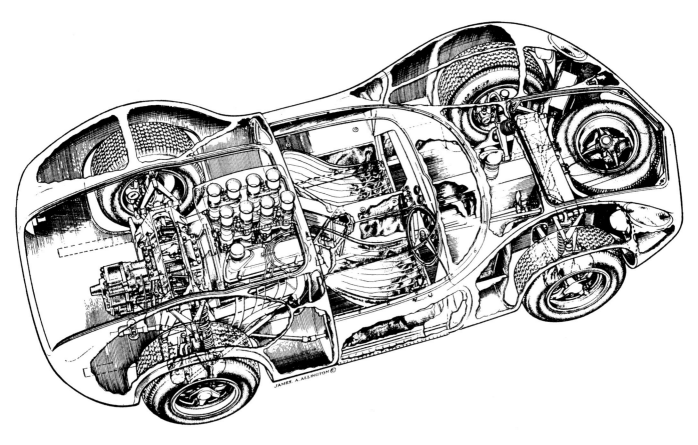

The Lotus 30's central backbone frame, containing its fuel, forced an offset driving position. Two radiators vented warm air into its front wheelbouses.

by Tom Killeen of Four Oaks, Warwickshire in 1951–52 for John Newton, who began racing the MG-powered Killeen K1 in 1953. During the war Killeen was in the RAF, restoring damaged Spitfires to combat readiness. The ruggedness of their structures gave him to think that something similar would work well for cars. While service manager for Jensen Motors after the war Killeen designed the K1 for Newton, whose company made lubricants especially valued for racing.

In 1952 Killeen patented his construction, which in the K1 was a pure monocoque on aircraft lines with top-

Pictured by Max Le Grand in 1964's British Grand Prix, the Lotus 25 marked a major forward step with the simplicity, strength and durability of its monocoque tub.

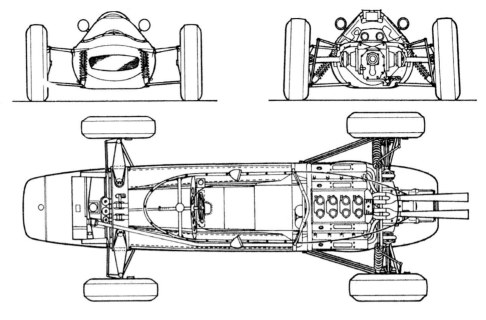

Consisting of two long fuel tanks joined by lateral bulkheads, the Lotus 25's riveted and bonded tub brought slimness, stiffness and serviceability to Grand Prix racing.

hat longitudinal stringers and hoops of steel, clad in Hiduminium sheet of 16 gauge. Supplied by High Duty Alloys Ltd, this was aluminium with some 4 per cent copper and a lesser amount of magnesium, to enable heat treatment, and other elements. Working on an assembly jig, the skin was attached to the hoops and stringers by snap-head rivets. At front and rear of the cockpit were bulkheads of Plymax, a wood and aluminium sandwich. The structure's stiffness, Killeen found, was sufficient to obviate the installation of bracing tubes that he'd planned for the engine bay.

Though it had no issue, apart from a handful of later K-series specials which became mid-engined after 1960, Killeen's K1 was a design of great merit that was completely contemporary with Colin Chapman's early work. Indeed, when competing in a September 1953 club meeting at Silverstone, Chapman saw Newton give his K1 its debut. Just at this time Colin was working on his Mark VIII for 1954, whose space frame as completed showed an attempt to use riveted-on aluminium sheeting to add stiffness to the overall structure.

'Among the many special features of the [first] Mark VIII Lotus,' wrote Chapman at the time, 'was a semi-monocoque-type of body panelling. Whilst this has quite a worthwhile advantage in weight saving I can now say that the snags which arise during routine servicing, repairs to accident damage and so on are such as to render it inadvisable for sports/racing cars. All the production Mark VIIIs have much more easily accessible components and more easily removable body panelling.' In retrospect 'semi-monocoque' was something of an exaggeration as describing a space frame with some

stiffening panels, but Chapman's experience with it was sufficient to deter further use of the technique for his sports cars apart from obvious floor panels.

By far the most apposite ancestor of the Lotus 25 was another post-war creation, Alvin 'Spike' Rhiando's Trimax. Hailing from Canada's Saskatchewan, Rhiando was a born showman who came to Britain in 1933 with the aim of importing American-style dirt-track racing. Though this didn't catch on, Spike took up Formula 3 racing after the war with a Cooper nicknamed the 'Banana Split' for its garish gold and chrome livery. In his trademark chequered shirt Rhiando won the 500cc race in the first Silverstone meeting of 1948. He's thought to be the first to install a big JAP 1-litre twin in a Cooper.

In April of 1950 Rhiando appeared at Goodwood's Easter Meeting with a completely new car, the Trimax, built to his concept by a specialist engineering firm that also refined his design. The name 'Trimax' indicated that it was designed to compete in classes of 500, 750 and 1,100cc. Stressed and built as well to compete in Formula 2 with – as the rules allowed – a supercharged half-litre engine, the Trimax was overly weighty in Formula 3 trim. 'Had the car been designed only as a Formula 3 machine,' said one of its designers, 'the weight would have needed ballast to reach [the class minimum of] 440 pounds.' For the mid-engined Trimax was of pure monocoque design.

Sheets of Duralumin – another high-strength aluminium alloy – of 16 and 18 gauge were formed and riveted to create the Trimax body/frame. Main elements of its strength came from side sponsons of D section which ran from front to rear, joined transversely by

Above: *An impressively tidy racing car for 1915, the Cornelian was powered by a Sterling four of 1,878cc. It was derived from the standard Cornelian, also unit-bodied.*

Below: *Louis Chevrolet was at the wheel of his monocoque Cornelian at Indianapolis in 1915. Fully independent suspension was another advanced feature.*

cockpit-facing bulkheads and tubular cross-members at front and rear. The floor was part of the structure as well. Inserted into the sponsons through access panels were synthetic-rubber fuel bladders giving a total capacity of just over 10 gallons.

Here was a design that closely foreshadowed the main elements of the Lotus 25. Unlike the latter, which was a 'bathtub' open at the top, the Trimax's nose skin was part of its structure. 'The torsional strength is provided by the large D-section sponsons,' said the aforementioned designer, 'both in direct torsion and in differential bending. Where it is necessary to reduce the width of those sponsons forward, to give wheel clearance, a double floor of box section is provided to maintain the torsion-box area.' This and other aspects of the Trimax design gave ample evidence of the care devoted to its construction.

There's no evidence or even likelihood that the brash Rhiando's creation influenced Colin Chapman. Its UK career was brief and inconclusive before its sale to America in 1951. In the 1950s two competition cars made partial use of stressed-skin structures – one successful and the other less so. The sheet-aluminium centre section of Jaguar's D-Type was fully stressed, acting as both body and chassis. Strongly influenced by

the Killeen K1, which Tony Rudd tested extensively at Folkingham, BRM's 2.5-litre P25 of 1955 adopted a 'semi-stressed semi-monocoque' based on a framework of steel tubes skinned in half-hard aluminium. In 1958 it was abandoned in favour of a space frame to the relief of the BRM mechanics who struggled to gain access through its various apertures.

By the early 1960s Chapman said that he'd 'got heartily sick of trying to unite structures that contained multi-tubular chassis and aluminium fuel tanks and drivers and bodywork – three elements which never seemed to fit together nicely. You'd build the steel structure to carry the loads. And then you'd cover the whole thing with a fibre-glass body.'

As mentioned earlier the challenge of fitting enough fuel into a successor to the 21, to take the V8 Climax, was on everyone's mind at Lotus in 1961. This was a hot topic during lunches at Waltham Abbey's Maple Leaf Inn for the company's top management consisting of Chapman, Fred Bushell, Mike Costin and purchasing

Frame and body were combined in the integral structure of the Voisin 'Laboratoire', one of which – from four entries – was fifth and last in the 1923 French GP.

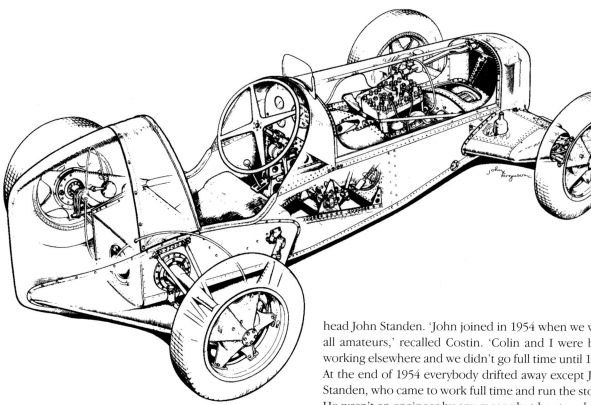

Completed in 1939, the Austin-powered Lightweight of Alec Issigonis was framed of aluminium-faced plywood panels like those used by Chapman in his first special. [LAT]

Partner of Issigonis in creation of the Lightweight Special, 'George' Dowson tended to its needs. The riveted assembly of its panels was exposed to view.

head John Standen. 'John joined in 1954 when we were all amateurs,' recalled Costin. 'Colin and I were both working elsewhere and we didn't go full time until 1955. At the end of 1954 everybody drifted away except John Standen, who came to work full time and run the stores. He wasn't an engineer by any means but he stayed with Lotus up to retirement.'

During one such lunch it was Standen who suggested solving the fuel-storage problem by using the tanks as frame members along both side of the chassis. 'Colin in his inimitable way grabbed a napkin,' said Costin, 'and started to sketch – this is how we should do it. We should do this and this and this – no great detail but I could see what he was on about immediately. How we would make the side skins and the engine – the whole thing. I went, "Crikey, that's a bloody good idea. Make it just like a monocoque aeroplane fuselage! That's great. Let's get on with it!" And that's where it started.'

'Some days later,' John Standen told author John Tipler, 'Colin came into my office, flung a roll of drawings on the desk and said, "Don't laugh, but what do you think of these?"' Thus was born not only the 25 but also a whole generation of monocoque racing cars. 'As in all sorts of design,' said Chapman, 'you can suddenly think of something so simple that you can't understand why you didn't think of it before.' The implication was that the thought was his, though in fact it was Standen's.

'In one fell swoop,' Chapman summarised, 'you reduced a three-element structure to a one-element structure – with a consequent gain all round in terms of lightness, stiffness and cost. Three elements could be replaced by one if you designed the aluminium tank in the first place such that it would hold a front and rear suspension. Then you could do away with the steel

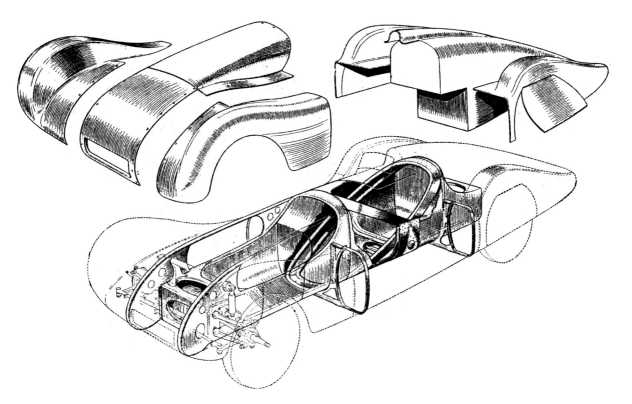

In his 1938 proposal for a British GP car, Laurence Pomeroy, Jr urged consideration of a monocoque structure that didn't incorporate the frontal exterior skin.

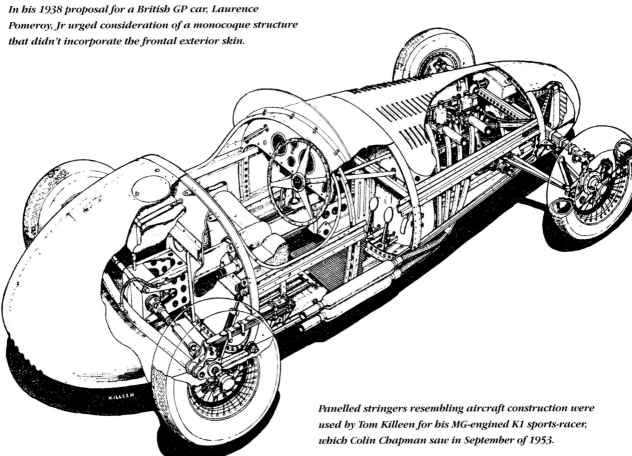

Panelled stringers resembling aircraft construction were used by Tom Killeen for his MG-engined K1 sports-racer, which Colin Chapman saw in September of 1953.

Preparing to compete in the Manx Cup on the Isle of Man in 1950, 'Spike' Rhiando was at the wheel of his impressive monocoque-framed Formula 3 Trimax.

frame. And then, if you could also design the aluminium fuel tank in the first place such that it conformed to the required body shape then you could do away with the body. So this provides an ideal solution.'

As with other Lotus projects at the time, the detail work on the 25 was carried out by a cadre of designers under chief draughtsman Alan Styman. 'Colin had the dominant influence,' said Styman. 'He would do the schematic layout

The Autocar *honoured Rhiando's Trimax with an article and a cutaway drawing by Vic Berris, showing its riveted construction of Duralumin sheet.* [LAT]

of a new design to one-fifth scale, showing wheelbase, track, suspension geometries, engine, gearbox and driver plus a few cryptic notes. He would give us a short briefing, then we would detail the overall concept.' Under Styman was the first full-time Lotus designer, former Vauxhall man Ian Jones. Working with him were David Shuttle, Mike Wardle, Bill Wells and Paul Wright.

'When I left in July of 1962,' said Mike Costin, 'we had just done the chassis jig which I made in wood because it was a good material to work from and hang things on. Because I'm from aircraft experience and design I knew what tools we wanted and I instructed who was going to do the riveting. I knew how, because when you do an aircraft you rivet thousands of rivets a day. As an apprentice I had to spend some time on the production line literally doing thousands of rivets. Rivets are always annealed before you

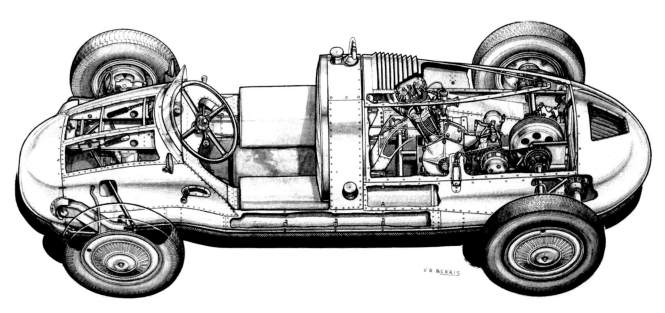

use them. In aircraft all the rivets are kept in refrigerators. They come out in boxes with a time on them because you're only allowed to use them for a certain time before they age-harden. But we didn't take it to that extent.'

Colin Chapman obviously had an advance look at the drawings by John Marsden that accompanied the description of the 25 in *Autocar* of 29 June 1962, because he used them in outline form for his patent application for the design, lodged more than three weeks earlier. Of the tub's D-section side members, he specified, 'the front ends of the tubular members can taper to a point or they may be finished square and provided with dummy fronts. Alternatively when required they can serve as headlamp housings.' The material used for the 25 and later cars was L72 Alclad alloy, similar in composition to the Killeen's Hiduminium and the Trimax's Duralumin.

The potential was obvious for a more complete true monocoque that made the nose and scuttle an integral part of the structure. This was the line taken by BRM in its response to the 25 and adopted by designer Len Terry for the Indy Lotus 38 of 1965. Of the latter Terry said that 'the integral top skinning increased torsional stiffness by something like 50 per cent – a very worthwhile improvement. It may be significant that since then I have never designed an open-top structure for a single-seater.' Stiffness in torsion of the 38 was 3,000 pound-feet per degree.

In the 1.5-litre era Chapman eschewed nose-top skinning for his Formula 1 cars. The reason, he said, was 'maintenance. BRM can get away with it because they have more mechanics and spend more on their racing team. In the Indianapolis car we accepted it because it's only the one race, but to work on the car all the year with

With the provision of adequate fuel in a compact Formula 1 Lotus a pressing concern, it was John Standen who suggested using the fuel tanks as part of the chassis.

the very tight schedule we had for the European season, standing on your head every time you look inside the tanks and things, would become a real nightmare. We feel that we've got the best of both worlds. Once you've got the body off you can get at everything.'

With Lotus first by far with this new technology, the next step was to disseminate it to lower categories. In 1963

Quickly picking up on the ideas of Standen and Chapman, aviation-experienced Mike Costin made the jig for the 25's monocoque, fashioned of L72 Alclad aluminium.

Colin Chapman favoured an open top for the tub of the 25 because it greatly eased service access to all its components. The shift knob wanted replacing here.

As seen with Jim Clark by Max Le Grand in 1964's French GP, the Lotus 25-Climax was the quintessential competitor in the 1½-litre Formula 1 years.

the Formula Junior Type 27 appeared, another monocoque. All-aluminium tubs were replaced by inner panels of 18-gauge aluminium married with a curved outer skin of GRP ¼-inch thick. Joining them were a bonding resin and pop rivets acting on wide washers.

Though the 27 started well with a debut win for Peter Arundell at Oulton Park, the marriage of the two materials in the monocoque deteriorated when their joining rivets began fretting. In panic mode new all-aluminium tubs were made in time for May meetings. Recovery and a string of wins took Arundell to the 1963 Formula Junior title by a single point. For the new Formula 2 of 1964 the 32 was built with steel inner and outer panels, lighter materials not being needed in view of the category's minimum weight. Its 32B version was strong enough to take a 2.5-litre FPF Climax for Tasman racing. Clark used it to win the Antipodean championship in 1965.

With a few exceptions, such as the Type 35 of 1965 and Formula 2 Types 44 and 48 of 1966 and '67 respectively, later Lotus single-seaters for lesser categories reverted to tube frames to take the fight to the Brabhams. Exemplary was the 41 of 1966, which led a comeback for Lotus in Formula 3. Ease of maintenance for private teams and owners was cited as a major reason for its adoption of a steel space frame.

With Maurice Phillippe on board in 1965, replacing the departing Terry, new designs were needed for the 3.0-litre Formula 1 of 1966. Their structures were tested

in the usual way, driver Jackie Oliver recalling 'going to see [Chapman] in the mid-1960s and he had the front of a chassis bolted to the floor and a big bloody scaffold pole on the back testing the forces. Colin knew the importance of rigidity.'

For Phillippe, however, the pursuit of higher torsional stiffness was not a be-all and end-all. The successful Type 33 Lotus-Climax rated 2,400lb-ft per degree, a good but not astronomical figure. 'Jack has shown us the way,' said Phillippe, a hint that the success of the space-framed Brabhams designed by Ron Tauranac demonstrated that a modicum of flexibility in the structure could compensate for any lack of precision, deliberate or not, in the rest of the chassis. But at Lotus there would be no return to space frames for Formula 1 cars.

Maurice Phillippe was at the structural helm when the challenge came, soon after his arrival in 1965, to build a new Lotus to take the 3-litre H16 engine that BRM leased to Lotus. As an expediency he and Chapman used a front end based on that of the Type 38 that won at Indy that year, using exactly the same nose bodywork. This also reflected their master plan, which was to use a 4.2-litre version of the BRM unit at Indy as well in the similar Type 42 chassis.

So radical and fascinating was BRM's Type 75 H16 at its launch that few men of the press took on board the manner in which it formed the frame's rear structure.

Some were of the opinion that it used pretty much the same monocoque as the preceding V8 BRMs, which carried their frames back alongside the engine. But from the start Tony Rudd and his BRM team were aware that the engine was so bulky that there was no alternative to using it as part of the frame. The H16's crankcase was so inherently massive that this imposed no structural deficit.

Engine structures had long been used to contribute to the frame strength of racing cars, in which the transmission of engine vibration to the driver could be tolerated, unlike road cars. Colin Chapman did it with his Austin-powered Mark III. Famously the cylinder heads of the Lancia D50 of 1954 were part of its space frame. First to rely entirely on the engine's strength in a mid-engined car was Ferrari, whose first F1 car of this type practised at Monza in 1963 and raced in 1964. This was a major breakthrough by Ferrari and its brilliant engineer Mauro Forghieri.

To its credit *Motoring News* highlighted this feature of the Type 83 BRM, showing how the H16 was bolted to the 'extremely strong' bulkhead behind the driver, cheekily adding that 'BRM seem unworried by the prospect of a broken con rod slicing the engine in half and detaching the rear end from the car!' In fact the H16 frequently disembowelled itself but never to that extreme, so overdesigned was it.

For their BRM-powered Type 43 Chapman and Phillippe used four longitudinal bolts to attach the H16

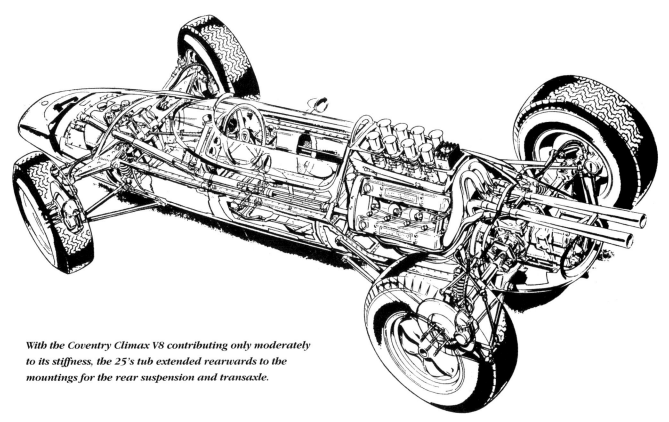

With the Coventry Climax V8 contributing only moderately to its stiffness, the 25's tub extended rearwards to the mountings for the rear suspension and transaxle.

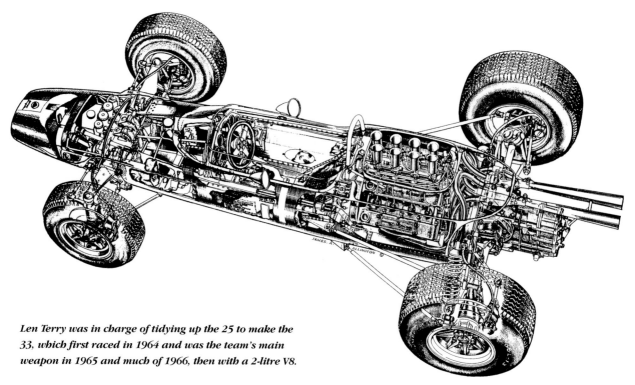

Len Terry was in charge of tidying up the 25 to make the 33, which first raced in 1964 and was the team's main weapon in 1965 and much of 1966, then with a 2-litre V8.

to the Lotus monocoque instead of the mounting beams and lateral bolts used by BRM. 'The 43 was the first vehicle we built by just bolting the engine on to the back of the hull,' said Chapman, 'and then bolting the suspension on to the back of the engine as it were.' The result gave adequate strength to a car that Jim Clark drove to the sixteen's only win at Watkins Glen in 1966.

Soon after laying down the BRM-engined 43 Chapman started work on the 49 to carry the new Ford V8 built by

On his way to victory in 1965's Dutch GP and that year's world championship, Jim Clark exploited the 33's simpler, stiffer and lighter monocoque.

Cosworth. Unlike the H16, a V8 did not demand to be used as the rear of the frame. Lotus had happily tucked the Climax V8 into its full-length monocoques with great success. Side-mounted exhaust pipes posed a problem, but that this could be solved was shown by the four-wheel-drive Type 63 of 1969, which had a full-length tub that didn't use the engine as the rear of the frame.

Self-evidently the BRM design provided a pointer to Chapman as he pondered his design of the 49. In co-operation with Cosworth's Keith Duckworth he decided on a similar concept. 'Obviously I liaised with Colin Chapman over this,' Duckworth told author John Blunsden, 'and once we had agreed what we wanted to do I went away, sketched my engine, looked at the situation and eventually came up with the fact that we could use plates from the top of the cam carriers, plus bolts from the bottom corners of the sump, to give us a suitable configuration of pickups for the back bulkhead of a monocoque.

'Chapman's monocoque had a very narrow base,' Duckworth continued, 'the two side sponsons being just nine inches apart at the back, so it made sense for us to locate the two lower bolts with nine-inch centres. Fortunately the position of my cam carriers when I had drawn them was such that the back face of a monocoque of appropriate size could be defined by the required positions of the mounting points.' In the engine's design the cam carriers were made especially rigid to accept the loads they transmitted without affecting the valve gear. As well the front of the V8 was shorn of all accessories so that it nestled close to the bulkhead that carried it. Four $3/8$-inch bolts attached the V8 to the tub.

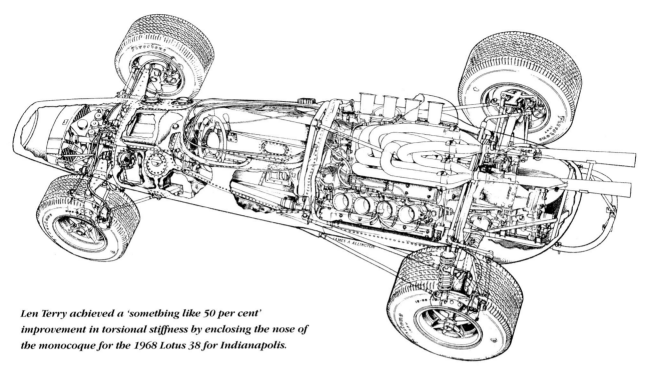

Len Terry achieved a 'something like 50 per cent' improvement in torsional stiffness by enclosing the nose of the monocoque for the 1968 Lotus 38 for Indianapolis.

'When we saw this feature we were all somewhat shocked,' recalled Italian racing-car designer Gianpaolo Dallara. "But this is crazy," we said. "The vibrations! The engine! That won't work!" But Chapman succeeded in implementing it in a very simple way that was logical and is still unsurpassed. He always had a mania to create, where possible, assemblies with a double function so that his cars were endowed with a lesser number of components.' Dallara's surprise seems odd as Italy's Ferrari was the originator of this concept, but memories in motor racing are often short.

In fact the layout was not without its problems. To simplify its exhausts the DFV V8 had a flat or 180-degree crankshaft that generated much more severe vibration than the conventional 90-degree crank. Though this allowed each bank to be tuned like a four-cylinder engine, a happy solution, it assailed the rest of the car with unprecedented vibration – especially when the engine was a major part of the car. When tasked with this Duckworth simply smiled and suggested that the teams build better cars.

Another disadvantage – not insignificant – was that

In 1966 the wide 3-litre H16 engine of BRM's Type 75 virtually mandated that it be an integral part of the car's structure, bolted to the back of its monocoque.

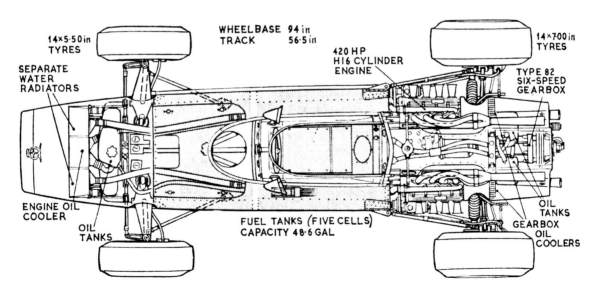

any major work on the engine or an engine change meant the car's complete dismantling. This resulted in much more work for the mechanics, who had not only their usual tasks but also the restoration of all the rear-suspension settings and weight balances to a high standard after putting the car together. Designers later found ways to cope with this while still relying on the engine as a major contributor to frame strength.

The same construction method was used for the Type 72 of 1970, which reverted to a more open tub-style monocoque. Shaped around steel bulkheads, it used inner skins chiefly of 20-gauge L72 Alclad aluminium alloy while outer panels were made of 18-gauge NS4 alloy, non-heat-treatable aluminium with a smidgen of magnesium. A feature of the new design was that all the external rivets were flush with the surface. An unimpressed observer was Len Terry, who

In the new 3-litre GP Formula 1 of 1966 the massive Type 75 BRM was the first car to use its engine as a main element of its frame. But Ferrari had done it earlier.

noted that 'a lot of labour, which might have been more usefully devoted elsewhere, had to be expended on countersinking hundreds of rivet holes, all for a minute performance advantage.'

The 72's steel sub-frame at the nose to carry the brakes and suspension was eliminated and its functions integrated into the monocoque in Ralph Bellamy's design of 1975's Type 76, which used heavier 16-gauge L72 aluminium. Geoff Aldridge took over to design the Type 77 of 1976, to which he added a reinforcing pyramid above the driver's legs. This was an important transitional model leading up to the ground-effect 78 of 1977.

'All that was inherited from the 77 was the rear suspension,' said Ralph Bellamy about the ground-effect 78 of 1977. Described by Tony Rudd as 'a typically outspoken Australian who did not suffer fools gladly,' Bellamy took the lead in sourcing a new material for the monocoque. This was Cellite, a sandwich of honeycombed aluminium between two sheets of Duralumin. A rigid yet light material common in the

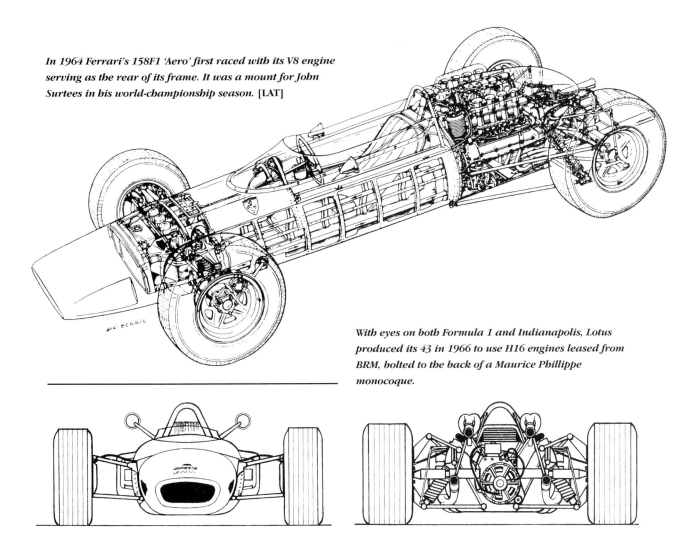

In 1964 Ferrari's 158F1 'Aero' first raced with its V8 engine serving as the rear of its frame. It was a mount for John Surtees in his world-championship season. [LAT]

With eyes on both Formula 1 and Indianapolis, Lotus produced its 43 in 1966 to use H16 engines leased from BRM, bolted to the back of a Maurice Phillippe monocoque.

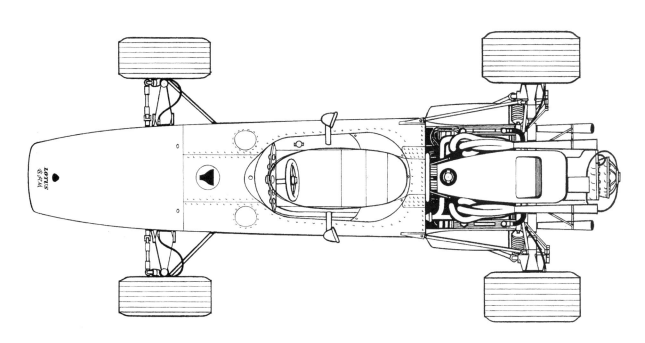

aerospace industry, honeycomb-core sheets were first used in racing-car frames by Ford for its J-Car of 1966, which evolved into the successful GT Mark IV of 1967.

Honeycomb had been insinuating its way into Formula 1 from the mid-1970s. Gordon Coppuck's M26 McLaren, first raced in 1976, made extensive use of the material. It was viewed with some caution by the conservative Grand Prix world because the integrity of its internal bonding couldn't always be assured and its fabrication into frames, needing bonding as well as riveting, was new to GP workshops. Nevertheless, said Bellamy, 'the 78's chassis comprised a central section with seat tank plus two side tanks. The side panels of the monocoque were all aluminium honeycomb sandwich material, so all told the tub was quite stiff.'

Exactly how stiff wasn't evident at first, because – to Tony Rudd's discomfiture – 'the stiffness test rig had been discarded.' Mechanic Glenn Waters rated the tub highly, saying that 'the 78 was one of the better cars I had to deal with at Lotus. It was the most structurally complete car. The 78 was nicely done because it had a completely full double-skin monocoque. From a racing operator's point of view we weren't continually having to rebuild the structure of the monocoque just to maintain the car.'

'We quickly found the Achilles heel of the Type 78,' said Tony Rudd, who although working on mainstream Lotus matters stuck his nose into Team Lotus business at

Ketteringham Hall from time to time. 'If it was crashed,' he found, 'the aluminium honeycomb panels buckled and could not be straightened, so the monocoque structure had to be thrown away. This was not so bad if you had plenty of spares – which we did not.'

When the 78 was designed the rules limited the size of individual fuel tanks, accounting for its three separate cells to give race-length capacity. For the 1978 season, said Ralph Bellamy, 'Colin got the rules changed to allow one big fuel tank, which meant that the 79 could have a thin central monocoque with composite wings hung on either side. It was lighter but not stiff enough. For the 1978 season, rather than introducing the 79 Team Lotus should have stuck with the 78 and put the 79's rear end on it. That would have been a better car than the 79 because the 78 was a lot stiffer and stronger as a result of its full-width chassis.'

Lest this be seen as prejudice on the part of the 78's designer, he had support from the people who worked on the cars. 'On the 77,' said Glenn Waters, 'and latterly the 79, we were forever fiddling with the engine mountings because they were pulling out. Various parts of the structure were actually failing. My definition of Lotus racing cars would be their structural inadequacy. We were always chasing inadequate structures while most of the other teams would build robust cars.'

Not helping the situation, added Waters, were the obsolescent techniques used by Team Lotus to build its cars. 'Chapman had a time-warp way of doing things,' he said. 'Everything on the car was fabricated, even though Gordon Murray at Brabham was already showing that CNC machining was better. Patrick Head took the

Closely co-ordinating their mutual design activities, Colin Chapman and Keith Duckworth decided that the 49's V8 would comprise the rear of its frame.

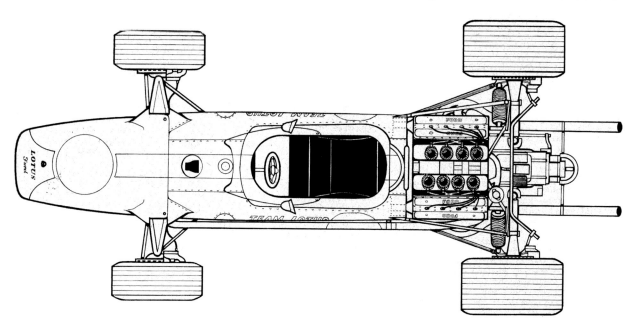

Although late to the 3-litre party in 1967, the Lotus 49 quickly made its presence felt. This was Graham Hill's for the Italian GP, which he led before engine failure.

Williams a step forward again. Lotus was stuck in 1960s thinking. I always felt that it was a negative thing at Lotus that the designers never got to go to the races, because they'd never see the other teams' solutions to the same problems.'

'The 79 was a very floppy car,' seconded designer Martin Ogilvie. 'In those days you used to get some quite good slow-motion shots at Monaco on the television. The 79 came down the hill from the casino and through the hairpin in slow motion and you could see the whole car was alive and twitching. It was not good! In fact when they were built they were originally about 3,000 pound-feet per degree, which is not high, but by the end of the season they were down to 1,500, which is about the same as a Caterham Seven without the side panels on.'

Visually as well as physically the 79's monocoque was an ephemeral-looking affair fashioned as a single skin of 20-gauge aluminium that carried all its fuel in one tank behind the driver and used honeycomb only in its floor. Though Chapman's commendable aim was to permit the widest possible underbody tunnels to the right and left, his design was in fact a throwback in principle to the ill-fated Type 30 – a wide motor car with a narrow central backbone frame into which, in this case, the driver was inserted. During development early in 1978 the structure was strengthened but the basic design remained flawed.

Pictured by Max Le Grand in the hands of John Miles at Monaco in 1970, the 49 was a Team Lotus mainstay for four seasons until the new 72 was fully ready.

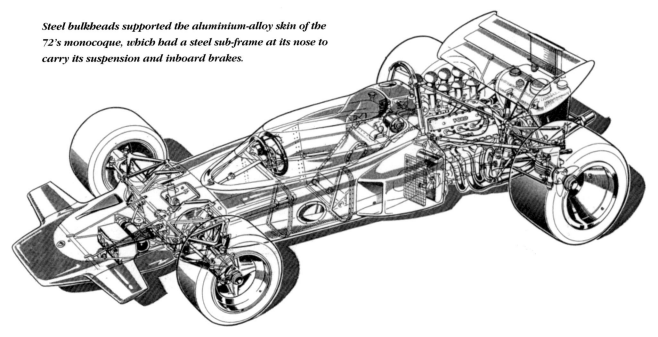

Steel bulkheads supported the aluminium-alloy skin of the 72's monocoque, which had a steel sub-frame at its nose to carry its suspension and inboard brakes.

With the added loads on the 79 from greater downforce generation, explained engineer Peter Wright, 'the suspension went stiffer and stiffer, the rocker arms then weren't stiff enough, the monocoque itself wasn't stiff enough, the suspension mounting points weren't strong enough. Basically the monocoques were all over the place. We found cracks and that was simply because the loads were going up much faster than the structural integrity of aluminium tubs could cope with. By totally subjugating the 79 to ground effect we made a slightly flaky car.' This was just when more strength, not less, was urgently needed.

Beauty though the 79 undoubtedly was, it frustrated its 1978 world champion driver Mario Andretti. 'In those days we were in the infancy of ground effect so there were big gains to be had,' said the Italian-American. 'But Colin would do nothing about the stiffness of the car. To be able to take advantage of the downforce you had to run very stiff springs. But to be able to feel the stiff springs you had to have a good stiff car. The torsional stiffness of the 79 was probably only 2,000 pound-feet per degree, which is ridiculous. Everything would pop!' The figure quoted by Mario was indeed between that of a fresh tub and the stiffness of one that had seen some use.

In 1979 Colin Chapman explained his philosophy of structural materials to Peter Windsor. 'We have been changing a lot recently,' he said. 'We have been using chrome-moly steel and we have been using some titanium, and we're getting round to using more of it than we did. But basically I believe in getting light weight from elegance of design rather than from exotic materials. It comes down to efficiency. If you can get the result with less cost and efficiency – it isn't only weight; it's cost as well – then you are being more efficient.

'Why build something out of titanium,' Chapman continued, 'if better thinking and more advanced engineering allow you to do the same job with steel or aluminium? In most applications the design criterion is stiffness, rather than the ultimate stress the material carries. The exotic materials are really no stiffer for any given load than the simple ones. Basic materials are easy to work, they are less critical, have less fatigue sensitivity and so on. So really they are much more amenable.'

In that year 1979 Colin Chapman returned to semi-exotic materials for the tub of his Type 80, intended as a further step forward in ground-effect downforce. Honeycomb panels akin to those used widely in aeroplane construction returned for much of the monocoque, which was selectively strengthened by titanium. This was the formula as well for the more conventional 81. For the 'twin-chassis' 88 and 1981's 87, however, Lotus went all the way to exotic. By then, with Chapman preoccupied with other projects, Peter Wright and Martin Ogilvie were key engineering players.

Within a week of each other, in early March of 1981, both McLaren and Lotus unveiled new Grand Prix cars with monocoques made from composites of woven carbon-fibre fabrics fixed in cured epoxy resin. This extremely strong yet light material was ideal for racing-car tubs. Initial concerns that such monocoques might not stand up to crashes were soon allayed when they proved at least as good as conventional constructions and in many situations much better.

Above: *For the tub of the first ground-effect Lotus, 1977's 78, Ralph Bellamy sourced Cellite, comprising aluminium sheets with honeycomb cores. It provided a robust monocoque.*

Below: *Hell-bent on downforce, Chapman dictated a narrow tub for the fast but fragile 79 of 1978, here with Ronnie Peterson following world-champion-to-be Mario Andretti.*

Above: *Reminiscent of earlier Lotuses was the cockpit-cowl hoop with lightening holes of the 79's monocoque, which new rules allowed to be narrow with a single fuel tank.*

Below: *Skinned in 20-gauge aluminium and criticised by drivers and mechanics alike as being insubstantial, the narrow tub of the Lotus 79 lost stiffness as the season progressed.*

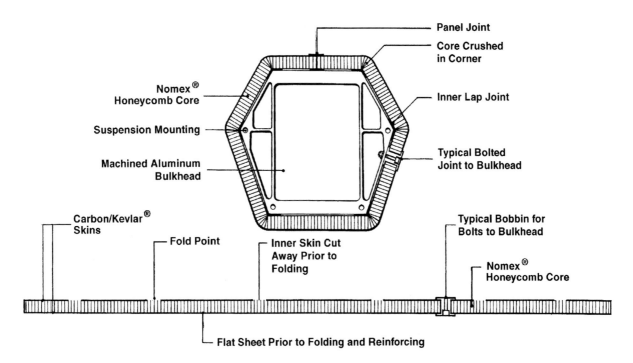

Panel Joint

Core Crushed in Corner

Nomex® Honeycomb Core

Inner Lap Joint

Suspension Mounting

Machined Aluminum Bulkhead

Typical Bolted Joint to Bulkhead

Carbon/Kevlar® Skins

Typical Bobbin for Bolts to Bulkhead

Fold Point

Inner Skin Cut Away Prior to Folding

Nomex® Honeycomb Core

Flat Sheet Prior to Folding and Reinforcing

The Lotus approach was to fold and join panels formed from a single sheet of pre-cured sandwich material that enclosed a core of Du Pont's Nomex fibre with skins made of a composite of carbon fibres with Kevlar, another Du Pont high-strength fibre. 'The inner skin was grooved and the sheet was cut out and folded into the monocoque around a jig,' Peter Wright explained. 'When the joints were reinforced and machined aluminium bulkheads were bolted in, it formed a stiff and lightweight structure.' The main reason for allying carbon fibre with other materials was, said Wright, 'because of concern over the crash performance of carbon fibre.' In the event, he added, 'of the seventeen monocoques made over four years, none was destroyed in an accident.

'However,' added Peter Wright, 'the techniques used on the McLaren showed the future.' Assemblies of carbon fibre were cured as a complete unit in huge autoclaves. That Lotus had been there at the outset, however, was a last brave gesture in the Chapman era by a team that had contributed so much to racing-car structure. Its introduction of the 'tub' to mainstream racing was as much a breakthrough as were the elegant space frames of the Eleven, Twelve and their successors.

'Chapman was only interested in what worked and didn't work,' said Glenn Waters, 'and he wanted to achieve results as quickly as possible. The actual execution of the engineering didn't concern him that much.' This reflects the Chapman of the 1970s, the

Peter Wright's fine book, **Formula 1 Technology,** *shows the manner in which Lotus folded and joined carbon-fibre-faced honeycomb panels to make monocoques in 1981.*

hyperactive engineer-executive who had many irons in the fire. It accounts for structural lapses that would have appalled the younger Chapman who took pride in his intuitive appreciation of stresses and strains. Now, however, good engineering was essential.

Lotus used its new composite tubs in both the controversial **88** *and the conventional* **87,** *pictured by Ove Nielsen in 1981 in the hands of Nigel Mansell.*

Chapter 6

WHITTLING WEIGHT

When we first got together, Colin said, 'Mario, I always want to make a car as light as possible.' I said, 'Well, Colin, I want to live as long as possible. I guess we need to talk.'

Mario Andretti

From the outset Colin Chapman had no option but to be obsessive about the weight of his cars. He had no access to the exotic twin-cam engines used by such sports-car-racing rivals as Osca, Porsche and Maserati. Not until 1957, thanks then to Coventry Climax, could he obtain power units that could match those of his rivals. So to achieve a competitive power-to-weight ratio with hopped-up Ford and MG engines lightness had to be a passion. It remained so throughout Chapman's career – though not always successfully.

Lightness was already high on the agenda in 1951 when Bill Boddy, editor of *Motor Sport*, visited Chapman to see his 'astonishing' Lotus special that was causing such a furore in club-racing circles. 'The principle on which Chapman worked,' he reported, 'was to put nothing into the Lotus which had not been carefully weighed first. "Simplicate and add lightness" was his motto, rather than drill everything full of holes afterwards (see sidebar on page 205).

'Throughout,' Boddy continued. 'the builders of the Lotus have carried a tiny 25-pound spring balance, and any component that brings this to its full reading is regarded with very deep distaste indeed! So we find a

At Trenton for a USAC race in 1964 Stanley Rosenthall caught Colin Chapman in pensive mood. Was he obsessing about fuel and start-line weight? It's possible.

front wing, complete with rigid 24-gauge struts and sidelamps, weighing a mere 10 ounces, and the beautiful little polished aluminium body shell only 65 pounds complete with hoops.'

During a visit to Lotus's Tottenham Lane workshops early in 1955 author and bookseller John Lello had direct evidence of the weight-reduction craving of the Chapman team. While watching work under way on the new Mark IX he overheard a technical discussion: 'The two-man conference which I had broken in on earlier adjourned from the office and concentrated on the car where various constructional details were proposed and discussed and it was immediately apparent that a great deal of thought was going into the final detail. Weight being a dominant factor, the elimination of unnecessary panels and outriggers appeared to be the immediate problem.'

With Williams & Pritchard the supplier of Lotus bodywork, inevitably they were drawn into debates about weight-reducing measures. When the Lotus Eleven was being created, a key issue was the spacing of rivets attaching the undertray to the frame. While Len Pritchard recommended one-inch intervals, Colin Chapman argued for two inches. The next day he bustled into the workshop with both trouser pockets bulging with rivets. 'Look at the extra weight you're costing me!' he shouted at Pritchard as he gestured at their useless mass.

Here driven by Ron Flockhart at Le Mans in 1955, the works Lotus Mark IX was bodied in 20-gauge alloy instead of the heavier 18 gauge used in customer cars.

Works Lotus Eleven-Climaxes, like the 1.1-litre car driven by Cliff Allison at Silverstone on 5 May 1956, were specially lightened.

'We were at the forefront of doing it lighter than anybody else,' said Mike Costin. 'He wanted everything light, didn't he?' This was especially the case in bodywork, Costin added, in which the works cars were higher-tech than those sold to customers. 'Bodies for sale were made in 18-gauge aluminium but our works ones were always made in 20-gauge. And of course our works Mark IXs were different from the production Mark IXs. One was in 20-gauge aluminium, the other was in 20-gauge magnesium. Nobody had made a body in magnesium before.'[1]

What were the benefits of this obsession with lightness? Cars could of course be stripped to the bone for short sprint races at Goodwood or Snetterton. Weights for long-distance races, however, indicate the level of preparation that a Lotus would require to do battle with the world's best. An apples-for-apples comparison is given by the weights of cars at scrutineering for the 24 Hours of Le Mans, a demanding race by any standards.

In 1956 at Le Mans a Lotus Eleven with a 1,460cc single-cam Climax engine weighed in at 1,022 pounds. This was 22 per cent less than a works Porsche Spyder of 1,498cc, which weighed 1,310 pounds. With the Climax developing 108bhp and the Porsche four-cam 127bhp, this gave the Lotus the advantage with 9.5 pounds per horsepower against 10.3 for the German car. On the Sarthe circuit only one of the Porsches turned a significantly faster lap than the Lotus.

Private Spyders were heavier than the works car at close to 1,400 pounds. Surprisingly a 1.5-litre entry from Gordini, the French maker renowned to be obsessive about weight, weighed in at a hefty 1,560 pounds. Two 1.5-litre Maseratis scaled 1,562 and 1,595 pounds. Only three cars starting the race were lighter than the 1.5-litre Lotus; all had half its displacement.

The special attention given to the works 1.5-litre Eleven in 1956, co-driven by Chapman himself, was shown by the higher weights of the 1,098cc Lotuses at Le Mans in 1956, which scaled 1,075 and 1,080 pounds – significantly more than the boss's car in spite of the changes needed to cope with the latter's greater power. A sign of the future, however, was the weight of the Cooper Bobtail with the same 1.1-litre Climax engine – only 1,024 pounds, seemingly obtained with little effort.

The 1.1-litre Cooper entered at Le Mans in 1957 was heavier at 1,142 pounds, while the three Lotuses similarly powered were around a hundredweight lighter at 1,046, 1,058 and 1,060 pounds. The lightest car in the

---

1   Starting in 1954 Mercedes-Benz was using magnesium for the bodies of its racing cars. The commercial alloy in Germany and elsewhere was known as Elektron.

race was a Lotus Eleven with a new 744cc Climax four. At 946 pounds it was the only car at Le Mans weighing less than 1,000 pounds.

For the 1959 season Lotus introduced its new Seventeen, on Eleven lines but smaller all around and wearing its controversial strut-type front suspension. That it was lighter as well was shown by the Le Mans scales,

Weighing 1,055 pounds on average, the Lotus Elevens at Le Mans in 1957 had been slimmed by a mean 23 pounds from their 1956 counterparts.

Winner of the Le Mans 1.1-litre class in 1957, the Eleven of Herbert Mackay-Fraser and Jay Chamberlain scaled a hundredweight less than the Cooper ahead.

which credited the two 742cc entries with a svelte 860 and 851 pounds. With a 981-pound Panhard these were the only three cars to break the 1,000-pound barrier in 1959. Three Elites entered weighed 1,371, 1,375 and 1,430 pounds in a field that offered no direct comparisons.

The ruthless methods that Chapman used to shed weight were often ugly. Bungee-cord salesmen flocked to Lotus. 'The big difference between our cars and, say, a BRM was the quality of the design and manufacture of the components,' said Mike Costin. 'BRM's were beautiful to behold while ours looked a bit scrappy. Ours were perfectly all right, other things being equal, which now and again they were.' Where they could and did fall down, however, creating what Costin called 'disasters and failures,' were often the consequence of the 'not very good bits we had. The company grew so quickly that we never did anything in the way of quality control.'

Controlling the quality of the early Lotus cars was a challenge in its own right for very good reasons, explained Keith Duckworth, who was in at the beginning of the Chapman legend: 'Nobody had a lot of money in racing in those days. Therefore you were also trying to manufacture pieces by cheap manufacturing methods. You didn't whittle everything from solid in those days.

Lightest car at Le Mans in 1957 was the 744cc Eleven of Cliff Allison and Keith Hall, weighing 946 pounds. They won their class by a 20-lap margin.

There were fairly simple welded-up structures. Quality control on those was very difficult.' Inspection of welds was a painstaking process well beyond the demands of time and cost of the early racing days at Lotus.

'With your mechanics and your system of looking at your cars and preparing them,' Duckworth told author Michael Oliver, 'you should be able to catch most things at the stage that either some stretch in the material – it's collapsed a bit – has occurred, or there is a crack forming and you can catch the crack before it is a disastrous failure. The only real way is to design light and then to have loads and loads of inspections and certainly lots of crack detection.'

Designing light and looking for failures to see what needed to be done about them was part and parcel of the Chapman philosophy. 'If you start off by designing everything conservatively and nothing fails,' explained Keith Duckworth, 'there is no way that you are ever going to lighten your car. You never lighten things under those conditions and therefore you don't learn quickly enough. If you start off light and it breaks, then you will in fact strengthen the pieces that break. An awful lot of bits that you might have thought would have broken, won't break. And that is the only way of getting a light car.'

At times, of course, Chapman had ready access to the skills of engineers who were well able to calculate the likely stresses on a frame or suspension. The difficulty was that they seldom had access to all the information that they needed to create a worst-case scenario. 'The

With their special 742cc Climax FWMA fours, the Lotus Seventeens at Le Mans in 1959 were stripped to the bone to make them by far the lightest cars entered.

Evident in the cockpit of one of the 1959 Le Mans Lotus Seventeens was ruthless weight reduction, not least in the driver's amenities – such as they were.

problem is that you don't know how hard your driver is going to hit kerbs,' said Duckworth, 'or you can't work out what the loads from hitting a kerb on any occasion are going to be. If you design it such that it will hit brick walls in all directions all the time, you will never win a race. Therefore you actually have to hang it out if you want to make a race winner.'

That it might have been hung out too far was the impression of Cliff Allison, who drove for Lotus from

1955 to 1958. Towards the end of the latter year, he told Graham Gauld, 'I was becoming unhappy about the reliability of the car. Vital bits kept falling off – like the steering wheel! He cut a lot of corners, did Colin, and made things lighter than they probably should have

As prepared for Le Mans in 1959 the works Lotus Elites weighed less than 1,400 pounds. One of them placed an impressive eighth, winning the 1.5-litre GT class.

Attachment of its fuel tank to the Lotus Twelve by bungee cords in 1957 was typical of Hornsey's early weight-reducing methodologies.

The cockpit of a 1958 Sixteen presented an inelegant spectacle with its obvious compromises. Low cost and lightness took priority in the early Lotus years.

been. There was a saying at the time that if you get Colin to design the car and John Cooper to build it, it would be a world-beater and I think there was some truth in that. John tended to make things a bit too strong and Colin made them a bit too light.'

Allison left to drive for Ferrari and become that rarity for the era, an old, bold racing driver. He had persevered with Lotus, he said, being 'absolutely convinced that Colin would build a world-beater because I had so much confidence in his ability as a designer. My theory was proved right because obviously he did make a world-beater and won Indy, the world championships and won everything. I was quite convinced he would do that. The only snag was I thought he might kill me first! It was just as simple as that.'

In 1958 Allison had been racing the Twelve, Chapman's first single-seater which was born the previous year as a Formula 2 car and upgraded to Formula 1. Even in Formula 2 form it had its problems, as driver Keith Hall discovered. In 1957's Gold Cup Race at Oulton Park, he related, 'I put up some quite good times in practice, but the car kept changing gear on its own. There was no way to stop it revving if it suddenly changed gear. The mechanics had a look at the car and found that the chassis was cracked in eleven places. What was happening was that the front and back of the car were moving apart. As the chassis moved, so did the rod controlling the gear-change.'

Following Allison into the Lotus works team was Innes Ireland. He had his own tales to tell from 1958 and '59 when he soldiered bravely on with the front-engined Sixteen Grand Prix car. He walked out to take the start of the 1959 Portuguese GP at Oporto, only to find that his car didn't look quite right: 'When I had a closer look at the front suspension I found a complete break in the main chassis tube – the big one that held the front suspension on! I could not believe my eyes!' Only minutes before the start he was equally astonished to see Lotus mechanics on the grid, welding his car's frame together.

Innes Ireland's experience with the Sixteen was nightmarish. 'In one car,' he recalled, 'at Monza in 1959, the mechanics found fourteen major breaks in the chassis. I had breaks in the steering, wheels fell off, wishbones breaking – anything that could happen to a car.' In those days failures usually happened in races because the Lotus budget didn't run to testing.

Things didn't get all that much better for Ireland and others with the mid-engined Eighteen. At the 1960 Belgian Grand Prix at the daunting Spa circuit, Stirling Moss, Jim Clark, Alan Stacey, Michael Taylor and Ireland himself were driving Eighteens with 2.5-litre Climax

Colin Chapman personally taped the cowl of a Sixteen at Reims in 1959. Preparation of the troublesome Sixteen posed constant challenges to his mechanics.

engines. During practice Taylor's car sheared its steering column and Moss crashed when his Walker-stable car broke its rear hub and crashed heavily at some 130mph.

'The Lotuses of Stacey, Clark and myself were wheeled off to the circuit garage,' wrote Ireland, 'to have their hubs examined for any fault similar to the one which had developed in Stirling's car. The results were just terrifying. Clark's was uncracked, Stacey's was cracked half-way round the hub and mine was all but sheared off! I suppose it was a gauge of how hard the cars were being driven at the time. Moss obviously drove his car harder than any of the rest of us and his hub went first. Chapman explained that a fault had been found in one of the machine processes at the works. He had new hubs flown out from England and they were fitted on to our three cars. I can't say, however, that I was filled with confidence when I got to the starting line.'

In 1956 Roy Salvadori was racing a Lotus Eleven at Goodwood for entrant John Coombs. Roy admitted that his sliding style of driving 'was hard on some rear suspensions.' When in practice the rear wheels were fouling the bodywork he discovered that the de Dion

Both Graham Hill, pictured at Aintree in 1959, and Innes Ireland survived numerous frame and suspension breakages in their Lotus Sixteens.

Though Lotus's change to simpler mid-engined designs eased maintenance, Stirling Moss insisted on having his Eighteen prepared by Rob Walker's stable.

tube had bent. 'We talked to Colin Chapman about the problem and he brought a stronger de Dion tube to the circuit the following day, informing us that this was one that we would not bend. By the end of that day's practice the new de Dion tube had bent. For the race Chapman brought an even stronger tube which happily did not bend until the end of the race.' Lotus had already clocked this problem; a de Dion tube had broken during tests of an Eleven at Goodwood in early April of 1956.

Looking back on his time with Lotus cars, as prepared for him by Rob Walker's stable or by his British Racing Partnership, Stirling Moss had little praise for Chapman's passion for reducing to the max. 'He was brilliant in what he could achieve,' Moss reflected, 'but the way that he did it was not very usable by most people. The cars were built too light – I don't know how many wheels I had come off but quite a lot. They came off because the stub axles broke, not because I hit anything but because – thanks to Chapman's ability in generating the lateral g – of the loading I put through the stub axles.

'His strength was in innovation, new ideas,' Moss continued, 'his skilful way of getting what he wanted mechanically; but his weaknesses were first that frankly he didn't seem to have the ability to make it easy to utilise his skills – his cars were too difficult to drive – and secondly that he was prepared to pare things down to the bone without leaving either sufficient safety margin or doing enough research to cut out problems. I think he took short cuts. He was perhaps a bit lax on fine detail.

'A man of his knowledge had no right not to be right on the dangerous things,' summed up Moss. 'At one time Rob Walker, whose team I drove for, was changing my stub axles and I think the drive shafts for every race and even then they broke. That shouldn't have been necessary. After all that I do have more respect for him as a designer than I have animosity for what he caused.'

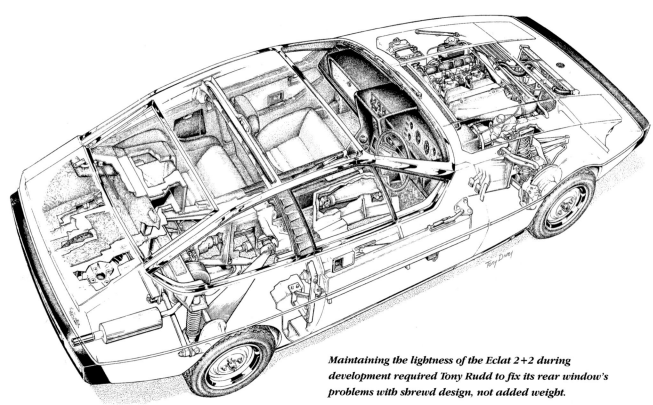

Maintaining the lightness of the Eclat 2+2 during development required Tony Rudd to fix its rear window's problems with shrewd design, not added weight.

These were the years in which, not without good reason, Colin Chapman gained a reputation as a designer who would sacrifice both strength and safety in search of lightness. When concerns were raised after the 1958 season that several Formula 1 fatalities might be the result of cars that were built too lightly, Chapman stepped in to argue to the contrary, pointing out that drivers died in crashes of cars that were among the heaviest (see sidebar on page 208).

The pressure on the Lotus chief's designers to reduce weight was unrelenting. One was Martin Ogilvie, who said, 'There's a lot of sayings I go back to Colin Chapman for, such as, "a quarter-inch bolt will lift a double-decker bus".' Designer Jo Marquardt recalled

Thanks to weight that was 9 to 11 per cent less than rivals and its relatively powerful 2.0-litre four, Lotus's Eclat 2+2 gave its owners a decisive performance advantage.

assisting Maurice Phillippe on the Type 56 turbine car for Indianapolis. It had a four-wheel-drive system made by Ferguson. 'Ferguson schemed it at one size,' said Marquardt, and Chapman said, "Make it half that size." Eventually they compromised.'

These strictures applied to road cars as well as racers,

Among performance sports cars the Lotus Esprit was a paragon of lightness at less than 2,000 pounds. It was true to Colin Chapman's abhorrence of excess poundage.

In its early months the Lotus 72 not only looked fragile, it was fragile. Chapman and Phillippe put lightness at the top of their requirements for an all-new design.

as Tony Rudd recalled. He led development of the 1975 Eclat 2+2, which was based on the Elite. 'The body was lighter,' Rudd related, 'and when I was travelling at a very illegal speed the rear window blew out! You do not put weight on a car in this company, so I had to trace to the heart of the problem, rather than just try and

Its finned hubs and slender suspension linkages testified to the Lotus 72's design down to minimum weight. In search of reliability it gradually put on poundage.

strengthen the rear-window surround or something like that. We discovered it was an exhaust-resonance effect on that lighter body.'

Peter Kirwan-Taylor, who not only assisted Chapman in financial matters but also took a hand in styling, recalled their debates over design features: 'Although my training had been very different from Colin's, we found each other's mental processes compatible, and there were few basic disagreements on design approach. That is not to say that we did not argue passionately over an inch here and a tenth of an inch there; it is a Lotus article of faith that nothing may be larger nor heavier than is essentially required.'

This approach had clear benefits in the resulting vehicles. Looking at the Lotus offerings of the mid-1970s, the Eclat 2+2 was a model that bore comparison with several rivals. It scaled 2,160 pounds, which was 9 per cent less than the Porsche 924 and 11 per cent less than the MGB Coupé GT – two sports cars of similar size and carrying capacity. The 165bhp from its 2.0-litre four gave a decisive performance advantage over both.

The Elite asks for comparison with the Porsche 911, both having comparable horsepower. While the German car weighed 2,470 pounds the Lotus rival scaled 2,335 pounds, 5 per cent less. A less decisive difference, this suggests that the Lotus technology of glass-fibre body on steel backbone frame was progressively less advantageous, compared to conventional construction, the larger and more complex the car.

Most impressive was the two-seater Esprit, which at 1,985 pounds was the only sports car of 2 litres and above to scale less than a ton. A contemporary rival was the Lancia Beta Montecarlo coupé, known as the Scorpion in America. The Lotus Esprit weighed 14 per cent less than the 2,295-pound Lancia. While the latter was more luxuriously equipped the difference was still impressive, to the credit of relentless pressure on weight reduction.

Grand Prix racing's rulemakers gave Colin Chapman a new target when, in 1961 at the beginning of the 1½-litre era, they established a minimum car weight for the first time. Set in the interest of safety, this was pegged at 450 kilograms, 992.3 pounds. Looking back at the end of this Formula, Chapman remarked, 'We've never had the car weighed properly. The organisers never drain the car. It always goes on to the weighbridge with an indeterminate amount of fuel in it. The mere design of a tank is such you can't tell what's in it. It's no use dipping it. The only way you know what's in there is by saying, well, we put five gallons in yesterday and we've run up the road in it a couple of times, so we tell the organiser

In addition to its adjustability the Lotus 77 had the advantage of lightness, as the scales showed early in 1976. This was Gunnar Nilsson competing at Monaco.

there are four gallons in it. So you take 28 pounds off what they weigh and it comes out to some funny number, because there is anything between 50 and 100 pounds scatter on their scales.'

Scatter or not, with his Type 25 Chapman was ready for the adjudicators. 'In South Africa at the end of 1962,' he said, 'the carburettor car was well below the weight and we had to put the top tank in and a lot of other little gimmicks to get it up to the weight for the race. It ran with the top tank which it didn't need, otherwise we'd have been about a pound under weight. Once we'd put the fuel injection on there wasn't the same worry because the weight of the fuel-pump "bomb" is about 12 pounds.'

Like team-mate Graham Hill, Jackie Oliver was lucky to survive the high-wing era with the Lotus 49 when heavy crashes followed wing failures with disastrous regularity. When a Lotus broke under Oliver, said the driver, 'Colin was never sympathetic. He used to have cars fail all the time; that was part of his stock in trade. He used to push things right to the limit and, as a result, he had very competitive cars.

'The analysis was done with the driver in the car to see whether it would break,' Oliver continued. 'When things went wrong, being the type of person he was, he would normally be suspicious of the driver and he'd also be suspicious that the mechanics might not have bolted it together properly. Then, if those possibilities could be eliminated, he would consider if it could have been a design failure.'

'The frailties were in the area of the 49's rear-suspension mounts,' said fellow driver John Miles, 'which were tubular frames bolted to the bellhousing/gearbox. These were redesigned a number of times but kept on breaking for much of the first 15 months or so of the car's life. The ZF gearbox also protested at the cornering stresses being fed though its housing and was ultimately replaced.'

Weight saving was evident in every aspect of the Ford DFV-powered Formula 1 Lotus 72 that made its bow in 1970. Immaculately detailed by Maurice Phillippe, it was an object lesson in design for purpose. 'Saving weight, of course, is part of every racing-car designer's philosophy,' wrote Anthony Curtis, 'but with Colin Chapman it amounts to a monomania accentuated in this instance by a desire to get ahead of three competitors using the same engine.

'It is to be seen in every part of the car,' Curtis continued, 'especially the suspension components which are fabricated from various exotic materials all of a high strength which is said to compensate for their unusual slenderness.'[2] 'But boy,' said John Miles, 'was it fragile. We seemed to be forever stitching things back

2   The front wishbones were made of nickel-chrome-molybdenum alloy steel and fabricated by argon arc welding. Uprights front and rear were cast magnesium.

Above: *Chapman's designs for four-wheel-drive cars, the Indy 64 and the F1 63 shown with Rindt at Oulton Park, were contemptuous of his usual strictures on weight reduction.*

Below: *With his 1968 49B – here Graham Hill's at Watkins Glen in 1969 – Chapman shifted weight to the rear to take full advantage of the latest wide Firestone tyres.*

together or making stronger bits. Nearly every time I got into 72/1 the engine blew or something fell off.'

Over time, as stronger bits were added, the 72 put on weight, so for 1974 the new 76 was designed to rectify that. 'It was meant to be a lighter 72,' recalled team manager Peter Warr, 'keeping the good bits and leaving out the bad bits. But it was a disaster; it was actually heavier.' This was addressed in the design of the 77 for 1976. When all the cars were weighed before the Brazilian Grand Prix, the team's two 77s scaled 1,281 and 1,283 pounds, a small safety margin over the minimum weight of 1,268 pounds (575 kilograms).

In the Brazilian weighing only one car was lighter, the 1,272-pound March 761-Ford. Ferrari was pretty good with the 1,301 pounds of its 312 T; this was an impressive result for a 12-cylinder car. The Tyrrell 007 was hefty at 1,380 pounds, as was Emerson Fittipaldi's Copersucar-Ford at 1,411 pounds. Its sister was the heaviest car weighed at 1,484 pounds. Not quite so bad at 1,475 pounds – albeit massively overweight – was the Brabham BT 45 with its 12-cylinder Alfa Romeo engine. These figures put into perspective the benefit achieved by Lotus with its concentration on lightness.

That concentration was still thought by some drivers to go too far. Among these was Mario Andretti, who raced for Team Lotus from 1977 to 1979. He was well aware of his boss's predilection for paring weight by all available means. 'Over time,' Andretti told Nigel Roebuck, 'I dealt with the problem straightforwardly. Colin wanted to introduce titanium suspension rocker arms. I said, "Well, give them to Ronnie [Peterson] if you want, but I will not drive with titanium rockers on my car." Same with the pedals – I had a titanium clutch and titanium throttle, but I had a steel brake pedal. Bob Dance was the overall chief, and I used to say, "Bob, in your practical experience, if you think that anything that is key, suspension-wise, is marginal or borderline, let me know and I'll deal with it with the old man."'

In the twilight of Mario's relationship with Chapman, a major sticking point involved weight. The new Type 80 of 1979 was intended to major on the Team Lotus aerodynamic know-how to generate even more underbody downforce, which it did. More downforce, however, meant stiffer springs to support the vehicle, and stiffer springs demanded a stronger monocoque. This, however, the 80 didn't have. Andretti gave his view:

This was when Colin and I started going off one another. He didn't want to recognise the importance of a stiff chassis. We'd put stiffer springs on, then the chassis would start torsioning even

Changes in the 49B for 1968 to move weight from front to rear included mounting of its engine-oil tank, complete with cooler, above its transaxle.

more. We were popping rivets all over the place on the bulkhead. I told Colin that we needed a collar round the cockpit, to stiffen the car in the centre. He hit the roof when he heard me, as a driver, offering technical advice. We had arguments like you can't believe. Colin's big concern was the additional weight. He just didn't want to make the car heavier. The Lotus 80 was the same lady as the 79, but with a totally new dress. In other words, the chassis was basically the same with a lot bigger dress on. So the presence of it was enormous, and it had the initial effect, but somehow the body needed more vitamins!

In happier days, Andretti's first experience with a Chapman-designed car was in the Grand Prix 49B at the end of the 1968 season. Mario's next Lotus outing was in the Indianapolis Type 64 of 1969. Here was a car that put completely at odds the Chapman strictures on weight saving. Without its body one of the three 64s scaled 302 pounds over the Indy weight limit – as if it were taking STP sponsor Andy Granatelli along for the ride. Mario's car weighed 166 pounds over the limit.

A major factor in the excess weight carried by the Type 64 was its four-wheel drive. At the time this was thought to be The Next Big Thing, thanks in part to the performance advantage that four-wheel drive had shown at Indianapolis in the turbine-powered Type 56 of 1968. The 4x4 Type 63 Formula 1 car was being

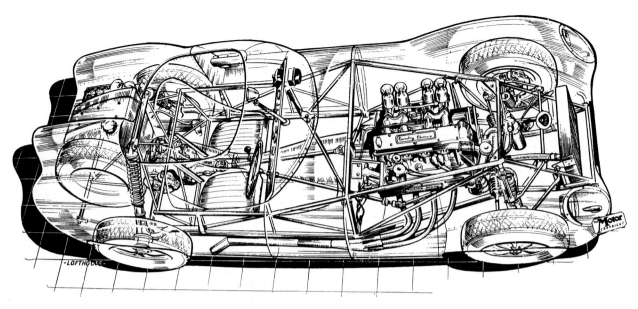

With the mass of its engine well forward and big fuel tank at the rear, the Lotus Fifteen was the result of Chapman's early belief in a high polar moment of inertia. **[LAT]**

developed in parallel. This was the car that Colin Chapman had in mind early in 1969 when he told *Motor*'s Charles Bulmer, 'I think we could produce a four-wheel-drive car weighing the same as our current car, although it would be a totally different car – we wouldn't just put four-wheel drive on any of our cars.'

The background for this was Chapman's response – 'Yes, I think it would be of that order' – to Bulmer's question, 'What about the weight penalty of four-wheel drive? The lowest estimate I've heard is about 90 pounds.' The engineer said that his 1968 Type 49 was already 'about 90 pounds heavier than it was last year. The Hewland box, heavy old drive shafts, solid discs, stiffer uprights, stiffer stub pins and heavier wheels have all been added since last year. Our car was bang on the weight limit last year and now it's about 90 pounds overweight.'

During 1969 Chapman managed to shed some of this excess poundage, quoting 1,160 pounds for his 49B against the minimum weight of 1,102 pounds. But his Type 63 was an altogether different story. The implication of his remark to Bulmer was that a four-wheel-drive Lotus would be a bespoke design that would use appropriate means to get down to the allowable weight. One would have expected nothing less from the combined talents of Chapman and Phillippe. Cited for the 63, however, was the portly figure of 1,246 pounds – the equivalent of putting an extra Jackie Oliver in the cockpit. McLaren's contemporary 4x4 effort weighed about the same while Matra's was almost 100 pounds heavier still.

Working against the usefulness of four-wheel drive

were the rapid advances of both tyre technology and wing-induced downthrust that allowed the new 3-litre Grand Prix cars to put down their power through the rear wheels alone. Wide rear tyres were the consequence of this, Colin Chapman said of his 1968 49B:

We're using such big rear tyres because we've got an abundance of weight on the rear. With two-wheel drive we concentrated on trying to get the maximum amount of weight on the rear wheels and this year we've got even more than last year. We've taken the oil tank from the front and put it at the back. We've got a much heavier gearbox and we've put the oil radiator at the back to save all the plumbing that went up to the front. We took about 50 pounds off the front and put 36 pounds at the back. We actually saved 14 pounds in weight but significantly increased the rearward weight distribution and that means you need larger tyres and larger wheels. Since we put the aerofoil on we've increased the tyre loading a lot more.

This trend in weight distribution continued into the 1970s. The Type 77 Lotus of 1976 had 65.5 per cent of its weight on the rear wheels. This was at the mean of the car's rivals between 63.5 per cent for the 312 T Ferrari and 68.5 per cent for the Hesketh 308 C.[3]

Front/rear weight distribution was a particular preoccupation of Colin Chapman when he attended the

3   The car weights measured at the 1976 Brazilian Grand Prix found the Lotus 77 to be the only car that had equal weighting on its left and right front wheels. The others, said engineer Enrico Benzing, had lateral weight differences of between 1.5 and 3.5 per cent.

COLIN CHAPMAN

Axiom Unmasked

In his entertaining 1951 autobiography, So Away I Went!, William Bushnell Stout explained the origin of the axiom, 'Simplicate and add lightness'. He and a small team were working on a new aeroplane design in workshops in Detroit in 1919. The resulting aircraft would fly in 1920. Their work would eventually lead to the world-famous Ford Trimotor transport.

I had some very colourful helpers – young draftsmen who wanted to get into aviation and who had not had their imaginations killed by having worked for a standard company too long. Nearly all of them made names for themselves later on – Evan Wright, Gordon Hooton, Frank Williams.

At this time it was difficult to put across the idea that there was necessity for original creative design work that did not follow tradition. I insisted that real engineering consisted in taking off parts, not adding new ones – that everything we adopted should eliminate weight by better structure.

Gordon Hooton summed it up at a conference one day. He said, 'I get it. You mean *simplicate and add more lightness*.' That became a slogan around our drafting room, a slogan to be heard of later from another source.

At about this time I read an article by C. G. Gray in a London magazine. A vitriolic piece of writing, it sneered at American aviation, stating that the United States Air Force had to hire 2,000 civilians to help it in its work, whereas the British (or, as he put it, 'we, of the more civilised race') got along very well having their stuff designed by Army officers and personnel.

Although Bill Stout was named president of the Society of Automotive Engineers, the American motor industry did its best to ignore his innovations and advice.

In 1919, before Bill Stout started working with Henry Ford, on the left witnessing a test flight, a member of his team came up with a slogan that was to become famous.

Having been at McCook Field and knowing the circumstances, I took up the cudgels and wrote Gray a letter in kind, questioning 'the more civilised race' which permitted plumbing (where it had plumbing) to run down the outside of the houses, where the pubs were filled with women feeding babies whisky over the counter, and so forth and so forth. I imagine I had the aim of stirring up in the cocky editor the same resentment I had experienced when I read his story on our American Air Service.

A letter came back from C. G. Gray in which he tactfully agreed with everything I said, in a very humorous vein. He thought the future of England depended on a 'steadily sozzled proletariat', which explained the babies in the pubs. In all, he got out of a dilemma rather gracefully, and from then on we became more or less regular correspondents.

In one of my letters I quoted our drafting-room expression, the fundamental of our aeroplane design, 'Simplicate and add more lightness.' This seemed to appeal to CG's sense of humour and he had placards printed and sent to all the aircraft drafting rooms in England so that for several years thereafter I received considerable correspondence on that slogan, and requests for new ones.

When Hooton first made this statement in our drafting room away back then, he had no idea what would come out of it eventually.

Although Bill Stout went on to build cars in the 1930s, his rear-engined Scarabs, he never built a racing car. What a pity.

landmark lectures on vehicle handling given by American engineer William Milliken and colleagues at London's Institution of Mechanical Engineers in October of 1956. 'He sat in the back row,' Milliken recalled, 'and didn't ask any questions.' During a subsequent lunch at the Steering Wheel Club, Lawrence Pomeroy, Jr said that 'a point Milliken immediately wanted to know was how Chapman set about the basic business of designing a new racing car. He was informed that a car should weigh five times as much as the engine alone and that stress calculations start from this premise.'

Chapman referred to the reciprocal of this recipe in 1957 when a colleague questioned his sale of two Mark VI chassis kits to Maserati. Don't worry about it, said Chapman: 'First of all, they'll put Maserati engines in the Mark VI frames and the frames will break. Our engines weigh 200 pounds; the Maserati is close to 400. So they'll stiffen frames in the conventional way and they'll be useless.' That this was so was illustrated by Vanwall's later purchase of a Lotus Eighteen chassis, in which it installed the Vanwall four. Much heavier than the usual Climax, this required a complete rebuilding of

At Indianapolis in 1968 Chapman personally monitored the fuelling procedure of Art Pollard's Type 56. For him reducing the amount of fuel on board verged on a religion.

the chassis that resulted in a correspondingly heavier car and the firm opinion of Tony Vandervell that Lotuses are 'all rubbish. They always fall apart.'

At their lunch Milliken and Pomeroy also learned that for Chapman a high polar moment of inertia was thought desirable. This referred to the distribution of masses along the chassis. A car with a low polar moment of inertia concentrated its main masses near the centre. Designers felt this made the car easier to turn – just as a sphere is easier to start in rotation than a dumb-bell of the same weight. To gain a high moment of inertia the masses were dispersed more to the front and rear, making the car more stable, especially in the hands of the less-skilled drivers who were customers for Lotus cars.

Colin Chapman's Sixteen single-seater showed design for a high polar moment with its engine well forward and all its fuel carried at the rear. The engineer underwent a Damascene conversion, however, when he sat down to pen his mid-engined Eighteen. In this, which Chapman considered his first true Formula 1 car, its mid-placed engine inherently reduced its polar moment. He put all the fuel forward over the driver's legs, another moment-reduction decision. From then onwards Chapman's racing-car designs had reduced polar moments which complemented the skills and quick reactions of the world's best drivers.

In the Monza paddock a Team Lotus mechanic followed strict Chapman procedures in checking a 25's fuel level. But he might add an extra gallon just for luck.

In no aspect of Colin Chapman's obsession with lightness did he test his team colleagues more than in fuel loadings in racing. 'It was all to do with the requirement to keep his cars down to weight,' said mechanic Bob Dance. 'He used to say, "A gallon of fuel weighs seven pounds. We spend hundreds of pounds on weight savings and you mechanics go and stick in an extra gallon or two of fuel!" So you could see his point.' 'We have always run things a lot closer on fuel than most of our rivals,' Chapman admitted in the 1960s. 'We carry out very careful fuel consumption checks. We have a log of each circuit and each engine and a lot of general know-how.

'If you can start the race with, say, three gallons of fuel less than anyone else, then you've saved yourself 21 pounds,' Chapman continued. 'Twenty-one pounds is very difficult to pare off a racing car…and worth a fifth of a second a lap. It's so simple. You've just got to have a nice, economical engine.' This was at the heart of the Chapman concept of motor racing. He aimed for a basic car that was down to the minimum weight that required the least fuel to finish a race. Whether it actually had the fuel it needed became a game of cat and mouse between Colin Chapman and his mechanics.

'We used to lose more points running out of fuel than were ever got winning races,' mechanic Billy Cowe told Michael Oliver. 'It wasn't that the capacity wasn't there, it was just that Chapman didn't like putting in too much fuel. The mechanics always used to put an extra gallon in because we knew we were always tight on fuel consumption. Then Chapman found out about this "mechanics' gallon" so he used to issue the fuel figures with a gallon off. And it got to an almighty showdown one day when we actually put in how much was on the ticket and it obviously ran out way before the end of the race.'

The problem was of course exacerbated in races where consumption rose from that measured in practice because a driver kept the hammer down more heavily than forecast. In 1967 this happened to Jim Clark at Monza, after he had to stop to replace a punctured tyre. 'He ran out of fuel!' said Keith Duckworth. 'Chapman would never have more than the odd extra ounce of fuel in and Clark's absolutely masterful effort – he was obviously going "Harry Flatters" everywhere – meant that he used more fuel, in catching up this lap and a half, than he would have done normally. An absolutely brilliant performance.' The same thing happened to

Jochen Rindt at Silverstone in '68 during a fierce battle with Jackie Stewart.

A decade later Colin Chapman's drivers were still suffering from his passion for razor-thin fuel margins. A lack of fuel knocked Mario Andretti's Lotus 78 out of the lead of the 1977 Swedish GP only two laps from the finish.[4] The 1978 South African GP at Kyalami was another case in point. Mario Andretti was hot on the heels of the leading Tyrrell and 'really pulling out the stops, and then the engine just started to die. Fuel! I was out of goddamn fuel. What made me so mad was that Colin had three gallons of gas taken out of my car on the grid. "Colin," I said to him, "If I run out of fuel I'll take it out on your hide!" "Trust me," he said. I could have died! That's the last reason you ever want to lose a race.'

Sometimes errors occurred because tank bladders were misshapen or because the foam filler, installed for safety, held petrol that a driver urgently needed. Nor were fuel systems always able to drain the tanks. Another source of error, said Glenn Waters of Team Lotus, was the way that fuel fills were counted. At Kyalami in 1978, he said, 'they had us remove some fuel from the car to begin with, which was always the Lotus way. Fill right up with fuel and then take so much out to get to the required amount, rather than pour in that specific quantity in the first place. If you were meant to put 10 gallons of fuel in the car, you had first to pump 90 gallons and then take 80 out, which made it easy to introduce errors. Not surprisingly that led to miscounting. So if we were told to take three gallons out, we'd only remove two gallons, just to be safe. But this time we were under Mr. Chapman's direct supervision so there was no opportunity to fudge.'

Chapman was a happy bunny at Kyalami because Ronnie Peterson, who had been trailing Mario, won the

---

4   Mario said afterwards that he realised that his injection metering unit had gone to a full-rich mixture early in the race and that he'd done his best to drive around the problem. An extra gallon or two might not have gone amiss, however.

Chapman on Lightness

The 1958 season was one of the cruellest in a cruel sport, with Grand Prix racing claiming the lives of Peter Collins and Luigi Musso, both in Ferraris, and Vanwall-driving Stuart Lewis-Evans. This was the first year of new rules that required petrol as fuel and shortened the length of Grand Prix races to 300 kilometres or two hours from the previous 500 kilometres or three hours. Both changes favoured the entry of smaller, lighter cars. Some, including reigning world champion Juan Fangio, suggested that the season's fatalities might indicate that GP cars were becoming dangerously light. This attack on his principles moved Colin Chapman to write this defence of lightness in racing cars.

Two fatal accidents in the *Grandes Epreuves*, which previously had a wonderful safety record, have been the subject of a great deal of unfortunate – and often ill-informed – publicity. Although perhaps purely coincidental, it should be pointed out that these accidents involved the heaviest of the current Grand Prix contenders. Thus, although it would be unwise to say that the 'minimum weight limit' addicts – and there are quite a few of them, even in Britain – have got hold of the wrong end of the stick, it would seem to be very easy to show that there is a very strong argument on the other side.

It must be obvious that the heavier the car the more difficult it is to control at the limit of adhesion and to slow it from high speed (due to weight increasing its kinetic energy) while in the event of impact with 'immovable objects' the extra inertia of the heavier car is likely to result in more damage to everything, and everybody, concerned.

As an example we can take Cliff Allison's practice accident at Oporto. On a left-hand bend Cliff got into a slide to the right, overcorrected, slid to the left and – at very considerable speed – the rear end of the Lotus struck a lamp post. The rear suspension was torn off – plucked off might cover it more adequately – and in a situation in which a heavier and more 'robust' car would almost certainly have slewed round and rolled over the Lotus remained on an even keel, lost its front suspension to the next lamp post and came to rest looking very much 'second hand'. The great point was that Cliff got out completely unhurt.

Examined slightly more scientifically, this accident had no ill effect on the driver (other than on his confidence) because firstly the lightweight car dissipated much of its kinetic energy in sliding across the road, in fact between the point at which the car was committed to an accident and the actual point of contact. In the collision with the lamp posts the extremities of the frame took the shock of impact and absorbed it in race. This was all the more galling to an angry Italian-American. 'I was livid, no question about it,' said Mario. 'When Colin wanted to take out that fuel, I didn't really argue with him because the guy's almost always right. But he's so paranoid about weight, and it's cost him so dearly so many times. But you can't convince him. Equally, you can't convince me that the weight of three gallons of fuel will make any difference to my competitiveness. There's no way.'

Even the amount of oil in the engine's dry-sump system was subject to Chapman's strictures, Tony Rudd said: 'Keith Duckworth was darkly suspicious of Chapman because he never put enough oil in, or so he reckoned.'

In 1979 journalist Peter Windsor pressed Chapman on his rigorous adherence to the minimum of fuel. 'Isn't there the philosophy that some things aren't worth cutting fine?' he asked. 'If one extra gallon gives you a safety margin, then don't you put in the extra gallon?'

'No, no, no,' came the unequivocal response. 'No, you've got to decide what you need and design for it. After all, if you started applying a "safety margin" philosophy you'd have to apply it to everything. You've got to decide what you need. You've got to decide what safety margin you want, and then you design to that limit.' For Chapman the precise amount of fuel in the car was just as much a part of its specification for a race as its wing, spring and damper settings.

That this philosophy made no allowance for the unexpected concerned Colin Chapman not a whit. Each designer brings to motor sports a set of criteria that they consider paramount. For Colin Chapman sheer speed was all-important. He ranked leading races rather than finishing them as a hallmark of success. Creating a car that was as light as possible, both dry and fuelled, was a major ingredient in his recipe for speed. In achieving this Chapman was, if possible, more ruthless than in any other aspect of his design activities. Virtually inexplicable, however, were his four-wheel-drive aberrations.

depth; the driver was not subject to a rate of deceleration at which he would be almost certain to sustain injury against parts of the car.

The suspension units, which have been shown to be strong enough for all normal use, did not provide sufficient resistance to throw the car into the air and overturn it, but rather aided the frame in absorbing shock. And although the extremities of the car were very much beyond repair (the engine also was damaged, and the radiator was found some distance away) that part of the frame which surrounds the driving compartment remained intact, so that Allison was able to climb out in the normal way as soon as the car came to rest; an expensive accident as far as the car was concerned, but at least Cliff was able to start in the race – even though it was only in another car.

Weight saving is a process which is naturally open to criticism if it results in unreliability, or breakages under normal use, but there is no doubt that a well-designed and properly constructed light-weight car can stand up to very hard use, the mechanical parts (engine and transmission) failing far more often than the chassis components.

In this connection it must be emphasised that design is more important than material; despite what might have been said about exhaust pipes dropping off our Formula 2 car it was the design – not the gauge of the tubing – which caused fracture, and it doesn't happen any more. In the same way the original Formula 2 car

suffered frame failures when the rear suspension was changed from de Dion to strut; the different load paths required for this layout have since been incorporated.

Instead of reducing weight, however, it is better to design light in the first place, modifying any components which may show signs of stress during development work. This, in the case of the frame, means having links which are all of the same strength. In this connection it can be said that the Ferrari, although it wins a lot of races (thanks to the most powerful 2½-litre engine in current use) has a frame which is inefficient.

The total weight of a racing car on the starting grid, with driver and fuel aboard, is in the limit determined by the weight of the engine; if this can be decreased by one pound then the rest of the car can be made four pounds lighter. In all this, however, tyres and wheels are the critical factor and their weight has a considerable influence on the car as a whole. The job of the designer is to keep the right relationship between sprung and unsprung weight and, above all, to keep the greatest possible amount of tyre tread in contact with the road.

So in the end it all comes back to roadholding. Given the suspension (and tyre) qualities which enable the driver to go round corners at very high speed without losing adhesion, the lightweight car will not only have the advantage of safety – in the event of the driver 'over-cooking it' – but will also be in a position to defeat cars with more powerful engines and perhaps greater maximum speed.

Chapter 7

AERODYNAMIC ADVENTURES

Aerodynamics is a very absorbing subject. It's quite difficult for a layman to appreciate the pitfalls and mistakes that you can easily make. You can't see what you're working with and you always get the impression that air flows where you want it to flow rather than where it wants to flow – and a lot of strange things happen. That's why I like it.

Colin Chapman

'It seemed to me that an efficient aerodynamic body would be the thing to have for the 1954 season,' wrote Colin Chapman at the time, 'if some sort of a march was to be stolen on the others.' Thus began the engineer's fitful flirtation with the beguiling art and science of aerodynamics, then and later exploited as a means of getting a step ahead of his rivals on the track. Chapman's career would witness important advances in the aerodynamics of the racing car – as well as a handful of howlers.

'Accordingly,' Chapman continued in his 1954 account, 'Frank Costin designed the now familiar Mark VIII body. This car was for myself and to serve as a mobile test-bed to try out the various new features I had included. The prototype was built during the winter of 1953–54 and weight was kept down to a minimum. Normally the main disadvantage of a streamlined body in racing was that of extra weight as compared with a "normal" body. We set out to produce an aerodynamic car which weighed less than most conventional sports-racing bodies – the never-ending problem of keeping ahead.'

Overseeing race activity from the Lotus pit at Monza during the 1967 Italian GP, Colin Chapman was at a track that favoured sleek aerodynamics for flat-out speed.

Apart from their enclosed rear wheels no aspect of Colin Chapman's previous Lotus cars suggested any preoccupation with drag reduction. In 1954, however, Colin planned to up his game as both entrant and driver, as colleague Peter Ross explained: 'He wanted to move into the more prestigious 1,500cc class at that time dominated by Porsche, Osca and Gordini. At events in the UK he would be up against cars such as the Cooper-MG, the Tojeiro-MG, the Leonard-MG, the Lester-MG and the Connaught, not to mention Peter Gammon who was putting his very powerful MG engine into his new Lotus Mark VI.'

An improved body design had to be part of the Chapman scheme for the new season. That this would be fully enveloping was self-evident. Up until 1952 the international rules had allowed sports cars to race with cycle wings. This had been popular during the transition years after the war, allowing sports cars to compete in formula-car events with their wings removed. For 1953, however, for the first time full wheel enclosure was mandated for sports-racers competing in FIA-sanctioned international events.

Chapman addressed the requirement for low drag with complete pragmatism. Familiar though he was with aviation technology, he saw no pressing need to apply it to the shape of an automobile. 'Chapman admits that he

Chapman's Mark VI of 1953 was still in a transitional stage from his first trials cars to a road/racing sports car. Only its enclosed rear wheels hinted at drag reduction.

does not love particularly the aerodynamic body,' reported Bill Boddy in a 1955 *Motor Sport*, 'But, as he said, you cannot sneeze at a free ten extra mph, apart from which his bodies enhance stability.' Boddy rightly called the

Frank Costin, shown holding the far end of a space-frame he designed for Lister, became Colin Chapman's first advisor on body design for aerodynamic performance.

resulting Mark VIII 'a pretty devastating car to emanate from virtually an amateur-inspired pocket-factory.'

Colin Chapman had a good idea of what sort of fully enveloping body his Mark VIII should have. In one-eighth scale on the draughting board in his sitting room at Cheshunt he modelled the shape of a car described as 'rather like a small C-Type Jaguar'. Since 1951 the C-Type had been the centre of attraction in sports-racing aerodynamics, its shape by Jaguar aerodynamicist Malcolm Sayer contributing to its wins at Le Mans that year and in 1953. Chapman reckoned that it couldn't be too far wrong.

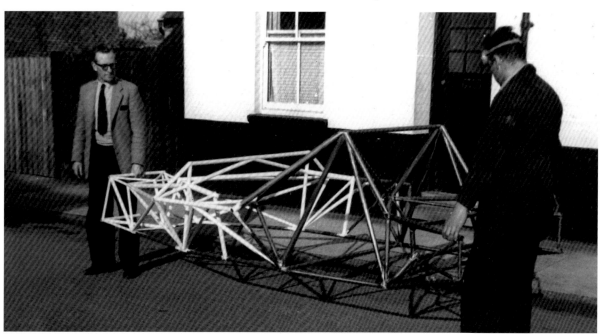

Colin commissioned David Kelsey to make a model of his planned design in one-sixth size to be used for wind-tunnel testing. Carved from balsa wood, his effort was finely detailed. 'When it was finished,' Peter Ross related, 'it was shown to Mike Costin, who didn't think much of it. It looked just like all the other competitors' bodies and "wasn't what I would call streamlined".' Mike suggested to Colin that it could be useful to let his brother Frank have a look at the model.

Briefly mentioned earlier, Mike Costin's older brother Francis Albert was universally known as Frank.[1] Passionate about aviation and trained by Britain's aero industry after leaving school at 17, the elder Costin was coincidentally working at de Havilland, the source of so much design talent in the formative years of Lotus. Unlike most others who were inveigled into Chapman's schemes, however, Frank was at Chester near Liverpool instead of at Hatfield north of London where his colleagues were more readily exposed to the tempting attractions of Lotus and Chapman.

Although Chapman didn't require abject servility of his colleagues a degree of respect or at least enthusiasm was required, so he was initially wary of Frank Costin, who in their only previous meeting had sniffed that his Mark VI frame was 'overweight' and not designed according to strict aeronautical principles. Nor was Mike sure that his brother would be keen, saying that 'Frank had never shown the least bit of interest either in cars or my activities with Lotus. On the telephone he perked up at the word "aerodynamic" and consented to have a look.

'I sent the model via inter-factory airlift to de Havilland's Chester plant where Frank was in charge of aerodynamic flight testing,' Mike continued. 'I rang him under the pretext of learning if the model had arrived safely and from the tone of his voice I could tell he'd swallowed the bait. As we were anxious to get on with the final design of the car I told Frank he could reshape the model to suit any ideas he might have. After a fortnight it returned completely changed from the original and to say the least it looked "different".'

'Frank Costin immediately took a hacksaw to the model,' said David Kelsey, 'carving off great lumps which he replaced with plasticine.' This allowed him to shape the vehicle on the lines he wanted, not only to achieve low drag but also to improve stability, an attribute overlooked by many early slippery designs. In de

Seen with Karl Kling as first shown in February 1954, the all-enveloping body of the Mercedes-Benz W196 encouraged Chapman to accept Costin's radical design.

Havilland's workshop he built a free-moving turntable for the model and an egg-box-like flow straightener for air from the company's high-pressure air system to allow him to ensure that he'd put big enough feathers on the arrow.

Among Frank's features for the P3, as the job was coded at Lotus in Edmonton, were spats for the rear wheels, long fins for stability, a single small, curved screen for the driver and careful ducting of air into and away from the radiator. Frank Costin drew these features full-size, extrapolating and refining from his model. Lateral sections every ten inches defined the surface of the skin.

Both to visualise the shape and to provide a guide for the body shapers, Nigel Allen and Peter Ross made up half-inch plywood transverse sections from Frank's drawings which fitted into a framework at Edmonton. 'Sitting in it,' wrote Dennis Ortenburger, 'one could look out over the framework of transverse sections and see what was turning out to be an extraordinary shape. An excited telephone call brought Chapman in at around 5am. Frank recalled that he exclaimed, "Aw, God, you know we'll never sell it. It's far too far out, far too advanced."

'As chance would have it,' Ortenburger continued, 'one of the lads came in later with the latest issue of *Autosport* and there on the cover was the Mercedes-Benz W196. Chapman's attitude changed in a flash; all of a sudden the Mark VIII wasn't that far out. Why, it was

1   With Francis Albert Sinatra only five at the time of Frank's birth in 1920, the future crooner's given names couldn't have inspired Costin's Italian-Irish mother. Both namings may have been inspired by the husband and consort of Britain's Queen Victoria, who was a Francis Albert.

In Britain one of the advocates of low-drag shapes was aircraft-maker Bristol, which first raced its Type 450 coupés in 1953. These are its 1954 versions at Le Mans.

The first Mark VIII Lotus of 1954 was a striking step forward. Its creator is shown driving to victory at Silverstone in the race for 1½-litre cars on 17 July 1954.

up with the gods for sure.'[2] Later in 1954 *Motor Sport* quoted Chapman as saying about aerodynamics that 'Mercedes-Benz knew something about that department!' Esteemed Daimler-Benz had indeed initially shown its W196 Grand Prix car with the all-enveloping body that it planned to use for fast circuits; an open-wheeled body was still in the works.

After completion at the end of March the P3 and its MG/ Morris-based engine were run in on the road. 'It poses special problems whilst being driven on the road,' Chapman said of his new creation. 'The good shape and lack of wind rush past the driver are factors which give a smooth ride and make speed very deceptive. In consequence it has been involved in three major shunts whilst being driven to and from race meetings by my mechanics, due possibly to misjudging just how fast the car was going.'

In fact the shunts took place both during the running-

2   Like many aspects of the early Lotus story this chronology poses as many questions as answers. For example it is unclear to this author whether Chapman ever saw Costin's modifications to Kelsey's scale model. Some accounts give the impression that Colin first divined the shape of the P3 from the full-size buck, while others have Costin only making the full-scale sections after Chapman had given him the go-ahead. By mid-January the buck was complete and beginning to be used by the panel beaters. However, the first issue of *Autosport* to show the W196 Mercedes was that of 26 February 1954. It appeared not on the cover but on page 259. This was some ten days after the body panels were virtually complete and waiting for the chassis. The P3's chronology is detailed in *Lotus – The Early Years* by Peter Ross while Dennis Ortenburger's account is based on his interviews with Frank Costin.

in and on a drive to Oulton Park with Mike Costin at the wheel. In the latter instance they'd reached 115mph while outrunning a police car, exulting in their first 100-plus miles per hour in a Lotus. 'With a power output of around 85bhp,' Chapman had said, 'we estimated that the car could reach a maximum speed in excess of 125mph.' His first serious high-speed effort had come close.

Competing in 1955 with the original Mark VIII, new owner Austin Nurse showed off its long tail fins, enclosed rear wheels and bulge over its MG-Morris engine.

During a hiatus in SAR5's busy racing schedule Costin and Chapman conducted instrumented aerodynamic tests on a disused airfield in Cheshire.

Especially in bare aluminium the Mark IX Lotus flaunted its clean lines, evolved from those of the Mark VIII to suit a new frame and the Climax FWA four.

Rear fins of the Mark IX were shorter, to fit in the Lotus van. A vent in the rear deck was carried over to provide cooling-air flow for the inboard rear brakes.

In 1954 Chapman raced P3 himself while building several more Mark VIIIs for customers. Said John Bolster in *Autosport*, 'This phenomenally successful 1½-litre sports-racing car has had a most spectacular season, in which victories and record laps have abounded. Perhaps its defeat of a formidable German car at Silverstone was its greatest triumph.' The vanquishing of Hans

Advanced though previous Lotus sports-racers were, the Eleven of 1956 marked a further leap forward with Frank Costin's deep enclosure of its wheels.

Herrmann's Porsche 550 Spyder wasn't quite definitive, because the poor German was last away from the Le Mans start after a mechanic left his gear lever in reverse instead of first. Placing third, pole-sitter Herrmann shared fastest lap with Peter Gammon's Lotus Mark VI, which was second behind Chapman.

'One does feel that this is a scientifically designed vehicle,' reported John Bolster, 'not the "lucky accident" that some sports cars really are.' He gave its top speed as 121.5mph, 'a phenomenal achievement,' saying that 'the rev counter remained steady at about 6,500rpm so a slightly higher gear ratio might increase the already excellent figure.' This was sufficient validation of the estimate cited by Colin Chapman.

'Above all,' concluded the knowledgeable and influential Bolster, 'I am completely converted to the fully aerodynamic type of body. It gives so much extra speed and such improved stability that one would be foolish to ignore its advantages except for the very slowest circuits.' This last was a suggestion that envelope bodies were inevitably heavier than the now-outlawed cycle-winged style, although with careful design it was Chapman's goal to prove this untrue. With substantial aluminium bulkheads supporting its body the Mark VIII hadn't achieved this but the demonstrable efficiency of its shape decisively advanced the state of the Lotus art.

Rightly enough, Frank Costin had doubted that the Lotus 'amateur-inspired pocket-factory' would be capable of building his ambitious body design. He reckoned without the skills of Chapman's moonlighters from de Havilland as well as the talent of Edmonton-based Len Pritchard and Charlie Williams. Their Lotus debut was with the Mark VI, said Pritchard: 'Colin brought us a frame, told us roughly what he wanted and left us to get on with it. We took a great deal of care over it, not only in the way it was put together but the way it looked, because we virtually styled it.

'When Frank came up with the Mark VIII it was a step forward and a challenge,' Pritchard added. 'From the beginning Charlie and I decided that we would only do our best work. A lot of competition cars of the time looked awful, with the body added as an afterthought. We felt that the body was important. It was part of the car. Its look established the car. We weren't prepared just to "skin" a frame, a term I detest.' Thanks to these attitudes and their attributes Williams & Pritchard became a byword for excellence in racing-car bodywork.

Frank Costin was generous in his praise of the partners' work. 'Both of them were absolute geniuses,' he told Mike Lawrence, 'the finest pair of metal bashers you'll ever come across. Not only did everything look so good, but everything fitted perfectly and they made it look so easy, a sure sign of genius. The Lotus Mark VIII's body was made of 20-gauge magnesium. Where do you

Starting in 1952 wide publicity was given to the Disco
Volante *Alfa Romeos, which featured enclosed wheels
and shapes with higher frontal area to gain low
form drag.*

important to Costin, who knew the drag penalty that
uneven surfaces could exact.

Eager to learn as much as possible about the new
medium in which he'd become involved, Frank Costin
organised tests of the works Mark VIII on a disused
airfield near Chester using pressure-measuring probes
that picked up effects near the skin and progressive
distances away. He was strapped to the bonnet to watch
movements of wool tufts taped in and around the front
wheelhouses. Another technique was the placing of tiny
blobs of dirty oil on the skin to see what the wind did to
them. Ingeniously, Costin carried his bottle of oil around
the paddock to deposit blobs on other cars in which he
was interested, observing their trails and dispositions
when they returned from practice.

Although later Lotuses would be even more efficient,
more refined, the Mark VIII glitters in the company's
annals as a major aerodynamic breakthrough. Albeit not
wind-tunnel-tested, contrary to assertions at the time, it
was as wind-cheating as it looked. When it was conceived
Malcolm Sayer hadn't yet unveiled his magnum opus,
the D-Type Jaguar, and few others were applying more

than eyeball aerodynamics.[3] Only Bristol with its 450,
introduced in 1953, Mercedes-Benz in 1954 and some
small-capacity French tiddlers were taking low-drag
science seriously. While the Mark VIII's shape was not
Colin Chapman's creation, it was his decision to go
forward with it after his concerns about its marketability
were allayed. When it proved quick, of course, it started
to look terrific.

Availability of the 1.1-litre Coventry Climax four, which
first raced at Le Mans in a Kieft in 1954, prompted Colin
Chapman to build a new car to carry it for 1955. It was
just the kind of engine he craved, featherweight – as its
FWA designation indicated – at only 215 pounds. For
the first time this new model, the Mark IX, would fully
integrate its frame design with Frank Costin's bodywork,
allowing the body to be directly supported by frame
tubes instead of now-redundant bulkheads.

Frank Costin considered the Mark IX 'more of a
developmental car than anything else,' wrote Dennis
Ortenburger, a transitional machine in his appreciation
of a car's problems, while also 'a quantum leap forward
in experience.' It was a clear evolution from the Mark

---

3 Some of the D-Type's aerodynamic principles, and indeed its monocoque
   construction, were foreshadowed in a one-off prototype, the 'light alloy car',
   used for record-breaking by Jaguar in October of 1953 in Belgium. Advanced
   aerodynamics for cars were much in the air at the time.

VIII with its wide, low frontal inlet for brake and radiator air, its low bonnet and its stabilising fins, though these were now shorter – to fit the car into Lotus's new Commer van – and taller, essentially extensions of the rear wings. The Mark IX was a pretty racer that began to establish a strong and distinctive visual image for the Lotus sports car.

In 1956 at Goodwood, Reg Bicknell's Eleven showed the new design's tiny radiator-air inlet, with ducted flow behind, and heavy body overhang of its wire wheels.

At Connecticut's Lime Rock an Eleven displayed the head fairing – a suggestion of Grahame Walter – fitted with a wraparound screen when regulations allowed.

It also advanced the aerodynamic art. With a similar MG engine to the Mark VIII he tried, John Bolster timed the Mark IX at a faster 128.6mph. Experience also contributed to a better-made body: 'The vibration of the panels at high engine revolutions has been noticeably reduced.' Its sister, a Climax-engined car, was timed at 127.7mph, even more impressive in view of its 25-per cent smaller engine.

The 'developmental' character of the Mark IX became evident in February of 1956 when the press were assembled to see a new Lotus model, the Eleven. It was the result of intense activity by Chapman and his moonlighting de Havilland team aimed at creating a new sports-racer that would synthesise everything learned with the Mark IX in a car that would be easier to build and sell, both as a complete car and in kit form to avoid purchase tax. In this they were destined to be phenomenally successful.

No small role in the Eleven's success was played by its shape, which was not only aerodynamically functional but also strikingly dramatic. 'It would be no exaggeration to say that the ultra-low streamlined appearance created a real furore,' wrote John Bolster, who took a Ford-powered car on the road. 'Crowds collected wherever I parked the car, and the interest it aroused was enormous.

When new rules required a full windscreen, the Lotus response was a low-drag design, as at Le Mans in 1958 on a French-entered Eleven duelling with a DB-Panhard.

It has a genuine, functional beauty, absolutely without decoration, and I heard numerous complimentary references from passers-by.' A less complimentary reference, said Bolster, was from 'a gentleman who tripped over the Lotus outside licensed premises and was very critical indeed from a prone position.'

By the time he tackled the design of the Eleven, Frank Costin had greater confidence in the ability of the car's chassis and suspension to cope with the various aerodynamic loads to which it was subjected. Having feathers on the arrow was still important, but not to the degree he'd originally thought. Low drag was still high on the agenda, with success at Le Mans a Chapman goal. Practicality was also paramount, with Colin specifying that the respective front and rear body shells would lift as single pieces and pivot upwards to expose their mechanisms. Another Chapman contribution was tilting the 1.1-litre Climax four ten degrees to the left to allow a lower bonnet and scuttle.

'Frank recalls that everyone was genuinely fired up about the project,' said Costin biographer Ortenburger. 'It was somehow more than the usual Lotus *esprit de corps*; it was a feeling that the Eleven was really going to be something.' For the first time Costin made a major commitment to his philosophy that shape was all-important in achieving low drag, even if it came at the expense of an increase in frontal area. This viewpoint was manifested in his design of the body of the 1956 Vanwall Grand Prix car, which looked tubby next to the

Maseratis but in fact was successful in reducing the body's all-important form drag, which is that caused by the shape of the car as distinct from the drag derived from its frontal area.

Though Colin Chapman was decidedly in the low-frontal-area camp when it came to drag reduction, he wholeheartedly accepted Frank Costin's approach to the Eleven's design. As with the Vanwall Costin concentrated initially on the car's main shape, ignoring the need for wings to cover the wheels. These would be added to the basic body as aerodynamically evolved shapes in their own right. In this Costin was true to the principles of pioneering aerodynamicist Paul Jaray, whose wind-tunnel-derived designs reflected a rigorous purity, each part of a body having its own integrity. Neither Jaray nor Costin admitted of any vagueness in their designs.

A similar approach to Frank Costin's was first revealed to the world in June of 1952. This was the Alfa Romeo Type 1900 C52, better known as the *Disco Volante* or Flying Saucer after its then-unusual ogival centre section, along which protruding blisters made room for the tyres. Here too was a form which focused first of all on the main body shape, designed for optimum penetration, and then added the contours needed to accommodate the wheels. It would be invidious to suggest that Costin was influenced by the various Alfa 'Discos', which were widely publicised in 1952 and '53, but they did demonstrate a similar approach to sports-car aerodynamics.[4]

Work on the shape of the Eleven was kicked off at a meeting at the Chapman abode in September of 1955. Joining Chapman and Frank Costin was Grahame Walter, a technical apprentice at the Royal Aircraft Establishment. Among the RAE's Farnborough facilities he and his colleagues had found a half-metre-section low-speed wind tunnel that had come from Göttingen after the war as German reparations. Making twelfth-scale models of various sports-car and calibration shapes, during 1955 Walter and colleague David Waters conducted tests of their drag and lift characteristics. The results were checked and assessed by the RAE's Dick Cawthorne, a principal scientific officer.

'Colin gave us a drawing of the car without a body,' Grahame Walter related, 'and a dimension which was to be the overall length. He explained that would allow

4 The Jaguar D-Type of 1954 and its 1953 predecessor show similar approaches to aerodynamics to those taken by Alfa Romeo and its body-design partner, Superleggera Touring. The *Disco Volante* shape was not used in racing by Alfa Romeo because its drag reduction was only at its strongest when the body was either so low that ground clearance was inadequate or so high that the centre of gravity was too elevated.

The Eleven's low drag was verified by independent trials including those of **Road & Track**, *whose editor John R. Bond was at the wheel during a test of a Club model.*

Following Frank Costin's lead with the Eleven, Peter Kirwan-Taylor's first design for the Elite envisaged deep enclosure of its road wheels and modest rear finning.

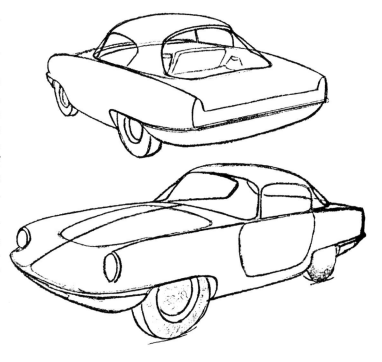

Unmistakably a Lotus with its tiny air inlet and downsloping bonnet, the Elite posed for the Rolleiflex of Edward Eves at the company's Hornsey headquarters.

With Stan Chapman's Railway Arms behind it, the Elite showed its cut-off tail and compound-curved side windows as specified by the meticulous Frank Costin.

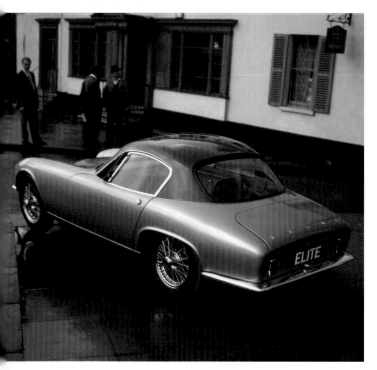

him to put a certain number of cars into his transporter without having to pay higher cross-channel ferry rates for a longer transporter.' The participants discussed the new car's aerodynamic features with Costin making initial notes and sketches.

Although Frank Costin was now of the view that tail fins weren't essential, Chapman felt that they'd become accepted as a distinctive Lotus characteristic and thus should be provided, albeit simply as extensions of the rear wings. Walter argued in favour of the aerodynamic benefit of a head fairing, which was accepted by Chapman and Costin for versions of the car that had a metal tonneau cover and wraparound windscreen where regulations permitted.

Although little remarked upon at the time, a striking feature of the Eleven was the deep enveloping of its wheels by the bodywork. Unique among its contemporaries, this was an attribute shared with the 'Disco' Alfa Romeos. At the front this feature required wider bodywork in plan view, creating an increase of four inches in width over the Mark IX and a two-inch reduction in track width. Even so the turning circle was a generous 42 feet in diameter.

Frank Costin chose this deep envelopment to reduce the amount of turbulence caused by the rotating front wheels, turbulence that would take its toll in increased drag over the rest of the car's surface. Gone were the cutaway front wheelhouses, which were subjected to many of Costin's runway tests on the Mark IX. Warm radiator air was still ducted into the Eleven's

wheelhouses.[5] Air entered the radiator through a small oval aperture based on the reduced size that had proven satisfactory on Chapman's personal Mark IX racer.

A new feature of the Eleven was its fitting of proper headlamps in the front wings. The previous envelope-bodied Lotuses had lamps under the bonnet that were swung up into place when needed, the only exception being the Mark IX that raced at Le Mans in 1955. For the three works entries at Le Mans in 1956 space was found for Perspex-faired driving lamps adjacent to the radiator-air inlets. These and other refinements were the work of Williams & Pritchard, whose Len Pritchard recalled that 'it was the Eleven that excited me more than any other car. The sketches were exciting and it *was* exciting as it took shape in the metal and came alive before our eyes.'

The result was by far the slipperiest Lotus yet. Meticulous testing of the finished vehicle contributed to this achievement. During February of 1956 Colin Chapman and Mike Costin carried out several tests that had aerodynamic content, using the Barnet bypass and London's North Circular Road. Tufts were attached to the body to reveal air movement behind the rear-view mirror and around the front wheelhouse, the latter observed from a Ford Anglia running alongside. Then in March Graham Hill drove a new Eleven the 80 miles to Southampton for shipping to the United States.

Dancing through the chicane at Goodwood during the 1963 TT, Mike Beckwith in Chris Barber's number 22 Elite beat a Porsche Carrera to win the 2-litre class.

Though Lotus Elites competed in North America – this one at Sebring in 1965 – their achievements in the New World didn't match their amazing Le Mans successes.

5   We can't be certain of the reason why the cutaway wheelhouses were abandoned. However the Ferrari Testa Rossa of 1957–58 had this feature as part of its 'pontoon' front wings, which were given up on the works cars of 1958 because they were thought to contribute to excessive front-end lift.

Afterwards he reported, 'Most marked was lack of de-acceleration on shutting off throttle, pointing to improved streamlining and little rolling resistance.'

Joe Lowrey's calculations based on tests by *The Motor* indicated that in the Eleven, compared to the Mark IX, 'already very low wind resistance figures have been improved by about 15 per cent.' *Road & Track* tested a racing model with headrest, finding 'some of the most startling performance data ever published.' With 83bhp from its Stage II Climax its top speed was 132mph on gearing that the car's owner said was good for 138mph at 7,400rpm on the long straight at Nassau. Acceleration from rest to 100mph took only 22.0 seconds while the standing quarter-mile was covered in 16.0 seconds. This was, judged *R&T*, 'fantastic performance with only 1,100cc,' made possible by both light weight and low drag.

At Le Mans in 1956 only one of the three Elevens entered completed the 24 hours, but it was seventh overall and winner of the 1,100cc class. This was a

Designed for minimum frontal area, his Lotus Twelve's body was little wider than Dennis Taylor as he prepared to do battle at Silverstone on 14 September 1957.

prelude to a sensational performance in 1957, when the 750cc and 1,100cc classes were won, as were the Index of Performance and the Biennial Cup. For reasons of visibility most raced without a unique tonneau cover that Frank Costin had devised to reduce the drag caused by the high windscreens mandated by new FIA rules. Fitting into new low-drag screens of Costin's design, this unique cover was air-inflated to maintain its rigidity.

The ultimate in Eleven streamlining was achieved in the car that Lotus prepared for Stirling Moss to attack 1.1-litre class records. Frank Costin capped his creation with an enclosed canopy to which he gave aircraft-style ventilation through entry and exit slots. Fixed in place, this required Moss to struggle into the cockpit through a folded-down door. Other preparations included taping of all seams, smoothing the belly pan and polishing the paintwork.

On the day after the 1956 Italian GP at Monza, won by Moss, he clambered into the Lotus. He soon showed its speed with a lap at 148mph, then settled down to average 135.54mph for 50 kilometres and 132.77mph for 50 miles. Partly owing to oversize rear tyres, however, the body took a hammering on the Monza banking with the rear frame and body breaking right away. After repairs the car ran again to reach 100 miles at 137.5mph in the hands of Mackay Fraser. A year later the speed for 100 miles was raised to 140.8mph by Cliff Allison in this, the sleekest Lotus yet.

Based on its tests, *Road & Track* estimated the drag coefficient (C_d) of the Eleven with headrest and wraparound screen at 0.40. This was satisfactory for an open sports-racer, especially as the Jaguar D-Type – often praised for its superb aerodynamics – returned a coefficient of 0.49 in a full-scale wind-tunnel test of an actual car. Both, however, were decisively outperformed by the first Lotus Elite of 1957–58. While the same tunnel test as the D-Type's showed a drag coefficient of 0.35 for the Elite, experts in the Lotus model tend to support a figure of 0.32.

Although not the 0.29 claimed by Colin Chapman, the Lotus Elite's C_d was ultra-low by the standards of road cars of the 1950s. Slippery though it looked and lacking an air inlet in its nose, the Type 356 Porsche had a drag coefficient of 0.40. In its 911 Porsche would reduce this, but only to 0.38. As well at 16.0 square feet the Lotus had a smaller frontal area than the 356 at 17.4 square feet. With this potent combination the Elite was able to perform out of all proportion to its modest 1.2 litres.

Credited with the original concept for the Elite's shape was Peter Kirwan-Taylor, an accountant whose conjoined abilities in finance and styling made him exceptionally useful to Chapman. 'I have always had a special interest in car design,' said Kirwan-Taylor, 'not just in styling but in the integration of form and function. When therefore in 1953 I read of the Lotus Mark VI kits being built in a little garage in Hornsey, I quickly drove up to have a look. The philosophy of Colin's design at once intrigued me – the simplicity of triangulation, minimum dimensions and weight saving. I decided at once to design my own all-enveloping body and build a Mark VI. I came to know Colin well, an acquaintanceship which with the subsequent development of the Elite became a lasting friendship.'

Ranked as the Fourteen in Lotus annals, the Elite followed quickly in the wake of the Eleven. Thus Kirwan-Taylor's first sketches and tenth-scale models followed its philosophy in accepting frontal area in search of a low drag coefficient. As a result its wheels were semi-enclosed at both front and rear. In a surprising about-turn, however, Frank Costin opined that in this case a lower frontal area should prevail. The body was narrowed and the wheel arches opened, more in the front than the rear.

Aero engineer Costin was ruthless about all the Elite's details that impinged on its likely aerodynamic drag. This affected the side windows, which had to have compound curvature to preserve clean flow around the greenhouse. This in turn meant that they couldn't roll down conventionally. As in the 300SL Gullwing they had to be either in place or bodily removed. Frank Costin specified curved instead of square sections for the drip rails above the doors to reduce their drag to the minimum. Credit for the superb final styling of the Elite was given by all parties to former Ford stylist John Frayling, the artist-designer who modelled its shape and specified its structure.

With between 1,000 and 1,100 produced in total, the Elite was a money-loser for Lotus but a great success as a racing car. Starting with first and second in class and placing in the top ten in 1959, it won its class at Le Mans six years in a row. In the Index of Thermal Efficiency, Elites were winners twice and second on four occasions.

At Monza in 1958 **Le Patron** *oversaw work on Graham Hill's Sixteen for the Italian GP. The new car had lower and wider lines than the previous season's Twelve.*

A Formula 2 entry for Graham Hill in the 1958 German GP, the Sixteen had an elliptical cross-section that took its bodywork close to the inner surfaces of its tyres.

Hotly pursued by John Surtees in his first car race at Goodwood in 1960, Jim Clark's Formula Junior Lotus Eighteen was more rectilinear in its cross-section than the chasing Cooper.

A feature of the Eighteen was the aperture in its tail into which – according to Chapman – air was to flow to cool its gearbox, clutch and engine.

Achieved on a circuit that demanded the ultimate in low-drag aerodynamics, these results pointed to exceptional achievement in that discipline.[6]

Beginning with the Mark VIII and culminating in the stunning performances achieved by the Eleven and Elite, Frank Costin made magnificent contributions to the designs and reputations of Chapman's cars.[7] Describing these years as 'entirely gin and enthusiasm', Costin was invigorated by his interactions with the creative Chapman and his colleagues, so much so that he decided to leave de Havilland late in 1958 to set up shop as an independent consultant with cars at the top of his agenda.

Would Chapman and Costin continue working together? Logic would suggest so but finance would have a role to play. All Costin's work for Chapman had been done from sheer enthusiasm, without payment.[8] Only when the two men spoke of the future did the subject of past compensation arise; Costin accepted a new Ford Anglia as retroactive pay. Then when the aerodynamicist told Chapman what he'd expect to be

---

6   For private teams Frank Costin developed front-end modifications such as a smaller air inlet and shrouded headlamps that he reckoned liberated an additional 16 to 20 horsepower at high speed.

7   Incredibly, early histories of Lotus make no mention of Costin's contributions. This was true of many of Chapman's collaborators but his is certainly the most conspicuous omission.

8   Although this wasn't his intention, Costin also worked for the March Formula 1 team without compensation. He agreed to design the body for the 1971 Type 711 March on the basis that he'd be paid in proportion to the demonstrated improvement in performance. Differences with March's Max Mosley over the interpretation of this meant that he wasn't paid at all.

paid for subsequent work, the Lotus chief decided that their co-operation was at an end. That may in fact have been inevitable, because neither man suffered fools gladly. In spite of their mutual respect, this boded ill for their future collaboration.

Subsequent front-engined sports-racing Lotuses were obviously derived from the Eleven by Chapman and his

Wearing an appropriate number, Dan Gurney's Eighteen at Goodwood in 1961 manifested the functionality that brought the new Lotus success in three categories.

From 1961 steeply inclined seating opened a new era in ultra-low racing Lotuses, of which 1964's 30 was a prime example. Jim Clark did his best to cope.

Designer Len Terry said that the Lotus 30 was 'a smoother version' of his Terrier Mark 6, three of which were built in 1962 contemporaneously with the taller Lotus 23.

team, especially Williams & Pritchard. The first Lotus single-seater, the Formula 2 Twelve of 1957, was a pure minimum-frontal-area design in line with Chapman's preferences. Quintessentially narrow, it used nose and tail shapes of extreme simplicity. Press-ganged into Formula 1 service in 1958, it showed a good turn of speed as Cliff Allison found at Spa: 'The car was performing very well, especially so through fast curves and, of course, Spa was super-fast. I was timed at 157mph on the Masta Straight.'

Although the Twelve's single-seat successor, the Sixteen, was dubbed a 'Mini-Vanwall' by many who assumed that Frank Costin was still designing Lotuses, it was in fact an in-house design that departed from the pure frontal-area regime. With an elliptical cross-section, the top and bottom of its body were symmetrically curved about a horizontal plane that extended from the nose to the rear of the cockpit. This gave the body a 'lateral streamlining' that was intended to reduce the effects of side winds and prevent power-wasting pressure build-up beneath the belly pan. This design made the Sixteen wider than need be – in fact astonishingly wide as seen in plan view. As with the Vanwall, the space was used to shroud suspension parts.

Colin Chapman returned to a rigorous reduction of frontal area with his Eighteen of 1960. 'In designing this body we had three factors in mind,' he said at the time. 'First, minimum frontal area commensurate with covering the essential parts of the car – especially the fuel tanks.

Second, the promotion of the maximum flow of air over parts requiring to be cooled. This means designing the front of the car around the smallest suitable radiator and channelling the air out so that it doesn't cook the driver. The third factor was to keep the weight down by keeping down the acreage of aluminium.

'In cross-section,' Chapman continued, 'the shape was dictated by the need to combine the minimum frontal area with the maximum radius of gyration of the chassis; this means getting the four main longitudinal tubes as far apart as possible to give the maximum degree of chassis stiffness. Thus the two conflicting requirements, maximum stiffness and minimum frontal area, have produced a square shape.' In a less guarded moment Chapman admitted to journalist Cyril Posthumus, 'Well, I couldn't have it looking like a Cooper, could I?'

Whether the Eighteen's rear brakes could be mounted inboard, said Chapman, was 'mainly a thermal problem. It's just a matter of how successful we are in maintaining low underbody temperatures in the engine compartment. The body is designed so that air will enter the engine compartment through the hole at the rear, flow forward from this high-pressure area over the gearbox, brakes, clutch and engine out through the hole in the undertray, the underside of the car being a low-pressure area. But if there is any danger of the rear brakes overheating, we shall mount them outboard, despite the increase in unsprung weight.'

Although the new Lotus wasn't exactly 'square' it was indeed boxy in cross-section. To counter it Cooper introduced its new low-line model, which combined reduced frontal area with less draggy lines. This gave it

In the Type 40 version of the 30, larger wheels and tyres required higher wings that added frontal area. At Brands Hatch in 1965 Jim Clark explored its braking limits.

As shown by Chris Amon in a Lotus 25-BRM at Rouen in 1964, moving the front springs and dampers inboard gave a small but significant reduction in drag.

the upper hand over the Lotus in top speed, as Innes Ireland ascertained at Spa in 1960 where Jack Brabham 'had the faster car, the Cooper, on the straight, but I knew that the Lotus's superior roadholding would always get me round and away from corners quicker.'

As discussed in Chapter 1, once committed to the rear-engined route Colin Chapman continued to emphasise reduced frontal area by reclining his drivers and making cars as low as possible. In sports cars his lowest of the low was 1964's 30, intended as the first of a family of ultra-low two-seaters. Launch stories of the new model spoke of 'a maximum speed which wind-tunnel tests suggest may be well over 200mph.' Designer of its body was Len Terry, who asserted that 'it wasn't wind-tunnel-tested while I had anything to do with it.

'It was, in effect, a smoother version of my 1962 Terrier Mark 6 sports car,' Terry said of the 30. 'Mind you, that body was a magnificent shape. Jim Clark, our New Zealand stylist – no relation to the driver – did it, but unfortunately he lived in an airy-fairy world. He had an aptitude for line and shape but forgot that wheels go up and down and the fronts also turn in and out, so he didn't provide wheel clearance. That was the only change I had to make.

'You must appreciate that aerodynamics didn't really come into race-car design until later in the '60s,' Terry added, 'when we began using wings. In '64 it was an unknown subject, basically, and we worked by guess

That the monocoque Lotus 25 achieved an almost unimaginable diminution of frontal area was dramatised by Jim Clark in Goodwood's paddock in 1965.

Above: *On the starting line at Goodwood in 1965, Graham Hill's BRM on the left showed the tucked-up underside that gave it a speed advantage over Clark's Lotus 25, at right.*

Below: *The minute dimensions of cars for the 1½-litre Formula 1 are evident on the grid at Watkins Glen in 1964, with Clark in front and Gurney towering over his Brabham.*

and by God – what looks right is right. I would think there was a lift problem with almost all sports cars of that period.' Certainly there was with the Lotus 30, which sprouted *ad hoc* whiskers and spoilers to curb its aviating tendencies.

In retrospect it can only be surprising that this situation was tolerated by Colin Chapman. He was well steeped in the value of aeronautical engineering. He'd earlier expressed his respect for Mercedes-Benz, which tunnel-tested all its post-war racing cars. Since 1961 Ferrari was exploiting the tail spoiler, a device that brought impressive aerodynamic benefits. In 1963 Ford was already using a wind tunnel to test models of its forthcoming GT40, which was launched without a spoiler but would desperately need one.

To be sure, many of these early tunnel-testing efforts suffered from inadequate simulation of the peculiar condition of a body running close to the ground. But Chapman's failure to appreciate and implement significant aerodynamic testing in the early 1960s is a puzzling gap in his *curriculum vitae*.

Drag reduction took on added importance from 1961 through to 1965 when Grand Prix cars were cut back to a mere 1½ litres and little more than 200 horsepower. Studies for BRM by the Norris brothers, famed for their work on land-speed-record cars, showed a clear advantage for front suspension that tucked the coil springs inboard out of the air stream as implemented by Chapman in the 21 of 1961. Brabham designer Ron Tauranac was sceptical, tunnel-testing inboard springs against his normal layout in Britain's Motor Industry Research Association (MIRA) tunnel and ascertaining a drag reduction of less than two per cent. This is either large or small depending upon how keen one is to gain every advantage.

In his monocoque 25 Colin Chapman achieved the minimum of frontal area in a car that seemed the epitome of drag reduction. At BRM, however, Tony Rudd claimed to have seized superiority. 'I treated ground effect as a nuisance,' he wrote, 'and deliberately gave the monocoques a V-shaped bottom like a boat. This reduced ground effect and consequent drag, hence the considerable speed advantage we enjoyed over the similar Lotus 25 and 33.' Jim Clark later told Rudd that at Reims, 'although he could hold Graham [Hill's BRM] out of Thillois on initial acceleration, it would then draw away from him and he had to pull out of the slipstream as he was in danger of over-revving.' With power from their V8s similar, BRM had gained an advantage over Lotus through aerodynamics.

Late in the Type 33's career, for the fast Italian Grand Prix at Monza in 1965, Chapman addressed this high-

Suggestions that the high nose of the Lotus 24 was detrimental to stability were supported by the lifting stance of Masten Gregory's car at Goodwood in 1962.

speed shortcoming. 'We felt that we were not as quick down the straight as we should have been,' he told Charles Bulmer, 'so we shortened the nose slightly, increased the radius on the air-intake lip, altered the outlet position and also put a complete undertray under the car. This, in fact, did give us about four miles an hour. We were in pole position at Monza in 1965 which we never were before.'

That the 33 benefited from an undertray surprised Bulmer, who thought reasonably enough that the underside of the monocoque served that purpose. Chapman explained:

One of the problems with a rear-engined car is getting the hot water and oil pipes through the cockpit area without roasting the driver or the fuel. This is something we'd had serious trouble with on the 24 and previous multi-tubular cars, where we'd put the pipes through the chassis so that the driver was sitting in an oven. Putting loose pipes up and down the chassis again wastes a lot of space. It's amazing how much space a pipe takes because you have to have clearance to mount it and each time it's put on again in a different place. So when we originally conceived the monocoque we thought it would be a jolly good idea if the pipes could be external. We had

Len Terry deliberately gave a downsloping nose to the Lotus 38 for Indianapolis in 1965. However, tests showed the new shape to be less effective than was hoped.

to get the maximum air-cooling effect and keep them away from the cockpit and the fuel area, so we put two V-section grooves in the underside for them. This tended to make the underside rather dirty with hose clips, hoses, pipes and wires, so at Monza we finally covered them all in which did reduce the drag.

Among the features of 1968's Lotus 49B were dive vanes at front and an upsweeping engine cover whose shape was modelled in clay to accord with a Chapman sketch.

Chapman and his team took a pragmatic approach to solving problems with the 25 and 33 that had aerodynamic aspects. 'Early on we found that we were in gearbox-temperature trouble,' Colin said, 'and that the best way of ameliorating the problem was to leave the tail cone off. Then, with the old cross-over exhaust system of the two-plane-crank engine, the underbonnet temperature was so high that we fried the carburettors. So we cut large holes in the side to promote airflow. We don't know whether it was coming or going. We work on the principle that if you cut a hole air will flow either into or out of it.

'When we did away with the carburettors and went to fuel injection,' Chapman continued, 'we still retained initially the high head fairing. We began to suspect that the depression behind the driver's head was sucking out hot air from under the bonnet and that in turn this was being sucked into the engine intakes. We confirmed this at Reims in 1964 by strapping an instant-reading thermometer on the air intakes and trying it with and without the engine cover in place. From that moment on we dispensed with the head fairing altogether. The actual body cowling just covers the cam boxes and then turns right down. We try to seal off heat radiating from the boxes and the heat that would blow up from the exhaust system.'

Stability was also an issue. Jack Brabham was unhappy with the aerodynamics of the Lotus 24 that he bought to race in 1962 until his own Formula 1 car was ready. 'At high speed,' wrote his engineer Ron Tauranac, 'the car was so inept that Jack couldn't even keep it in a straight line as it blasted through the grandstand complex at Reims. My guess is that the root of the Lotus's trouble was its high nose. I had always been an advocate of a low nose, so as to allow the air to bear down on the front of the car and give it some stability. With the Lotus, due to its high nose the air was getting underneath the nose and tending to lift the car, which of course was the last thing you wanted.'

In 1965 this problem was addressed by Len Terry in his design of the Indianapolis-bound Lotus 38. 'This car was the first single-seat Lotus to have a "droop-snoot",' said the designer, 'and a semi-wedge-shape body profile designed to give some aerodynamic downthrust at high speeds.' The 38's ground-snuffling nose set the style for subsequent Lotuses up to the introduction of the wedge look. It was especially prominent in the successful 49 of 1967.

The nose-down design feature was further emphasised in the changes made for 1968 to create the 49B, whose snout sprouted small adjustable dive vanes. Balancing this was a sloping engine cover, intended to reduce lift at the rear. 'One might imagine that hours of extensive wind-tunnel research had gone into determining the optimum shape and angle of attack for this engine cover,' wrote Lotus 49 historian Michael Oliver, 'but this was not so.' In fact it was the result of a modelling-clay exercise based on a sketch by Chapman, carved on the back of a 49 by mechanic Bob Dance. 'I started scraping away,' said Dance, 'and the Old Man would come along every now and then and look and say, "No, no…that's not what I meant at all!" until it was how he wanted it.'

The 49 had another aerodynamic feature that originally made its bow in 1963. 'At Spa I tried out a new type of windscreen which Colin had designed,' wrote Jim Clark, 'based I believe on a principle used on the bridges of some destroyers. This gadget trapped some of the air passing over the bonnet of the car and channelled it under the windscreen. The "funnel" which trapped this air narrowed towards its exit, forcing the air through at a high rate. The powerful jet of air thus created was directed upwards in front of the driver's face, deflecting the main blast of air, and any dust it carried, over his head. This jet of air acted, in effect, as a windscreen,' Clark added, 'without the visual obstruction which a normal windscreen presented. The real windscreen could thus be brought down below eye level, giving the driver unrestricted visibility.'

Explaining the background to this development, Colin Chapman said that 'the drivers were complaining of a lot of buffeting in the cockpit. To get the screen high enough to stop the buffeting would have reduced visibility, particularly in the corners. So we went to the slotted-type screen – a double-screen enclosing a converging passage in which the air is speeded up to emerge from the top in a high speed stream which deflects the ordinary air. It

In the foreground of a 1968 confab between Colin Chapman and Graham Hill was the slotted-type windscreen that was first fitted to the 25 during 1963.

meant that we could lower the leading edge of the screen by about two inches which improved visibility tremendously. The drivers were delighted.'

Jim Clark only practised with the new screen at Spa in 1963, perhaps for the best as it was a wet race. Later in the season he started using it in races on the way to his first world championship. 'Then at Monza in 1965 we put

Designed to create an upward curtain of air that would give its driver clear vision, the slotted screen was on the 49B being discussed by Jochen Rindt and Chapman in 1969.

In 1967 the 49 was fitted with a vee-shaped engine-oil reservoir, like that successfully introduced on the 25, to reduce aerodynamic congestion behind the radiator.

With rearwards movement of the 49B's oil tank, the addition of more space for exiting air behind its radiator allowed the latter to be reduced in size and weight.

the old screen back,' added Chapman, 'just to see if there was any measurable difference in drag. There wasn't, but the drivers said they couldn't drive with the conventional screen after they'd been used to the slotted one.' The distinctive screen was used on several later Lotus single-seater models including the 49.

Chapman evolved a special version of his air-injection screen for his Indianapolis entries, as he explained: 'At Indianapolis, which lasts for 500 miles and where speeds reach 200mph, the buffeting was intolerable. We did a lot of wind-tunnel work at MIRA. We found that there was a lot of spill-over from the sides of the screen due to the cockpit depression, so we extended the double-skinned screen round the sides. We shall do this on our Formula 1 cars this year.' By that he meant 1966; the new Type 49 of 1967 had this feature.

Internal aerodynamics in the Lotus 49B of 1968 improved after the oil tank and cooler were moved from the nose to the tail, allowing the radiator size to be reduced. A similar benefit had arisen for the 25 during its development. Seeing that the oil tank behind the radiator had only a gently curving front that blocked flow away from the radiator, Len Terry 'veed' the front of the tank and reduced its size. 'The better airflow allowed me to reduce the radiator thickness by four rows' of ten, said Terry. 'Almost 40 pounds weight was saved by these changes because of the lighter tank, smaller amount of oil, lighter radiator and reduced water volume. This was pure gain because oil and water

temperatures stayed where they had been with the old set-up.' The smaller vee-shaped tank was carried over to the 33 of 1964 and to the 49.

Radiator design also figured in the all-new Type 72 Grand Prix Lotus of 1970. Its wedge-shaped profile derived from efforts to reduce lift and add downforce, as discussed in the next chapter. To achieve this the radiator had to leave the nose. It could have been placed in the extreme rear, as tried – unsuccessfully – by Copersucar Fittipaldi in 1975. Instead the radiator was split in two and mounted in nacelles flanking the fuel tank behind the driver.

This was not the first appearance of side-mounted radiators. Several sports-racing cars had used them as had a modified Cooper of 1961. But this was the first time they'd been fitted as part of an integrated design in which they made eminent sense. Certainly the radiators and their housings added to frontal area, a Chapman bugbear, but the Ford V8's exhausts were crowding the rear tyres so the passage of air along the car's flanks was already congested. Chapman and Maurice Phillippe installed the cores inside nacelles that expanded from their entries to allow the air to decelerate before reaching the radiators.

Gradually this Lotus execution was followed by the rest of the Grand Prix field, the 72's example thus shaping the Formula 1 car of the 21st Century. At the 72's launch much was made of the 'wind-tunnel tests' that had dictated its design. This was a reference to the tests with scale models that Lotus had conducted when preparing the design of its 1968 Indy entries, tests that led to the wedge profile as described in the next chapter.

Introduction of a pair of side-mounted radiators on the 72 – Fittipaldi racing one in 1971 – ideally complemented the new Lotus's striking wedge profile.

The nacelle at the front of each 72 radiator was designed to decelerate incoming air so that it would enter the screened core at a more moderate velocity.

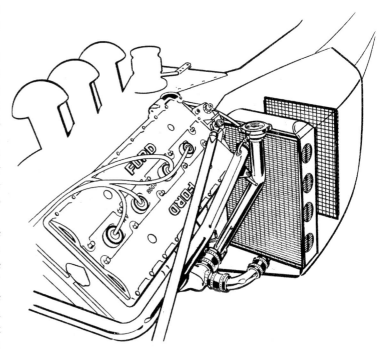

Aerodynamic development of road cars for racing, begun with the Elite, continued with the Elan, including this low-drag coupé evolution by Ian Walker Racing.

Meeting at 1972's Turin Salon, Colin Chapman and Giorgetto Giugiaro were among motordom's most creative spirits. They were the parents of the mid-engined Esprit.

Had specific tests been carried out on the 72, they would certainly have revealed turbulence over the exposed engine that degraded the effectiveness of the three-element rear wing.[9]

For the development of Lotus road cars the wind tunnels at MIRA in the English Midlands began to be used in the 1970s to ascertain both the drag and lift of scale-model and full-sized vehicles. There a baseline drag coefficient of 0.30 for the original Elite was established. As modified for the twin-cam engine the Europa measured 0.33 while the Esprit registered 0.34. Initial tests with the Esprit showed significant lift at both front and rear, so both a chin spoiler and a lip on the tail were added during development.

The 1975 Esprit, said its stylist Giorgetto Giugiaro, 'grew out of the Maserati Boomerang concept car which was pure folly really. Colin Chapman saw it and asked me to do a proposal along similar lines – that was the time when I was really beginning to push the folded-paper origami style. Of course when it was time to make the car ready for production I had to be pragmatic. In order to keep costs down the windscreen was

---

9 Michael Oliver's definitive history of the 72 makes no mention of wind-tunnel tests. However, still preserved at Classic Team Lotus is what appears to be a wind-tunnel model of a 72 in its early configuration. Its tests may not have revealed the shortcomings of the wing's positioning.

Above: *Inspired by his Maserati-engined Boomerang that had intrigued Chapman, Giugiaro rendered this design for the Esprit. Creation of styling models followed.*

Below: *True to Giugiaro's vision, the original Esprit show car was crisply executed. Compromises required for its production brought changes its designer deprecated.*

completely flat, the door handles and lamps were basic and I was never very happy with it.'

Chapman took a close personal interest in the styling evolution of the Esprit at Giugiaro's Turin studio, making key decisions including the shape of the windscreen. Twice he was accompanied by Peter Kirwan-Taylor, who recalled the trips to 'review and argue over the design concept and full-scale model with Giugiaro.' Former Lotus sales chief Robin Read credited Chapman with 'a remarkable eye for style, form and aesthetics. Hence the immortal beauty of the Climax Elite, the Lotus Eleven and the Lotus 25 plus so many others, all of which were designed by others but given their final, subtle shaping by Chapman himself.'

A new direction in the styling of Lotus road cars followed the 1965 Geneva Salon, where Fissore displayed a coupé body styled by Briton Trevor Fiore on the TVR chassis. Its sharp, rectilinear lines appealed to Chapman, who told his staff that future roadgoing Lotuses would need to have squarer, crisper styling that marked a sharp break from the Elite and Elan. Instead of Fiore, who could well have styled some striking Lotuses, former Jaguar man Oliver Winterbottom became the company's house designer in January of 1971.

Since Chapman's sight of this TVR Trident by Fiore and Fissore in 1965, he favoured crisp styling lines that he felt would aid his effort to move the Lotus range upmarket.

Winterbottom, who was responsible not only for style but also for body engineering and aerodynamics, produced as his first complete car the new Elite of 1974. This was a major move upmarket for Lotus. Previously, said Winterbottom, 'John Frayling had styled a car, but the wind-tunnel tests for John's model showed extreme lift at both axles. In March 1971 I presented a quarter-scale model that was officially adopted by the board – meaning Chapman – and full-scale design work started soon after.'

With its wedge-shaped profile and squared-off tail the new Elite polarised opinion, but functionally it was an advance for Lotus. An under-chin spoiler showed the result of tunnel testing to reduce both lift and drag. Constraints on in-house design capacity led to Giorgetto Giugiaro's design of the Elite's interior, which Oliver Winterbottom considered 'too traditional. It was also rather complex to make.'

In the meantime in Formula 1 Colin Chapman was looking for ways to get to grips with the Ferraris, which in the mid-1970s had found renewed speed with their flat-12 engine. Hitherto his attitude to aerodynamics had been surprisingly hit-and-miss. Save for his early alliance with Frank Costin and his adoption of side radiators, Chapman hadn't been a party to important innovation in exploiting the air. Now, however, he would be midwife to an historic breakthrough. He would find the answer in the harnessing of the wind in a revolutionary way.

Above: *Wind-tunnel tests of scale models by John Frayling and Oliver Winterbottom led to selection of the latter's design for the 1974 Elite, a new direction for Lotus.*

Below: *Setting a new course for Lotus road cars, the new Elite – here in its 1980 S2.2 version – was aerodynamically sound with its under-chin spoiler and truncated tail.*

Chapter 8

DISCOVERING DOWNFORCE

In the 1960s and 1970s aspiring race-car engineers and indeed anyone with a technical interest in cars hurried to the news stand to collect the latest magazine with the announcement of a new Lotus Formula 1 car. The anticipation of discovering what Colin Chapman had created this time was seldom disappointed.

Peter Wright

A new era in the application of aerodynamics to racing cars opened during two days at the end of August 1967. In co-operation with Firestone, tests were conducted at the Indianapolis Motor Speedway with a symmetrically suspended Type 38 Indy car that had been run but not qualified earlier in the year. It was equipped with transducers that measured the car's suspension movement and recorded the data on paper. 'We first produced a datum calibration line,' recalled designer Maurice Phillippe, 'and after each run we were able to gauge from the trace exactly what the relative wheel movements were.'[1]

The results astonished the Lotus men. 'The thing that staggered us more than anything,' said Colin Chapman, 'was that the lowest the car ever sat relative

A 1979 portrait by Ove Nielsen captured Colin Chapman in the midst of the ground-effect era that he and his team had launched. It brought him both glory and grief.

to the ground was when it was stationary. Even on the banking, where the extra normal load is 25 to 30 per cent of the weight of the car, it was riding above static ride level so the aerodynamic lift was something more than that. And all these years we'd been designing the suspension so that when it really sat down on the banking it would still be as required.

'For some time we had been feeling that the cars weren't behaving the way they should,' Chapman continued, with 'relatively small changes having disproportionate effects. We were getting a lot of nose lift at Indianapolis and we were finding it terribly difficult to get the car into the turn at 160–170mph. The normal weight transfer effect when you change from acceleration to braking was magnified by the nose-up, nose-down change of attitude which completely alters the lift and therefore the weight distribution.'[2]

This gave Chapman and Phillippe a lot to think about in the design of their 1968 Indianapolis entries, which were to be powered by gas turbines. They prepared quarter-scale models for testing in MIRA's small wind tunnel. 'We did a lot of work on basic body shapes and their effect on pitch and yaw,' said Chapman. They

---

1   Chapman told Charles Bulmer that 'what I was trying to arrange with Firestone was some sort of electronic measuring device to fit on a wheel hub and measure the actual distance from the wheel hub to the road surface to see how much [a tyre] grows and how much of this could be attributed to centrifugal tyre growth and how much to reduction in weight, but I haven't really got around to that. And, of course, it would be necessary to produce a suspension where you didn't have any real camber change, otherwise that would destroy the whole experiment.'

2   It will be noted that this effect was being measured on the Type 38, which Len Terry had already given a more downsloping nose than its predecessors as related in the previous chapter. Contrary to Terry's assertion the reshaped nose didn't dissuade the Lotus from being lifted by aerodynamic effects.

evaluated some 30 different configurations. 'We started to concentrate on minimum lift rather than minimum drag although quite often the two are interrelated insofar as a lot of the drag is induced drag [drag due to lift]. We tried to evolve a body shape which would produce the maximum amount of negative lift but also with an acceptable pitching moment which is very important. This is how we arrived at the wedge shape which does work very well from this point of view.' The wedge profile of his Lotus 56 was destined to dominate thinking both at Indy and, later, in Formula 1 for the next few years.

Validated in tunnel trials of models, the wedge design of the Lotus 56 for Indy in 1968 was a response to 1967 tests at the Speedway that showed surprising amounts of lift.

In 1956 Swiss engineer Michael May and a colleague fitted this downforce-generating wing to their Porsche Spyder. High-level official objections kept them from racing it.

In mid-September 1966, just under a year before the revelatory Indy tests, the racing world first saw another new way of exploiting aerodynamics when Texan Jim Hall decanted his brace of Type 2D Chaparrals at Bridgehampton on New York's Long Island. Here for the first time was a racing car with a high-mounted wing whose support struts were attached to its rear-wheel uprights. A joint invention of Jim Hall with Chevrolet engineers Frank Winchell, Jim Musser and Jerry Mrlik, the wing was designed to apply added downforce directly to the rear tyres without the intermediary of the sprung bodywork. The driver used a foot pedal to feather the wing to reduce drag on straights.

Because the high-mounted wings proved fragile, so much so that their supports broke in the truck on the way to Bridgehampton, the 2D scored only one victory in its 1966 season. Can-Am rivals were slow to copy the Chaparral innovation, partly for lack of the necessary engineering know-how and partly because some, like McLaren, didn't want to be seen copying arch-rival Jim Hall. Nor were Grand Prix teams fast off the mark in exploiting high-mounted wings.

First to use a wing to generate downforce for a Formula 1 car was Ferrari, in 1968. In 1963–64 a Swiss engineer, Michael May, was a consultant to Ferrari on its successful adoption of Bosch direct fuel injection to its racing engines. May had been the first to exploit a downforce wing in circuit racing (as distinct from record-breaking). His privately entered Porsche 550 Spyder went so quickly in practice at a 1956 Nürburgring sports-car race that the Porsche team manager supported those who argued successfully for the removal of its big wing. May mentioned the function and the success of this device to Ferrari's chief racing-car engineer Mauro Forghieri.

Early in 1968 in New Zealand, during practice for the Tasman-series race at Invercargill, Ferrari engineer Gianni Marelli witnessed experiments with a primitive

Made by Bruce Crower, this wing was fitted to Smokey Yunick's Indy car in 1962. Its inappropriate design created much more drag than downforce so it wasn't raced.

wing fitted to a Lotus 49 driven by Jim Clark. At the end of November 1967 Clark had driven a car built by Rolla Vollstedt in an Indy-car race at Riverside, California. While a few cars had vestigial rear spoilers, Vollstedt had equipped his with a substantial free-standing wing-like deflector. Flying down under to race in the Tasman series, Clark told the Lotus crew how impressed he was with the deflector's influence.

Responding to Jim Clark's enthusiasm, the mechanics scrounged a helicopter rotor blade from Christchurch airport and cut off a section, about the width of the Ford V8, which they mounted to the frame on two side struts and a third one to the rear, adjustable to allow the angle of attack to be varied. Clark only drove the car briefly in this configuration because Chapman forbade its running as soon as he heard about this unauthorised modification of his design.

While Indy in 1968 saw the arrival of the door-stop-shaped 56, Colin Chapman's approach to the aerodynamics of his Grand Prix car produced the 49B with its nose-mounted dive vanes and its serendipitously sculpted engine cover. In fact he had wanted to build a 'wedge' Grand Prix car as well at the time, he told Charles Bulmer and Philip Turner: 'Having got a body shape that works reasonably well – and it's not easy to copy it quickly because you've got to design a whole car and suspension around the body – we thought we'd build our Formula 1 wedge and have a season while

everybody was trying to copy it. But events overtook us and we couldn't build it in time.'[3]

In the meantime Ferrari's Mauro Forghieri had been mulling over the potential of a wing. He and his team engineered, built and mounted a small but aerodynamically sound wing on the rollover bar of their 312 F1 and tested it early in 1968. The results were good enough for two of the team's cars to appear with wings at Spa in Belgium for the Grand Prix on 9 June. On this fast circuit, where the wing would have maximum effect, both Ferraris qualified on the front row of the grid. One raced without its wing but the other, driven by Chris Amon, used it in the race – marking the first deployment of a downforce-generating wing in Formula 1 competition.

During the rest of the 1968 season the Ferrari team experimented with various positions and heights for its wing to gain the best overall benefit. For the Italian Grand Prix at Monza Ferrari introduced hydraulic controls which allowed the angle of incidence of the

---

3 In fact he did manage a modified-wedge Formula 1 car in the shape of 1969's 63, which with the Indianapolis 64 – both cars with four-wheel drive – imposed a huge workload on Lotus and its suppliers. The solid-axle Type 57 also represented a potential wedge-shaped Formula 1 car.

wing to be changed by the driver. Like the Chaparral counterpart it could be left in full-downforce position for turns and then feathered by the driver to reduce its drag on the straights.

Although Ferrari tested rear wings whose struts were attached directly to the hub carriers, it preferred to race with less-fragile chassis-mounted wings. The potential for danger that high hub-mounted wings could offer was clear to Mauro Forghieri, who organised a meeting with other makers of Grand Prix cars to discuss a possible agreement on banning them. Enzo Ferrari was willing to give them up but the others weren't.

Colin Chapman responded quickly to this new paradigm. He was no stranger to wings, he said, having tested some in the wind tunnel along with the work that led to the wedge shape. 'We did do some airfoils at that stage,' he said, 'and we realised that they were much more efficient at producing downloads but they weren't legal at Indianapolis so we had to try to get the same results from the body shape.'

In the second race after Spa, the French GP on the Rouen circuit, Chapman's cars appeared as the 49B Mark II with huge rear wings on struts that were

A wing mounted on struts from its rear hubs was part of the design of the 1966 Chaparral 2D, whose novel features rivalled Chapman's creations for innovation.

mounted to the rear hubs. Although the rules affecting body width at the time constrained their size within the inner edges of the tyres, Chapman reckoned that this didn't apply to wings so his were considerably wider. In practice, however, Jackie Oliver's Lotus crashed heavily. Whether the collapse of the wing was cause or effect wasn't easily discerned at the time.

Downforce was just the job at the twisty Brands Hatch track for the British GP on 20 July, where Oliver and Graham Hill were first and second on the grid. Victory went to a private 49B driven by Jo Siffert, also fitted with a high rear wing. The wet German Grand Prix was inconclusive and the fast Monza circuit didn't favour the use of wings. In the last three races of the year, however, the starting grids were forests of high wings, some (not Lotus) adding them at the front as well.

Monza, Watkins Glen and Kyalami, at the beginning of 1969, found Mario Andretti added to the Lotus strength. 'If there was no limit' to the height of a wing, Andretti recalled, 'obviously the higher the better, the cleaner the air. That's Colin, you know! He always understood all that. We used to have a fourth pedal on the left of the clutch where you could feather the wing. Down the straight you could just use your left foot to press on that pedal and that would trim the wing out. It was almost like having an overdrive gear.'

Feathering the wing was Colin Chapman's re-invention more than two years later of the system

Above: *With victory in a six-hour race at Brands Hatch in 1967 by Phil Hill and Mike Spence, the Chaparral 2F rubbed British noses in the merit of a high-mounted rear wing.*

Below: *His new 2H not yet ready, Jim Hall raced his Chaparral 2G in 1968's Can-Am series with wider wheels and tyres. Its wing pylons were well engineered.*

used by Jim Hall on his 2D Chaparral, whose wing was so big that leaving it in the downforce position would have imposed excessive drag. It was first tried in the high altitude of 1968's Mexican Grand Prix as Jackie Oliver explained: 'Because the air is thin there, you had to run a lot of incidence, meaning the wings were at a steep angle to be effective. But Mexico also had long straights where the wings would slow you down. So Colin said, "Lads, what we're going to do is lower the wings on the straights and we'll put them up again in the corners."'

'We did it, literally there, in the garage,' Bob Dance told Michael Oliver. 'We took the wings to pieces, moved the static pivot point to a dynamic pivot point – which was a fabrication job – and then reskinned the wing. We fitted a Bowden cable and made up a little pedal, and then there were springs which were bungee straps on the wing to counteract the downforce. The Old Man reckoned that we'd pick up 200 or 300rpm. It was not a lot but it would give us a little edge. But it took about 14 hours work by four people to do it.' Though one of the bungee cords broke early in the Mexican race, the modified 49B was Graham Hill's race winner, bringing him the world championship.

A better-engineered wing-feathering system was used from the start of the 1969 season, including the Tasman Series. A problem, however, was that the reversion to

Looking modest by later standards, a wing was introduced to Formula 1 by Ferrari on its 312 F1 in 1968. Hydraulic control allowed driver adjustment of its incidence.

the high-downforce setting imposed severe loads on the support struts, said Mario Andretti: 'When you got down to the braking point, when the wing would take the maximum pitch it would be such a jolt that it could collapse the wing support tubes. We saw a couple of them collapse with dramatic results. One time I got away with it was at the end of the straight in Kyalami, under braking. That could have been a total disaster for me because there wasn't much of a run-off at the end of the straight. It was probably much more downforce than Chapman ever calculated, and the wing just didn't have strong enough struts to support it.'

Over the 1968–69 winter Colin Chapman mused about his wing-related findings to Philip Turner and Charles Bulmer. 'We haven't actually measured the effective lift/drag ratio of the airfoil as fitted on a car,' he said. 'We work on the lift/drag ratios of the base airfoil section and calculate it that way. But the drag seems to be significantly higher than is shown from the pure calculation which predicts around 400 pounds of download at 150mph with only about 4½ drag horsepower. Well, we seem to lose more on the straight than that – about double that – and I don't see why the little verticals that hold the thing up should add all that much.'

What about changes in downloads when following another car? 'We don't know the full effect of this,' Chapman admitted. 'When we first ran with the wing at Rouen and Jackie Oliver had his shunt – which could have been attributed to loss of effect from the wing due

to the slipstream of another car – we then mounted the wing a lot higher and since then the drivers haven't complained about any really bad effect. They say they notice when they get into the slipstream of another car but it isn't disastrous and doesn't catch them unawares any more. The main thing is not to rely on its full effect when you're really in close company with someone going through a very fast corner.

'We haven't got down to a full analysis of the situation yet.' Chapman added. 'The biggest argument against airfoils which people advance at the moment is that when the car starts going sideways it loses the effect of the wing, but that means the driver's lost it anyway. Let's face it, there are a lot of other bits of the car that don't work as well when it's going sideways – the tyres for instance haven't anything like the adhesion. The suspension will get into a roll position so that your contact patch is nowhere near where it should be – in all designs basically if you optimise the thing for one set of circumstances it tends to become less effective in other circumstances. I don't see that this is a valid criticism of the fact that you are using airfoils. You may as well say you've lost adhesion once you get off the concrete on to the grass so let's not allow grass.'

Working closely as he was in these years on tyre development with Firestone, Chapman was well aware of the advances that wings allowed him to exploit. 'The more load you put on, the more cornering power you get,' he said. 'This is what made the airfoil possible. In

In Grand Prix racing Chapman was the first to fit a high wing attached directly to the rear uprights, as jointly pioneered two years earlier by Chevrolet and Chaparral.

the old days if you loaded a car to the extent we are doing now you'd get less cornering power rather than more. This, I think, is where some of the Japanese are wrong – they think it is disadvantageous to continue to load the outer wheel and are trying to put their aerodynamic load on the inside wheel only. This is not really necessary because you haven't got near the peak of the curve' of the tyre's increase in grip in relation to downward pressure on its contact patch.

Twilight of the big high wings followed the second race of 1969 on the Montjuich circuit in a public park in the heart of Barcelona. In the early running the Lotuses of Jochen Rindt and Graham Hill – both qualifying on the front row using wings that had been extended at both ends – crashed into the Armco barriers as the result of wing failures. 'One of the drawbacks was that the aerodynamic oval tubing that Colin was using for the uprights was never as strong laterally,' observed Mario Andretti. Later in the Spanish race the rear wing of Jacky Ickx's Brabham buckled.

Although the teams arrived at Monaco four weeks later with wings erect, rulings based on safety banned them for the race. Henceforth wings were only allowed if they were an integral part of the bodywork. For the Monaco race the Lotus mechanics fabricated a likeness

Visible in 1968 on Jo Siffert's bouncing Walker-stable Lotus 49B were the stresses that racing imposed on the supports of the big wings used by Chapman.

In March of 1969 at the Brands Hatch Race of Champions all the F1 cars wore substantial wings, several even doubling up with wings at the front as well as the rear.

of the ducktail that had been introduced on the 49B for 1968 but then abandoned during the brief and hectic high-wing era. Short of aluminium to make the deck, they scavenged some from the interior of their racing transporter.

Starting with the Dutch GP in June of 1969 the team's 49Bs were fitted with wings mounted to the frame at

the rear, establishing with others the look of the modern Grand Prix car. Later similar wings were fitted to the four-wheel-drive 63s, on which they were more effective because the Lotus's engine, mounted further forward to suit its transmission, was less in the way of airflow to the wing. During the season end plates were added to the wings to increase their effectiveness, those on the 63 being the largest.

Meanwhile the Chapman-Phillippe team was producing its fully-fledged response to the wing ban, the 72, which made its bow in 1970. Derived directly from the Indy Type 56 of 1968, its wedge profile was intended to defeat lift. Downforce would come from a new three-element rear wing and adjustable dive vanes flanking the nose.[4] 'It was immediately obvious that the Lotus 72 belonged to a new generation of cars,' said Ted Simon in his book about the 1970 season. 'Like a Concorde among Boeings it belonged to a class of its own.'

Bourne-based BRM, the racing team owned by the Owen Organisation, took a different approach to the wing issue. BRM's first wings were designed by a Cambridge graduate who had joined the team in 1967, Peter Wright. He was put to this task by BRM technical chief Tony Rudd, who arranged for Wright to liaise on the project with legendary engineer Sir Barnes Wallis. Wright quietly got on with this interesting job, using the quarter-scale wind tunnel at London's Imperial College to test his designs, the first of which appeared late in the 1968 season.

Early in the winter of 1968–69 Tony Rudd became uneasy about the high wings and their failures, said Wright: 'He asked me whether it would be possible to generate downforce without the use of separately mounted wings.' Assuming that the entire plan area of the car's body was available and producing downforce, Wright calculated that it could be much less efficient than a rear wing yet capable of the same amount of downforce.

'Tony Rudd agreed that a wind-tunnel programme should investigate the possibilities in greater depth,' Wright continued. 'Working with chassis designer Alec Osborn, I drew an inverted-airfoil-shaped body with a slender central fuselage for driver and engine. Internal radiators were fed by NACA intakes while nose wings and a trailing-edge flap permitted the overall downforce and its distribution to be adjusted. Wind-tunnel tests at the Imperial College indicated that overall downforce would be similar to that of a winged car.' With this came

In 1968 – as here on a Brabham – and early in 1969 collapses of wings and their supports were alarmingly frequent. This ultimately led to their prohibition.

the bonus that the drag caused by the generation of downforce would be significantly less.[5]

On his return from the South African GP at the beginning of March 1969 Tony Rudd 'found Peter Wright in a state of suppressed excitement.' Wright explained his promising tunnel findings to Rudd, who was 'rather sceptical that he had managed to get so much from an open-wheeled car, and suggested further tests which he rushed off to perform. Peter's results from his second set of tests were even better than the first, so I had to decide what to do next. Obviously we had to build such a car.'

These early months of 1969 coincided with changes at the top of BRM. Raymond Mays, the BRM founder who had long managed driver affairs, was shunted aside in favour of author and racing-safety pioneer Louis Stanley, who was married to Jean, sister of company chief Sir Alfred Owen. The Stanleys recruited 1964 world champion John Surtees, who was on the rebound after two frustrating seasons with Honda. Surtees joined BRM at the beginning of 1969 on the condition that 'the team planned a down-to-earth, straightforward race programme.' Understandably enough this meant total dedication to the cars to be driven by John Surtees.

4   The new design of rear wing was also used on the Type 49 during its run-out season of 1970.

5   These results were achieved without the side skirts and fences that were used on later ground-effect cars. In the wind tunnel Wright did see added downforce with little increase in drag by fitting the model's wings with side plates.

Above: *At Monaco in 1969, the first race after high wings were banned, panels cadged from the Lotus transporter's interior completed a spoiler for Graham Hill's winning 49B.*

Below: *Continuing with adjustable dive vanes attached to the nosepiece, from mid-1969 Lotus fitted substantial chassis-mounted rear wings with end plates.*

Tony Rudd soon realised that life with Surtees wouldn't be easy. During an early visit by the driver to Bourne for his seat fitting, said Rudd, 'he did not say much but it was obvious that he was not impressed.' After Surtees questioned long-established fuel-injection practice at Bourne, Rudd found himself overruled. How should he handle BRM's demanding and well-connected Number One driver in relation to his plan to build a radical new car? Rudd's decision was to keep it secret. 'If Surtees hears about this he'll only bad-mouth it,' he told a colleague.

Late in March Rudd set up a secret 'skunk works' in a rented machine shop on Exeter Street on the other side of Bourne. While Osborn completed the car's drawings at Bourne, Rudd installed Wright, a panel-beater and a welder to get on with building a car with the Italian Grand Prix in September as their target. He told all concerned 'to keep their mouths shut. If the car was as good as the wind-tunnel results, we would have a few months to make a killing before everyone copied it.' He would also have some explaining to do to John Surtees. When strut-mounted wings were banned at Monaco in 1969, Rudd knew that he was sitting on a gold mine of an idea.

While work on the wing car was progressing Peter Wright tried fitting one of the existing BRMs, the P126, with 'stubby, airfoil-section panniers, bolted to the sides of the monocoque to try to replicate the new car.' If they worked they were also a possible replacement for the banned wings. Although Wright recorded that subsequent tests of the podded car at Snetterton 'were inconclusive due to a lack of measurement equipment,' Tony Rudd averred that 'the side pods had little effect' with Jackie Oliver doing the testing.

Though Alec Osborn didn't attend the test his view as well was that they were inconclusive. 'The attachments were rather flimsy and on reflection very sensitive to position in both height and longitudinal location. I suspect that the transfer of any downforce through this fragile arrangement needed further development.' With the tests being interrupted by the alarming explosion of an experimental high-silicon-aluminium brake disc, the results didn't deter work on the radical new BRM.

By June of 1969 good progress was evident. The tub, with its rear longerons alongside the BRM V12, was almost complete. Radiators were inside the side pods, which were being skinned in aluminium. Wright and Osborn were working on diversion of the radiators' warm exhaust air from the engine's induction system, which wanted cool air. Some engine changes may have been needed to get the best from the radical new design.

Matters came to a head before the Dutch GP at Zandvoort on 21 June, the first race after the banning of wings at Monaco. Surtees was sniffing that something was up, said Rudd: 'It was clear that he had noticed the absence of some of the key people now in Peter Wright's team.' Called to a meeting at Zandvoort, Rudd was told by the Stanleys that 'whatever project I had running on Exeter Street at Bourne was to stop at once and the staff returned to their regular work.' Mere days after the Zandvoort meeting Rudd resigned, ending almost 19 years at BRM. Chapman had a job waiting for him at Lotus.

Only after Rudd's departure did John Surtees find out exactly what had been going on at Exeter Street. 'He was extremely unhappy to discover the existence of the project,' recalled Alec Osborn. 'He demanded the shop's immediate closing. Everything was scrapped. The real issue was that he hadn't known about it. As the Number One driver he probably should have!'

So much for BRM's wing-car project. Had John Surtees nipped a promising new initiative in the bud? It seems so. In his autobiography Surtees acknowledged his discovery that Wright 'already had all these drawings for a ground-effect car,' but claimed that 'BRM's budget was too restrictive for him to be allowed a free hand, so it was agreed that Peter Wright's concept would be something of a second-stage development of the P139' – the new Osborn-designed conventional car that BRM was just launching. The second stage never arrived. At the end of August both Osborn and Wright left Bourne.

Peter Wright's next stop was Specialised Mouldings, set up by Peter Jackson to make bodywork for racing cars including those of Huntingdon neighbour Lola. 'One of the first tasks I was given,' Wright said, 'was to work with Robin Herd, chief designer of the new March company, on the design of bodywork for its Formula 1, 2 and 3 cars. The Formula 1 car, the March 701, needed additional fuel capacity in certain races, and I suggested inverted-airfoil-shaped side tanks. Robin Herd agreed.'

'At that time there was a terrific differential in the fuel required from race to race,' said Robin Herd, 'so add-on tanks were a good idea.' In its central and side tanks, within its monocoque, the 701 carried 34 gallons of fuel. To carry more fuel Wright suggested that foam-filled bag tanks, each holding eight gallons, be fitted into bulges that would be permanent features of the side bodywork, to bring total capacity up to 50 gallons. Based on his recent work at BRM, Wright proposed shaping these bulges as inverted airfoils.

'Peter recommended this idea,' said Robin Herd, 'and it worked. There was no doubt that we were getting some benefit from the pods. We might have found a little additional downforce and it certainly carried extra fuel without a drag penalty.' However any hope of serious downforce from the wings, in Herd's view, 'was wasted by the fact that the rest of the design was fairly messy with the springs in the slipstream and so on.' Nevertheless he later reflected that 'here was this new concept, staring us in the face, and we were never in a position to realise it fully. It was just that we had so many other things to concentrate on.'

The introduction of the March 701, a completely new car from an ambitious new company building a wide range of racing cars, was a minor sensation. Although its designer Robin Herd called his 701 'dead boring, really.' its side-tank bulges were distinctive. The March press release described them as 'low aspect ratio side wings along monocoque designed for optimum performance in turbulent conditions.' Its author, March's Max Mosley, called his description of the stunted wings' function as 'absolute rubbish, but we were living on hype.'

Not quite 'absolute rubbish', it turned out. None other than Mario Andretti testified that the stubby wings were effective. During a tyre test at the high altitude of Kyalami in South Africa, Andretti suggested that the engine's power loss in the thinner air could perhaps be

Augmenting the downforce expected from its wedge shape, the 72 had front dive vanes and a three-element rear wing mounted close to the engine.

compensated for by removing the drag of the side pods. 'Why don't we take those off and see what reaction we get out of the car?' he suggested to his STP-sponsored team.

'So we did that,' Andretti continued, 'and my straight-line speed didn't change at all. However I noticed that I lost some front-end downforce. We lost direction entirely, like suddenly I needed 2½ degrees extra front wing. So I knew they were working. Even though the pods were between the wheelbase – and you would think that we should have got just overall downforce – the pods actually moved the centre of pressure forward and affected the front end more than the back.' Magpie that he was for useful racing insights, Andretti didn't forget this experiment.

With the March 701 turning out to have little long-term development potential, its design features were ignored by the other runners. Instead, with the burgeoning success of the 72, the 'Chapman wedge' was the speed secret to have. It was soon copied by McLaren, for both Indy and GP racing, and evident in new designs from BRM, March, Brabham and even Ferrari.

Popularity of the 'wedge' look didn't escape the attention of Mike Warner, in charge of Lotus Components, the company arm that made cars for lesser categories. 'Chapman always left me to get on with my thing,' said Warner, 'and to be fair to him I work

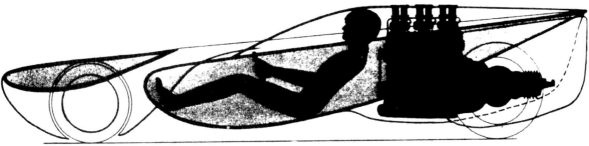

best like that. I had a design team of Dave Baldwin and Martin Waide, who was ex-Team Lotus – diminutive and very, very clever. He designed the Type 70. Dave Baldwin designed the Type 60, the 59 and the 69.

'It was totally my marketing philosophy to do the wedge-shaped Formula Ford because of the success of the Indy car,' added Warner, referring to the Type 61, which had its cooling radiator canted sharply forward to give it a chisel-sharp nose. 'America was the market that I was aiming at.' The 61 was never within miles of a wind tunnel, he added: 'Aerodynamically it made no bloody difference at all – it just looked good. It was a bit of a wedge of cheese. With the speeds that were around in those days in Formula Ford, you were only just beginning to get to the stage where aerodynamics had an effect.

'We built a huge number of them,' Mike Warner recalled. 'We had a flow line which at one point in time was pumping out twenty-five a week. The 61M – which was M for modified – was a far better car. We got rid of the engine cover at the rear and made it a lot smaller and lowered the profile so it became a narrower wedge.

In 1967 Berlin-born Luigi Colani envisaged a racing car of inverted-wing design. He was on the right track, although like the BRM engineers he hadn't twigged the importance of side skirts to manage underbody airflow.

It was a better-balanced car. At one point we won all the European Championships – we won the lot – and the International Championship. We really put Lotus Components back on the map.'

Introduced for the 1970 season, Martin Waide's Formula A/5000 Type 70 started out as a pure wedge with a razor-sharp nose thanks to the mounting of its engine-cooling radiator behind the engine above the transaxle. Testing, however, showed that this cooled inadequately so the radiator was moved to the nose, angled at only 30 degrees from the horizontal to preserve a sloping front deck. Though not the most successful Lotus, the 70 did enjoy some wins for George Follmer in the USA using Boss Mustang horsepower.

Meanwhile experimentation by a talented Brazilian was advancing the state of the art of wings to produce downforce. Starting in 1970 Emerson Fittipaldi raced

Tasked in late 1968 by BRM's Tony Rudd to ascertain whether downforce could be generated without wings, Peter Wright began testing a model of this configuration.

Testing early in 1969 in the Imperial College tunnel, with its moving ground plane, showed promising results for the BRM model with its rising sponsors on both sides.

Lotuses in Formula 2, driving Dave Baldwin's 69. In 1972 he was still active in F2 with the 69 but as a private venture. 'The car belonged to Lotus but I was running the team,' Fittipaldi related. 'There were no Lotus people involved because it was a private team.' Assisting Emerson and his brother Wilson was Brazilian engineer Ricardo Divila.

They began experimenting with the rear wing, designing their own airfoils and mounts. Starting out, said Emerson, 'the car was understeering terribly on fast corners and oversteering too much on slow corners. I put the wing *right* back, completely beyond the limit of where it should be, just to see what happened. And then I had different positions to move it forward to get the right position. One thing that we found that was good was that we could have much less frontal area. Because the wing worked like a lever, so far behind the wheels. And in cleaner air. The problem was to keep the front down because the lever was behind the rear wheels. What we found was that we could make a smaller rear wing, to have the same effect, and then we had to change the front wings too.'

By 1972 Colin Chapman was beginning to have more faith in the ideas and opinions of his young Brazilian driver. 'I spoke to Colin,' Emerson recalled, 'and said, "I would like to try the Formula 2 wing because I've had this experience in Formula 2. Moving it backward you have more effect and you can have less frontal area." He

said, "What? A Formula 2 wing on our Formula 1 car?" They didn't want to try it. I said, "Please, just take it along to try it." It was a yellow wing; they painted it black! We tried it at Nivelles and I raced and I won with the Formula 2 wing!'

Though much smaller than the 72's usual wing, the airfoil developed by Fittipaldi's team functioned in a much more wing-like manner thanks to its greater separation from the car's machinery. This helped Emerson dominate the proceedings at Nivelles in Belgium with both pole and victory. Seizing on the successful idea, Chapman began moving the wing even more to the rear. He also conceived a flexible-rubber mounting, fitting invisibly inside the wing, that allowed it to feather itself automatically at high speed. Contravening the new rule that barred movable aerodynamic devices, the flexi-wing gave a useful high-speed dividend until it was rumbled by an attentive Jack Brabham.[6]

The rear-wing improvements were among the many refinements that made the 72 one of the most successful Grand Prix cars ever conceived. But it was forced to race much longer than expected because the model built in 1974 to replace it, the 76, didn't work. Chapman and

---

6   For 1972's British Grand Prix, a crucial home event for Lotus and sponsor John Player, bracing struts were added from the rear of the wing to the gearbox to suggest a rigid mounting. In fact the 'struts' were telescopic so had no deterrent effect on the wing's self-feathering.

Phillippe had designed the 72 to take advantage of the special tyres that Firestone provided. A switch to Goodyear for 1973 was initially successful but the American company soon began to tailor its tyre designs to the needs of other teams, especially a resurgent McLaren. 'The 72 had worked fine as long as we could obtain the tyres designed for it,' Chapman said. 'Once we found ourselves building up cars to suit what tyres we could get, we were in trouble.'

In 1973 Lotus won the Formula 1 constructors' championship though Emerson Fittipaldi was pipped for the drivers' title by Jackie Stewart, having shared wins with team-mate Ronnie Peterson. In 1974, however, Lotus dropped to fourth among constructors, headed by McLaren, Ferrari and Tyrrell. Peterson and Jacky Ickx were struggling with both the 72 and 76. In 1975 the position was even worse with both Peterson and Ickx departing and other drivers drafted in to make the running, including John Watson, Brian Henton and Jim Crawford. Lotus plummeted to seventh among constructors after finishing in the points in only four of 14 races.

A reduction in support from sponsor John Player was only part of the reason for the Lotus decline. The main cause was that Colin Chapman's energies were being applied elsewhere. At Lotus Cars the company's own four-cylinder engine was being created, the task Chapman had assigned to Tony Rudd in 1969. The Elite and Eclat were being developed for launch in 1974 and 1975 respectively. Requiring much of Chapman's attention, the mid-engined Esprit made its bow in 1975.

An additional burden on Chapman's time had arisen. After one of his corporate arms acquired a Norfolk pleasure-boat company, Moonraker Marine, in 1971 Colin applied himself with his usual diligence to learning all about the maritime industry. Plastic technologies for both cars and boats were provided by another Chapman company, Technocraft Ltd. Its head from 1974 was Peter Wright, recruited to the job from Specialised Mouldings.

Small wonder that the Formula 1 effort failed to command its traditional share of Colin Chapman's attention. 'When he was distracted, as at one time he was by his boat-building business, the team suffered tremendously,' said a driver who hadn't given up on Chapman, Mario Andretti. 'After Long Beach in 1976 Chapman was somewhat down.[7] At breakfast I said to him that if he gave 100 per cent and let the boats go to someone else, I would give 100 per cent.'

BRM's Peter Wright and Alec Osborn used small nose wings and an adjustable rear flap to trim their proposed 1969 car, whose downforce was less 'draggy' than wings.

Foreseeing the look of ground-effect cars to come, the BRM engineers provided generous space at the rear for air to exit from the racing car's underbody.

In fact the engineer, stung by Lotus's 1974 results and the poor start to the 1975 season, had already decided to right his racing ship.[8] He described the turning point to biographer Gerard Crombac: 'It was in Ibiza, in August 1975, when I was there on holiday. I was sunbathing at the time and thinking about various ideas and in my mind I drew up some lines of investigation that I thought were necessary in order to decide what

---

7   One Lotus 77 failed to qualify (Bob Evans) and the other (Gunnar Nilsson) started dead last and crashed out on the first lap after a suspension breakage. Andretti too had retired, driving a Vel's Parnelli entry. It was a sign of their mutual respect that the two men breakfasted after the race.

8   Chapman never did voluntarily let the boats go to someone else, but his loss of interest in the company contributed to Moonraker's voluntary liquidation in 1980.

Asked by March to provide extra fuel capacity for its 1970 Type 701 GP car, Peter Wright recommended and designed side pods that were shaped as inverted airfoils.

could be done to produce a negative pressure beneath the car which was greater than that above it. Then, if you could do that, it would produce the stabilising forces necessary to hold the car down on the road without the need for wings.'

In this later recollection Chapman overstated the insights that he brought back on his personal plane from Ibiza, leaping ahead – as was his wont – to the end result. In fact, as the main text of the dossier in the page 261 sidebar shows, he brought back more questions than answers. Playing an important role in finding the answers was Ketteringham Hall, a remodelled 15th-Century stately home that had been headquarters to the American Second Air Force during World War II. A mile and a half north of Lotus at Hethel, the multi-roomed mansion had been a school until it was bought by one of the Lotus companies and leased to Team Lotus, which by now was a separate business.

'Ketteringham Hall was a quiet environment,' said designer Martin Ogilvie. 'The drawing office was in the old orangery. You could walk out of the door and stroll down to the lake, which was a fantastic environment for being creative. Ketteringham Hall also encompassed boat-design people, so it was really quite fun up there. It was all youngsters, fighting for position

in the company, supercharged people, with Colin Chapman driving us on like mad, churning out boats and racing cars. He certainly was an amazing bloke to work with.'

Colin Chapman's office in the Hall was the scene for a meeting with Tony Rudd after the Lotus chief's return from Ibiza. 'He gave me the armchair and sherry treatment,' said Rudd, 'which was always dangerous. He handed me a 27-page folder in his neat handwriting saying, "You have had a long enough holiday from Formula 1. It's time you got down to some serious work." He listed all the unknown factors – as far as he was concerned – for the design of an F1 car. "When you have all these answers we will know how to build a good car."

'I was sent away,' Rudd continued, 'to read the 27 pages, prepare a programme to obtain the answers, together with the names of the project team I needed. I asked for Peter Wright, as most of the questions involved aerodynamics, Charlie Prior to make the models and Ralph Bellamy to draw my schemes.'[9] Chapman was shocked by the request for Wright, who was running an important company in the group, but he had to acquiesce. Wright brought in the Imperial College's Frank Irving as an aerodynamics consultant.

With their focus on aerodynamic research to provide what Chapman called 'maximum non-dead-weight

---

9 A reading of the dossier shows that most of the questions did not in fact involve aerodynamics, but those that did certainly demanded the kind of testing that Rudd put in train.

FORMULA FORD WEDGE FROM LOTUS

At Lotus Components, Mike Warner lost no time in exploiting the radical wedge look of the 56 Indy cars with his 1968 introduction of the 61 for the popular Formula Ford.

download, ie aerodynamics,' the team used the Imperial College quarter-scale tunnel in the evenings, both to stay out of the way of daily activity and to preserve confidentiality. 'We used to have a big session at Imperial College on Friday night,' said Tony Rudd, 'and then be back at Ketteringham Hall on Saturday morning to compare notes. At about 10:30 am Colin used to come in. We'd tell him what we'd found and what we thought we needed.' But Rudd knew better than to reveal prematurely what they'd learned: 'We didn't tell Colin about anything until we were pretty sure of what we'd found, because once he'd got the idea into his head, he would move the whole caboodle full speed in that direction.'

One of Colin Chapman's objectives for the new car, said Peter Wright, was to make it 'aerodynamically more pitch-sensitive than the 72,' which was suffering from inadequate front-end grip. 'He believed that if the downforce on the front increased under braking, it would improve turn-in.'[10] An associated aim was to get more heat into the front Goodyears. The 77 had only begun to perform after its front brakes were moved outboard where their heat could contribute to tyre warming.

The researchers' first step was to model the 72 to

serve as a baseline for the testing. Subsequent work was based on a slender new fuselage designed by Bellamy to carry driver, fuel and Ford V8. The final design would carry fuel both centrally and in the car's side pods. After a wide chisel nose was eliminated as giving too much drag for the downforce it generated, wind-tunnel work concentrated on a narrow nose with airfoils at the front of Bellamy's central core.

An invaluable feature of the Imperial College tunnel was that it had a ground plane that moved, simulating the effect of the road under the car. A rubber belt, it began to lift under the nose wings. To counter this the Lotus team rigged suction under the belt to hold it down. After this was done, Rudd reported, 'we confirmed that an inverted aerofoil close to the road had its effect magnified by the interaction with the road, particularly if used with end plates. We discovered that if we moved the nose airfoil closer to the road surface, say to within six inches at full scale, the downforce it produced increased dramatically. When we reduced the gap to only four inches, it became much greater still, on the order of twice as much.'

This went right against the accepted thinking at the time, said Ralph Bellamy: 'Conventional wisdom was that ground effect was bad. If you look at F1 cars of that

---

10 These instructions were included in part of the dossier, not reproduced here, which contained Chapman's observations on his cars' behaviour at the Austrian Grand Prix which he had attended on 18 August before going on holiday.

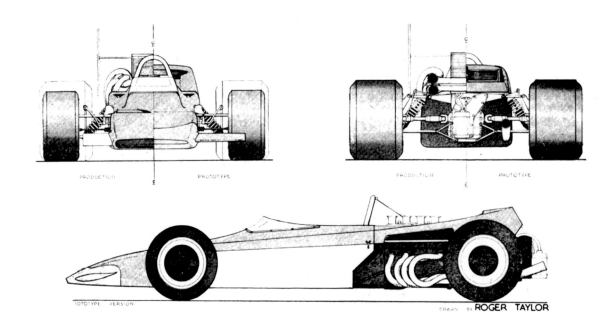

Roger Taylor's drawing shows, on the right, the Type 70 prototype with its rear-mounted radiator and on the left the final design of Lotus's Formula A/5000 racer.

As raced at Oulton Park in 1971 the Lotus Type 70 gained downforce from wings at front and rear. Ford power disadvantaged it against the Chevrolets.

period, their front wings were always mounted quite high, clear of the ground. Suddenly we were finding that if you put them lower they worked better.'

When this finding was reported to Colin Chapman, he asked, 'What happens if you make the whole car like an inverted wing?' Ready for this moment, Peter Wright proffered his Polaroids of the BRM wing-car

experiment.[11] An excited Chapman green-lighted development in this direction. 'Colin showed a great deal of initiative with the direction of all our investigations,' Rudd recalled. 'He would hear our reports at the weekend and then would say, "I think we should investigate this or that." He really was the stimulus – the catalyst – that got us all going.'

'By late summer' of 1975, wrote Peter Wright, 'the overall configuration of the 78 was defined – slim nose with oil cooler and front wings, airfoil side pods to house fuel and accommodate the water radiators in the leading edge, similar to those on the de Havilland Mosquito aircraft.' As with the BRM project and the March 701, added Wright, 'the side pods had been found to generate little downforce but they packaged fuel and cooling radiators with no drag penalty. A large conventional rear wing completed the aerodynamic configuration.' This would achieve the Chapman objective of front downforce sensitive to pitch, with the front wings gaining in effect the closer they were to the ground as the car nosed down under braking.

'Through the winter of 1975 we continued to refine the aerodynamics and tune the pitch sensitivity,' Peter Wright related:

By the end of a week of tunnel testing the strong wooden model would have been so modified with card, modelling clay and sticky tape that it had

Belgium's GP at Nivelles in 1972 saw a breakthrough when Emerson Fittipaldi persuaded his team to try his smaller remote-mounted wing from Formula 2.

usually lost most of its structural integrity. Towards the end of one of the weeks in the tunnel I noticed that it was becoming almost impossible to obtain consistent balance readings. Something was wrong. Looking carefully at the model, it became clear that the side pods were sagging under load and that as the speed of the tunnel increased they sagged even more. That indicated two things: (1) that the side pods had started to generate downforce and (2) that it had something to do with the gap between their edges and the ground.

Thin wire supports restored the side pods to their correct position and stopped them from sagging – no downforce and consistent balance readings. Next, we taped card skirts to seal the gap between the edge of the side pods and the ground. leaving only approximately 1mm (0.04in) gap. The total downforce on the car doubled for only a small increase in drag! Ralph Bellamy looked somewhat startled. I do not think either of us believed the results, so we repeated the tests, with and without the skirts. Ground effect was real, powerful, and efficient, if the outer edges of the side pods were sealed to the ground.

This was the breakthrough – entirely serendipitous – that led to the full exploitation of ground effect by Lotus. Colin Chapman explained the phenomenon his team

---

11 Success of course has many fathers. Tony Rudd's recollection of the crucial moment was that 'Peter [Wright] and I trotted out the idea that we felt the answer was to make the whole car like an inverted wing and he latched on to this immediately.'

As shown by Ronnie Peterson in Austria in 1973, the 72's rear wing moved much more to the rear, where a rubber mounting made it self-feathering at high speed.

The search for answers to the questions posed by Chapman's 1975 dossier led to scale-model tests at the Imperial College that ultimately achieved skirted downforce.

would exploit in the 78: 'We produce a depression underneath the car by taking the air in at the front, accelerating it through a throat – rather like in a carburettor choke – and then expanding it again as it goes out through the back. The negative pressure created at the throat thus forces the car down on to the road surface. Although the car itself is a relatively large object, it is not as efficient as a wing in terms of the total download it can produce. However, what it does produce it does with less drag and that is important. So what we have been working on is to use a contoured underside to the car so as to run less conventional "wing" and by doing so produce the same downloading but with less drag.'

Encouragement of this design direction came from another source. Mario Andretti remembered sitting in on a design discussion with Colin and colleagues. 'As a driver I would love to have downforce without drag penalty,' he told them. 'I started explaining to them about the March 701 that I had driven in 1970. I said, "You know, there is something to those wings; we were getting downforce without drag penalty." There were no fences – the side pods were just a clean shape. Can you imagine if maybe we had put fences on there? We would control the flow better, there would be no spillage.'

Vital to the successful achievement of downforce, in the early years of its use, were the fences or skirts that channelled air under the car through the shaped underbody and its venturi. Here there were some

(text continues on page 264)

Future Spec for F1 Car

17 July 1975[1]

1. A racing car has only *ONE* objective: to *WIN* motor races. If it does not do this it is nothing but a *waste* of time, money, and effort.

    This may sound obvious but remember it does not matter how clever it is, or how inexpensive, or how easy to maintain or even how safe, if it does not consistently win *it is NOTHING!*

2. Having established this what do we have to do to make it win:
   (i) Simply stated it must firstly be capable of lapping a racing circuit quicker than any other car, with the least possible skill from the driver, and doing it long enough to finish the race.
   (ii) After this, and only after this, and with absolutely no compromising of objective (2)(i) one has to consider how expensive it is, how simple, how safe, and how easy to maintain, etc. *NONE* of those aspects must detract *one iota* from (2)(i). 'Good enough' is just *NOT* good enough to win and *keep* winning.

3. What makes a car capable of lapping quicker than any other car:
   Simply stated there are only two basic considerations which govern this.
   (i) The surplus of power available over total resistance.
   (ii) The surplus of total cornering force generated over total dead weight, and its optimum distribution.

4. Dealing with the second first:

    As it is the *surplus* we are talking about, before we go into all the intricacies of increasing cornering force etc, the simplest way of increasing this surplus is to

DECREASE DEAD WEIGHT!

This will also incidentally have the significant effect of also increasing the surplus of power available over total resistance.

Quantitatively it is *BY FAR* the most paramount item of importance in racing car design – *every* other consideration *MUST* be secondary to achieving absolute minimum dead weight.

Our target design weight must initially be *well below* the legal minimum regulation weight.

It must be such that the practical realities of racing car operation are fully allowed for and only then will the car come up to weight. For instance a car is always weighed semi-wet, ie after all fluids have been added, fully topped up in the case of water, oil, hydraulic fluid etc, and half heartedly drained in the case of fuel.

It must have a 'built-in' weight provision for a certain about of 'rethink' weight additions plus the inevitable multiple coats of paint etc etc.

So our design target should be something like 100lb underweight. When all the above increments have been added the rest can be temporarily made up with ballast until ennui catches up with us.

There is *no* other aspect more important than this!

On the first page of his dossier, dated 19 June '75, Colin Chapman set out the imperatives for a Formula 1 car. He posed many issues for his engineering team.

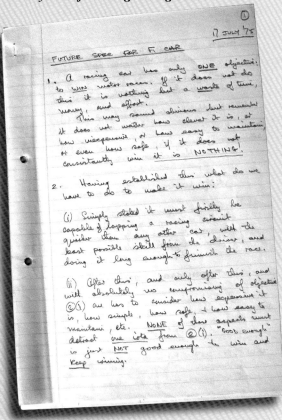

---

1 The dating of the first page of the dossier shows that Chapman had begun working on it before his August holiday.

5. Having achieved minimum dead weight we must get maximum cornering force from the tyres. This is maximised by:
   (i)   The largest possible contact patches.
   (ii) With the softest compound.
   (iii) Kept in contact with the ground as long as possible.
   (iv) With highest possible download.
   (v)   Spread as evenly as possible over the contact patch.
   (vi) And spread as evenly as possible over the four contact patches in proportion to the sideloads they have to carry.

6. Contrary to what our Mechanical Engineering Professors taught us, friction between two surfaces is *NOT* independent of area.
   But it is dependent on load, and in the case of a flexible tyre tread, will be maximised with, as nearly as possible, uniform distribution of load, ie no relatively highly loaded areas.
   To maximise all these aspects of (i) to (vi) we must:
   1. Use the largest possible tyres.
   2. At the softest pressures consistent with stability.
   3. Minimising the weight transfers due to cornering, braking, and acceleration.
   4. Keeping them on the ground with the most uniform pressure fluctuation arising from suspension and tyre deflections due to road irregularities.
   5. And keep them *upright*.
   6. And arrange actual downloads to match sideloads at a common slip angle.

7. This in practice means:
   (i)   Long wheelbase.
   (ii) Wide track.
   (iii) Lowest possible CG.
   (iv) Least possible roll under side load.
   (v)   Maximum non-dead weight download, ie aerodynamics.
   (vi) Softest possible springing with large travels.
   (vii) Optimum distribution of aerodynamic download.

8. But here we start to run into the compromises we must make eg:
   1. Low CG with large wheel travels!
   2. Soft springs with low roll angle!
   3. Long wheelbase & wide track with light weight.
   4. Maximum aerodynamic download with minimum drag etc etc.
   Surely the only way to settle these compromises is to QUANTIFY their effect and optimise the selection.

9. Total cornering force can also be increased aerodynamically.
   Should we try to use vertical lifting surfaces to provide additional side load derived from the speed and yaw angle of the car whilst cornering?[2]

10. We have now decided to maximise 'The *surplus* of total cornering force generated over total dead weight,' by:
    (1) Absolute minimum dead weight.
    (2) Maximum aerodynamic weight.

---

2 This is a fascinating suggestion. By this Chapman meant vertical wings on the car that would generate an additional lateral force in corners and be feathered on the straights. There was at least one precedent for this. For its planned attack on Indianapolis in 1951 Mercedes-Benz tested such cornering aids on its W154. At each side of its cockpit vertical airfoils were mounted, reaching up about as high as the top of the driver's head. A scale model of the planned addition was made and tested in a wind tunnel. Then the twin fins were mounted on one of the cars. They were placed as close as possible to the laden centre of gravity and mounted on fore-and-aft sliding tracks to permit their fine-tuning to the right location. The fins were pivoted on their vertical axes so they could be angled into action as the car entered a turn, then feathered to reduce drag on the straights. This was done hydraulically with a control lever worked by the driver's knee. Testing this radical rig, works driver Karl Kling found that it was surprisingly effective.

(3) Most evenly spread tyre loads with
(4) Minimum change due to road profile, and
(5) Minimum camber change with roll.
(6) Lowest possible CG.
(7) Optimum distribution of aerodynamic load.

DESIGN PROCESS

1. First find the range of lateral stiffnesses of the tyres we intend to use.

2. Arrange for the car centre of weight at a predetermined running condition, say at constant speed through the apex of a medium speed constant radius turn, to watch these tyre lateral stiffnesses.

3. Calculate, and measure eventually, the dynamic shifts of the centre of weight due to braking and accelerating etc.

4. Design and test prove an aerodynamic system, which caused the centre of lift to exactly follow the centre of weight with pitch change.

5. Then arrange for all other mechanical aspects of the car such as suspension rates, roll bar rates, roll centre weights, roll couple distribution to maintain an exact proportional balance in all phases of operation ie

   (i)   All straight line speeds from min to max.
   (ii)   Braking and acceleration.
   (iii)   Nose down roll. Nose up roll.
   (vi)   Over a crest, through a dip etc etc.

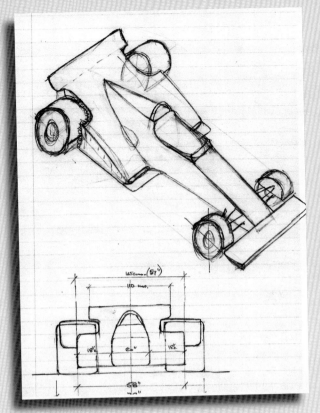

Included in Colin Chapman's July 1975 dossier were dimensioned sketches of a possible racing-car design, based on his appreciation of the requirements at the time.

Chapman's 1975 concept envisaged a wide front wing mounted above the nose and steeply wedged rear bodywork that included low-drag installation of the radiators.

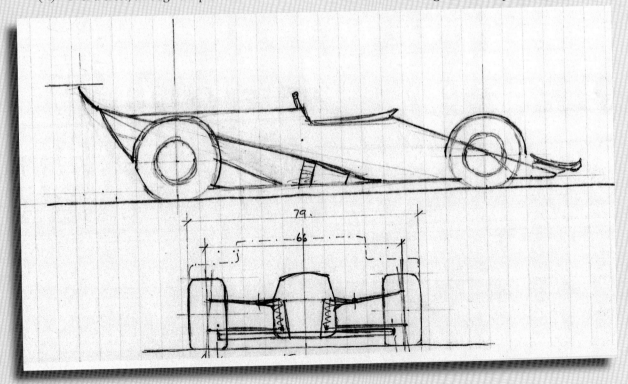

For his 1973 Foyt Coyote for Indianapolis, Bob Riley shaped the underbody as an expanding venturi in plan view and fitted fixed skirts along its flanks.

remarkable precedents, some of which were under the nose of Mario Andretti. Designing cars to race at Indianapolis for A. J. Foyt's team, American engineer Bob Riley produced a superb skirted design in 1973. Based on tests in the wind tunnel at Texas A&M University, Riley gave the car's flat underbody an expanding venturi shape in plan view. 'We found that actually closing off the sides you got even more downforce,' Riley related. He also put a downforce-generating duct in the nose that Foyt insisted be concealed by a snap-on canvas cover when the car was at rest.

For Pat Patrick's 1976 Indy team the creative Riley built a brace of Wildcats that exploited a similar concept. Flanking its clean underside were skirts of hard-wearing GE Lexan plastic that channelled underbody airflow. The Offy-powered Wildcats placed a solid third and fourth in 1976. However, Riley hadn't yet lifted the rear of the underbody to enhance its venturi effect. 'I never really used that again,' he admitted. 'I always meant to get back and do that, to kick up the rear of the car, but didn't have the time – just never did.'

Bob Riley's use of Lexan for skirts was an echo of the design of the radical 2J Chaparral 'sucker car' fielded by Jim Hall in 1970. This pathbreaking car had not

only sliding side skirts, running all the way back past enclosed rear wheels, but also a system of hinged Lexan plaques across the underbody behind the front wheels to seal off the area sucked to the road by the car's twin suction fans. Height of both side and rear skirts was controlled by Bowden cables and a linkage from the car's suspension.

These examples support the contention of Peter Wright that 'there were a lot of people dabbling in what turned out to be ground effect, without necessarily realising it. Funnily enough, Chapman had funded a guy in the States called Buckley, who had a Citroën DS with venturii underneath and suction fans leading on to the boundary layer, but he didn't have skirts. Chapman came to the conclusion that it was "rubbish". To a certain extent it was.' Only with skirts were the full benefits of underbody downforce liberated.

Most relevant to the Lotus effort was the experimentation with skirts carried out in 1974 by Gordon Murray on his BT44 Formula 1 car. With a very wide and flat surface close to the road, his BT44 naturally generated a modicum of downforce, Murray learned through manometer tappings. He sought to augment this by fitting transverse strips of glass-fibre under the tub that were normally clear of the road but touched it under braking. Murray ran the strips in five races during 1974 but didn't pursue the technology further.

This precedent was of great importance to Peter Wright. In fact before Wright told Tony Rudd of his breakthrough findings he and Ralph Bellamy 'had a lengthy discussion about skirts, their legality and their practicality. According to the Technical Regulations, movable aerodynamic devices were not allowed.' Whether or not they would be movable remained to be seen at that point. Either way, the precedent that had been set by Murray's skirts – which had not been protested or judged illegal – was reassuring.[12]

'When we'd finished the testing,' said Ralph Bellamy, 'Colin asked me whether I wanted to build a car along these lines. I said yes, and to his credit he said okay, let's do it.' To the credit of John Player, it stumped up additional funding that allowed the 78 to be built. 'By the end of January 1976 we had the basic design complete,' said Tony Rudd, 'and called upon Team Lotus, still based at Hethel, to supply people to detail and build the car.' Later in 1976 Colin Chapman decided to move the entire Team Lotus operation to Ketteringham Hall, a process that was

---

12 In due course skirts would be sanctified by a CSI ruling that allowed the distance from the chassis to the road to be joined by a 'flexible device'. In 1981 sliding skirts were banned and from 1983 Formula 1 cars had to have no skirts and flat bottoms between their axles.

completed by mid-1977. It had ample nooks and crannies in which to conduct secret projects.

Meanwhile the Lotus 77 was recovering from its early-1976-season malaise thanks to major changes to its braking and suspension. Soon an opportunity arose to apply the new-found aerodynamic expertise. 'We were testing the 77 at Hockenheim,' Mario Andretti related, 'and we were running the car fairly soft in those days. I noticed that through the Bosch Curves, when we were getting roll in the car, all of a sudden I was experiencing a heaviness in the steering. The car was sticking more on the left side because we were closing the gap to the ground.'

Andretti continued, 'I said to Colin, "Something is happening aerodynamically here, when the car gets closer to the ground under roll." He sent Bob Dance into town to buy some plastic strips and they pop-riveted them down the side of the car to close the gap entirely. I went out and immediately, on the first lap, set a new lap record. Of course the more I kept running the slower I was going, because we were wearing the plastic away and it was becoming less and less effective. But it told us what we needed to know – that we had to close that gap.'

With wide side pods housing its radiators, the 77 was eminently amenable to this experimentation. Nylon brushes, the first skirts used on the 78, were raced on the 77 during 1976, Andretti related: 'The brush didn't wear out as much as the plastic strips, but it wasn't as

Bob Riley's Offy-powered Wildcats for the Pat Patrick Indy 500 team in 1976 had smooth underbodies that used skirts of GE Lexan to channel the airflow.

Using fans to generate downforce, Jim Hall's Chaparral 2J of 1970 enclosed the front of its skirted underbody with a row of downwards-sprung Lexan plaques.

During the 1976 season the Lotus 77 – seen at Monaco – served as a test horse for plastic strips and Nylon brushes as means of channelling underbody airflow.

effective because air would still slip through the bristles. We raced the 77 with brushes a couple of times. Colin hired David Phipps to photograph the car everywhere on the circuit to see what the brushes were doing. We saw that, at speed, the forward part of the brushes were sucking in and, just in front of the rear wheels, they were blowing out. Whatever was blowing out ahead of the rear wheels was loss of velocity – downforce – because we were wasting all that energy.'

The same problem was experienced with the 78, which was first tested at Snetterton in August of 1976 by Gunnar Nilsson. 'Initial testing,' said Peter Wright, 'indicated that the brushes were quite incapable of sealing the sides. For winter testing at Kyalami, polypropylene skirts were tried, but they too sucked

inwards and became distorted. Andretti and the race engineers wanted to abandon messing about with all this trick new stuff that did not appear to work and to concentrate on developing the car. Colin Chapman would have none of that and insisted on continuing to work on the skirts until the potential of the car gradually became apparent. On returning from that test, Chapman instructed me to spend 100 per cent of my time on skirt development.'

With a test rig towed behind a Renault 4, Wright evaluated skirts and ground-rubbing facings. His final design used underbody negative pressure to hold a ceramic-faced aluminium skirt against the road. 'A 78 was modified for Gunnar Nilsson to try at Snetterton,' said Wright. 'After only a few laps he was one and a half seconds per lap faster and came into the pits with eyes bulging and a big grin on his face, saying, "I go quicker than I ever go before and I look over the side of the car and there is a metre of track left!"'

So promising was the 78 that Colin Chapman took the unprecedented decision to keep it under wraps in 1976 and race it only in 1977. This required a different kind of meeting, 'the hard chair in the window', for Tony Rudd, whose team had put so much effort into the 78. But Chapman didn't want to risk a premature rumbling of its secrets. Rudd could only agree. He told his chief, 'Well, the first time everybody sees it going back up the ramps into the truck and sees the underside of it, they'll see what we've done and suss out how it works, and they'll copy it.'

In the event it took the competition a while to twig the speed secret of the 78 after it was revealed to the press on 21 December 1976. In the first races of 1977 it was more consistently competitive than its predecessor but not spectacularly fast. The evolution of its skirts was only beginning. As well, an important and unexpected breakthrough came in Brazil when the car went out in practice with rear wheels and tyres that were set more

Pictured with Peterson in charge at Monaco in 1978, the 78 showed its pace in the 1977 season after skirts were fitted and more space was cleared at the rear for air to exit.

outboard. Better lap times suddenly came much more easily because airflow under the rear of the 78 was less congested.

'Even when new cars appeared for 1978 it was clear that many other designers hadn't an inkling of what the 78 was about,' said Ralph Bellamy. 'Other designers, looking at the wing-shaped side pods, dismissed them as a gimmick,' Peter Wright recalled. 'When the 78 started to go quickly, an elaborate deception concerning the differential put many people off the scent.' 'There was a campaign of disinformation that was incredibly successful,' added designer Bellamy.

'The 78 first ran after the August Bank Holiday in 1976,' said team member Glenn Waters. 'We took one of the 77s along to Silverstone with it to use as a

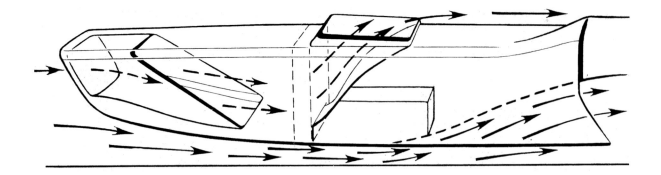

Redesign of the sponsons for 1978's 79 provided dedicated passages for air through the radiators above the lower surfaces that generated downforce, rising at the rear.

Cleaner and more handsome than its 78 predecessor, the 1978 Lotus 79 was faster too after an initially faulty underbody was reshaped to unlock its potential.

benchmark. The only other team there was Tyrrell. Ken Tyrrell came up to look at the 78 and walked away quietly, talking about it. A lot of people were curious about it because by contemporary standards it was enormous. Everybody else was trying to make small cars and suddenly Lotus brought out this car which, superficially, looked like a tank.'

Though no 'tank', there was no denying that the 78 lacked the elegance that the world had come to expect of a Chapman design. 'I didn't think the 78 was a very good-looking car,' Colin reflected. 'It needed a lot of tidying up. But then it was a car that sort of evolved. While we were building it we were still carrying out our wind-tunnel programme. We were still trying out various things, so we made changes of direction even while we were designing and building the car. And it looked it.'

The 78 showed plenty of pace in 1977. Mario Andretti won four championship races and placed third in the driver table while Lotus was again among the leading constructors, second to Ferrari and two points ahead of McLaren. 'On a damp race track we usually fly with that car,' said Andretti. 'In Sweden, when it was drizzling on Saturday, I was putting four seconds on everybody. I was driving right at the top of the corners, right on the edge, just opposite of the groove. That gets slick when it's wet. The dirtier the surface is, the better it is when it's wet.'

The 78's advantage was there in the dry as well, said Colin Chapman: 'It's been eight years since anyone's had such an advantage. We had two seconds a lap on the others in the damp and a second and a half in the dry.' A convincing demonstration of the new car's advantage came at Monza where Mario passed the Wolf-Ford of race leader Jody Scheckter on the outside of the ultra-fast Parabolica bend on lap 10 of 52 to take a dominant victory.[13]

In turns the 78 was unbeatable but on the straights it was disadvantaged. 'We knew for sure we'd be right in the ballpark on slow and medium circuits, places with very short straightaways,' Andretti related. 'Anywhere else we were in trouble. I had this problem with Reutemann at Kyalami. That Ferrari was awful around the back of the circuit, but we'd get to a straightaway and he was just gone.' 'The 78 suffered from the downforce generated by the side pods being located too far forward,' Peter Wright explained, 'with the result that it was always necessary to run a lot of rear wing to balance it. As a result the 78 had a reputation for poor top speed.'

'Just build me a 78 that's quick in a straight line,' was Mario Andretti's request of Colin Chapman when the car for the 1978 season was discussed. To many at Ketteringham Hall it seemed that a cleaned-up 78 would be the answer. Indeed, the 78 handily won the first two races of 1978. But this wasn't Chapman's style. 'He said

we were tearing up all the old drawings,' said one of his designers, 'and starting again with a car that would be a total ground-effect car. Colin was absolutely adamant about it. We'd started on the first drawings by Easter of 1977.'

Chapman's commitment to an all-new car was even more intense after his 1977 holiday. In a repeat of 1975's events he was full of ideas after his summer break, said Peter Wright: 'He came bounding back from his holiday home in Ibiza and said, "Right, now we've got to do it properly."' This time he produced his customary precise drawings showing what he wanted: a pure wing car[14] with a narrow central monocoque to take all the chassis stresses and side pods that had no function other than providing venturi surfaces and internal radiators for water on the right and oil on the left. 'When we got to the 79 we were a little bit surer of what we needed,' Colin said later, 'and were able to lay out much more of a one-piece design.'

As conceived by Chapman, the 79's driver sat more forward to provide the space needed for a single central 34-gallon fuel tank. The detail design was by Martin Ogilvie with Geoff Aldridge and input from race engineer Nigel Bennett, Bellamy having left to work for the Fittipaldi brothers' team.[15] An important change from the 78 was inboard springing for the rear suspension to reduce airflow blockage. A curious blind spot, however, was Chapman's retention of inboard rear brakes. Moving them outboard inside the wheels would have streamlined the rear passages further. 'There wasn't a problem at all with the brakes' on these cars, said Glenn Waters, 'because they didn't have to slow down. They could go round the corners without having to kill the speed.'[16]

'Chapman told us to compromise the rest of the car for the aerodynamics,' said Peter Wright. 'The layout of the 79 chassis was different: the engine was all tucked in, the exhaust tucked in, the suspension designed for the aerodynamics, so we had a lot more freedom. The side pod was something you could just fit whereas on the 78 it was part of the chassis structure so it wasn't easy to change.

---

13 One of the shrewdest racing engineers, Harvey Postlethwaite, didn't miss this indicator. For Wolf he was the only designer to field a properly skirted car for 1978.

14 Perhaps deliberately to mislead, 'wing car' was a misnomer for these new racing cars, as for that matter was 'ground effect' as the term was used in aviation. The function of an underbody venturi had some features in common with the aerodynamics of a wing but it was in fact a new and unrelated vehicular phenomenon.

15 Bellamy fell out of favour with Chapman after the publication in Motor of 16 March 1974 of an interview with Mike Doodson in which the engineer was indiscreet about design and development features of the new 76 and claimed much of the credit for the car's design.

16 This wasn't entirely true in 1978, when porous magnesium calipers of the rear brakes allowed high-temperature seepage that degraded brake performance.

With its structure deliberately compromised to achieve maximum downforce, the 79 had only its radiators extending into the side volumes that comprised its sponsons.

'The brief for the 79 was to move the centre of pressure of the underneath of the car rearwards,' Wright continued, 'and to increase the pitch sensitivity further. In tunnel tests the cleaning-up of the suspension and engine ancillaries that Chapman had achieved was immediately apparent in better downforce figures. I extended the throat of the venturi as far rearwards as possible and worked on profiles that maintained attached flow with as sharp a recovery as I dared, bearing in mind that testing was only one-quarter-scale.'

Wright's reservations about the validity of wind-tunnel testing with models was well founded at this early state of the wing-car art. The 79's first test was at the Paul Ricard circuit near Marseilles in December of 1977. 'In lots of ways it felt basically nicer than the 78,' recalled Mario Andretti, 'even right out of the box on the first day – but it was actually worse in a straight line! It was a basic design problem. We weren't getting the downforce we expected from the underneath of the car – or rather we weren't getting it where we wanted it. Consequently we had to use more rear wing than we wanted.'

A major underbody redesign had the 79 in a fit state by the non-championship race at Silverstone, but Chapman promised Andretti even more progress. Not until mid-May at Zolder for the Belgian GP did the 79 race again, this time for Andretti to win from pole. However, said Mario, 'the more we developed the car, sometimes the worse it got.' The solution was the design of underbodies to suit circuits. Andretti: 'Where your diffuser would curve up, that's where your downforce was fat. Slow tracks like Monaco, you'd want it to turn up early. Then for a high-speed track like Hockenheim, we had diffusers with a centre of pressure much further back. We were testing those until we were *blue.*'

The first time Mario Andretti felt the full potential of the revised 79 was in practice for Monaco. 'The back end of the car was unreal!' he enthused. 'It turned in as good as the 78, but the back end was at least as good as the front. It seemed like here was the perfect race car with grip at the front, grip at the back and incredible traction.' For public consumption Colin Chapman told journalist Alan Henry that 'what we've done on the 79 is to trade download for wing. The car isn't *significantly* quicker than its rivals on any section of a given circuit. It's just that some cars are good on fast corners, some good on straight-line speed and some good on slow corners; we're good on all of them. That's where we score with the Lotus 79.'

And score he did. Including its victory at Zolder the 79 won six races in 1978, taking Lotus to clear victory in the constructors' rankings over Ferrari with Brabham third. Mario was world champion ahead of team-mate

Ronnie Peterson, a tragic posthumous ranking after Peterson's death following a crash in the 78 at Monza. Lotus fielded the 79 in the early 1979 races with Carlos Reutemann joining Andretti. The cars were still good enough to score points finishes but others – especially Ligier, Ferrari and Williams – had finally twigged the new technology. They finished ahead of Lotus by engineering their cars more robustly so that they could cope with the extremely stiff springs that downforce demanded – springs that Chapman was loath to provide.

Blazoned with the emblems of new sponsor Martini & Rossi and again wearing British racing green, the proper Lotus contender for 1979 was unveiled on 16 March in the reception area of the race headquarters at Brands Hatch. Rushed to completion to suit the sponsor, the 80 wasn't race-ready but had shown sensational numbers in the wind tunnel, promising almost twice the 79's downforce. When he was shown the test results, Colin Chapman jibed, 'Good. Now go and show them to the guy with the chequered flag.'

Neither of the two Lotus 80s made was destined to be first to see the guy with the chequered flag. The aim of the new design was logical enough, as Chapman explained: 'We pioneered a solution which was very successful in 1978 and which they're all copying. But we intend to introduce another solution later in 1979 that'll make the cars look different again. Hopefully it will be better – and by better I mean it will produce the same negative lift effect with even less drag. We're not seeking to produce more and more download to increase cornering speeds. What we're trying to do is produce the download necessary to go through the critical corner of a circuit – the one that everyone tunes for – with less drag than we currently have. Less drag means less power, which means less fuel.'

At its introduction the Lotus 80 exemplified drag reduction with phenomenally sleek lines and a complete lack of conventional speed-robbing wings. Instead it had a dedicated venturi and skirt system under its long proboscis and principal sliding side skirts that extended all the way to the rear of the bodywork. Starting out at full body width behind the front wheels, the skirts curved inwards to be able to pass inside the rear wheels. 'It was very complex,' said designer Geoff Aldridge, 'and, because of the constraints of ground-effect, fitting everything else in became very difficult.'

Neither skirt system was satisfactory in practice. The front skirts couldn't cope with the movement needed when the nose dived under braking, so they were removed and conventional wings fitted. With their ess-bend in plan view the side skirts were prone to jamming under longitudinal loads, requiring ever-stronger springs

Seen from the rear, the Lotus 79's detachable sponsons were easily changed – as they often were – to adapt their downforce characteristics to different circuits.

to keep them free. 'A huge amount of effort went into solving that,' said Nigel Bennett. 'There were teams of people working on it. But in the end, if you hit a kerb the skirt would stick and you lost some of your downforce. And without wings it became very unbalanced. So we added wings, which made it more consistent but spoiled its very low drag figures.'

When the skirts were working the phenomenon of 'porpoising' manifested itself, as it already had with the 79. Bouncing on the springs occurred when downforce fluctuated with changes in the distance of the venturi surface from the road. 'The porpoising would tell you that we were way too aggressive on the downforce,' said Mario Andretti. 'It needed to be controlled by the springs and the springs were too soft, so the car was getting sucked down and then bouncing up, down, up. The minute it started you just had to back off the throttle. The chassis was never stiff enough to take the heavier springs that the car should have been using.

'We didn't carry on with the 80 because Colin refused to make it stiffer,' Andretti continued. 'We went back to the 79s but in retrospect it was a mistake to do that, and it turned out to be a botched-up situation. I felt we weren't going anywhere with the 80. I knew what it needed and he

Ove Nielsen's unusual perspective on the 79 in its 1979 livery shows its nose wing, right-side sponson and dual front-brake calipers.

wasn't about to do it. There were disagreements that took the focus away from the overall effort and we paid for it dearly. That was a year best forgotten.'

Behind the scenes Chapman was vituperative about the 80's problems. His favourite adjective 'useless' came into frequent use to describe unsatisfactory executions. He ridiculed the car's rollover hoop as 'elephantine'. His first job list for the car had 104 items, which shrank slightly to 97 after tests at Jarama in April of 1979. The only chink of light for the 80 was a third place for Mario

Pictured with the nose wing that its creator had hoped to avoid, the 1979 Lotus 80 was the result of Chapman's all-out effort to implement nose-to-tail downforce.

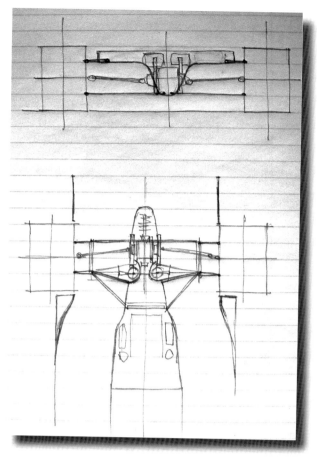

Chapman's drawing for the rear venturi of the Type 80 showed its inboard brakes and the curved side skirts that defied many attempts to make them work properly.

So dedicated to downforce was the Lotus 80 that its venturi and side panels extended to the extreme rear, with a small adjustable spoiler for trimming its attitude.

in the Spanish GP behind the 79 of Reutemann. By mid-season the costly 80 had been abandoned.[17]

'Looking back on the last few seasons,' Colin Chapman reflected at this point, 'I suppose you could say that we have paid the penalty for innovators. We did all the

pioneering work on ground effect, starting with our Lotus 78 and moving forward to the 79. Then we realised that we were still only in the infancy of studying the principles of ground effect and, I suppose, we took too big a step forward again to the 80. That step cost us the 1979 season. With the 80 we got ourselves into a stability problem which we didn't fully understand, in fact is only just becoming fully understood now. We had devised an aerodynamic system which wasn't matched to the chassis, the suspension and the springing system. So we decided to abandon the 80, continue development on the 79 and develop the 81 as an "interim" car for the following season.'[18]

Chapman made one last effort to see what could be learned from the 80. If the drivers wanted stiffer springs, he would try them in the off season. One car went to Paul Ricard in November of 1979 for three private test sessions with driver Stephen South. Fitted to the 80 were the stiffest springs in the Lotus inventory, their rates of 2,500 pounds per inch more than five times stiffer than in pre-ground-effect days. 'Definitely better,' was South's assessment, 'but the car still moves around too much. Super-stiff springs cause so much vibration that I have difficulty in keeping my feet on the pedals and my backside's pretty bruised.' South's complaints resembled those of many drivers in the stiffly sprung skirted-car era.

'If only the car could be sprung even stiffer and yet isolate the driver and the fragile parts of the car from the shocks and bumps that would result, maybe the concept would work,' said an internal Lotus report of

---

17 Lotus wasn't the only entrant to be led up the garden path of ultimate downforce by great wind-tunnel readings in 1979. Designer Tony Southgate had been at Lotus during the discovery of venturi underbodies. 'Colin Chapman and I were of the opinion that we must be able to make a car that did not need conventional wings,' Southgate related, 'one that could perform just off the ground effects generated by the chassis bodywork. That became a challenge. There was a bit of a race between Arrows and Lotus to see who could be the first to produce a car without wings.'

By now at racing newcomer Arrows, Southgate 'had been playing around in the wind tunnel with a new design that was no more than an aerodynamic exercise. It was producing terrific numbers – we were up to around 1,500 pounds as opposed to the 750 pounds of the better pre-ground-effect cars. Eventually we all got carried away and blinded by the numbers that were coming out of the wind tunnel. We thought, "We've got to make this car."' The result was the wingless Arrows A2, whose all-enveloping bodywork carrying long, straight skirts contributed to excess weight. In an echo of the Lotus 80 experience Jochen Mass, whose two sixth places in the A2 were its career highlights, felt that 'rock-hard springs' might have made it raceable.

18 The 81 and longer-wheelbase 81B, driven by Mario Andretti and then Nigel Mansell and Elio de Angelis, were unsuccessful in 1980 and 1981, as was their similar successor the 87. None of these cars brought Lotus victories.

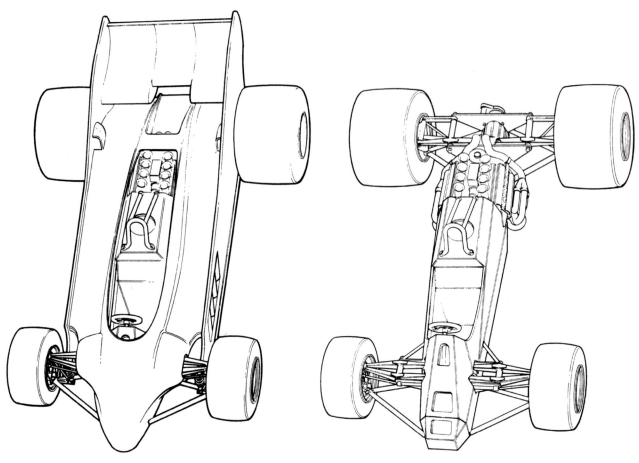

Based on results with the 86 test car, which had curved skirts, the 'twin-chassis' Lotus 88 of 1981 was designed as rectangular in plan view with straight side skirts.

At the heart of the 88 of 1981 was a complete racing-car chassis with Lotus's new folded carbon-fibre tub, completely capable of independent operation. It could and sometimes did carry a small nose wing.

February 1981. 'It was evident by now that the aerodynamic loads exceed the inertia loads on the car, and that the primary structures must be designed to absorb and distribute these loads and the suspension to feed the loads to the wheels while maintaining body attitude.' What was needed, it continued, 'was an attempt to resolve the mutual incompatibility of suspension requirements between those parts of the car which affect its aerodynamics and those parts which insulate the driver from the road shocks. So the concept of two separate chassis with two separate suspension systems was born.'

'While Team Lotus stepped back one pace and raced the 81 in 1980,' said Peter Wright, 'I set out to investigate and attempt to solve the porpoising problem. The 80 had proved that there was more downforce to be had but unless it could be controlled it was unusable.' Wright conferred with Cranfield's David Williams, whose conclusion was that 'it was an aero-elasticity problem, akin to flutter in an aircraft wing. The changing aerodynamic loads, as the car bounced and pitched, excited the pitch

and heave modes of the sprung mass on its springs and tyres.' This occurred because the downforce was applied to the vehicle through its main sprung body and chassis, which passed the increased force to the wheels and tyres through the suspension's springs.

How was this to be dealt with? 'While I was contemplating how one might apply ground effect to a high-performance road car, such as the Lotus Turbo-Esprit, a possible solution occurred to me. There was no reason why a ground-effect underbody could not be connected directly to the outboard ends of the lower suspension members and not to the sprung part of the car. In this way the problems of excessive deflection of soft road springs, and the need for skirts to maintain the gap between the edges of the underbody surface and the road, would be avoided. Now, if we could do that on the racing car – where is that rulebook?

'Having read the regulations thoroughly, including a detailed look at the definitions section,' continued Wright, 'I highlighted the relevant sections and went to see Chapman (his office in Ketteringham Hall was next

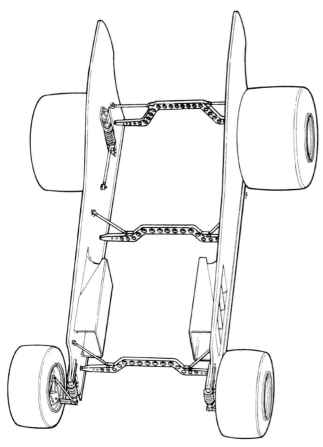

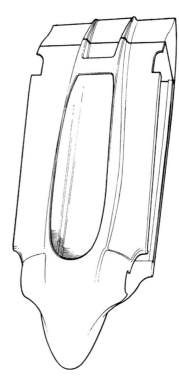

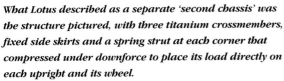

What Lotus described as a separate 'second chassis' was the structure pictured, with three titanium crossmembers, fixed side skirts and a spring strut at each corner that compressed under downforce to place its load directly on each upright and its wheel.

Integral with the 'second chassis' was the 88's bodywork, comprising all its upper and lower surfaces including the downforce-generating underbody. It transmitted downforce directly to all four wheels when the springs became coil-bound.

door to mine). Within hours chief designer Martin Ogilvie and I had moved upstairs to a locked office in Ketteringham Hall. A veil of secrecy was drawn over what we were doing.'

What they were doing was designing and building a test car, the 86, based on a third unused Type 80 monocoque. In spite of the 80's problems the 86 had curved skirts running to the extreme rear, with a low wing at the back for balancing the downforce. Like that of the 81, the 86's nose was snubbed and wingless. It was a bulky-looking car as it had to be because its body – including the all-important underbody – was entirely separate from the chassis and suspension. The only point of contact was at the four hub carriers, where downforce was applied directly to the wheels and tyres.

In his thoughts about a road car using the principle, Wright had planned to attach the body directly to the hubs. His reading of the rules, however, suggested that there had to be a 'suspension' between hubs and body: 'The regulations stated that any part having an aerodynamic influence must be mounted to the entirely

sprung part of the car. Therefore, we surmised, the body must have a suspension system. To help people think of this in the right way, we decided to describe the car as the "twin-chassis" 86 – not the "twin-body". The "suspension" characteristics we were looking for were very stiff, just hard bump rubbers.' The aim was to meet the letter of the rules.

During 1980, said Wright, with Nigel Mansell the driver, 'an exclusive test session was booked at Jarama, away from prying eyes. The performance straightaway showed great promise. The curved skirts were, as usual, a problem to get working reliably, but the downforce was there and the car did not porpoise. The decision was made to proceed to a new car, based on these principles, and including sliding skirts.' While they were gearing up to build the 88, as it was designated, the authorities imposed their ban on skirts. As well they required all cars to have at least 6 centimetres clearance to the road, without saying when and how it would be measured. These were linked to a new Concorde Agreement governing Formula 1 racing.

'It took us about 30 seconds,' said Wright, 'to realise that in the twin-chassis concept we had the perfect solution, provided we could come up with a suspension system for the body that raised it at pit-lane speeds and allowed it to sink down on to the bump rubbers at racing speeds. We found these characteristics in the type of pressurised-gas strut used for bonnets and tailgates on road cars and found a supplier who was prepared to tailor the exact characteristics we required.' As related in Chapter 5 on structures a folded carbon-fibre tub was built for the 88 to provide the stiffness that had been lacking in earlier monocoques. Instead of the 86's curved periphery the 88 was straight-sided from front to rear – a by-product of a design that was originally conceived to carry the now-outlawed skirts.

An early indication of the new car's potential came in a test at Paul Ricard before the season opened. 'Most of the initial tests involved standing out by hairpins to see if the outer chassis [the body] would come up on slow corners,' Peter Wright recalled. 'To prevent this we put in very-high-rebound damping so that it would come down quite easily but take a long time to rise up again. Alfa Romeo was also there to test their 179C. It rained a lot and when the car first ran it was on a damp track. Alfa immediately sent out their car to "calibrate" the 88's performance. If I remember correctly, the 88 was about one second a lap quicker.'

Wright and Chapman, who shared a patent on this

The first 88 of early 1981, pictured, mounted its radiators in the 'second chassis' bodywork. In the 88B presented later they were integral with the inner chassis.

technology, were convinced that the concept was legal. 'The rules banned cars with no suspension,' Wright averred, 'but they hadn't thought of two suspensions.' Against this was the prohibition of movable aerodynamic devices. The entire body with its underside venturis was just such a device. As well, the transmission of downforce directly to the car's hubs – as had been the case with the 49's rear wings – was now forbidden. The 88 did exactly this at all four corners, once its gas struts had collapsed. It looked like Lotus was in for a fight.

The fight duly commenced with the presentation of an 88 at Long Beach for the first Grand Prix of 1981. 'If that car passes scrutineering,' threatened Frank Williams, 'I will withdraw my cars.' Having already been obliged by the Lotus innovation of ground effect to build entirely new cars, the other teams weren't eager to open the Pandora's box of yet another Chapman advance. Responding to their official protests, the Long Beach officials initially allowed some running but then black-flagged the 88. Much the same happened in Brazil and then in Argentina.

Was the 88 actually achieving its potential? After the Argentinean race, said engineer Nigel Stroud, 'Chapman left me with the 88 and driver Elio de Angelis and a few mechanics and said, "You have a go." I think we concluded in Argentina that the chassis within the bodywork had no aerodynamic load at all, so it was literally being tossed around through suspension forces inside the body. Consequently all the cambers were going all over the place and the driver never felt confident in the car because the car was never the same.' De Angelis eventually crashed the 88 in what Stroud called 'a very unusual place.'

Departing from Argentina, Chapman issued a bitter statement that included the following remarks:

It is a particular disappointment for this to have happened at the Argentine Grand Prix which has marked more pleasant points in the history of Team Lotus. It was here, in 1960, that we were welcomed into the band of sportsmen competitors with our first full Formula 1 car, which was as innovative then in its way as the Essex-Lotus 88 is today. It was also here in 1977 that we ran the first ground-effect car ever in motor racing, a principle which every Formula 1 car has since copied.

Throughout these years we have witnessed the changes which have taken place in Grand Prix racing and unfortunately seen what was fair competition between sportsmen degenerate into power struggles and political manoeuvrings between manipulators and money men attempting to take more out of the sport than they put into it.

We have a responsibility to the public of the Grand Prix and to our drivers and this has stopped us from withdrawing our cars from this event. But for the first time since I started Grand Prix racing, 22 years ago, I shall not be in the Team Lotus pit during a race for this reason. During this period no team has won more races or more championships than we have, nobody has influenced the design of racing cars the way we did through innovations which are already finding their way into everyday motor cars for the benefit of increased safety and energy conservation. And yet we are being put under unbearable pressure by our rival competitors, who are frightened that once again we are setting a trend they may all have to follow.

Colin Chapman appealed against the decisions that had excluded the 88. After a meeting in Paris on 23 April the authorities upheld the ban, referring to a rule which in their view required the bodywork to be attached to the chassis. Countering that no regulation in the Concorde Agreement required such attachment, Chapman considered that he'd been denied a ruling based solely on 'the letter and intent of the rules in force, presented in coherent and comprehensive manner.' Calling the Court of Appeal's conclusion 'bizarre', he said that a lack of raceable cars meant that Lotus would not attend the San Marino GP on 3 May, the first time the team would miss a Grand Prix since 1958.

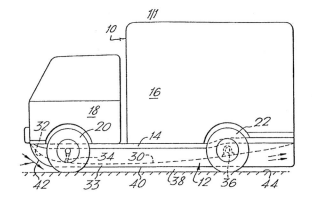

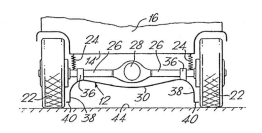

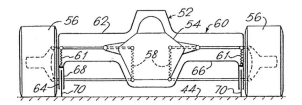

Shown by the patent of Chapman and Wright were two versions of the 'twin-chassis' concept, the example of a lorry making its purpose and function completely clear.

Hoping for better treatment at home, Team Lotus regrouped. It prepared new versions of the controversial cars for the British GP on 18 July, dubbing them the 88B. Radiators were repositioned and the cockpit fairing and windscreen were mounted to the body instead of the monocoque. With this came new terminology. The word 'chassis' was no longer used. Instead the 88B was described as having two 'sprung structures': an inner one carrying the driver, fuel, engine and transmission, and an outer one comprising the bodywork and aerodynamic devices.

Well in advance of the British race Lotus asked the RAC's scrutineers to inspect the 88B and give their view as to its eligibility. Finding no evidence that the rules barred a car with either two sprung structures or two sets of springs, they passed it as eligible to race at Silverstone. Although Ferrari, Alfa Romeo and Talbot-Ligier tabled protests before practice began, two 88Bs did practice on the Thursday. The FIA intervened,

Effort devoted to the 88 meant that little care was given to the conventional 87, wearing a big front wing at Monaco in 1981. Only rarely did it score points finishes.

however, saying that the cars didn't comply, so the times set were annulled and Lotus hastily prepared two 87s.

Only on this occasion were practice times for the radical Lotus published. Neither was particularly quick, 17 of the 30 drivers setting faster times than Nigel Mansell in the 88B. His deficit to the fastest runner, a turbocharged Renault, was 3.8 seconds. Were they exploiting its full potential? It seems likely. In his hastily prepared 87 Mansell was slower in second practice, too slow to qualify in fact – an immense disappointment in his home race – while de Angelis was slightly faster. 'The development was very much in its infancy when the chassis was banned,' testified Mansell later. 'The big problem was the transition from slow speed to high speed.' Nevertheless he loyally defended its potential: 'It was a brilliant idea.I have no doubt that, fully developed, the car would have been very quick and a winner.'

The 88 saga petered out with appeal hearings at both the RAC and the sporting authority, the FISA in Paris, the last of which judged the 88 and 88B to be illegal. Publicly, Colin Chapman was philosophical. 'Away from the pressures of racing we had developed the 86 and 88 throughout 1980 and the following winter,' he said. 'In fact I finalised the 88 design two days after the Concorde Agreement had been signed. Hopefully, the regulations were now frozen for four years because we knew that, although the 88 complied with the regulations, if we had introduced it before the Concorde Agreement had been signed, then sure as fate they would have changed the regulations against us. We believed we would be okay, once that agreement was signed.

'What we didn't realise,' Chapman continued, 'was that – despite the fact that the car conformed to the regulations – political pressure could be such as to overturn the rules and that the car could be excluded, totally against the integrity of those rules. We believed, and still believe, that the 88 concept is legal and every competent observer says that the car is eligible. Yet we've been bashing our head against a machine which, for some purely political motive, has been trying to get it excluded. With the regulations in such a state of flux, there was no way I was going to introduce the new car. So we left it.'[19]

Privately Colin Chapman was profoundly frustrated and disappointed by what Tony Rudd called 'a terrible mess. Chunky refused to admit defeat at the hands of the bureaucrats and wasted a whole season in fruitless argument.' Nigel Mansell put it well: 'Colin had seen his most radical and brilliant design banned without anybody being able to produce a valid article in the rules which the car was supposed to have contravened. He had spent hundreds of thousands of pounds on developing the car and almost as much again on lawyers and court cases to appeal against FISA's decisions.'

Adding to Chapman's exasperation was FISA's failure

---

19 Two 88Bs survived in their original format and were raced in Historic Formula 1 in the 21st Century, one of them by Clive Chapman's Classic Team Lotus.

Updated for 1982 by Peter Wright and Martin Ogilvie from the 87, the sleek 91 scored a lucky victory in the Austrian GP for Elio de Angelis, seen here at Brands Hatch.

to address what was manifestly a blatant breach of the new regulations, said Peter Wright: 'He was particularly incensed that Brabham were permitted to race a car that raised itself hydro-pneumatically to pass the six-centimetre test in the pit lane and then lowered itself on the track, and ran flexible skirts.' A brainwave of Brabham's Gordon Murray, this cynical cheat was quickly adopted by other teams.

'That 88 business infuriated him because he felt it was inhibiting his basic right to come up with genuinely different ideas.' Wright added of Chapman. 'He spent an enormous amount of time and money consulting legal advisors about the legitimacy of the 88's interpretation of the rules and he would never accept that it was illegal in his own mind. It was an affair which severely dented his morale. After he lost, in the face of a coordinated effort by his competitors and the Formula 1 organisation, he never again really enjoyed Formula 1 racing. He went off to develop his new interest – ultralight aircraft – in which he immersed himself right up to the day he died.'

Colin Chapman's defence of the 88 concept was more than determined; it bordered on the obsessive. At the age of 53 in 1981 he had joined Enzo Ferrari as one of the Old Guard of Grand Prix racing. Callow newcomers were nipping at his heels. Although he had many other issues on his agenda, including Lotus Cars, ultralights and the controversial DeLorean project, Chapman nevertheless found the time and money to defend the twin-chassis concept.[20]

By now the Lotus founder was used to getting his own way. His record of success seemed to justify all his actions. A whiff of megalomania infused his impassioned defence of the twin-chassis idea, as if the stupid idiots running motor racing didn't grasp that they were dealing with *Colin Chapman*. The more irritated with them he became, and the more publicly, the more adamantly the establishment rebuffed his arguments. Chapman's inability to break through with the 88 was the most severe setback of his life in racing – indeed the most severe setback of his life.

Was Chapman judicious in being so quick to seize the idea presented to him by Wright? An idea that Wright had only cursorily subjected to a rulebook analysis? That he did so smacks of desperation. 'One of the wonderful things about working for Colin Chapman,' said Peter Wright, 'was that as soon as you took an idea to him, he picked it up (if it was any good) and extrapolated to where it might take one, while at the same time scrutinizing it carefully for weaknesses.'

A drowning man after his struggles with the 80 in 1979, Chapman seized Wright's 'twin-chassis' life preserver in a desperate *coup de foudre*. He was quick to take it up, too quick in the event, for the concept's shortcomings turned out to be legal rather than technical. And confident though he justifiably was in his technical and persuasive skills, legalities were not a strength of Colin Chapman.

---

20 The documentation resulting from Chapman's effort to prove the 88's legality fills a complete file drawer, preserved at Hethel by Classic Team Lotus.

Chapter 9

MAN MANAGING

Even down to his smallest gesture, Chapman is quick and neat. A man of intense vitality – volatile, quick-tempered and impatient of mediocrity. Has been admired and criticised in almost equal proportions. Can be refreshingly blunt. Has no time for the amoebic mass of clichés and prejudices which surrounds Grand Prix racing.

Louis Stanley

'His persona is ebullient, buzzing, fast-moving, joke-cracking,' wrote Robert Heller about Colin Chapman, 'but for all that outwardness the personal armour is difficult to pierce and the man is dangerous to cross. One businessman claims that Chapman is the only person who has ever thrown him out of an office. He reacts vigorously to failure, real or imagined: his language in that event fits the image of the brisk, efficient commanding officer.'

Of medium height, with a physique that fluctuated between sleek and well-padded – the state that gave rise to his 'Chunky' nickname – Colin Chapman was the personification of the purposeful and successful businessman. Warm though he could be when required, he offered few apertures through which his inner feelings could be discerned. This was an asset, an armour behind which he shielded when necessary from people or events not to his liking. He also deployed social correctness, warding off the unwashed at Indianapolis by saying, 'In my country you don't talk to people until you've been introduced to them.'

An oft-quoted resemblance to film star David Niven was largely evinced by a neat moustache and features

Colin Chapman liked to be in control. He could best exercise this characteristic at the track, where he could shut out other concerns and focus on racing.

that were regular rather than remarkable. Erroll Flynn might have been more apt as an archetype albeit more flattering as well. In visage and carriage Chapman oozed the confidence and sincerity that were his stock in trade. These were important assets as he built the businesses that stood behind his ability to innovate in engineering.

'His features are neat,' wrote Ted Simon in 1970, 'his hair carefully tended, his body compact. He is, as the old song has it, "dapper from his napper to his feet" and moves with brisk agility, sometimes swinging a key chain from his hip.' Judging Chapman a 'tight-lipped titan,' Simon called him 'a millionaire at forty, controlling his Lotus empire with a strong, personal hand. Usually impassive, he released his pleasure at the success of his car in short bursts of enjoyment.'

Chapman gradually gained an aptitude for the skills of personal presentation. In earlier years he didn't worry much about his turn-out. Engineer Bill Milliken recalled lunching with him at London's Steering Wheel Club in 1956 when Colin was 'very poorly dressed, wearing a long, threadbare top coat.' Milliken was driven in an 'undistinguished' Morris Minor to Hornsey to see the Lotus facilities. 'His office was a stand-up office,' Bill recalled, 'it was so small.' In those days his lucky Clydella tartan shirt and chinos often sufficed at the track.

Later Colin Chapman adopted neat single-breasted suits and sober ties that bespoke a businessman in

At Monaco in 1963, listening to Jim Clark, Chapman was wearing a short-sleeved version of his lucky tartan shirt. Clark led easily but retired with gearbox trouble.

whom it would be prudent to invest. He wore a tie at the track as well, sometimes with a vee-neck pullover that saw frequent use. Later he established a trademark image with the fisherman's cap that he famously flung to the skies at a victory.[1] He could wear a sponsor's kit with the best of them, tailored trimly in the glory years of John Player and Essex sponsorship.

Never one to embrace the *hoi polloi*, Chapman grew even more remote in later years. He became 'much harder and more cynical,' said close associate Tony Rudd. 'He made a cult out of his impatience and intolerance of anything that appeared to him to be wasting time. This applied to everything. He had learned the meaning of the rosettes in the Michelin guides, stayed at the best hotels and used the best restaurants, when before a Kit-Kat and a bag of peanuts in the aircraft sufficed.' However, added Rudd, 'there would be whole days when he was his old cheerful self. It was just as if

he devised the character that he thought the world wanted him to be, and he was playing that part.'

John DeLorean and Essex Petroleum's David Thieme introduced Colin Chapman to the Good Life, to 'staying in the Hotel de Paris,' said Peter Warr, 'the black and gold helicopter to ferry him from airport to circuit, the black and gold Lotus to get him from helipad to paddock. Instead of being in the garages until 11pm trying to work out solutions to problems and writing job lists, fifteen minutes after practice he was gone, back to the five-star hotel.'

This *modus operandi* challenged the opportunities for his people to interact with Chapman. Designer Ralph Bellamy found a solution in hitching a ride with his chief. 'Going to races was the time when we used to talk a lot about the new car, principally when we were flying in his aeroplane. Nobody could interrupt so we'd hammer it out right there. A tough engineering session at 5,000 feet!' Private flying allowed confidentiality, which Colin dealt with in his own way on commercial flights, said Dan Gurney: 'He used to write notes to himself. When on an aeroplane he'd write them so small that nobody could read them over his shoulder.'

From beginning to end of his three-decade career Colin Chapman never lost his voracious appetite for information. His deep dives into the technologies of suspensions, structures and materials were related earlier. During the gestation of the first Elite he was driving a Porsche 1600 because, said Denis Jenkinson, 'he felt that Porsche standards would have to be the very minimum in the way of detail finish on his own Gran Turismo car,' adding 'and with that we could not agree more.'[2] A passion for lightness and low drag, however, kept the Elite from achieving the Porsche-like amenities that Chapman had come to comprehend.

'He was an absolute past master at soaking up knowledge,' Tony Rudd said of Chapman. Looking to replace the costly aluminium bodies of the Eleven, Rudd added, Colin needed to learn about glass-fibre: 'He read all the books that he could find on the subject and soaked up the knowledge. It was the same with boats and again with microlights.' This thirst for knowledge was evident from an early age, said his father: 'Even before he could read it was remarkable. Colin collected cigarette cards concerning aircraft. I would read aloud the details on each card to him and, days later, he would recount them to me – technical information, performance, history… and it was always amazingly accurate.'

His ability to absorb and retain information made

---

1 He couldn't very well have copied the ebullient somersaults that John Cooper turned on such occasions.

2 The Porsche had belonged to Paul Fletcher, who traded it to Lotus for the only one of the special Climax-powered de Dion-axled Sevens built in 1957 to be fitted with a 1,460cc FWB engine.

Colin Chapman a formidable discussion partner. 'He got up much earlier than most people!' said Keith Duckworth. 'He could marshal his arguments in a superhuman fashion. You'd be having a discussion about something and he would say "Well, this follows" and I would look doubtful, without having been able to sift into my mind why I didn't like what he said.

'At that stage,' Duckworth continued, 'realising that he might be out-argued, or that there was something fallacious about what he'd said, he would change the subject and throw in a red herring and I would lose the main argument while chasing this useless red herring. And I'd find that I'd agreed to something which I shouldn't have done! I gradually learnt that all I could do was to say "Yes, Colin, I've heard your arguments, I need time to think about them. I'll let you know my view in the morning." And with that proviso, there wasn't a problem.'

'Colin has an inquisitive, logical and demanding mind,' said his close associate Peter Kirwan-Taylor. 'He has to understand "the moving parts". He tests his ideas in discussion "at the limit" and thus determines the critical factors which will result in the successful solution to a given problem. Then he develops and refines an elegant answer. I have seen him apply this scientific method to cars, factories, boats, houses, mortgages, aeroplanes, price/earnings ratios, labour relations, wage structures and racing formulas with equal success. It is a formidable ability admitting no compromise.'

Allied to this analytical ability was an awesome resourcefulness. Alvin Cohen heard from a friend about an adventure he had with Chapman after the war when the two of them, the story went, were tasked with inspecting London's bomb-damaged buildings. In the cellar of one of them 'they discovered an Aladdin's cave of hundreds of shelf supports, racking and shelving, all in precious steel. Knowing that this damaged building had long been abandoned, Chapman concluded that this particular treasure horde required liberating!'

The two of them, Cohen continued, 'commandeered a flatbed lorry and loaded it with all the steel components and went touring London, flogging off their windfall to all the engineering companies so desperate for steel.' Chapman's gains from this enterprise, the tale continued, produced the capital he needed to start dealing in used cars, another discipline in which his resourcefulness was well rewarded.

A friend of Colin described his business technique as 'a dazzling combination of charm and calculation,' adding that 'Colin will sell you the right time, and probably get a commission from the chap who owns

A brown pullover was a frequent sight on Chapman in the Lotus 72 years. Sunglasses were worn more rarely, however.

the watch!' His resourcefulness was well expressed by Tony Rudd: 'I think it was part of his mystique that he imparted confidence in the people around him. You had the feeling, however bad things were, that somehow or other Chunky would get you out of it. You forgot that he probably got you into the mess in the first place.'

An indication of Chapman's resourcefulness came from the early proliferation of his operating companies. 'There were a lot of them,' said Mike Costin: 'Lotus Engineering, Lotus Components and Racing Engines Limited. The reason why there were so many companies was that the buyer of a kit car could buy the chassis from one company and the engine and gearbox from others, so that he could legitimately avoid purchase tax by buying the components from different sources.'

The multiple companies posed puzzles on occasion. Driver Trevor Taylor recalled filling up his racing-car transporter, signpainted 'Team Lotus', at a Cheshunt petrol station. 'Just as we were filling up,' he said, 'a voice came out, shouting, "Stop, stop!" We wondered what was going on. "You can't fill up here, not as Team Lotus anyhow." I said, "What about Lotus Cars?" "No,

Chapman could brush up well as he did in 1969 when he and Andy Granatelli met to confirm the burly STP chief's sponsorship of Lotus at Indianapolis.

A greying Chapman donned John Player garb at Monaco in 1976, wearing his armband on his belt. He was conversing with designer Tony Southgate.

no," was the reply. "Lotus Components?" I said. "No, no," again. I was trying to think of another Lotus company. "What about Lotus Developments?" I said. "I'll just check – yes, that's all right. Fill up with that account." Lotus had very little money then and what they had was made to go around the best it could.'

The multiple companies also facilitated jiggery-pokery with funds in later years. 'Team Lotus's financial year used to be about six months different from Lotus Engineering and Lotus Cars,' recalled Martin Ogilvie. 'They used to swap the money around. [Finance director] Fred Bushell got the money in and looked after it and Chapman used to spend it. He would say, "Fred, your job is just to get the money so I can spend it." But the money was never there, so they had to do a sponsorship deal as early as possible. Sponsorship got more and more difficult to come by, as it was realised by sponsors like Camel that their money was paying off the previous year's debts.'

The financial struggles of his companies' early years contributed to Chapman's passion for good hard cash. 'I formed the view of a shrewd, tough businessman,' said Bill Milliken, who as chief steward at the rich US Grand Prix at Watkins Glen had many dealings with Chapman. 'He was a smart guy, pretty shrewd, pretty tough. An hour or so after each race we paid out the prize money. Chapman always insisted on getting everything in cash. He got it in 50-dollar bills. The other teams seemed much more relaxed about this.' Colin took the same line with other race organisers.

That Chapman was both Lotus's design brains and its entrepreneurial spirit was seen by company insiders as an advantage. 'One of the great things with Chapman,' said Peter Wright, 'was the fact that he was involved on the business side as well as the design side. As a result he was able to commit finance to high-risk projects which he believed passionately to be correct.' Among such projects were the Indianapolis 'wedges', the radical Type 72, the research leading up to the 78 and 79, the 88 – for good or for ill – and the active suspension that was under development at his death.

Hand in hand with this duality of disciplines went Colin Chapman's ability to persuade people and companies to fund his initiatives. His persuasiveness was legendary both inside and outside Lotus. Mike Warner recalled that 'the best tip I ever had' was given by Fred Bushell before he went in for a meeting with Chapman. 'Colin's a terrific chap,' said the finance man, 'but he can charm the birds off the trees. I'm just giving you that tip.' It was fair warning for Warner as the company chief asked him to take on new responsibilities.

This talent was evident at an early age, said the senior Chapman: 'I don't want to give the impression that Colin was one of those pale schoolboy wonders we sometimes hear about. He was a perfectly happy, lively child with a normal instinct for mischief. There always seemed to be a gang of some sort, with Colin invariably its leader.'

Among the earliest to fall under the Chapman spell were the Allen brothers. 'As a dentistry student I lived with my parents and two brothers in a large house at Muswell Hill in North London,' Nigel Allen related. 'As a hobby my brother Michael and I had put together a very well equipped workshop with up-to-the-minute set-up of hoist and sliding gantry, pit, welding gear, lathe, valve grinder, small tools, benches and all the other paraphernalia that back up a complete car workshop. We used this to buy and refurbish old cars and then sell them on to make a bit of money.

'One day,' Allen continued. 'a young man stopped at the garage where we were at work and introduced himself as Colin Chapman. To cut a very long story short by the time he left that afternoon he had persuaded us – and we had agreed – that together we would design, build and race a new make of car, the Lotus!' Colin had opened this historic 1950 meeting by criticising an Austin Seven the Allens were building, saying it was too heavy to race. From having no thought whatsoever of racing the Allens were soon converted to the urgent need to build a car to compete under the 750 Club formula.

Big enough to hold three Austin Sevens, the Allen workshop was a major advance from the lock-up behind girlfriend Hazel's house where the first two Chapman specials were born. Now Colin and his new colleagues were fuelled with tea and biscuits by the brothers' mother. 'My associate in Lotus Engineering was Michael Allen,' Chapman would later grandly explain, 'whose brother Nigel has since become well known in competition with Lotus cars. We two shared the financial responsibilities of the company and there has not been any other financial backing.'

'It was quite an experience and there's no doubt about it,' Michael Allen related. 'Colin was a very special sort of bloke. Talk to anybody who has known him for a long time – he was a ruthless bugger who wanted to be successful whatever and he really did use people to get the thing on the road, anybody who would come and work for nothing. As soon as they started to make a fuss, then, "all right, there's someone to take your place." He

During practice for the US Grand Prix of 1977 Chapman stationed himself in the pit lane, ready to plug into his driver's electronic communications.

While chatting with Lotus-driving New Zealander Tony Shelly at a sunny Goodwood in 1962, a sandwich sufficed to keep Colin Chapman going.

would be all over you one time and next time he would have no use for you. You've got to have a dictator really to make it work.'

Dictators, however, can soon wear out their welcome. Chapman, too, was prone to look to the exciting new person as the one who would solve all his problems. He needed help, however, because he was working full-time at British Aluminium and would do so until 1955. With the move to former stables on Tottenham Lane in Hornsey at the end of 1951 and the subsequent intake of de Havilland boffins starting with Mike Costin, the Allens left the scene.

'I think we had just had enough at that stage,' said Michael Allen. 'We felt that we were rather on our own. Colin was on the other end of the phone saying, "Oh, do it this way – do it that way," making promises to customers which we had to fulfil. In the end when the Mark VI was pranged and the insurance paid up like a lamb, it sort of cleared all debts in the firm and we said we'd had enough. So we got out. Looking back on it I should have stuck it out, but you don't know, do you, at the time?'

The accident referred to by Michael took place on 2 August 1952 after the brand-new prototype Mark VI Lotus had only competed in two race meetings. Related Chapman, 'Nigel Allen, taking the car to Boreham where it was to be raced one Saturday in 1952, was involved in a pile-up which completely "wrote-off" the car. Nigel was unhurt, happily.[3] It was heart-breaking to have the only Mark VI wrecked when it was just one month old. We had lavished so much thought and work on it but fortunately the other driver was convicted of "driving without due care" and the insurance money obtained just about put our finances straight again!'

Although never one to coddle his workforce, Chapman felt obliged to make the occasional gesture in the Hornsey days, as Ernie Unger recalled: 'When in his more expansive mood, at about 5pm, when the day shift was ending and people were preparing to become the night shift, Colin would load us all into his 100E Ford (and you'd be amazed at how many could squeeze into a 100E – especially when Mike Costin is prepared to occupy the boot!) and whisk us up to a fairly nondescript café at the top of Muswell Hill. There we'd be plied with

---

3   The front end of the Lotus was demolished by its collision with a bread van, Nigel Allen related. A knee injury was suffered by his passenger, his wife-to-be Pauline.

COLIN CHAPMAN

egg and chips, a slice of bread and butter and a mug of tea, which largesse was supposed to keep us fuelled till the wee small hours.'

The men of Hornsey saw many of those wee small hours. Although they were both employed elsewhere until the beginning of 1955, the arrival of Mike Costin at Hornsey at the beginning of 1953 was a godsend for Chapman. 'We all used to work,' said Costin, 'but I was Colin's right-hand man. I was responsible for putting into action and doing all the things that he was involved in. We had chief designers and people in various departments. Nominally they headed up to me as technical director, but everybody really knew that they were headed up to the great dictator. Colin was always there or thereabouts but I was at the sharp end of the work being done.

'We all fell under the spell of Colin,' added Costin, 'getting us to do things that we knew we shouldn't be bloody doing such as making bits which we were fairly sure were going to break – or staying all night to work. Colin was really an impossible person to deal with, but he and I had a relationship that was extremely good. We only had two or maybe three major rows. He knew he could push me a hell of a long way – he was a very fine judge of that limit.

'All-nighters were taken for granted,' continued Mike Costin: 'In the motor-racing season, if I got to bed on a Friday night three times in a season I was lucky. Every night was an all-nighter. It was standard.' Getting in needed parts from suppliers could be tricky as well, Costin added: 'Lotus were very slow at paying their bills, which really meant they shot themselves in the foot because people stopped working for them. Bushell would delay and delay.

'Colin could leave on the Tuesday and leave me with the work of three unfinished cars for the team,' Costin added, 'and say, "Well, I'll see you at the scrutineer at four o'clock on Thursday night." His words to me would be, "Look, we've got to get that boat, you know, get 'em in." And it was impossible. People used to say to him, "Oh, you've done it now, your bloody car's not here." He'd say, "Don't you worry, Michael will be here. Give him half an hour," and of course idiot Costin would drive in with a transporter. "There you are, I told you." Because he knew that I would leave it right till the end.'

Soon Jim Clark was watching the master persuader at work. 'Colin is a hard taskmaster,' said the driver, 'yet he still retains that knack of getting people to work near-miracles for him. Many a time I've seen him talk mechanics into doing what they genuinely think is impossible. But somehow he fires them with some of his own tremendous enthusiasm and the job gets done.

Essex Petroleum's flamboyant David Thieme brought big bucks to the Lotus racing effort that accustomed Colin Chapman to a more lavish lifestyle.

The thing is, if it's really necessary he'll always be prepared to roll up his own sleeves and lend a hand and I think people respect him for that.'

'You were aware that you were on a team headed by a genuine creative genius,' said Dan Gurney about his Indianapolis years with Chapman. 'In his era he was the guy. There were many other excellent creative people, but Colin had a special element about him. There was a special feeling about Chapman. All the people around him had absolute faith in his ability to outsmart the next guy. It was a very special group of people.'

A later Lotus driver, Nigel Mansell, had much the same view: 'Colin was a great motivator and a great designer and an incredible entrepreneur. He had incredible charisma, too. It just oozed from him. So you couldn't help but be motivated by his directional abilities and plans he had, a few of which were completely crazy, but it was very exciting to try and do them.'

'He had charisma,' seconded Mike Kimberley, 'when he cared to use it.' The Lotus engineer and manager recalled a winter when he and his family were snowed in at home. 'I was on the phone to Colin about this and that,' he related. 'Then I heard one of my youngsters: "Daddy! There's a helicopter outside!" Sure enough, it was circling around the yard. In it was Colin, shouting, "I brought your work!" He threw out a box, giving me a big grin and a thumbs up.'

Mike Warner had a ringside seat to observe the Chapman charm: 'What I saw was this ability, not just on the racing side but also on the engineering side, of pulling people beyond what they even contemplated they were capable of. Chapman would come up with this concept and would often draw people beyond what they had taught themselves and their abilities. Len Terry is a classic example, a brilliant designer the peak of whose career was the work he did under Chapman. There are several other people like that – Maurice Philippe, very, very similar, did nothing after Lotus.

Although the Essex Petroleum backing – David Thieme on the right – brought splendid presentation to Lotus, it coincided with poor performance on the track.

'He was like a chameleon,' Warner added. 'He could tune his shade to the exact shade of the person that he wanted to work for him.' 'He had everybody around him analysed and catalogued,' seconded Tony Rudd. 'He used a different technique with different people. He always argued he did not understand high finance, but it was surprising how many finance people he managed to charm into providing him with millions to fund Team Lotus. Despite the criticisms, they certainly got value for money from their investments.'

Rudd was among those around Chapman who knew they were being manipulated yet succumbed to the Lotus chief's charm. 'His talent as an engineer was matched by his understanding of what motivated people,' said Rudd. 'He knew that the way to get me to perform was to say, "When I am in trouble I always know which of my old friends to turn to." I would confront him breathing fire and brimstone and flatly refusing to do something. A few minutes later I would be completely talked around and trying as hard as I could to make it work.'

Another such colleague was sales chief Graham

Arnold. 'Behind the smile that could charm money out of the trees, or more usefully out of bankers and sponsors, Colin did indeed have a nasty streak,' found Arnold. 'His reputation for using people until they were used up, like old toothpaste tubes, was not anecdotal. In 1971 he sacked me as sales director, after seven years, then invited me back for a stint of five or more years when my many replacements didn't deliver. His exact words were, "Come back and do what you did before, but quicker."'

Another swinging-door employee at Lotus was Peter Warr, Chapman's last team manager. 'There was always a complete lunacy about working for Colin,' he told Simon Taylor. 'He believed there was no reason on God's earth why an idea he'd just had couldn't be on the cars for the coming weekend. But his leadership, his ability to motivate, was such that people would start to believe it could be done, and they would perform way, way beyond their self-believed capabilities. If he said, "Right, lads, today we're all going to jump off the cliff," they'd do it. He'd jump first and they'd all follow him.' 'He was a man who could persuade people to climb mountains,' said Fred Bushell, 'who only thought they could climb over stiles.'

'Chapman was first and foremost a very good engineer, far-thinking and innovative,' said one of his last designers, Geoff Aldridge, 'and he was also a very shrewd businessman. Thirdly – and more important than both those things – he could motivate people and he could charm the birds off the trees. He'd come in, put his arm round you, and you'd work all night. And with those three things going for him, he couldn't fail.'

The flip side of the Chapman charisma was a contempt for underperformers, the 'ruthless bugger' referred to by Michael Allen. 'His temper was fairly violent,' recalled Peter Warr, 'and he had a very short fuse. He'd come round and say to someone on the shop floor, "You're meant to be the welder. I could weld that, so why the hell can't you do it right?" He could perform pretty much any task in the factory and everybody knew it.'

Graham Arnold had sight of this side of Chapman when he wrote a speech to be delivered at the Lotus shareholders' meeting after going public. Its text ended with, 'To me, the workers at Hethel are the real Team Lotus. Without them you, our shareholders, would not be reaping the benefits of your investment.' Recalled Arnold, 'He left this out and walked down from the podium towards me, asking, "How was that, then?" I showed my anger by saying, "Colin, why on earth did you leave out the bit about the employees?"

Juggling responsibilities of racing, road cars, outside contracts like DeLorean, boats and microlights, by 1981 Chapman had come under relentless time pressure.

He just snapped, "They get paid, don't they?" and walked away.'[4]

Arnold also saw the callous Chapman one year 'when we were even more strapped for cash than usual. Colin landed his even-bigger new aircraft at Hethel to join us for the directors' and executives' Christmas drinks party one Friday afternoon in late December. Halfway through he took a fellow director by the elbow and said, "I noticed as I was coming in to land that the employees' car park is completely full. That means we employ too many people. Get rid of a few, will you." On the following Monday, Christmas Eve, a number of employees received their free turkeys and their P45s in the same parcel.'

The 'nasty' Chapman was quick to make his feelings known in language that demanded forbearance from his colleagues. Michael Allen recalled the reaction of *le patron* when he saw the bodywork that Allen and Frank Hine had just completed for the Mark IV. 'Completely and utterly bloody useless,' said Chapman. 'It will have to be done again.' 'That was a favourite expression of his,' Allen recalled: '"Completely and utterly bloody

4   The author was reminded of this when he read of McLaren's Ron Dennis in David Coulthard's autobiography that 'Ron's not a big hand-shaker. I can tell you that Ron once told me, "I don't shake hands with employees," so read into that what you will. It is what it is.'

useless." Which wasn't very helpful when you had just worked all night to do it.'

Ron Hickman, who worked chiefly on Lotus production cars, would be less than thrilled when Colin Chapman would return from a race weekend and rubbish his efforts and those of his colleagues. On one such occasion the Chapman verdict on a prototype was 'a heap of fucking shit' which he also derided as 'the biggest white elephant in the motor industry.' Not surprisingly, soon after this demoralising meeting Hickman decided he'd had enough of Lotus.

With or without bad language Chapman could be tough on his designers, said one of them. 'He'd go into the drawing office and look over the draughtsman's shoulder and say, "No, no, no, that's not what I want at all." He'd grab his pencil and sketch on the side of the drawing to show him. And if the draughtsman didn't produce exactly that, Colin would go on at him until he did.' Wife Hazel remembered this attribute from the early days: 'He would become annoyed when someone tried to improve on instructions he had left. That's because he invariably got it right first time.'

Flying, which Chapman learned with the RAF, became a vital time-saver. He was snapped in the 1970s preparing to take off from Hethel in his Piper Seneca.

On one occasion, Mike Kimberley related, Chapman came into the design office holding a steel bracket. He flung it ten feet into the office shouting, 'Who the hell designed this? If ever I see welding on a bracket like that, come into my office and I'll show you welding and stiffness!'

At Hethel Chapman would make his rounds through all the design offices, 'Components, Team Lotus and Lotus Engineering,' said Mike Warner. 'He'd go round all of them going, "What are you doing, what are you doing?" And the red pencil would come out. "No, no, no, no, no, no. What you want to do is that, that, that and that." This was part of his boost, what he needed. It was his meat and wine.

'Components was the tail-end Charlie,' Warner added, 'after he'd been in Engineering and Team Lotus, and he kind of drifted through Components. By then he was on his way back to his office. He left a kind of half-thought squiggle on a drawing. Of course the designers were mesmerised enough to think, "Well, Christ, he'll be back in two weeks' time. I'd better do what he says."'

Given the chance, however, designers rebelled at this demoralising Chinese torture of their schemes. 'Why are we building crap?' was the question Mike Warner asked his designers when he arrived at Components. 'Dave Baldwin – I can see his piercing blue eyes now – said, "Get Chapman off our back." I said, "What do you mean, keep him off your back?" And he said, "We get half-way through a design and he's been to America, and he comes back in and he goes round all the drawing boards…"'

'What are you actually saying?' was Warner's reaction. 'Are you saying that if you were given a free run for six months, something like that, you'd come up with the designs that could make big improvements to the product range?' Getting their assent, Warner found some extra space in his stores complex. 'I created what was a very quiet, secret design room, two boards down there. They worked a rota – Dave Baldwin, Pete Lucas and Martin Waide. 'I got all my designs. That's how the 59 and the Seven Series 4 and the Type 70 came about.'

A standard Chapman technique in dealing with issues of racing cars or road cars was production of a hand-written job list on lined paper, numbering each item. These job lists, for which the boss was renowned, covered a wide variety of topics. He wrote things down as they occurred to him. Among specific instructions for things to do on the car would be thoughts about aspects of design that needed investigation over the longer term (see sidebar on page 307).

Sometimes the boss's notations were cryptic. His job lists sometimes included the notation 'MCTR' at the end of an item. An example was a job list for the 77 which appended 'MCTR' to 'The clutch is presently FAR too difficult to adjust'. 'None of us knew what it meant,' recalled Martin Ogilvie, 'and we didn't dare ask him. We had this bloke called Mike Cook who was more of a development engineer – he did the test work and fibreglass information – so I came up with the idea that "MCTR" stood for "Mike Cook To Rectify" so he got given all the difficult jobs to sort out. In fact it was "More Careful Thought Required". It meant that Chapman didn't know the answer himself; he was just saying, "It's not right so have another go." It was ages after that we found out what it really meant: Chapman thought it was quite funny.'

'If you couldn't do what he wanted for very good reasons,' said Geoff Aldridge, 'that was fine, but if you couldn't do it because you couldn't be bothered, or it was too difficult, he got quite angry. I never saw a bad side to him but I know lots of people did. There were stories of him tearing drawings up. It never happened to me. I always found him very approachable; he would sit down and explain things to you if you said you didn't understand.'

Speaking of angry, Chapman and engineer Mike Kimberly had a set-to over the design of engine mounts for the Lotus Europa. 'We fought about those mounts for four days,' Kimberley recalled. 'I tell you now that it will fail,' Kimberley told Colin about his preferred design, giving him a forecast of the likely time of failure as well. 'Who's the chairman of this company?' Chapman shouted. 'Do it my way!'

'We put the Europa into production,' Kimberley related, 'on time and on budget. After three months the engine-mount failures started to come in. There were 120 cars out there; we made new mounts and put them in. A while later Chapman came by my desk. "I was wrong, you were right," he said, handing me an envelope. In it were 500 shares of Group Lotus plc! He genuinely appreciated good people. If he could walk all over you, you wouldn't survive.'

'Contrary to other people's opinions since,' said Alan Styman, chief designer under Chapman in the early 1960s, 'I always found him relaxed and sympathetic to our problems when he was in the drawing office. His comment, "Let's lean on the board," would incite a response of togetherness. Knobs in the ear would also be handed out, but always with a whimsical smile. He would remind us that "a man who never made a mistake never made anything" and "let's rather have something wrong than not at all."

Creation of the profusion of Lotus companies and management of the transactions among them were included in the responsibilities of finance chief Fred Bushell.

Though thought a dictator by many among his long-suffering staff, Chapman seemed ready to admit to Clark, left, that he didn't know the answer at Trenton in 1963.

'Producing work for both race and road cars caused unhappiness between Colin and design engineer Ron Hickman,' Styman added. 'Each wanted his work done first but Colin nearly always won because his cars were more exciting! My impression was that he was never happier than when he was involved directly with racing cars. Anything else for him was a complete pain in the arse.'

Ron Hickman poured out his frustrations on 21 October 1963 in a six-page single-spaced memo to Chapman titled 'Points Awaiting Your Decisions'. In it he referred to a 'mammoth report' on production-car design issues and proposals that his chief must have found even less digestible. Hickman's complaints concerned work on the M20 project, later to be the Elan +2, which was competing for resources at the time with the ill-fated Type 30 family of two-seaters.

Having set out a vast laundry list of detailed topics needing resolution, down to mounting methods for window-guide channels, Ron Hickman concluded as follows:

There are many other matters on which your advice and help is needed from time to time in one of your various official or 'unofficial' capacities; but whilst not always important

enough to write down or 'scream' for, it should not be assumed that when you are not available we are 'forced to do things for ourselves'. Quite the contrary, there is a universal reluctance to proceed if we know that you are either interested in a thing, or have not even seen or tried it to give it your blessing or otherwise.

Hickman's litany of unresolved issues provided a perfect illustration of the minutiae of production-car development that interested Chapman not a whit. One can picture him tossing the memo aside with a deep sigh. This was a business in which he'd decided to engage, but he often found its demands intolerable. Later he devolved authority for production-car decision-making to others.

As his business activities expanded and proliferated in the 1960s Colin Chapman tried to put suitable management techniques in place. In 1963 he set out this subdivision of decision making for the benefit of his team:

The Policy:	*What* we want.
The Plan:	*How* we intend to do it.
The Programme:	*When* we intend to do it.

Colin hoped that this *modus operandi* would liberate him from having to resolve the same problem twice. He deeply disliked revisiting issues, though he would do so if pressed. For this reason Chapman sought to establish policies, wherever possible, that covered matters that needed resolution. In this can be seen his recent exposure to the Ford Motor Company and its policy 'blue letters' that set out the positions that had been adopted by the company at the highest level on both internal and external topics.

Some of his staff were open to learning from the Lotus chief. 'Chapman was an exceptionally good teacher,' said Peter Collins, Team Lotus manager for three years at the end of the 1970s. 'He didn't sit you down and tell you what to do or what was wrong, but he was a fantastic teacher. You learned by his example in many respects.' 'Lotus was a university of motor sports for me,' said driver Jackie Oliver. 'I learned a lot from Chapman, watched his methods, listened to him. He told me, "Lad, it's easy having the ideas; it's getting things made, getting things done that's the hard part." I remembered a lot of this when I started my own F1 team.'

Chapman's tutorial patience had distinct limits, however, as his dialogues with Keith Duckworth

A pleasurable moment for a relaxed Colin Chapman at his home circuit, Snetterton in Norfolk, was shared in 1963 with his daughter Jane.

demonstrated. 'Colin couldn't stand that this bloke was so bright,' recalled Mike Costin. 'Keith was very forthright and he wanted an explanation of everything. He wanted to discuss everything. Colin didn't want to know; he wanted to do it *that way*, even if it proved to be wrong – and, by the way, he wanted it done yesterday.'

In the early days of Lotus, Duckworth was typical of the intake that was attracted by the opportunity to work with Colin Chapman. 'People are just interested and come along to ask us for jobs,' Colin said. 'Take Keith Duckworth for example. He was secretary of the Car Club at London University and asked me down to speak. I gave him a job working in the vacations on gearboxes; then he came full-time. Later he went off to do independent research and now he has his own firm. We give him 100 per cent of our engine business.'

At Lotus, said Tony Rudd, 'The work was stimulating and exciting. Chunky exploited the idea that people looked upon Lotus as a post-graduate course and were willing to work there for less than the going rate anywhere else.' Even paying them, of course, was a concession made by the man who at the outset used his Tom Sawyer-like skills to persuade hugely talented people to work for nothing.[5]

Chapman's employees approached the predilections of their boss in different ways. 'Most of his young men thought the way to promotion and prosperity was to implement his every word,' observed Tony Rudd. 'One of them once remarked to Chunky that he was always in trouble for following his dictums yet I, who often challenged or ignored them, never seemed to get into trouble. "Because he uses his loaf," snorted Chunky. "I wish you would sometimes."'

In Team Lotus, manager Andrew Ferguson made a game of trying to anticipate Chapman's needs and desires. Calling it 'nursemaiding Colin,' he said that he 'thoroughly enjoyed it. I treated the whole thing as a highly competitive game, always striving to stay one step ahead of the Guv'nor and trying to imagine what might come into his mind next so as to be well prepared. To win was mighty satisfying, especially when Colin suddenly realised that I had read his mind well in advance and had all details catered for! His knowing smile and accompanying comment were ample reward. Mind, you, there were also explosive blasts when I expounded my theory only to discover that I had picked wrong.'

---

5   Widely read as he was, Chapman may well have envied the architect Frank Lloyd Wright, whose charisma was such that acolytes paid to be allowed to work with him at his romantic Taliesens.

No such latitude was granted to Chapman's engineers. 'The worst time to deal with Colin was when he got enthused about something,' remembered Martin Ogilvie. 'We had to deliver in no time at all and work all hours. His mantra was always to "double it" or "halve it". There was one occasion when Colin said to me, "I want you to design the rear anti-roll bar to be twice as stiff. And I mean *twice as stiff*." He was quite explicit. So I built this huge, heavy anti-roll bar which was totally hopeless, of course. He was aghast and told me, "Ah, Martin, you must always design what I mean, not what I say. I was just making a point for emphasis."'

Such challenges to his designers were intense because Chapman was often enthused about something. This began at a young age, according to his father. 'He soon began to invent things,' said Stan Chapman. 'There was his automatic peashooter. He showed me the drawing first, all professionally laid out with materials specification, stress points and what have you. His prototype worked perfectly. When Colin was 12 he built a warplane of his own design, finished to the last detail. It was a twin-engine job and when the propellers were turned, the wheels retracted and the bomb doors opened. That model 'plane really set us thinking. It was so extremely good, a really mature and beautiful piece of workmanship.'

For Chapman the businessman it was essential to be on correct terms with key allies such as sponsor Andy Granatelli, right, and Lotus racing-car customer Rob Walker.

Jim Clark saw the joke at Goodwood in 1962 but Colin Chapman was deadly serious. Charming when need be to achieve his aims, he also had a ruthless side.

During his 1968 Indianapolis campaign Chapman looked sceptical in his conversation with Vince Granatelli. Relations with the Granatelli brothers were always lively.

When he arrived on the world stage, Colin Chapman's timing was good, he admitted: 'I was helped by the times, because just after the war everything was new and business was starting again and everything was a lot more fluid. Where I've been lucky is in having a number of opportunities presented to me which I've been able to take. I think you make a lot of your own luck in that respect, in that you've got to be quick – but you can never really tell. It's too subjective.'

'Back in those grey post-war years,' said Sid Marler, 'Colin showed how established thinking and stifling conventions could be severely bucked in contrast to the many union-ridden and badly managed companies of the day. Lotus also brought a welcome splash of colour to Hornsey, especially with their dark green cars with yellow wheels.'

In 1955 *Motor Sport* had found the 'Hornsey home of Lotus rather cramped due to the car's very quick rise to fame, and discarded body shells, new frames and other components are apt to stack up outside on fine days, where they mingle with the delightfully early-vintage Austin Seven saloons of the employees.' 'That so much can be accomplished in such cramped quarters verges on the miraculous,' said a 1957 visitor.

The latter year saw the opening of an office block and showroom which finally provided room for on-site car design and a proper sales activity. Squeezed among Tottenham Lane, the British Railways main line and Stan Chapman's Railway Arms hotel were the cramped workshops and car-assembly area. Williams & Pritchard had a workspace there while frame-maker Progress Chassis was just over the Lane.

Management of bustling Lotus was a decidedly top-down affair. 'The whole of the Lotus "empire" was run as a dictatorship,' recalled Mike Costin. 'Colin was a total dictator. It didn't bother me that Colin was a dictator. It was his company, it wasn't anybody else's. Later on, when I had a three-year service agreement, I had five per cent of the shares of Lotus Components. Should I leave, the shares had to be returned to the company at par. In fact when I left Colin after ten years my total remuneration left just enough money to buy my wife a Mini – it cost £362. It was part of the build-up of life.'

A major breakthrough for Lotus – indeed *the* major breakthrough – was its alliance with Ford to build the Lotus Cortina. 'I think without Ford, Lotus would not have made it to that higher division,' said Mike Warner. Although Walter Hayes was the public face of the Ford/Lotus relationship, Warner credited Ford of Britain executive Leonard Crossland with important behind-the-scenes assistance. In the mid-1960s, when the Lotus relationship with Ford was forged, Crossland became Ford UK's managing director and then its chairman in 1968. He was knighted in 1969.

'Leonard Crossland was very close to Chapman,' Warner recalled. 'I think his patronage in the early days helped Colin grease the wheels, if you like, with Ford of America because Colin didn't get on too well in the beginning with Ford of America, with Henry Ford II, having this brash young UK upstart come over and say, "Yeah, we'll win Indy for you, don't worry about it!" I don't think Crossland's place has ever been fully recognised.'

'We have been working with Ford and using their engines for Formula Junior races,' explained Colin Chapman when asked about his Ford relationship. 'They then asked me to meet them and try out the new Cortina which they thought had a good weight/size ratio and could be made in a high-performance version, but in small numbers. I was quite impressed with it. When they asked if I could make 1,000 I found it would just fit in with our production plans. We put in aluminium doors, bonnet and body lids. We modified the front suspension, gave it wider wheels, widened the front track, fitted disc brakes, altered the camber of the wheels and gave it a different rear suspension. If you did that with an ordinary production car it would take two years. We were able to do it in three months.'

In 1965 Chapman went into more detail about the Lotus relationship with Ford, as follows:

I am often asked what the actual connection is between Lotus and Ford Motor Co Ltd, so I will outline the actual position. Firstly we are not partly or wholly owned by Ford nor have they ever tried to buy us out.

For Ford of Britain we act in the following capacity:
a. *We developed the Cortina-Lotus and are still going ahead with certain production and improvement development work on the car.*
b. *We manufacture the Cortina-Lotus at Cheshunt assembling our engine, gearbox, suspension and interior into a slightly modified Cortina two-door body. These cars are then returned to Ford's Dagenham factory and are distributed through the Ford distribution network with full Ford Warranty and Service backing. By special arrangement our Sales Division is permitted to market a proportion of these cars direct to the public in standard, 'Special Equipment' or full race form.*

Peter Wright, left, got the one-eyed treatment from his chief. Colin Chapman tailored his approaches to his staff to suit his knowledge of their needs and motivations.

c. *We prepare and race the Team Lotus Cortinas which won the 1964 National Saloon Car Championship.*
d. *We hold a Lotus-Cortina spares stock for Ford Dealers.*

For Ford of America we produce the Indianapolis-type cars which after Indy won the Milwaukee and Trenton races and run, in America, a team of Lotus-Cortinas for the English Ford Line Division at Dearborn.

These were important responsibilities for the budding Lotus operation, which in 1959 had moved to new premises in Cheshunt. The Ford involvement obliged Lotus to raise its game in all the areas mentioned while bringing cash flow that transformed the company's prospects. Sir Leonard Crossland's contribution was recognised by his appointment as deputy chairman of Lotus Cars, the car-building operation, after his retirement from Ford in 1972. During the run-up to the launch of the new upmarket Elite 'Sir Leonard grew much more actively involved in the company,' Fred Bushell related. 'Soon he was personally controlling the activities of the managing director and was therefore performing the monitoring, motivating and target-

Fired and then rehired by Chapman, Graham Arnold was a long-serving sales director for Lotus. He doubted that success at Indianapolis helped sales in America.

setting which on previous new-model launches Colin would have carried out himself.'

Cheshunt was soon outgrown. 'Twenty-five years from now,' Chapman said in 1965, 'we will look back on the Cheshunt plant and smile at its smallness just as Sir William Lyons must think of the early Swallows built in two small sheds. We now have some factory space in Norfolk which produces glass-fibre body moulds, some body sections and certain tools and components. We chose Norfolk mainly because experienced glass-fibre labour and technicians were locally available due to the decline in the glass-fibre boat business and because the premises were vacant. There are therefore no grounds for the suggestion that Lotus will soon move to Norfolk.'

His last remark was disingenuous, for Lotus was already planning its move to Norfolk. Cheshunt had been resistant to any further expansion of its operations. Land at the disused airbase at Hethel had been acquired and plans for the new works drawn up. In November of 1966 Lotus moved lock, stock and barrel to Hethel, with office staff enjoying an open-plan environment that was

then novel in Britain. This was a Chapman innovation, based on offices he'd seen at BP in Germany. Hangar space for company aircraft was organised while a test circuit was laid out on the airfield.

'We don't really want to make many more cars than we are making at the moment,' Chapman said in explaining the move to Hethel. 'What we do want to do is make more of the car ourselves. Our main objective in moving from Cheshunt to Norwich, where we have three times as much floor space, is not to make three times as many cars but to make ten to twenty per cent more cars and to make very much more of the car ourselves. We're already fully manufacturing and painting Elan bodies. We make our own chassis and we've just started making our own engines. We are making our own trim and we will carry on making more and more bits of the car ourselves.'

At Hethel Chapman and Bushell were still using the multi-company structure that they'd found amenable to financial flexibility. In 1965 Chapman put the position as follows:

> *From the original Lotus Engineering Co Ltd we have grown to become the Lotus Group. Each company has a set objective within the Group and has to stand on its own feet both financially and in its management.*

Lotus Developments Ltd
designs and develops all passenger cars to the production stage.

Lotus Cars Limited
manufactures the Elan and Lotus Cortina, produces fibreglass bodies and handles all outside purchases and supplies.

Lotus Cars (Sales) Ltd
markets and distributes our products at home and abroad as well as operating the service, parts and technical literature sections.

Lotus Components Ltd
manufactures production racing cars, racing versions of passenger cars (Elan and Cortina) and produces the famous Lotus Seven sports car.

Team Lotus Limited
develops and designs racing cars and operates or controls the various teams which race from the factory or represent the marque on our behalf.

Chapman and tall Peter Warr were dead centre in a portrait of 1972's Team Lotus. Chapman's staff did not always receive the appreciation that this image implied.

After the move to Hethel three more companies were added: the Cheshunt Lotus Centre, to continue retail sales near London; Lotus Cars (Service) Ltd for after-sales service and Racing Engines Limited. Each company had an executive director. In only one, Team Lotus, did Chapman hold this post. After little more than a decade in business he successfully devolved responsibility to trusted colleagues, with former Ford man Dennis Austin heading Lotus Cars. All were under the umbrella of Group Lotus Car Companies Ltd, where Chapman, Bushell and Kirwan-Taylor were the only directors. Although cosmetically disguised, a dictatorship was still in effect.

Especially when privately held, such an enterprise didn't go unnoticed. Jaguar was actively looking for acquisitions. Ultimately it would absorb not only Guy trucks but also Coventry Climax. 'Jaguar came down,' said Mike Warner. 'Sir William Lyons came down and inspected Lotus with a view to absorbing Lotus. I think he weighed it up with Colin Chapman, but Chapman was too free a spirit at that point.'

Though Mike Warner wasn't among those who made the move to Hethel – 'not because of anything other than I'd been offered another damned good job and I wanted to stay in the Home Counties' – he kept the confidence of Fred Bushell, who had been offered a senior post with one of the big accounting companies. Bushell had once told Warner that working for Chapman 'was like trying to run up an escalator the wrong way, and if you paused for a second...' Now, said Warner, 'Bushell was tiring of that escalator.'

Meeting with Chapman, Bushell expressed his thoughts. His chief wasn't at a loss. 'Colin mapped out – for the first time in the years I've known him – mapped out this extremely clever strategic plan where we're going,' Bushell told Warner. 'Now I know what we're heading for.' That was the plan of Chapman and Kirwan-Taylor to take the Group public. 'The chameleon had to change his colour to meet Fred at that point,' Warner related, 'and the only thing that could encourage and motivate Fred was a brilliant strategic plan. Whether Colin had planned it or whether he thought it up at the time, God only knows.'

In 1967 journalist Bill Gavin took the measure of the man who was about to go public. 'Like every successful person Colin Chapman comes in for a great deal of criticism,' he wrote. 'Many people claim that he is self-centred, avaricious, heartless, even irresponsible. Colin does possibly have these faults in some degree, but I would certainly not regard them as character defects, for without them he would not have achieved the great success that he has.

'The manufacture of racing cars is a very borderline sort of business,' Gavin continued. 'A host of British firms have tried it but less than half a dozen have managed to make money at it. The production runs are relatively so small that a good percentage of the overheads has to be lumped on to the price of every car or spare part. The fact that Lotus has made money in this business reflects on the business acumen of Chapman and his co-directors as much as on Colin's abilities as a designer.

'All the Lotus successes have brought Colin Chapman fame and a certain amount of wealth,' Bill Gavin added, 'but his first love is still motor racing. If he applied himself to the production-car side of the Lotus operation with the same verve as he goes about his racing activities, the whole operation would be more successful; but then the racing would possibly go to pot as it did in 1958 and 1959 when he was concentrating on getting the Elite into production.'

Fred Bushell told Jabby Crombac that he warned Chapman about the pitfalls of going public: 'I said that I

During practice for Canada's Grand Prix in 1967 Chapman worked on his job list. Marrying action items with musings on the future, these lists were management tools on which he relied.

At Indianapolis in 1967 Chapman checked on a damper's function. His engineers, workmen and mechanics knew he was able to carry out most tasks.

felt he would not be particularly happy since it would place considerable restraints upon his own freedom of action which, from experience, I felt he would be unwilling to accept. He said that he was changing and was quite sure he could rise to the challenge.'

Although Bushell said that a public share issue was likely to take two years, as usual Chapman wanted to do it faster. 'Colin threw himself into the undertaking with his usual drive and enthusiasm,' said Bushell, with the result that only six months passed before the flotation in October of 1968.[6] Team Lotus remained a private Chapman family property.

Colin Chapman retained 52 per cent of the shares in the new company, which at its launch valuation made him a millionaire four and a half times over. From now on, however, the City would demand regular reports on how his businesses were doing. While the rosy forecasts for 1968 were met by a 50 per cent increase in profits, thanks to cost-cutting and diligent sales efforts from Graham Arnold, losses during a recession in 1970 were a wake-up call.

'The crisis forced Chapman to pay attention,' wrote Robert Heller, 'not only to the financial control of the company but also to its management systems. Like all tough taskmasters who are fanatical about perfection and detail, Chapman had in any case tended to delegate either inadequately or inefficiently. He was both doing too much himself and not getting enough information on what others were doing in his name. A man who runs motor racing teams is used to coping with crisis and calamity: Chapman gets highly excited but doesn't panic – and he didn't panic in face of his management pile-up.'

'We didn't actually have a slump,' Chapman explained to Ray Hutton, 'but we did suffer from two major financial setbacks of a non-recurring nature: excess expenditure in sectors of the Group other than our main car-manufacturing company. One of them was in the marketing division, where we wasted a lot of money – really through imprudent management – and the other was in our racing-car division where the manufacture of competition cars for sale became unprofitable. These two activities detracted from the profit made by the car-manufacturing company.' This signalled the end of the line for Lotus Racing as Lotus Components had been renamed.

---

6 Notably he did this in the shadow of the death of Jim Clark at Hockenheim. Engaging so completely with a novel challenge may well have been good therapy for Chapman.

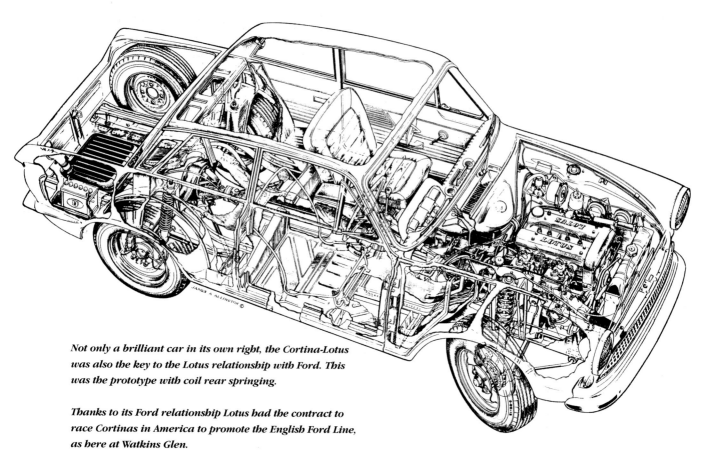

Not only a brilliant car in its own right, the Cortina-Lotus was also the key to the Lotus relationship with Ford. This was the prototype with coil rear springing.

Thanks to its Ford relationship Lotus had the contract to race Cortinas in America to promote the English Ford Line, as here at Watkins Glen.

When cutbacks were necessary, Colin Chapman was able to make them. 'Other people in the past had sometimes succeeded in elevating meanness to the status of a fine art,' wrote Leonard Setright, 'but it was left to Chapman to perfect it as an instrument for winning motor races. Just as his demands for credit were notorious in business, so his insistence on the utmost efficiency of men and machinery became a byword in automobile engineering. Sometimes this niggardliness took curious forms: no visitor to the factory (in the days when it was at Cheshunt in Hertfordshire) ever enjoyed any hospitality, even a cup of coffee, the boss having decreed that anybody found consuming food on the premises was liable to instant dismissal on the grounds that it made the place untidy. He could not offer perfection, but he could demand it.'

'His strong self-control enabled him when necessary to avoid wasteful self-indulgence,' added Robin Read about the Chapman of the 1960s. Charles Fox echoed these verdicts, saying that Chapman 'is known as being Cockney-shrewd in matters having to do with money. He's never seen grabbing the check for drinks but is notorious for carrying great wads of presumably unmarked bills and buying such things as aeroplanes with them.'

Having joined Lotus in 1969 from Jaguar, engineer

Mike Kimberley rose through the ranks of the Lotus road-car company. He became operations director and then, in 1975–76, managing director to prepare for its spin-off as a separate company in 1977. The launch of the new Elite in 1974 had been a deliberate strategy on the part of Lotus to move upmarket, to produce a car that could cover its costs and produce a profit. It was the first of a new generation, later adding the Eclat and Esprit, in which £6 million was invested.

However, the introduction of more costly Lotuses meant abandoning the lower-priced segment that the Elan had served. 'I supported the move upmarket,' Kimberley said, 'coming from Jaguar and seeing the way Jaguar was protected from the recession in the 1960s. I believed it was a move in the right direction. The only proviso was that I believed we should have kept an Elan-priced car.'

Kimberley's proposal had been for a new model akin to Porsche's 924, but because 'Chapman was concerned with image' it wasn't progressed. 'Chapman had developed fairly fixed ideas on the basic parameters of the company,' Kimberley added, telling journalist Daniel

In the 1960s a Cortina-Lotus pitted at Bridgehampton during an endurance race. The Lotus-run team wasn't shy about advertising the source of its support.

Erected in 1957, the Lotus office block in Hornsey brought respectability to the budding company. Its showroom soon succumbed to the need for offices.

For the Lotus 50th anniversary, celebrated in 1998, Autocar produced a map of its various locations. Beech Drive in Muswell Hill was the Stan Chapman family residence and Tottenham Lane the site of his hotel and the birthplace of Lotus as a company. Hazel Williams lived on Alexandra Park Road, just south of which was the home of Michael and Nigel Allen on Vallance Road. Lotus moved progressively northwards to Cheshunt and then to Hethel.

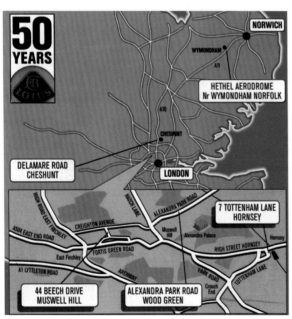

Ward that 'Chapman was very autocratic over production and design issues alike, while also keeping an uncompromising rein on the finances.' The company chief's 'lack of enchantment with the car company,' said Tony Rudd, was exacerbated by what Chapman called 'Kimberly's incessant bleating for money.'

Its new upmarket product range didn't keep Lotus from suffering in the Energy-Crisis 1970s. From a staff of 900 at the beginning of the decade Hethel cut back to 600 by 1974. Monthly production of 200 cars in the 1960s fell to 100 by 1978 and in 1979 to only 30. 'Of course we were short of cash,' said Mike Kimberley, 'so in 1976 we were working on the levitation principle of picking yourself up by your own boot laces.' Respite came in 1977 when American Express, essaying the world of venture capital, provided loans and overdraft facilities. Lotus Cars was still struggling, however, and late in 1982 at Chapman's death remained in what the *Financial Times* called 'deep financial trouble.'

Meanwhile the car company was committed to annual support for Team Lotus ranging between £75,000 and £100,000, justified as a marketing expense, and the provision of interest-free loans. 'I was often told that Chunky operated Lotus cars to fund his motor racing,' said Tony Rudd. 'He never said this to me. By the time of the 1978 championship, F1 costs had exploded. Team Lotus's annual budgets far exceeded the best profits Lotus Cars had ever made (about £1.25 million). Most of Team Lotus's income came from sponsors.' In the mid-1960s annual racing budgets had been nearer £150,000.

Certainly Team Lotus hadn't been guilty of gilding its facilities at Ketteringham Hall. While other Grand Prix teams were building up their in-house capabilities, Team Lotus was if anything shrinking them. 'We were down to just four fabricators' in 1978, said Peter Riches, 'whereas at one time we had eight. There were two machinists and we had two lathes and a mill, and that was it. It was only a small machine, and that was all we had to make any turned or milled components for the car. If those two machine tools couldn't do it, the job had to be farmed out.

'We had suppliers whom we could phone on Monday,' Riches continued, 'and say, "We need this by the end of the week," and they would make it. People like Hesketh made their money like that. We probably paid well over the odds for it.' After Hesketh pulled out of Formula 1 it maintained its fabrication facilities as a service to other teams while also building monocoques for Lotus.

Ketteringham Hall's remote location was ideal for security. However it was well away from the Oxfordshire epicentre of British motor racing, justly famed as

Soon after its completion the open-plan office block at Hethel glistened with glazing. The factory buildings began on the right.

'Carburettor Valley'. 'It was nice being out in the wilds,' said mechanic Steve Hallam, 'because we were doing stuff that only we had thought of doing and it was interesting, but you need movement of staff to keep up with developments. The Team Lotus factory – a wonderful Elizabethan manor house – was great, but it wasn't good enough.'

Frustrated by all the legal constraints placed on his Lotus road cars, in 1977 Colin Chapman moved his base of operations from Hethel to Ketteringham Hall. There, said Peter Riches, 'Chapman was in dispute with his home-base staff. He wanted to negotiate longer guaranteed working weeks and all sorts of things, and it was getting very messy. I arrived on the scene just as four of them were made redundant. The Old Man always had to have a scapegoat. That's why not many people ever held grudges against him, because they knew that eventually it would probably be their turn to be the scapegoat.'

Occasions when Chapman took his staff into his confidence about future projects were rare. Keeping his cards close to his chest increased his power over his associates and gave him the flexibility to make sudden changes in direction. 'Although we all worked as a team with great success – usually,' said Mike Costin, 'Colin automatically worked with his people on what is now called a "need to know" basis.'

'Chapman is a fanatic about keeping technical information under his hat,' said one of his early co-workers. 'The first anybody at Lotus knew about the projected Formula 2 car was when the welders delivered a new frame one morning. Of course they had an idea that something new was cooking: Chapman hadn't been putting in as much time as usual at the plant. This meant developments, for he does designing at home.'

'He was paranoid about secrecy,' added Martin Ogilvie. 'If something got out he would come storming in, saying, "I told you it was a secret! If someone's been blabbing down the pub I'll dock people's pay!" But it always ended up being him because he was always blabbing to his mates because he had a massive ego.'

Artful misdirection was part of the Chapman armoury, as in the case of the 'trick differential' explanation for the 78's performance. However Keith Duckworth thought he carried this to extremes:

I didn't understand why, during 1967, when we went around to all the GPs together and were frequently wandering around the paddock, he'd tell different tales of what had gone wrong with the car and/or engine to various journalists. I decided in the end that he just wanted to complicate life because he found it too simple if he told the truth all the time. I almost think that 'a stranger to the truth' is what I have thought might be a description. His dealing fibs of course made it very difficult for most commercial or most straightforward people. He gave them great difficulty in living with him. Which of course was of great value to me – why I was able to get Mike Costin to join me – because he couldn't really live with Colin's deviousness.

This character trait played its part in the relationships of Chapman and Lotus with their customers. In Britain Mike Anthony was an early and supportive Lotus customer. For his 1955 season Lotus was building a special Mark VIII to take a Bristol six, the prototype of the Mark X. 'That winter,' Anthony related, 'with the car under construction, Colin rang and asked, "Would you like disc brakes?" Up to then no Lotus had been fitted with them. I thought it a fabulous idea but when I asked, "How much?" he replied, "An extra £1,000." That was more than I was paying for the rest of the car, minus engine and gearbox. I told him that I didn't have the money. But he said, "Well you needn't pay me until it's convenient." I thought that was fair, so the car came with disc brakes.'

During a race meeting at Charterhall, Anthony conferred with the representative of Dunlop, the maker of the brakes, who asked the driver, 'How are you getting on with the experimental brakes we *gave* Chapman for your car?' The light dawned. Said Anthony, 'He told me that Dunlop had an agreement with Chapman to sponsor my car with [the brakes]. If they were successful they would fit them to other Mark Xs. I wrote a letter of complaint to Chapman but had no reply, and later Lotus sued me [for the £1,000]. I put in my defence that it was all a con, that I would have been

Expanding on its estate at Hethel Aerodrome near Wymondham, Lotus had immediate access not only to a runway but also to a perimeter-road test circuit.

quite happy to pay for the conversion fittings but not the whole sum. It went to the High Court. Lotus was not represented, the action was adjourned and I never heard any more. But I didn't speak to Chapman for several years after that.'

In 1955 racer Peter Ashdown was buying the parts he needed to build up a Mark IX. 'Dealing with Chapman at the time was impossible,' he said. You'd arrive at the lock-up in Hornsey to collect a part only to find it had been sold to someone else.' 'This was still happening in 1970,' said enthusiast Mike Holland. 'Early that year I ordered a kit Elan S4. By late May it hadn't arrived so I threatened to cancel the order and buy a BMW instead. "My" car arrived within seven days. It was in a different colour – which I had to agree to – and the labels on the car were in the name of a different customer.'

Even prominent race winners received the 'bait-and-switch' treatment from Lotus. After lengthy negotiations over the specification and price of a special Nineteen, Dan Gurney remarked, 'Well, that is the first car I've ever bought where the clutch was an optional extra!' Gurney's patron Frank Arciero had previously bought a Nineteen for Dan, but when the driver came over to collect it he found the car unready. 'In fact,' said Robin Read, 'Chapman had sold it to one of the more experienced Lotus customers who knew the ropes of jumping the Lotus queue.'

Another important American customer for Lotus cars was Texan Jim Hall. After acquiring a Formula Junior Lotus and a Fifteen sports-racer Hall decided to step up to Grand Prix racing. 'When I was trying to buy a 2.5-litre Lotus Eighteen,' Hall related, 'Chapman kept telling me he could do that, but when it got right down to shipping it, it got shipped with a 2.0-litre engine. The

price was different and everything, but it was a bit of a bait-and-switch deal. That means you offer something you can't really deliver and deliver something else. That was an experience with Colin Chapman, bless his soul. As they say, he was sharp.'

Speaking of sharp, the 1962 Grand Prix season gave an example. Sleeker than its predecessor the 21, the Lotus 24 was introduced for Formula 1 in 1962. Private teams were quick to buy them, among them Jack Brabham until his own car was ready and BRP, the British Racing Partnership headed by Stirling Moss's father Alfred and manager Ken Gregory. BRP engaged former Lotus team driver Innes Ireland.

'We had been promised the very latest Lotus cars in time for the start of the season,' related Ireland. 'Chapman had made this promise in writing to BRP and assured us that we would get the best possible service and consideration from him. In fact our cars were to be basically the same as those raced by Team Lotus.' In the light of this it was no small shock to arrive at Zandvoort for the Dutch Grand Prix to find Jim Clark sitting in the new monocoque 25. 'Chapman told me that this was not for BRP because it was Lotus's 1963 car – pretty extraordinary, since it was only May 1962.' The promises made earlier in the year were seen as deceptive at best and sharp practice at worst.

Having had a new idea, Colin Chapman saw no reason either to delay its introduction unduly or to share it with rival teams. He was dedicated, above all, to new ideas

Racing at Brands Hatch in 1955, Mike Anthony had disc brakes on his Lotus-Bristol. Only after being billed for them did he discover that Chapman had them at no cost.

and their successful exploitation. This was one of his great strengths, said wife Hazel: 'Many of his ideas are "borrowed" by others, and it always makes me fume. Colin is quite unperturbed. He just says "Oh, I'll think of something better next year." What's more – he does!'

'Colin was never satisfied,' found early business partner Michael Allen. 'You'd get a car going well at a race meeting and something would break. You'd come back on a Saturday night, have a bit of rest, then be prepared to mend what had broken on the Sunday. But no – that wasn't enough! It wasn't enough to be winning all the 750 Formula races. "We've got to modify this, we've got to modify that, we've got to improve the other," he would say. It just took all our efforts.

'This was the trouble,' Allen continued, 'he would never settle. I say if it's going well let's keep it going well. You never knew if you were improving it or not because you had done so many different things. You never really knew when changes had worked. But he always gave the impression that he knew exactly what he was doing. It was for us all a bit of an adventure.'

It never stopped being an adventure for all Chapman's later colleagues. 'I think that Chapman is a terrific engineer,' said driver Jochen Rindt, 'But he sometimes takes off into the sky, you see. If you've got a bloke who tries to stop him – which is very difficult to stop

A long delay after he'd ordered an Elan S4 kit prompted Mike Holland to threaten cancellation. Though he specified a white body he had to accept yellow instead.

Promised parity with the works team's F1 equipment in 1962, the BRP team bought Lotus 24s – Innes Ireland's here. Arrival of the 25 in May came as a shock.

Chapman because he has his own way whatever he does, really.'

A common complaint concerned Chapman's lack of interest in development. One of his stock phrases – later adopted by Keith Duckworth – was that 'development is the last refuge of an incompetent designer'. A stricture meant to encourage more consideration in depth before cutting metal, it could be taken to extremes. 'Chapman was not very interested in development,' said engineer Nigel Bennett. 'He would find the current situation totally boring. It was new ideas that kept him going, trying to stay ahead.' Peter Warr saw flaws in this philosophy: 'If Colin had a failing it was that he always looked for the next thing no-one had rather than develop what he had.'

Bennett and Warr were exposed to this Chapman characteristic in the 1970s when advances in GP car design were hectic thanks to the exploitation of downforce in its various forms. Colin had became even more impatient, much less tolerant of the status quo. Earlier exceptions that proved the rule were his successful evolution of the 25 into the 33, the Indy 29 into the 34 and 38 and the long careers of the 49 and 72. When needs must, Colin Chapman could develop with the best of them.

Chapman's biographer Jabby Crombac recalled being startled during the introduction of the Lotus 76 by his friend's statement: 'The era of radical innovations has now passed. From now on we will proceed by detail

Next New Car Requirements

Absolute MAXIMUM of low drag aerodynamic download – ie large negative lifting body surface ahead of the rear wing.

1. Rear wing double tapered super banana.
2. Rear wheels which *both* remain virtually upright in the corner under heavy side G. (Longer top links for more negative camber on droop.)
3. Outboard front brakes – but double caliper for extra capacity with free wheel transmission.
4. FRICTIONLESS suspension links when under maximum load, front and rear.
5. FRICTIONLESS plunging joints on rear drive line. (Susp geometry to minimise plunge anyway).
6. As the McLaren is about the fastest car down the straight through the speed traps why can't we have maximum legal tracks front *and* rear? Quantify what %age we would lose.
7. We MUST solve the UJ boot problem. We just cannot use boots to hold the grease in! – let's use hookes joints and roller splines.
8. Add large gearbox spacer so as to get all the airbox disturbance over before the rear wing. Also minimum overhang airbox fairing.
9. We MUST have a fuel system which does not make the car 70 lb heavier down the wrong side after a little running!
10. Water pipes that *never* break.
11. Driver's seat which is *absolutely* rigid – and sits him low in the car.
12. 100 L petrol – Calorific value? Elf oil etc.
13. Wheel hub bearings that *cannot* fail. And keep their grease in!
14. Investigate null point in toe curve procedure.
15. Are we sure that a single lower link at rear is no problem?
16. 6 speed gearbox.
17. Really effective limited slip differentials – why not go to Wiseman diffs – make our own?
18. Really massive suspension link attachments so there is *NO* possibility of *any* deflection.
19. Lower bottom reversed wishbone for maximum rear wheel rigidity.
20. Front and rear wheel mounting systems to be absolutely rigid. Present wheel bearings suspect.
21. Really wide base for lower w'bone on rear upright casting – like 49?
22. Can we devise a selective fuel system that will use outboard fuel first!

improvements.' And this on the very threshold of the introduction of the venturi underbody that was to revolutionise the Grand Prix car. 'Coming from such a man as Colin Chapman,' said Crombac, 'this was indeed a surprise but it just goes to show the frame of mind he was in at what was a critical time for all car manufacturers, but especially for Lotus, due to the fuel crisis which had struck throughout the world a few months earlier.'

Was Chapman sincere in his comment to Crombac? Or was it yet another of his classic misdirections, calculated to throw his rivals off the scent? Of the two options the latter is the more likely. The 76, after all, had an automatic clutch to allow left-foot braking – an innovation destined to mature years in the future. Colin Chapman had no intention of taking his foot off the throttle.

Friend and sometime colleague Charles Bulmer explained 'the way in which Colin worked – he would draw a number of people into a discussion, listen to their arguments and often give them further assignments. Then he would come to some decision or compromise using his own intuition or his own assessment of the knowledge and abilities of the various participants.' Invariably his decision would disappoint and even disenfranchise some of his team. But this was of absolutely no concern to Chapman.

'He was not an easy man to know,' said close observer Louis Stanley, 'but watching him in action was revealing. It told a great deal about him. He was a tireless, unceasing worker. As with all perfectionists, incompetence came under withering attack. He was often ruthless in decisions; shrewd and astute when it came to business deals. A fiery temper made him unpredictable, often leading to uneasy relationships. He talked about achievements without false modesty.'

From this assessment, and from our overview of Chapman the manager, the word 'ruthless' jumps out. He brooked no argument, shared no decisions, spared no egos, confessed no fallibility. He had a dedicated sense of purpose rare in any manager. Coupled with an arrogance that repudiated rules that he judged applied only to others, this brewed a volatile cocktail. It was part and parcel of the unique character of Colin Chapman.

Chapter 10

DRIVER
DEALINGS

Colin Chapman is regarded as a very good judge of a driver's abilities. This no doubt stems from the fact that he was a fine race driver himself. One is often left thinking that if he had continued racing he might have reached the very top.

Bill Gavin

'He has a name for discovering new drivers,' said Hazel Chapman of her husband. 'I think this has only been possible through his own track experience. He gave Graham Hill his chance when Graham was in the gearbox assembly section at Hornsey. He noted what a good driver Jim Clark is and invited him to join us. Colin's a great driver with a natural track sense. And quite fearless.'

Chapman the driver was in fact phenomenal. This was of immense benefit to the early success of Lotus because the man himself was not only an extremely capable driver but also indefatigable in preparing and racing his cars – with the help of his able band of aides. As was later the case with Clark, it was difficult to separate the success of Lotus from the skill of Chapman. But the latter certainly counted. 'I had an admiration for his skill,' said track rival Stirling Moss, 'and he was a good driver too.'

Colin Chapman's first cars were built for mud-plugging trials. He began competing in his Lotus Mark II at the end of 1949 and enjoyed trials successes early in 1950. 'It went so well,' he said, 'that although I had built it for trials I began to think about racing it.' His first taste

In his early Indy campaign Chapman had the towering talents of Dan Gurney, here in 1963, and Jim Clark. Dan decided he'd rather try to beat Colin than join him.

of track racing was on Silverstone's Club Circuit in an Eight Clubs race meeting on 3 June. It may well have appealed to Colin that the organisers shared out the gate receipts among all the entrants, a novel gesture that attracted a good field.

Chapman took part in one of the one-hour regularity trials designed to sort the competitors. Then in the five-lap scratch race for 1½-litre sports cars he started from the front row alongside the road-equipped Type 37 Bugatti of Dudley Gahagan, a well-tuned and much-raced car. 'To my intense delight I won,' said Colin, 'after a tremendous "dice" with Gahagan.' *Motor Sport* called it 'a really furious duel between Chapman's Lotus and Gahagan's GP Bugatti, the latter cornering wider at Stowe and duly losing ground so that they finished in that order.' A week later Chapman competed in another Silverstone club race but had 'no success largely due to suspension trouble.'

As a first racing success for Lotus and for Colin Chapman the Eight Clubs meeting was historic. It also went down in history for staging the first race to the new 750 Formula, devised by the 750 Motor Club for sports cars based on the ubiquitous and available Austin Seven. The race was won by Holland Birkett, prime mover of this new initiative. Having started with Sevens Chapman saw this as an exciting direction in which to travel so made plans to build

Colin Chapman drove his first Austin special, with its 'Rolls-Royce' radiator, over hill and dale in off-road trials, often accompanied by plucky girlfriend Hazel.

Success in trials required weight well to the rear but enough on the front for steering plus the finesse in throttle control that Chapman was able to provide.

a suitable car for the 1951 season. He duly dominated that year's 750 Formula racing in his brilliant Lotus Mark III.

It was not entirely a quirk of fate that Colin Chapman found his way into circuit racing by this route. The obvious alternative was the then-booming world of racing for 500cc cars, Formula 3. Though launched as a series for home builders using motorcycle engines, the half-litre formula soon benefited from the neat and efficient cars produced in series by Charles and John Cooper, John often taking the wins. Stars Stirling Moss, Peter Collins and Cliff Allison were nurtured in the cradle of Formula 3.

Formula 3 however required a modicum of professionalism. Cars were trailered to races, which implied a tow car, and required alcohol-based fuels to give of their best. It was thus a rung above club racing, attracting both established *équipes* and those with some financial backing. This was not the world of Chapman and the Allen brothers. They drove their cars to events on the road, as the 750 rules required, and substituted ingenuity and elbow grease for pound notes. The 750 Formula would also nurture the careers of such resourceful racers and designers as Maurice Phillippe, Len Terry and Eric Broadley.

Colin's switch from trials, which required a passenger, to racing was a disappointment for wife Hazel, who was now on the sidelines. In compensation he offered her drives in the Marks III and VI. 'Colin used to give me instructions after a brief look at the circuit,' she recalled. 'I drove it flat out as he instructed and it took him several white-knuckle attempts before he matched my time. If he said I could do it, then I would. He had that effect on people. I must have been mad.' Here was a nurturing of the talent that would make Chapman one of the great driver coaches.

A notable Chapman cockpit success was his victory in the 1½-litre sports-car race that started the proceedings of the British Grand Prix meeting at Silverstone on 17 July 1954. This 17-lap race was billed as a showdown between the Lotuses, all-conquering in British races, and the then-new Porsche 550 Spyder with its four-cam engine. The German car was driven by Hans Herrmann, who had won his class in the Mille Miglia two months earlier.

Unusually for such a short race a Le Mans-type start was used. 'For this kind of start I had a proven technique,' said Herrmann. 'First gear is already engaged. Thus I can jump into the seat, step on the clutch, start the engine, release the clutch – and away we go! No fooling around with the shift lever. But when

I started up I slammed back against the pit wall. Somebody must have manoeuvred the car and left it in reverse. This involuntary bump was only brief and fortunately the obstacle was only planks. So the damage was light, but I came away last and had to tackle the whole field from the rear.'

While at the front Chapman in the aerodynamic Mark VIII overtook Peter Gammon's quick Mark VI, Herrmann was eighth on the first lap, fourth on the third and third by the seventh lap, where he finished. By then he had run out of laps to catch Gammon in second and Chapman, a popular winner on the grandest stage that British racing had to offer. Although it's unlikely that Herrmann would have beaten the Lotuses on home ground, the circumstances that delayed his start were soon forgotten.

At this stage of the Chapman career journalist Dennis May gave this assessment of the designer as driver:

Chapman the driver is a good deal like Toscanini the singer: adequate but blood-curdling. Nobody is very surprised that he's prematurely grey, for the consensus is that if he had any nerves at all he'd frighten himself into general paralysis every time he came up to the starting line. Described as a 'press on regardless' driver, it is a rare event for him to lift his foot during a race. Only his highly developed mechanical sympathy keeps him from blowing up engines right and left, and only a benign providence keeps him safe and

Towards the end of 1949 Chapman began competing in trials in his second Austin-based special, the first one to be given the Lotus name.

sound to collect the winner's garland. As an engineer he maintains that any driver who spins off ought to be shot. As a driver he is constantly spinning off. But he hasn't shot himself yet. His friends explain this very simply: there's no money in shooting yourself!

That Chapman could have moments of red mist at the wheel was recalled by David Kelsey: 'Colin was always given to sudden flushes of adrenaline when things went well. I remember an occasion when he won a race, or at least his class, with, I think a Mark IX, among much exotic machinery which included Duncan Hamilton in a D-Type. After crossing the line Colin drove into the paddock behind Duncan, flushed with success and waving to all and sundry. As they motored slowly through the throng, Duncan suddenly stopped and Colin didn't. Result, two bent cars and an equally out-of-shape Hamilton, who loomed over Colin threatening to rearrange his features.'

'People ask me why I don't give up racing and concentrate on design,' Colin Chapman said in 1954. 'The answer is that I must race the cars myself to find out design faults. Drivers are always a bit vague about handling and similar details so the only thing to do is to find out things yourself.' The 1956 season

On the inside here, Colin Chapman deeply relished his defeat of Dudley Gahagan's Bugatti with his Mark II in his first-ever race at Silverstone on 3 June 1950.

Conspicuous for its advanced design among other Austin-based 750 Formula cars, Chapman's Lotus Mark III (12) started a race at Silverstone on 2 June 1951.

was the last in which Colin raced actively. He practised his new single-seater Twelve at Goodwood on Easter Monday of 1957 but failed to start. He won the Chichester Cup, a ten-lap race for 1½-litre sports cars, against heavy opposition. Though entered in his troublesome Twelve at Reims in July, his car wasn't ready.

'The drivers respected him because in the early years he could drive as well as any of them,' said Mike Costin. 'Maybe, maybe – with a few excursions out on to the outside of the grass around the track which meant more work for me. We used to go testing, Colin, myself, Trevor Taylor in the early days, Jimmy – and we'd all drive the cars. Of course when Graham Hill first came along he used to come testing with us. We'd compare notes and try this and that on bends and camber angles and build it up from there. But obviously Colin made all the decisions. We only contributed.'

No makeweight, Mike Costin was in the thick of the development testing. 'In those days nothing happened in motor racing until Easter Monday at Goodwood,' he recalled. 'Jim Clark joined us in 1960 and we were testing the Lotus Eighteen with the Ford engine – the Cosworth engine – so we were all flashing around. Trevor Taylor tells a wonderful story. He says that that day neither of them could match my time around Goodwood in the Junior. I don't recall it, really, but it's a wonderful tale to tell.'

During tests at Brands Hatch on 1 March 1956 a development 1.1-litre Eleven was driven by Graham Hill and Mike Costin as well as Chapman. Hill was quick, taking much of the testing burden and lapping at a best of 1:07.8, while Costin's fastest lap was 1:13.2. Chapman, however, turned 1:07.6 early in the day and then towards the end clocked a best of 1:05.7. Though changes in the

Winning the 17-lap race for 1.5-litre cars at Silverstone in 1954, a curtain-raiser for the Grand Prix, was a triumph on an international stage for Colin Chapman.

car affected these comparisons, there was no doubt that on the day Colin Chapman was fastest.[1]

In April of 1956 Chapman, Reg Bicknell and Cliff Allison took 1.1- and 1.5-litre Elevens to Goodwood to ready them for the new season. In the bigger-engined car Chapman lapped at a best of 1:45.5 but when the track turned damp the others couldn't break two minutes. In the smaller Lotus the next day Allison's quickest was 1:41.4, after which Chapman turned several at 1:41 flat in spite of a 'terrible flat spot – carburation useless below 5,500.' He was still every bit as quick as Allison, who with Graham Hill would lead Lotus into Formula 1 in 1958.

Asked near the end of his life whether he thought he could have had a driving career, Chapman answered jocularly, 'Oh, I don't know. I used to have too many accidents. Too brave, I suppose.' More seriously he continued, 'No, I don't think so. I built cars because I wanted to see if I could build a better machine than the next man and in the early days that meant driving it yourself. But even in the reliability trial days – mud-plugging and all the rest of it – I was always trying to

---

1   Guest driver on that day was Coventry Climax engine designer Harry Mundy. Harry had two tentative laps of Brands and spun on his third lap, after which he demurred further driving.

build a better car rather than saying "I'm going to drive better than the next man." I always regarded the competition as being on the engineering side of it rather than on the driving side. I enjoyed driving, sure I did. But it wasn't the all-consuming passion for me and I found I was getting just as much enjoyment from the engineering side of it.'

Before he was 30 Colin stopped driving competitively. 'I can get a great deal of satisfaction from designing and developing cars,' he said. 'Therefore I was able to stop racing. I feel rather sorry for some people who are jolly good drivers and can't get the same satisfaction from anything else and therefore they keep on racing when they just shouldn't.'

Colin Chapman explored the heights and depths of his driving career at Reims before the French GP on 1 July 1956. Short of drivers for his Vanwall team, Tony Vandervell decided to act on Stirling Moss's suggestion that Chapman would be worth a try. Colin's only previous experience in a single-seater GP car was in a backmarker Aston Martin-engined Emeryson in the same race – the 1954 International Trophy at Silverstone – in which a Vanwall raced for the first time.

A test session was arranged at Goodwood for Colin to have a chance to drive, for the first time, the car he and Frank Costin had designed. After the test, invigilated by demanding team manager David Yorke, Chapman was given the green light to compete at Reims. There he took it easy – breaking in a new engine – on Wednesday, the first practice day. Late on the Thursday

At London's Crystal Palace circuit on 18 September 1954 Chapman and SAR5 'ran away' with the ten-lap race for 1½-litre sports cars.

team-mate Mike Hawthorn was on an out lap when Chapman approached him at some 120mph, both heading for the right-hand Thillois Corner. It wasn't the time for his Vanwall's rear brakes to seize. With Hawthorn's Vanwall on the left, ready to take Thillois, the route to the escape road was blocked. Colin's green racer punted the rear of Hawthorn's and then bounced nose-first into a concrete pillar.[2]

'Mr Vandervell was not amused, to say the least,' wrote Denis Jenkinson. For the race the mechanics managed to make one good Vanwall out of two but Colin was not its driver. No clamour for Chapman's cockpit services arose afterwards, from Vanwall or other stables. A heady experience had ended in disappointment for all concerned. Lotus spirits were lifted a week later at Rouen where Chapman won the 75-minute race for 1.5-litre sports cars from pole, setting fastest lap in his Eleven, with Allison's Lotus winning the 1.1-litre class.

Chapman remained quick, continuing to test-drive his cars well into the 1960s. 'Despite the fact that he hasn't raced regularly for years,' wrote Bill Gavin, 'he usually manages to get down to a very good time. I was at Silverstone the first time that the 24 Formula 1 car was ever run. Colin had only a short spell in this car, during which the power from the new Climax V8 took him unawares, and he spun. Later in the day he took out the works 22 Formula Junior car which Peter Arundell had been testing. Arundell was then king-pin in junior racing and was a very surprised man indeed when after several laps Chapman took about a second off his best time.'

Considerable excitement attended the 10-lap race for GT cars at Brands Hatch on Boxing Day of 1958, for Colin Chapman was unretiring to race a blue Lotus Elite. He qualified on pole with Mike Costin next to him in a red Elite and Jim Clark on the outside in a white Elite. In qualifying the trio far outpaced all the bigger-engined cars including a 300SL Mercedes-Benz. 'I was hanging around in the paddock,' said Costin, 'and I'm thinking, hey, side by side – there's no way Colin's going to lift off and there's no way Jim's going to lift off – looks like I'm elected!'

Meanwhile, according to Mike Lawrence, in the Brands men's room Clark overheard Costin and Chapman discussing which of them should take the win. He decided to upset their applecarts. As the red, white and blue Elites exploded from the start Clark grabbed the lead ahead of Colin. 'This situation did not meet with Chapman's entire approval,' reported *The Motor*, 'but try as he may he could find neither the speed nor the room to pass Clark.' When they lapped

2   The brake lock-up is evident in the video of the incident preserved on YouTube.

tail-enders, however, it was Clark who came unstuck, gifting the win to Chapman with Costin third.

What the Elite was like from the inside was vividly described by passenger Robin Read:

My enduring memory is of the extraordinary noises of protest made by the Elite at speed. With standard suspension the demonstrator Elite assumed amazing angles of roll under fast cornering, so much so that I found myself looking

With the rest of the 1½-litre sports-car field 'nowhere', Mike Hawthorn (leading) and Chapman had an epic battle in Elevens at Goodwood on 21 May 1956. After both spun on lap 15 of 26, Hawthorn pitted for a quick check that gave Chapman the win.

Seen at Goodwood on 1 April 1961 in his Rob Walker Eighteen, Stirling Moss judged the Lotus a demanding car to take to its limits but rewarding to those who could.

Above: *On 3 June 1961 Stirling Moss won a 200-mile race at Brands Hatch in a UDT-Laystall 18, rebodied after Esso barred Lotus from selling the BP-backed team its latest 21.*

Below: *Keith Hall, leading a Cooper at Goodwood in 1956 in his immaculately prepared Eleven, was persuaded by Chapman to come under the Team Lotus umbrella.*

COLIN CHAPMAN

down at Chapman while at the same time being barely able to see out of the window on my side of the car. Meanwhile the fibreglass structure creaked and groaned incessantly as it was subjected to these extraordinary cornering and braking forces, Chapman again darting around the puddles and passing cars to left and right. His mastery of the Elite was absolute and as he drove he shouted comments about tyre pressures, wheel alignment and brakes, never relaxing for a second.

'By comparison with this track-driving experience,' Read continued, 'travelling with Chapman on a public road was very relaxing. He would rarely drive so unreasonably fast as to cause one the slightest nervousness.' This may have been a more settled Chapman than the one of earlier years. 'Colin was a very fast driver on public roads who asked no quarter and gave none,' said Peter Ross. 'If this meant forcing an articulated lorry to mount the grass verge to avoid a head-on collision, then so be it. He once told me that his worst fear on a long journey was to have an accident which forced him to stop, because he knew that for the next 30 minutes there would be a stream of drivers arriving from behind him eager to give evidence against *"that madman"*.'

That Colin Chapman was capable of driving them to the limit inevitably influenced the design and behaviour of his racing cars. In 1957 Denis Jenkinson held the view that Chapman took into account the abilities of lesser drivers in his designs, saying that he 'is capable of pure design yet allowing a factor X for the inabilities of the human machine, even to the Fangio or Moss standards.' This was not, however, the view of the man who was the first to win a *Grande Epreuve* in a Lotus, Stirling Moss.

'His main problem was that the design he did was aimed at a very narrow band of people,' said Stirling. 'If you were really good as a driver a Lotus design was brilliant. If you were not very good, it was impossible to exploit the benefits you could get from the car. I think that probably the lateral g you could generate on a Lotus was better than on a Cooper but there were very few people who could get up into that echelon. Getting there was difficult and the experience was not fulfilling except in achievement. I never had the pleasure of driving a Lotus other than finishing the race in the lead. That is to me where the pleasure started and finished.

'If you were a moderate driver or even a good driver with a Cooper you could get away with it,' Moss continued. 'You could do anything you liked because it was a blacksmith thing and it worked wonderfully well

Although a home-brewed member of Lotus staff at Hornsey, Graham Hill only won a place in Chapman's team in the 1958 and '59 seasons after proving himself elsewhere.

and did everything it should do and it never bit you. The pleasure and exhilaration of driving a Lotus was only there for a fleeting moment of success. It was a tool with which to win in the right hands but it was a car that I was always worried about. It was waiting to bite you. You could liken it to going out on a date with a bad-tempered girl. If you made the wrong move at the wrong time you may get your teeth knocked down your throat.'

Colin Chapman was unapologetic about having produced a car that demanded the ultimate in driving skill. He described his approach to the task in the following terms:

The roadholding of a Formula 1 racing car is obviously far superior to that of most road cars but this alone demands a far greater awareness of the eventual limits of adhesion on the part of the driver. A close analogy can be drawn between driving and flying, for in the latter context there is a critical angle (related to speed) at which the wing of an aeroplane will lose all its 'lift' and consequently will stall; much the same is true of tyre adhesion on a racing car. Whatever the

Driving ahead of Phil Hill's Ferrari on the Avus's infamous North Banking in the 1959 German GP, Graham Hill retired in the first heat with 'queerbox' maladies.

design of the aerofoil section there is a point at which any aeroplane will stall. In the same way, whatever the design of the suspension there is a definite limit to a car's roadholding, and that is largely determined by the tread pattern of the tyre – and, of course, the condition of the road.

As the pilot can judge the stability of his plane by correlation of speed and flying altitude, so the driver should be able to balance the car against the forces which are tending to send it off the road; the best drivers have this faculty in the seats of their pants. The maximum slip angle which the tyres can adopt without losing all adhesion is thus the criterion, but the chassis designer can delay the point at which all 'grip' is lost by endeavouring to keep as much of each tyre as possible in firm contact with the road and by equalising weight distribution.

Having established a separate racing entity as Team Lotus, at Fred Bushell's suggestion, Chapman proved a master at inveigling promising privateers into associating themselves with Team. Drivers like Keith Hall were reluctant at first, seeing no advantage to themselves,

but were persuaded by Colin's assurance that they'd get spares, even engines, when they needed them and would benefit from Lotus's starting-money negotiating skills. Hall joined up, 'provided I could maintain and tune my own car. He asked me why I wanted to do that so I told him that his kept falling apart and I obviously have mine in better nick.'

Colin Chapman's home-brewed Grand Prix driver, Graham Hill, competed in Formula 1 in 1958 and '59 with the Twelve and then the Sixteen. At the end of the latter season, he said, 'I had just about had enough. In two whole seasons of Grand Prix racing I had finished once and scored just two world championship points, and I didn't want to face another season of constant failures. I told Colin that I had been approached by BRM and that I wanted to leave, and I told him why.' Chapman showed Hill his plans for the new Eighteen, which he considered his first pukka Grand Prix car, but the disappointed former Lotus gearbox builder was not dissuaded.[3] Chapman chose Jim Clark as his replacement.

When Innes Ireland joined Team Lotus in 1959 he was on a three-year contract with an escalator that gave him one-quarter of the starting money at first, one-third in the second year and half in the third year. Half of any

---

3 In his first season at BRM Graham Hill faced similar disappointment. He finished the 1960 season with only the four points he gained from a third place in Holland, retiring for one reason or another in all the other races. In 1961 Hill scored only three points and in 1962 he was world champion.

Gathered in 1961 at New York's Idlewild Airport were, from left, Jim Clark, John Cooper, Bruce McLaren, Graham Hill, Jack Brabham, Tony Brooks and Colin Chapman.

prize money also went to the driver. Like Hill, Ireland suffered from the congenital breakages of the ill-favoured Sixteen, saying that his confidence 'kept getting badly shaken by the series of mechanical mishaps which occurred in the team.'

After feeling that he was 'getting the hang of the Lotus…getting it to move quickly and getting the back end hung out a bit on corners,' Innes Ireland then had to manage his transition to the rear-engined Eighteen and the more precise driving style that it demanded. In the United States towards the end of 1961 Ireland won the first *Grande Epreuve* for Team Lotus. In the light of this the driver was surprised – to put it mildly – not to have his contract renewed for 1962, when Jim Clark and Trevor Taylor comprised Team Lotus in Formula 1.

'From an impersonal point of view,' said Ireland, 'Chapman had every right to do what he did.' What galled the driver was that Colin hadn't dealt with his dismissal in an up-front manner. 'It may be that Chapman felt that in his other driver, Jim Clark, he had someone who might be prepared to be more dedicated to motor racing than I was. If only he had said that, well, it would have been perfectly legitimate. Clark is much more dedicated than I am, or than I would be prepared to be.'

At a less elevated level two American drivers had a taste of the Chapman style of driver dealing. Millard Ripley, a VW dealer in Elmira, New York, arranged with

Colin to compete at Sebring in 1959 with an Eleven, which he would buy after the race. 'Chapman agreed to sell him a car,' related Ripley's friend Bill Milliken, 'if we would pick it up from Miami.' Ripley asked Milliken, an experienced racer, to be his co-driver.

'We picked up the car from a ship,' said Milliken, 'and trailered it to Sebring. Chapman took charge of setting it up, the carbs, ignition and so forth. He was extremely knowledgeable. Ripley and I drove it in practice. It seemed competitive. But then Chapman reneged on the deal. "I think I've got somebody who can do a better job than you guys," he told us. He refused to sell the car to Ripley because he wanted it driven by more experienced drivers. We were out and they were in. Rip and I were more than a little disappointed.'[4]

'Chapman has come under fire for the "heartless" way in which he has fired drivers from time to time,' wrote Bill Gavin. 'Seemingly the worst case was when he fired Innes Ireland just after he had won the United States Grand Prix for Team Lotus in 1961. But people

---

4 Observers said that the works-entered Lotus Eleven arrived too late and insufficiently prepared to have a chance of doing well. Driven by Tom Fleming, Bill Schade and Harry Dager, it was unclassified, having completed 123 laps against the 160 of the Elva that won the 1,100cc sports-car class.

Although admitting that he wouldn't have matched Jim Clark's dedication to Team Lotus, Innes Ireland had the skill to score its first F1 victories in the Eighteen.

Driving the Formula 2 version of the Eighteen in which he won his race, Innes Ireland headed for the Goodwood pits during the meeting of 18 April 1960.

forget that the manager of a racing team should have the same right as any other employer, the right to hire and fire at will until he's satisfied that he has absolutely the best person for a given job. A team manager will want to be sure that the man he chooses is morethan just a very fast driver. Because he must travel and live with the rest of the team for a large part of theyear it's essential that there should be no clash of personalities.'

As in the episode with Ireland, which found Chapman meekly examining his shoes when delivering the bad news, the Guv'nor could be remarkably reticent in his dealings with drivers. Then Lotus's European sales manager, Roger Putnam recalled a visit to Hethel in the 1960s by his Swedish importer with a would-be Lotus driver, Ronnie Peterson. Chapman's secretary 'told me to keep them entertained while Colin finished a meeting. I returned to look after the pair and saw out of my window Colin and his Galaxie 500 heading for the main gate at high speed. He had disappeared for the rest of the day. I had a very uncomfortable few hours with a very angry Ronnie and an embarrassed importer who felt they had been stood up.

'I must have done a good job in protecting Colin's back,' Putnam added, 'because the same thing happened to me twice more. A short while after Ronnie's visit a Brazilian called Wilson Fittipaldi arrived at Hethel. He had a portfolio of photographs showing his brother campaigning something called the

"Fittiporsche" in South America and was convinced that Colin would sign up Emerson on the spot. Once again I contacted Colin's office and once again was greeted by the sight of Colin's car leaving at high speed. Colin wouldn't believe me several years later when I told him that both drivers had been refused a meeting with him. The third unexpected visitor was a wealthy man named Mike Rahal who had a meat-packing business in Chicago. He was sure Colin would like to sign up his son Bobby. He was much more insistent and I had to spend two days with him while Colin avoided coming to the office.'

For the 1962 season Innes Ireland joined the BRP team. His team-mate in 1963 was American Jim Hall, who was assigned a BRM-powered Lotus 24. The mechanically minded Hall was frustrated in his efforts to get the best from this combination. 'Neither the chief mechanic nor the mechanics were able to help me much to develop the chassis during that season,' he related. 'I was disappointed. I thought: "Here I am in Grand Prix racing and this is one of the top teams and these guys don't seem to know what to do to improve the car." So I asked Colin a time or two. I went to him and said, "I'm a customer driving one of your cars. What am I meant to do about this?" and he was totally evasive – he just didn't answer. He said, "Yes, that is a problem we've got," that kind of answer, so I didn't learn anything from him either. I suspect he knew but he didn't tell me if he did.'

Chapman would have seen the lanky Texan as fairly far down the Lotus food chain, driving an outmoded Lotus for a team that had built its own monocoque car for Ireland because it couldn't buy the Lotus 25. 'Colin Chapman was very good at motivating people,' recalled mechanic Eddie Dennis, 'but he could destroy people too – he had a razor-sharp tongue on him. He had his favourites – Emerson was one and Andretti was another – and basically the number two driver had to toe the line.'

Emerson Fittipaldi didn't have the easiest of times at Lotus at first. The 72 wasn't handling at the beginning of 1972, he and Reine Wisell told Chapman, who felt 'my bloody drivers' were at fault. 'Reine and I were still so new to Formula 1 racing,' said Fittipaldi, 'that Colin just didn't believe us. When we were explaining a problem to him we had a job to convince him that it was a real one and not simply our lack of experience.' Soon, however, test sessions began to reveal the problems and the solutions.

'In 1971,' Fittipaldi added, 'we spent one year developing the car and trying to work together well. I

Unceremoniously dropped from Team Lotus after 1961, Innes Ireland moved to the BRP team for whom he competed at Brands Hatch in a Lotus 24-Climax in 1962.

Drinking and driving? Emerson Fittipaldi enjoyed the champagne that he won by setting pole time at Brands Hatch for the Race of Champions in March of 1972.

Above: *On 19 March 1972 Emerson Fittipaldi gave a hint of his season to come with a decisive victory in the 106-mile Race of Champions at Brands Hatch.*

Below: *Chapman had a firm grip on the trophy for Fittipaldi's victory in the 1972 British GP. Also present were the RAC's Dean Delamont and Maria-Helena Fittipaldi.*

After seven years with BRM, Graham Hill returned to Lotus in 1967 at the urging of Ford's Walter Hayes, who wanted strong support for the user of Ford's DFV V8.

think when we started the next year everything worked, the whole organisation, with the right combination between the driver, the mechanics and the team manager. Chapman was like a teacher or a tutor. Going through the problems you normally face with any Formula 1 car with Colin behind me was just fantastic. He could be very difficult sometimes but he knew a lot about motor racing and racing cars, more than anybody I ever worked with.'

The Lotus boss returned the favour. 'There's no doubt that, at his best, Emerson was a fantastic driver,' Chapman said. 'He was keen when he came to us and demonstrated tremendous willingness to learn. We thrust him into the Grand Prix world pretty early and he responded with that fantastic win at Watkins Glen. By 1972 he was right at the top, driving tremendously well.' 'Now Chapman and I get on well,' said Emerson in 1972. 'People always get on well when they're winning. Maybe things weren't so good at the beginning. But now they're okay!'

For 1971 Colin had rejected the idea of employing a known star, accepting instead the risk of starting the year with two young drivers. 'Very rarely in my career have I bid for established top-line drivers,' he said in 1981. 'I would far rather a driver come into the team

and grow with us, developing a relationship gradually like Nigel Mansell. I've never been quite so keen bidding for an established star because I would find myself wondering if he was just here for the season to collect a large pot of gold before moving off to fresh pastures. It doesn't make for such a good relationship within the team.'

On several occasions Chapman had squads of drivers who were undeniably of the first rank. The first instance was in 1967, when he brought Graham Hill into the team as partner to Jim Clark to satisfy the request of engine sponsor Ford that he have strength in depth. 'Also,' said Hill, 'if they had two top-rank drivers, obviously no other team could have them and this would reduce their opposition – so it had a two-fold benefit.' 'I think Graham honestly came to us feeling that he was quicker than Jimmy.' Colin related. 'Of course he found out that Jimmy was the quicker driver. But what impressed me was the way in which Graham then came to terms with this reality with good grace and no bad feelings.

'And remember,' Chapman added, 'to be second-best to Jim Clark certainly wasn't any disgrace. Graham was a real trouper. Whereas Jim would simply rush out and produce a couple of inspired laps, almost out of a hat, Graham would grind round and round for most of the session to almost match his time.' Ford's precaution proved tragically prescient. Taking the demoralised team by the scruff after Jim Clark's death, Hill became world champion in 1968.

'For 1973,' related team manager Peter Warr, 'we felt it was time to have two top drivers. I had infinite admiration for Ronnie Peterson, so he joined us alongside Emerson. Colin engineered Emerson's car, I ran Ronnie's. Of all the drivers I worked with I got on with Ronnie best, as a friend. It was obvious to me he was the fastest thing out there, by a long way. The only way he could drive a car, testing, practice, race, any time, was flat out. He wasn't perfect, because if there was a problem with the car he'd just drive around it.'

'Two drivers of the calibre of Emerson and Ronnie obviously have their own problems,' Chapman said at the time, 'and we'll just have to see how we get on. I think they're both very sensible drivers…probably one of the few pairings that you can envisage which would get on harmoniously throughout the whole racing season and who realise that by pooling their resources and co-operating with each other they are in fact helping each other.'

Although the Fittipaldi-Peterson relationship in 1973 has gone down in history as troubled, Emerson didn't

At the 1967 US Grand Prix, Colin Chapman listened intently to Graham Hill's representations. At this race Hill seized one of his season's three pole positions.

At Indianapolis in 1968 Derek Gardner, left, Dick Scammell and Colin Chapman lent their ears to Graham Hill. Keeping meticulous notes, Hill knew what he wanted.

see it that way. He was aware of its risks, he said at the time: 'I have already told Ronnie it will be very difficult. There is a good understanding between myself and Ronnie; we don't want anyone to come between us. We have agreed this. If Ronnie has any problems he will talk to me, and if I have any I will talk to him. We will talk to nobody else.'

Although Ronnie outqualified Emerson by 11 races to 4, the results in racing terms were much more balanced. The Brazilian had five fastest laps to his credit against two for the Swede. In two events, Holland and Germany, Fittipaldi was hampered by ankle injuries from a Zandvoort practice crash. 'I enjoyed every minute of working with Ronnie,' Emerson said afterwards. 'Ronnie was a great team-mate. He was one of the best friends I ever had in racing. And, of course, we had some fantastic races together, really fantastic.'

This didn't gainsay occasional inter-team irritation when Peterson and Warr would go wildly out on their 72's set-up and fall back on the settings arrived at after meticulous development by Fittipaldi and Chapman. 'We'd put Emerson's settings on his car,' said Warr, and Ronnie would 'go out and put it on pole.' The 'equal Number 1' philosophy brought Lotus a manufacturers' cup but left its two drivers behind Jackie Stewart in drivers' points.

Peterson left Lotus at the troubled beginning of the 1976 season, only to return in 1978 to drive first the 78 and then the 79 as team-mate to Mario Andretti. This

was Chapman's next teaming of two top drivers, this time in his black ground-effect beauties. Andretti saw Peterson as a roadblock in the way of the championship he hoped to win in the revolutionary Lotus. 'Tell me where it's written we need two stars in the team,' he told a friend. 'I had nothing against Ronnie – I'd always liked him – but I had my doubts that the arrangement would work out.'

This time Peterson had the benefit of the set-ups that Andretti would painstakingly craft from his deep bag of tricks. 'The big difference between Ronnie and Mario's cars,' said Glenn Waters, 'was that Ronnie could normally be quicker than Mario. And Chapman would try to slow him down by putting more fuel in the car. Interestingly – and this didn't really come out until afterwards, because Ronnie was quick – they would often not let him use the qualifying tyres and Mario would use them.' The result was a resounding Lotus championship year, the drivers' cup for Mario and a posthumous vice-championship for the much-missed Peterson, fatally injured in a 78 at Monza.

After his successes of 1977 and '78, Colin Chapman had no problem finding and funding another top pilot to join Andretti in 1979 to drive the exciting new 80. This was Argentina's Carlos Reutemann, who had been third in the championship in 1975 with Brabham and in 1978 with Ferrari. After a strong start to the season in the 79 Chapman was ecstatic about his acquisition. 'Isn't Carlos

With Chapman and Jack Brabham, Graham Hill lived up to his reputation as a raconteur. His 1968 championship revived his team's spirits after Jim Clark's death.

a fantastic driver?' he said to the driver's friend Peter Windsor. 'I hardly knew him when we first met. All I'd heard were these stories about him being moody or difficult. I'm going to make Carlos world champion this year. You watch!'

In spite of problems in 1979, Reutemann would soon be similarly positive about Chapman. 'There's no question he's a genius,' he said. 'The best thing of all would be to drive your whole career with Lotus.' The problem was that team-mate Andretti – who got there first – was of much the same mind. Mario was outspoken about his desire for a different team-mate. 'This is the second time he's caused disruption in the team,' said Chapman of Andretti. 'He did it with Ronnie. Now he's doing it with Carlos.

'I've never had a driver of his calibre and not won a championship with him,' added Chapman. 'I want Carlos to stay until we win that championship.' Colin even told the driver that he'd arranged to have Andretti move to Alfa Romeo in 1980 so that he could run Carlos as his unrivalled Number 1. Unconvinced, however, Reutemann checked with Alfa and discovered that this wasn't so. Instead he took up an offer from Frank Williams which led to his best-ever season, second in the driver table, in 1981.

Helping present the new 77 for 1976 was Jacky Ickx, right, who bolted from the team before the season started after two years as team-mate to Ronnie Peterson.

Another driver to whom 'moody or difficult' would definitely apply was Jochen Rindt. 'God, was he arrogant out of the car,' said Chapman. 'Not a sympathetic personality, I would say.' Self-assured to a fault, Rindt was one of Chapman's most controversial choices. 'I just don't think you have to eat, sleep, think racing all the time,' said the Austrian. 'I try not to get hundred-per cent involved with it. I start thinking about the next Grand Prix when I get there. Everything's going well, let's not worry about it. I'll wait until somebody starts going quicker.'

Rindt's protestations of disdain for the nitty-gritty of racing rang hollow against the background of his behind-the-scenes machinations. With Alan Rees he ran a Formula 2 team, a relationship that made him the original target of the people who ultimately founded March Engineering with Chris Amon instead of Rindt. He maddened Chapman with his twists and turns, urging him to develop a four-wheel-drive car and then

all but refusing to drive the 63 when it arrived. 'But when he was out on the circuit,' said Colin, '*what* a driver. Sheer lightning reflexes. When he was in the mood he was quite fantastic.'

Neighbours in Switzerland, Jackie Stewart and Jochen Rindt were close friends. 'Jochen was a driver I rated very highly,' said Jackie. 'It took him an absurdly long time to win a Grand Prix, but it took him changing his technique – so he was sideways less of the time – for him to start to achieve sustained success. His problem was that Lotuses were not robust cars, unlike my Matra, so if you bullied them, like he did with his F2 cars, they'd break. Before 1970 he retired from a lot of races that he could well have won.'

Rindt's death in a practice accident at Monza in 1970 was a blow to Chapman, lightened only by Fittipaldi's subsequent success at Watkins Glen. This caused Tony Rudd to reflect on the relationship between driver and engineer, which he considered 'absolutely vital to success. Chapman and Team Lotus suffered when they lost Rindt, but they had enough momentum and Colin enough ability to keep it going for a few years. It really needed the Andretti input to make the Lotus 78s and

Undeniably fast, Sweden's Ronnie Peterson drove three seasons with Lotus before jumping ship to March early in 1976 after racing the recalcitrant 77 at Buenos Aires.

79s into winners and then it sank back again.' Rindt's superiority in his last season was sufficient to make him F1's only posthumous world champion.

Jochen Rindt's predecessor at Team Lotus was Jackie Oliver, who was plunged into the deep end at Monaco in 1968 after Jim Clark's death. Though Oliver's credentials had been proffered to Chapman by team manager Andrew Ferguson, this didn't cut much ice with the Guv'nor. 'As to my views on racing drivers in general,' Ferguson wrote, 'Colin always considered that I was too lenient in my judgement of their merits. He soon dubbed me "President of the Down-and-Out Brigade"!' The recommendation of race engineer Jim Endruweit carried the day for Oliver.

'Colin was not too helpful,' Oliver recalled, 'not that he didn't like me – but he wasn't in the right frame of mind so soon after losing Jimmy. Colin was impossible, a whirlwind, all over the place. Then Jimmy died and he was even worse. For me it was a hard opening at the

Pictured by Ove Nielsen in a Lotus 78 at Monaco, Ronnnie Peterson returned to Lotus for the 1978 season. He scored victories in South Africa and Austria.

Justly famed for his car control, Peterson got his 79 out of shape at Zandvoort in 1978. Killed at Monza, he placed a posthumous second in the world championship.

Mario Andretti, left, made no secret of his reluctance to have Peterson in a team for which he had worked hard for two years to develop the downforce advantage.

coal face. I wasn't fully prepared. I didn't know the circuits. There was never any question of going testing with any new bits. Colin would have an idea and insist it was on the cars for the next race.' This was spectacularly the case late in 1968 with the huge hub-mounted rear wings. Oliver: 'I was plunged in without any knowledge of what to expect or how the car would handle or any data like that.'

Oliver found a vast wing on his 49 for the French GP at Rouen. 'I looked at this thing up there on stalks,' he recalled. 'Nobody on the team could tell me anything so I asked Chapman what it was all about. "Aerodynamics, lad," he said. "It's the future." There was no, "Go out, do one lap, come in for a check." It was, "Go out and get on with it." So I went, and the grip was unbelievable, grip I'd never experienced before.' On his third lap, however, Oliver had an almighty accident which he was lucky to survive after flow over the wing was disturbed by passing another car.

Oliver led the British GP at Brands – a circuit he knew well – before retiring and was third in the last race in Mexico. 'My performance didn't alter my relationship with Chapman,' Jackie reflected. 'Colin only wanted to use me when it suited him and he'd got Rindt signed for 1969. He liked to think that a problem with the car was a problem with the driver, especially with drivers he didn't fully support. Graham used to go through hell with that. He never thought Graham was quick enough. Beside Jimmy no one was quick enough. Well, Jochen was. He was very involved with Jochen.' Jackie Oliver signed for a full-time drive with BRM in 1969.

Playing second fiddle to Jim Clark in 1964 and '65 was the fate of Surrey-born Mike Spence, who was promoted from Formula 2 after Peter Arundell – dominant in Formula Junior for Lotus until he moved to F1 in 1964 – was injured in a crash at Reims. Spence had five points finishes in two seasons, then moved to the Reg Parnell team's BRM-powered Lotus 25 for 1966.

In the view of Parnell's son Tim, Spence 'was, without any doubt in my mind, the most technically brilliant of all drivers. If we were testing a car or setting one up and qualifying for a race, after a couple of laps on the track Mike would come in to say that this or that was wrong or some changes were needed with settings. The mechanics worked on the car to his stipulations and off he went again. You could bet your bottom dollar that the following laps were instantly quicker.

'A great technical man and a terrific asset to the team,' Parnell continued. 'I don't really think that Colin Chapman wanted to lose him; he appreciated what a good test driver he was. It was that knowledge of his testing abilities that gave way to Colin Chapman calling me and asking if he could have Mike to drive in the 1968 Indianapolis 500.' This invitation, granted by Parnell and enthusiastically taken up by Spence, led to tragedy. During a practice run at the Speedway in the turbine-powered 56 he drifted too high in Turn One and hit the wall. The right front wheel swung back and struck his head. Mike died in hospital later that day.

This was the last straw for Colin Chapman. He left Indianapolis, releasing a statement that included the following:

I am filled with grief at the loss of my long-time friend and associate Jimmy Clark, and the additional loss, just a month later to the day, of Mike Spence. As an understandable result I want nothing more to do with the 1968 Indianapolis race. I just do not have the heart for it. I thank my good friend Andy Granatelli for taking over in my stead and allowing me to carry out my decision. As entrant and owner of these cars, Andy will have an added burden and responsibility since things must go on. I appreciate his action.

Before qualifying started, however, Chapman was back. 'This was completely unheralded,' said Andrew Ferguson. 'He merely gave his customary "Hi", picked up his briefcase and proceeded as if nothing had occurred.' 'I thought Mike and Jimmy would want me back here,' Colin said, 'so it's only right that I return to Indianapolis.' In the interim he'd attended a packed

On the podium in his first two races for Lotus in 1979, Carlos Reutemann made a good first impression. He checked data with Chapman and engineer Peter Wright.

memorial service for the popular Mike at Indianapolis and his funeral at Bray near Maidenhead. He absented himself from attending the Spanish Grand Prix. It had been a gruelling few weeks for Colin Chapman.

'After Jimmy's death,' related Graham Hill, 'the Lotus team was in despair and Colin Chapman seriously considered giving up racing. He had always said he would stop the day Jimmy Clark stopped racing. Jimmy had been killed in April. The next Grand Prix was the

In his second season with Lotus, 1970, Jochen Rindt scored his second win for the team driving a 49C with his customary brio as pictured by Max Le Grand.

Spanish, in May. It made me more determined than ever to go out and win that one.' This he duly did with the 49, although an improved 49B was sent out to Spain. As Chapman was not attending he forbade its use. 'I think that victory made Colin and Lotus think it was worth carrying on. Colin said he would continue until the end of the year and see how he felt about things then.'

Chapman's idea of giving up racing when Clark retired was referenced elsewhere. 'Once or twice Jimmy talked about retiring,' Colin told Nigel Roebuck, 'and it gave me mixed feelings. The idea of going racing without him was almost unthinkable, but at the same time I loved him as a human being and didn't want him to get hurt.'

'Jim Clark's tragic death in Germany left him distraught,' Louis Stanley said of Chapman. 'His distress was evident as we waited in a charter plane at Frankfurt. Colin's grief was heart-breaking. I thought then that he would quit altogether. I shall never forget the moment when the coffin containing Clark's body was lashed to the floor before we took off for Edinburgh. Shortly after take-off a cockpit window shattered, pressure dropped and the plane lost altitude and had to limp back for an emergency landing at Frankfurt, narrowly avoiding a further tragedy. The death of Mike Spence in Indianapolis was a further blow. Time eased the shock. Something of the old resilience returned.' Coincidentally a blessed diversion came from Chapman's need to concentrate on the Lotus Group's stock-market flotation later in 1968.

'I was terribly distraught about it all,' Chapman told John Ezard, 'because Jimmy had been my very close friend, in fact my best friend for a number of years. And we'd built up a very close relationship. It made it all so interesting and such fun to do what we were doing, to race and develop new cars and go and race in new countries and tackle new problems and achieve success and failure together. I was very upset indeed when Jimmy had his accident. It's something that one has to recognise, that all racing drivers are capable of having accidents. But somehow I felt that Jimmy was such a good driver, so much head and shoulders above any other that…well, somehow or other I never felt it would happen.

'I don't think it'll ever be the same again – for me, anyway,' Chapman continued. 'I worry a great deal, I'm afraid – in fact possibly more now than I used to. Because it is a terrible responsibility having drivers going round this fast in your cars. And it gets harder to bear, I don't mind telling you, as you get older. It's a terribly exciting life and it gives tremendous satisfaction when you're successful at it. I think that the risk is there. No one lives for ever.'

'I think Jimmy's death made Colin a much harder

person,' said Jackie Oliver, inadvertently overlooking the subsequent death of Mike Spence. 'I think there was a "Phase One Chapman" which existed before Jimmy died, followed by a "Phase Two Chapman" afterwards, who took a complete change of direction. People like Rindt and Andretti managed to survive in such an environment where perhaps the younger and more sensitive drivers did not.

'While Ken Tyrrell was probably the best team owner when it came to bringing on new young drivers,' Oliver told Jabby Crombac, 'Colin was probably the worst. He would never spend time considering other people's difficulties and problems because he was too impatient. Colin would never sit down with me and say, "Now,

Excited about the potential of 1970's new 72, Rindt worked through its teething troubles to win four races in a row en route to his posthumous world championship.

young Oliver, I understand all the difficulties…" He wasn't that sort of person. He was too brash.'

In this there was a curious dichotomy. At least after the deaths of Clark and Spence, Chapman was disinclined to deploy with his drivers his 'chameleon' strategies, his insightful assessment of the other person's needs and wants and associated adjustment of approach and appeal that proved so successful with his managers and in business. He'd used this sympathetic approach previously to attract talented drivers to the Lotus family. As far as drivers were concerned, however, the 'Phase Two Chapman' was more inclined to take the 'hard man' approach.

By his own lights, at least, one driver succeeded in penetrating the 'Phase Two' reserve. 'He was just like a second father,' said Nigel Mansell of Chapman. 'There isn't anything I wouldn't have done for the man. He was so genuine and straight with me. He helped me through all my difficult situations and taught me an awful lot. I still think of his words and guidance. I remember him very dearly for the life lessons he taught me.' By the time Mansell came along, first as a tester and then as a racer in 1981 and '82, a mellower Chapman – for whom racing was a welcome diversion from his business

Jochen Rindt's win from pole in the 1970 British GP at Brands Hatch was especially gratifying to Chapman. Nina Rindt shared the podium with her lavishly laurelled husband.

travails – was willing to take more time with this driver.

Although raw, Nigel Mansell was unrelenting in application. This scored highly with Chapman, as we saw in his preference for Clark over Ireland. Of Mansell's team mate Elio de Angelis he said, 'He is a brilliant driver, but like so many brilliant drivers he doesn't always tackle the task with all the application which is necessary. It's very rare to find the combination of sheer talent and dedication. When you do, the result is a Jim Clark. When they don't have the application the result is that they appear no better than drivers with slightly less natural ability who apply themselves with great dedication.'

In the wake of another driver death, that of Jochen Rindt, came young Emerson Fittipaldi. He too was capable of application combined with a winning personality. 'I was Jimmy Clark's number one fan,' Emerson told the author during his time with Lotus. 'I liked to ask a lot about Jimmy because I never had the opportunity to know Jimmy personally. I always ask, how was Jimmy and how did he drive, and Colin always tells me fantastic stories about Jimmy. I know that he loves Jimmy Clark still. When he worked together with Jimmy for so many years, after Jimmy got killed it must have been very bad for Colin, a bad feeling. Jimmy meant so much for Colin.

'Colin didn't talk a lot about that,' Fittipaldi added. 'He didn't like to talk about it. He always tried to keep his opinions about drivers to himself. When I first went

Lotus's 1970 British GP victory was a surprise with Jack Brabham running out of petrol on his last lap. A protest that the 72's rear wing was too high was overturned.

to the team, Colin took me to one side and said, "Emerson, I don't want to get too close to you. I have already had a great deal of sadness losing Jimmy and Jochen." But I can tell you, I had a great relationship with Colin. We were very good friends. But he always tried to keep a certain reserve.

'He knew how to get the maximum out of the combination of both car and driver from the feedback of the driver,' Fittipaldi added. 'Some designers I've worked with, since my time with Colin, have had the ability to get the most out of the chassis of a car, or they know how to get the most out of a driver's performance. But many fall short of being able to get the maximum out of the combination of the two.'

In 1960, early in Jim Clark's career with Lotus, John Surtees joined him and Innes Ireland in the team for some races. 'We weren't buddy boys,' said John of Jimmy, 'but we were close and we always talked about the cars, what changes we were making. You never took anything for granted with Jimmy. There was never any suggestion of favouritism towards him from Chapman – I never saw that – and you had to like Colin, even if he was a bit of a rogue. He was a bubbly character, always full of enthusiasm, and clever.' Points from the trio took Lotus to second in 1960's makes standings behind

Cooper and ahead of Ferrari, eclipsed by the new mid-engined racers from the pesky British *garagistes*.

Colin Chapman made no secret of his admiration for Jim Clark as both driver and person. He told Gordon Wilkins that he felt Clark had matured during his first championship season of 1963: 'The reason, I think, was that he had by then built up a high degree of confidence in his machine. He was completely happy with the car and was prepared to push it to its limit if called upon. Up until Aintree he had always seemed to be keeping a little in reserve.

'Jim has always been very, very quick,' Chapman continued, 'but now he has learned to go fast in traffic and keep his concentration in company. He is a lot more relaxed. I think he has proved to himself that he has the measure of the opposition. He has certainly gained in experience. The fact that he has had a lot of diversified racing has helped – Indianapolis, the Ford Galaxie, the Lotus Cortina and so on – and I think that in the next year or so he will continue to improve at a tremendous

Jackie Oliver, left with Graham Hill, was plunged with little guidance into the turbulent winged world of Team Lotus in 1968. He was lucky to survive.

Testing as well as racing was a particular strength of the well-liked Mike Spence, right with Jim Clark at Watkins Glen in 1965, his second and last season with the team.

rate. We have been working together for three years now and he is also becoming very much better in his analysis of the car. He has now developed into a fine test driver as well.'

'I think he's grown to recognise now that there's more to be gained by letting Jimmy do most of the testing,' said Bill Gavin of Chapman. 'He figures Jimmy will drive the car just that much faster and what Colin really wants to know is how the car behaves when being driven to its very limit. Despite Jim's lack of technical training, Colin has no difficulty interpreting from Jimmy's remarks just what is wrong with the car or how it might be improved.

'Of course one difficulty with a natural driver like Jim Clark,' added Gavin, 'is that he might automatically overcome some fault in the car's behaviour simply by altering his style of driving slightly, but Colin is now well aware of such tendencies.' So was designer Len Terry, who had a solution: 'When you went testing you allowed him only one flying lap and then brought him in. That way he could tell you what the car was doing. Leave him out any longer and he would simply adapt himself to all the car's faults and drive through them.'

'By now I was learning fast,' said Jim Clark of his 1962 season. 'Colin was a first-class teacher in the rudiments of chassis design. He could explain to me just why the car handled the way it did. With his assistance I found that I was taking much more interest in the mechanics of the car than ever before. I was never really mechanically minded but now I was beginning to see what Colin was driving at.'

'Jim will always have a go and give his very best,' testified Colin Chapman. 'In all the time I have known him, I have seen him have remarkably few "off" days. This is a tremendous morale-booster for the team as a whole. The mechanics will work really hard preparing the cars when they know the man in the cockpit is going to make the most of what they give him. It means that all the hard work is converted into race-winning potential. He gets on better with mechanics than most drivers. He has a good personal relationship with them and even when things go badly wrong he's far more likely to let me have it rather than to moan to the mechanics.'

'I remember once when Jim had a big argument with Chapman at Oulton Park following a steering breakage,' said 1962–63 team mate Trevor Taylor. 'He came over to me, fuming, and said, "I wonder what this is all about,

Opposite: In 1965 Mike Spence was centre of attention between Jim Clark and Colin Chapman in his 33-Climax. His best result for Lotus was third in that year's Mexican GP.

Nigel Mansell drove the gorgeous but uncompetitive 87 at Monaco in 1981, the last race for Team Lotus in Essex livery. He competed for Lotus for three more seasons.

Pictured in the cockpit of the 87 at Monaco in 1981, Elio de Angelis joined Lotus in 1980 and raced for the team until 1985.

Trev. This motor-racing lark sometimes seems to be a mug's game." He didn't often fall out with Chapman, probably because Colin knew how good he was and didn't push him too far. I always got the impression that Chapman would dominate everything and everybody if he got the upper hand, but he respected you if you decided to stand up to him and confront him.'

For Mike Costin, Jim Clark's performance in the big sports-car race at the Nürburgring in 1962 typified his skill and resourcefulness. He was driving the new mid-engined 23 in its first outing with the 1.5-litre twin-cam engine. 'Jim came over the top at the end of the first lap without any of the big-capacity sports-prototypes in sight and was round the South Curve before they appeared,' said Costin, who was in charge of the effort. 'I wouldn't have expected Jim with our 1,500cc car to be anywhere near the front of the field, but that was Jim. That is why I – and a lot of other people – regard Jim Clark as the greatest driver in the world – ever. The track was partly wet and partly dry and it was in those sorts of circumstances that he really shone.'

Roman Elio de Angelis, right with his 1980 team-mate Andretti, was only 22 when he joined Lotus. He was second in Brazil and placed fourth twice during the season.

Another reason that Clark and his mechanics got on so well was that he succeeded without taking it out of the car. Engine builder Keith Duckworth was a close observer of the state of their respective Ford V8s. 'You could actually tell the difference between a Graham Hill engine and a Clark engine.' Keith told Michael Oliver, 'by the fact that Clark would have apologised for having over-revved it on two or three occasions and the valve gear would show no signs of having been over-revved, whereas Graham's had never been over-revved and the valve gear was quite often tatty! Clark just changed gear gently, didn't he? There was never any hurry about anything; he had bags of time because he was incredibly good. Graham was really an exceedingly courageous driver because I think that he was running at a higher percentage of his "tenths" than Jim ever did. I think Jim had prodigious natural ability whereas Graham was working hard at it.'

Of course no one was closer to this comparison than Graham Hill. 'Jim Clark had all the requirements for his profession to a very high degree,' wrote Hill. 'He was a

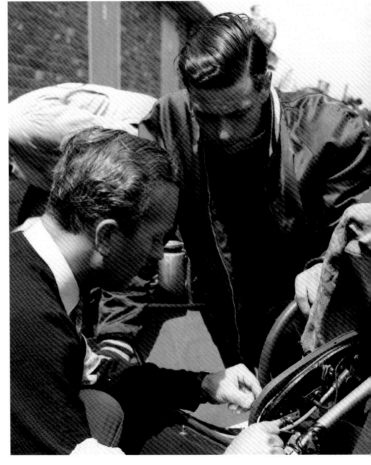

Calm, friendly and knowledgeable co-operation was the hallmark of the Chapman-Clark relationship, pictured in 1963 at the Dutch GP, which Jimmy won.

In the 1963 season – here Station Corner at Monaco – Jim Clark so dominated in his Lotus 25 that he won seven of ten championship races and set six fastest laps.

natural athlete; he had very good muscular and mental co-ordination; he had a very good eye – he could hit a ball well – his timing was extremely good and so were his reactions. To be any good in motor racing you've got to be a very competitive person and this he certainly was; in his driving he could be aggressive too, but he didn't take undue risks. You can be aggressive and competitive; you can also be boorish, aggressive to the point of being dangerous – and this he was not. In fact you could say that he was a safe driver in that his judgement of situations was particularly good.

'He had the will to win,' added Hill, 'this tremendous urge to win, which you've just got to have. Some people have it more than others and he had it more than most. He was a fighter whom you could never shake off and whom you never dared underestimate. He invariably shot off in the lead and just killed the opposition, set up

a lead and just sat there, dictating the race. He was an ideal racing driver.'

Ideal or not, Clark sometimes required winding up. Mechanic Alan McCall recalled a troubled 1966 Indy campaign in which Speedway regular Al Unser was coping well with his 38-Ford 'while Jimmy kept complaining. The night before the first day of qualifying Chapman gathered us all in the garage and sat Jimmy on a chair in the middle of the room. He said, "These boys are working their asses off and they've done everything they can. What about you, Jimmy?" Clark was livid but he never said a word and finally got up and stormed out. The next day he qualified in the middle of the front row.'

His trips to Indianapolis and other American tracks like Milwaukee and Trenton acquainted Colin Chapman with the talent available on the other side of the Pond. One such was the incomparable Parnelli Jones, who beat Jim Clark by 34 seconds in the controversial 1963 Indy 500. 'Chapman wanted me to run F1 as Jimmy's team-mate,' said Jones, 'with the understanding I would be the number two driver. I told him I'd be on the gas the last

50 laps regardless of who my team-mate was so it never happened.'

Another Indy-car driver, keener on the idea of Grand Prix racing, quizzed Clark about it at every opportunity. 'Jimmy had been named rookie of the year in 1964, so we ended up attending the same pageants. I probably asked him 5,000 questions about Formula 1,' said Mario Andretti, 'and he answered every one. I asked him what I needed to work on and he said I needed to be quick in the slow corners and carry speed into them. I always appreciated his honesty and friendship and that's how I got to meet Colin.

'I believed in Colin from way back,' Andretti added. 'My first time at Indianapolis was 1965, the year Clark won in a Lotus, and I remember asking Jimmy to speak to Colin about keeping me in mind for a ride sometime. Jimmy reported that Colin had said he would do that but I didn't really believe it. Then the results started coming. Colin said, "Whenever you think you're ready, call me". In 1968, after I'd won every USAC road race I'd entered, I knew it was time to get my feet wet. I wanted to do the last two races of the season, at Monza and Watkins Glen, so I called up Colin and he agreed immediately.

'The first time I drove the 49 at Monza that year I just flat fell in love with that car,' Andretti enthused. 'I knew I was designed and painted to be a Formula 1 driver! I'd never been in an F1 car before but I'd thought about it so much. It was exactly what I'd expected – taut, precise and a little underpowered compared with what I was

Wearing – as often – his driving gloves, Colin Chapman debriefed Jim Clark during a practice session. The two men were destined to become close friends.

Carrying the number earned with his 1963 championship, Jim Clark won the 1964 British GP at Brands Hatch from pole and set fastest lap in his Lotus 25.

Chapman and Clark communicated closely in the pre-headphone era at Watkins Glen in 1964. Numerous retirements marred Clark's season, which brought only three wins.

used to in Indy cars. It was a very sincere car, in that it gave you something for nothing. I knew it was a car that would pay you back something. You don't put any more effort in than normal – you just get more than usual in return.

'That first day at Monza we were quicker than Chris Amon's Ferrari,' Mario recalled, 'and he was pretty much

That racing wasn't always effortless for Jim Clark was evident at Monaco in 1966, where Max Le Grand caught him putting his 2-litre Lotus 33-Climax on pole.

top dog that year.'[5] Conflicts kept Mario from racing the 49 at Monza, but sensationally in his next outing in the 49B at Watkins Glen he seized the pole by seven hundredths of a second from Jackie Stewart. 'What really annoyed me was that everyone was saying I lived at the Glen – that I'd been testing there and brought up there – but I'd never seen the place before! I never even went around the circuit in my road car.'

In 1969 Andretti started three races for Lotus, two of them in the unbiddable four-wheel-drive 63, then went off to drive for others in Formula 1. 'You kept going to all these silly places like March and Ferrari,' Chapman joked with Mario, 'and then you went to Parnelli – thought you could do a Lotus without me! You stole all my guys [Andrew Ferguson and Dick Scammell], all my designers [Maurice Phillippe], hired premises ten miles down the road and moved Lotus there!'

'Yep, sure did,' Andretti rejoined. 'I paid for it, though. That Parnelli aged me ten years in two years. Maurice always used to talk about cycles, but as I didn't understand all that I asked him to convert to something I did understand, like wheel rates. He did and we were still lost.' In his between-Lotus years Mario won once for Ferrari in 1971 (South Africa) and eked into the points twice for the Vel's Parnelli Jones team in 1975.

With Vel's Parnelli not sending a car to the Brazilian GP at the beginning of 1976, Andretti had another of his one-off drives for Lotus, joining Ronnie Peterson in what would be the Swede's last drive for Team Lotus until 1978. This was the first race for the 'adjustable' 77, which competed at the twisty Interlagos circuit in its narrow short-wheelbase guise. 'Man, that car was terrible!' said Mario later. 'That Lotus was just frightening. I don't think I scare easily, but I sure as hell scared myself that weekend. I just didn't want to see that car again.'

On the fifth lap in Brazil the two Lotuses collided, Andretti retiring immediately and Peterson a few laps later. No worse fate can befall a Grand Prix team. Denis Jenkinson, at his most waspish, said in *Motor Sport*, 'When you have two really hopeless drivers in your team the only worse thing that can happen is to have no drivers at all. Andretti's efforts in the new Lotus 77 were an insignificant gnat's whisker better than Peterson's and I'm afraid I have become tired of waiting to see Andretti shine; you can wait forever. He may be a big wheel in USAC and SCCA kiddy-car racing, but he's a dead duck in European-style Grand Prix racing.'

Bonhomie at the British GP in 1965 was shared by Jackie Stewart, Jim Clark and Chapman. The loss of Clark in 1968 was a bitter blow to the motor-racing world.

Chapman's latest Lotus looked set fair to obliterate the Formula 1 ambitions of two great drivers.

After two more Grands Prix for the Vel's Parnelli team Mario was at liberty. 'My last race for Vel's Parnelli was at Long Beach in 1976,' said Andretti. The team withdrew thereafter. 'I retired – again. Worse, I didn't really know what I was going to do next. On the Monday after the race I sat down for breakfast in the Queensway Hilton, near the old *Queen Mary*. Colin was sitting there, too, and was just as unhappy as I was because his cars had gone awfully badly in the race too.[6] He came over and we started talking. I told him that I was completely committed to F1, that Champ Car was out the window and I would even take a sabbatical if it meant I could get a decent drive. And he said, "Why don't you drive for me?"'

It didn't happen right away. 'I said I'd do it only if he made me the number one driver and worked things around me, simply because Lotus never had the resources to run equal equipment for both drivers.' There was also the nightmarish recollection of the skittish 77 at Interlagos. Mario had already accepted an invitation from Frank Williams to drive one of his cars in the International Trophy race at Silverstone a fortnight after the GP in California. 'During the course of that,'

5   After testing at Monza in the Lotus-Ford during the week before the race, Mario turned only eight laps in the heat of Friday mid-day and was indeed quickest of all when he left the track. When temperatures dropped in the early evening seven others went faster – but not by much.

6   This was putting it mildly. In one Lotus 77 Bob Evans was too slow to qualify for the race while in its sister Gunnar Nilsson was the slowest qualifier. He crashed out on the second lap after his suspension broke. Andretti, starting in the third row from the back in his Parnelli VPJ4 after troubled practice sessions, was up to eighth place but retired on lap 15 of 80 with a coolant leak from a broken pump casting.

When Mario Andretti joined Team Lotus full-time in 1976 his team-mate was Gunnar Nilsson, F1 newcomer who arrived in a swap with fellow Swede Ronnie Peterson.

Towards the end of the 1977 season Andretti and Chapman were regretting their failure to take full advantage of their 78's downforce superiority. Engine failures didn't help.

said Andretti, 'Nilsson passed me and I could see they'd made a lot of progress with the Lotus. Let's see if we can help each other, Colin and I decided.'

'It was just what we needed,' said Chapman of Andretti's arrival. 'I'd always told Mario that if and when he ever took up Formula 1 full time, he was my number one. I was absolutely delighted when he came back to us. I think quite seriously that we might still be in the doldrums if he hadn't. He has this ability to get people's enthusiasm going. I know he had that effect on me and it extended to the designers, mechanics, everybody. Quite apart from his talent, he is such a genuinely nice guy that people want to do their best for him.'

Importantly, as with Michael Schumacher and Ferrari later, Mario Andretti represented an acknowledged driving standard. If the results weren't coming Chapman had to acknowledge that it was the fault of the car, not the driver, whom he was often prone to blame for lack of results.

By the next 1976 *Grande Epreuve* in Spain Andretti was at the wheel of a black and gold Lotus. Nilsson finished on the podium while Mario retired as he did in the next race in Belgium. He missed Monaco to race at Indy, then led in Sweden from second on the grid before retiring. 'The first race I ever finished in a Lotus – any Lotus! – was the French Grand Prix in '76,' said Andretti. 'It was only fifth, but it really broke some kind of barrier. From here on in, we felt, things could only get better!' The season ended with a win in Japan overshadowed by the drama of the Hunt-Lauda contest for the world championship.

'The best thing that could have happened to us as a team was putting that win together in Japan,' Mario Andretti recalled, 'and having that winter to work from that last thought. Psychologically, that's gold. Especially when Colin said he was going to put his whole heart into things. His wife said, "I've got a new husband again. He's got a whole new incentive. He's really, really keyed up about the whole thing. It's all brand-new, the way he used to be, instead of being in a rut, the way we were for a long while." It was nice to hear.

'I remember sitting around at the end of the season,' Andretti added, 'when Colin routinely told me, "Mario, your next car will make this one look like a London bus." And he was right. That was the beauty of Colin. If you rode with him through the peaks and troughs, he'd always deliver. Of course there were plenty of troughs – but he could make you a champion.

'The troughs were apparent in 1977,' Andretti added, 'when I dropped out of so many races. We had a fast car but Colin was always doing little things to make it lighter or faster. He was an unstoppable tinkerer.' So, for that matter, was Andretti, who was expert at such minutiae of racing as the handling 'stagger' caused by different tyre diameters. 'At Indy,' he pointed out, 'you've got four caster angles, four camber angles. I had my own notes and circuit maps and I tried to find the extra angle the others didn't have. If you look at a circuit with, say, eleven corners, there may be seven or eight that are key for passing or for speed on the next straight and two or three that you have to throw away. I always tried to maximise the car for the key corners.'

Neither party to their relationship took the other for granted. 'I felt safer in the Ferraris,' Mario said, 'and Colin Chapman knew it. He knew I had concerns. Let's face it, his track record in that respect was not brilliant. I almost killed myself at Indianapolis in a Lotus in 1969 with wheels coming off.' Andretti on the other hand seemed accident-prone. In 1977 he had collisions with Reutemann, John Watson and Jacques Laffite. 'We've had some shunts,' Chapman admitted, 'but this is probably due to frustration, when slower drivers were holding him up. He does put himself in situations sometimes where he's relying on the other guy to give way a bit.'

This was a small price to pay in Chapman's view for a driver who asked and gave no quarter. 'He's the sort of guy that unfortunately I like,' he said. 'What impresses me most about Mario is that he is still, first and foremost, a racer. That's the way to win races: just piss off and leave 'em. Okay, he asks top money and he gets it. He doesn't sell himself short. But the racing comes first. That's how it should be. But I think it's difficult for a driver to sustain this level of enthusiasm.'

Mario Andretti agreed. 'You've got to maintain a sparkle,' he told the author after the 1977 season. 'You've got to be able to keep looking forward to going there. Back in the late 1960s I found towards the end of the season I hated to get into the goddamn race car! And I figured, "Come on, Andretti, sit down and let's talk about it. Why? Because, too much!" Too much can be too much for anybody.' Thus for the talented Italian-American his Formula 1 debut, thanks to Colin Chapman, was a much-needed tonic.

'I thought I'd be in Formula 1 maybe a couple of years,' Andretti added. 'In 1975 when I got in I figured, well, I'll do '75, '76 and '77 and I think I'll have my fill. Now I find there's no way I could leave this for anything else! No way! First of all, it's more lucrative than anything else I can do. Which is important. I won't hide that. And secondly, there's nothing else that comes close to giving me the satisfaction! I mean, *not even close!* I find that

It all came good in 1978 for Andretti and Chapman, here with Peterson behind them. The Swede's death at Monza cast a pall over a year of hard work and rich reward.

instead of losing interest, I'm *gaining* it. Because now I know what it's all about. I've got the feel of it. And I don't feel like I want to give it up.'

For both men 1977 was an 'if only' season with the first 'wing car', the 78. 'It's been *eight years* since anyone's had such an advantage,' said Chapman. 'We had two seconds a lap on the others in the damp and a second and a half in the dry.' They achieved second among teams and third among drivers in a season undermined by unforced driver errors and Ford V8 failures. But Mario was undaunted. 'When you win races, and you've got the championship right' – reaching out with a grasping right hand – 'just about there, you feel you can go for it. And I don't think I'll be satisfied until I give it a valiant, valiant try.' This he did to epic effect in 1978.

'Colin was a wonderful chapter in my life,' said Andretti. 'He was such a maverick. Working with him was no trip to Paris, but I guess you're always going to have problems with a genius. Of all the cars I ever drove, I guess the Lotus 79 was my favourite. Okay, it was the car that took me to the world championship, but every time I went into a race with the 79 I felt I could win it if the car would stay under me. I totally understood that car – including its flexing, which of course Colin would never admit to! Everywhere we went, I was just thoroughly satisfied. It's just knowing that the man is really trying to give you every possible help, instead of sitting around the table talking.

'Everybody was highly motivated to create something different and pursue whatever we needed, including a lot of testing and good preparation,' said Mario Andretti of his championship season in 1978. 'Colin really wanted to make the difference. As a driver, to have Colin himself so motivated was a good chance for me t o go for the championship. Every time Colin was on that particular path he produced a world champion and that was awesome, tremendously motivating for all of us. We were making these strides because we were constantly searching for that elusive unfair advantage.'

'From being flat on their back on the floor at the back of the Formula 1 grid,' wrote Denis Jenkinson at the end of 1978, 'Team Lotus has soared back up to the forefront. While everyone at Hethel can be proud of their efforts over the past three years, no one will deny that it has all been due to the dynamic leadership of Colin Chapman.' Sticking to his guns, Jenkinson was unwilling to give a scintilla of credit to Mario Andretti.

One of Colin Chapman's finest drivers, Mario Andretti brought determination, loyalty, experience and intelligence to the perfection of ground effect in 1976–78.

Yet beyond peradventure his partnership with Chapman made all the difference in the team's spectacular breakthrough. 'Looking back on the last three years,' said the driver, 'I guess one of my biggest worries was being the guy *not* to win the championship for Colin. So many guys had done it before, I didn't want to be the one to let him down.'

The next trough came all too quickly in 1979 with the disappointing 80. The 1980 season with the hastily conceived 81 was an embarrassment for both Chapman and Andretti. The latter earned his single solitary point in the last race at Watkins Glen, where he'd been lapped by the Williams of winner Alan Jones. Mario left Lotus for a final full season with Alfa Romeo.

'I would honestly have liked Mario to stay on with us,' said Colin Chapman at the end of 1981. 'We enjoyed a long relationship which started in 1976; we were thrown together at a time when both our fortunes were at a low ebb and we needed each other.' Never again would Chapman enjoy such a fruitful relationship with a racing driver, one that was a happy echo of the golden years with Jim Clark and, indeed, Emerson Fittipaldi.

Having been a first-class racing driver himself, Colin Chapman could be a harsh judge of his pilots-for-hire. With characteristic ruthlessness he was decisive in his selections and rejections. Although not

Lured by the potential of the 80, Andretti stayed on at Lotus in 1979 and persevered in 1980 with the ineffectual 81 before leaving for a last season with Alfa Romeo.

renowned as a talent spotter, he was in fact shrewd and forward-looking in his driver choices, helped in the 1960s and early 1970s by Lotus's presence in feeder categories Formula 2 and Junior. He was opportunistic in harvesting talent from these for Formula 1 at the lowest possible cost.

Life in the second rank as a Lotus driver was anything but easy. Andretti put his finger on it: the team was seldom able to field two cars prepared to equally high standards. But for the lead driver the full benefit of Chapman's unrivalled insights and expertise was available – if he were prepared to apply himself. Chapman saw little point in expending energy on a driver whose application did not match his own. When he found such drivers he was indeed capable of taking them to the world championship.

During 1980 the Chapman-Andretti partnership was still wired up, as at Monaco, but retirements were frequent. Andretti could muster only a sixth and two sevenths.

Chapter 11

RACING
REALITIES

There was something in Chapman's philosophy that said when things aren't working you either start again or you change the personnel or you do both. I think that's why Lotus ceased to be successful in the later years because there was more to motor racing than just tearing it all up and starting all over again.

Geoff Aldridge

'I enjoyed my trials experience and successes,' said Colin Chapman of his early mud-plugging outings, 'but I had taken up competitive motoring largely to prove that I could build a motorcar better than the next man and I was finding out rapidly that trials were not the best proving ground. Luck enters so much into the results – you may have a "dry" climb whereas the next competitor goes up after a shower of rain.[1] To go on improving the design of your vehicle under such conditions is a bit frustrating at times whereas racing seemed to offer just about every opportunity for "improvement of the breed", so I decided to concentrate wholeheartedly on that aspect of the sport.'

In racing, too, Chapman never denied an acquaintance with Lady Luck. When asked late in his career what the factors were that contributed to racing success, he gave what he considered to be 'the standard answer: 20 per cent car, 20 per cent driver, 20 per cent management, 20 per cent mechanics and 20 per cent luck.' Juan Fangio too was a believer in the influence of luck. 'There is a formula for success,' he said, 'and it is

Having stepped back from a successful career as a driver, Colin Chapman diverted his competitiveness into team managing, at which he was among the masters.

not difficult to analyse. It is made up of 50 per cent car, 25 per cent driver and 25 per cent luck. All my life I have been lucky.'

Colin Chapman never vouchsafed whether he considered his luck good or bad. 'You won't win a race by luck,' he said, 'but you can lose one. You can be in a commanding position to win – have the car, driver, engine, mechanics, everything – but still not win because luck wasn't with you. We have, say, 40 engine rebuilds a year and we know we're going to have between six and ten blow-ups a year. That's just human fallibility. The luck is whether those blow-ups occur when you're leading the race or when you're in the middle of a test programme somewhere.'

When asked by Peter Windsor whether he was superstitious, Chapman admitted that he might be. 'That's a funny thing,' he answered, 'because when people ask me that I always say no. But when I think about it, I suppose I am. I must be, with all this nonsense with the hat – throwing it in the air when we win a race. But I don't wear any lucky charms or anything.' Early in his career he did have a 'lucky' tartan shirt which Hazel doused in Borax to make it fire-retardant.

That Colin Chapman was prepared to be so forgiving of 'human fallibility' in the assembly of engines is surprising, as was his readiness to accept a failure rate of 15 to 25 per cent. Had any supplier other than

---

1   The author would define such random variations as 'chance' rather than 'luck'.

With its Eighteen in 1960, Chapman's Lotus shouldered its way into racing's front rank. Two of its team cars were readied for racing at Silverstone on 14 May 1960.

Spotted with fellow motorcyclist Geoff Duke at Silverstone in May of 1960, John Surtees, left, felt Lotus wasn't adequately funded to prepare safe and reliable cars.

Coventry Climax or Cosworth delivered goods that failed with such frequency they would have been on the Chapman carpet. This spoke to a relationship with engines that was arm's-length in his later years as described in Chapter 2. It's easy to see why he persevered with the ultra-reliable turbine in GrandPrix racing.

Ultimately, when the chips were down, for Chapman speed was more important than reliability. 'He was less concerned about not winning than at not being at the front,' recalled mechanic Glenn Waters. 'You could be a yardstick or an embarrassment. He was okay working at the back of the grid. He still loved the fight. But if you were finishing second or third, then he could see no reason why you shouldn't be winning. That was when the wick really got turned up. That was the racer in him.'

With speed – a pole or fastest lap – Chapman could manifest his virtuosity as a designer. Finishing a race was a bonus. It was important, of course, but secondary to speed. 'Colin, above everything else, wanted to win races,' claimed John Surtees. But he was often resource-constrained, his 1960 driver added: 'His budget in those early years would have meant cutting many corners, part of the reason for the cars at times being referred to as "frail".' Surtees had a grandstand view during a Tasman campaign in which he had three steering failures 'and ended up feeling quite jaundiced about the whole programme.

'Colin lacked concern about the final quality of the product,' Surtees maintained. 'The fact that it fell apart didn't seem to matter to him provided it had gone quickly before it did. He was a brilliant engineer when it came to creating the concept of a racing car. I've often said that the Eighteen was probably the most competitive car that I ever drove relative to the opposition – in any of my motor-racing years. Having said that, though, his budget and consequently the number of experienced personnel and the quantity and quality of the parts that were available left something to be desired in the early Sixties.'

The arrival of Jim Clark in Chapman's world brought a new sense of responsibility. Clark's genius demanded closer attention to reliability, which in any case was intrinsically enhanced by the 25 with its abandonment of tubular frames with their many welds, only one of which had to be faulty for disaster to result. 'I felt right from the beginning of 1962 that the only thing that could beat Jim Clark on a Lotus 25 was unreliability,' Chapman said. 'In fact, the 25 *was* a reliable car in 1962, insofar as it had a higher percentage of finishes per start than the BRM. But unfortunately it had its troubles in the wrong races – the *Grandes Epreuves*!

'I was convinced that there was nothing wrong with the design of the car,' Colin continued. 'But Jim did have disappointments during the major races of 1962. At Monaco he went out with faulty gearbox adjustment and at Zandvoort because of clutch adjustment. Then at

With the inherently better durability of the monocoque of his 25, pictured in the 1964 season, Colin Chapman vowed to develop more cautiously to improve reliability.

Rouén a tension pin was omitted from the front suspension and at the Nürburgring the driver beat himself by forgetting to switch on his fuel pump. At Monza we had the wrong oil in the gearbox and in the final and vital race in South Africa a bolt fell out of the crankcase.[2] But in every one of these cases Jim had either put up the fastest lap or was leading the race before he retired.' Speed was Chapman's recompense.

In a non-championship race at Solitude 'Jim had a new type of drive shaft on his car and it twisted straight off when the flag fell. You see, we'd never done a competitive start with the shafts with a full load of fuel on board.' At the time Chapman drew a salutary lesson from this: 'One lesson I have learned in motor racing is that improvements in cars have to be tackled slowly and progressively. We have stopped experimenting in major motor races. We won't try anything new on a car in a major event.'

Meritorious though it was, this mantra was soon shelved. There never seemed to be the time, money and personnel

---

2 Though this was indeed thought to be the case at the time, the actual failure was discovered when the engines were dismantled and rebuilt at Coventry Climax. The shaft driving the two oil scavenge pumps had sheared, which allowed the engine to fill up with oil which was dumped out of the rear oil seal and the breather system.

Always eager to absorb new technology, Colin Chapman was joined by Jim Clark to examine the radical STP-Paxton turbine car on its first appearance at Indianapolis in 1967. A year later he was fielding Lotuses powered by its Pratt & Whitney turbine.

to conduct methodical testing away from the races. There's no better example of this than the high wings of 1969 and '70 that grew like Topsy from race to race with little or no validation testing. A victim of this policy, Jackie Oliver, attested to 'how little testing was carried out. Chapman was at full stretch and there were no spares and no spare car; they just couldn't keep up with development. They'd design a fantastic new rear-suspension component – and build two of them. If one got bent you had to put the old one on. It was very frustrating.'

Chapman himself was often frustrated. In 1976, when he was struggling with the 'adjustable' 77, he bemoaned to his colleagues Team Lotus's apparent inability to shake its cars down before races: 'Once again we have PROVED that there's NO WAY that we can take ANY race car to a race meeting without *full* circuit testing beforehand. The so-called "impossibility" of achieving this is all in the mind. What happened to the two weeks we "saved" by not going to Argentina?'

Colin Chapman never failed to give lip service to the importance of reliability. Asked by David Phipps about his plans for the 49 for 1968, he said, 'We are certainly going to carry on with developments of the existing cars as our mainstay for next year. We've gone through one season trying to sort out the bugs with something new and I certainly wouldn't want to go through another season doing exactly the same thing. We are going to have experimental cars which will come along during next year and we will start running them as soon as we think they are raceworthy, but we won't be putting our main effort into them until we are satisfied that they are as reliable as the existing cars.' Here was a reference to the 49B, which in fact he did phase into use with some circumspection.

Testing during race meetings wasn't sufficient, testified Lotus champion Emerson Fittipaldi: 'You cannot concentrate the same way that you can in a private test. In the official practice the driver is in the cockpit and the team manager, the mechanics, are just worried about him going quicker. Everybody is looking at the stopwatch, waiting, expecting him to go quicker! The team manager isn't thinking of what you can do to improve the car. He just thinks, "Oh, somebody else is going quicker!".

'In a private test,' Emerson continued, 'everybody is thinking about what they have to do to improve the car, not to go quicker. Not to do a quick time, but to improve the car. That's the big difference. You arrive at the track and you know that you can spend nearly all day just trying to get the car right, thinking about the ratios and wings and tyres. You stop at the pit and talk to the team manager and the mechanics. You say the car is doing this and that; they have time to think before making a decision. That's the difference. Who started doing that a lot is Jackie Stewart, with tyre testing. Now everybody is doing it.

'It takes a long time and many hours of testing to get a Formula 1 car to work right, to work on the limit,' Fittipaldi added of his experience with the 72. 'Because you have so many options now, when you stop at the pit you must give the right information to the team manager and the mechanics because if you give the wrong information they can start going the wrong way. You can drive *very* quickly but the car isn't going to be on the limit, where it should be. The Lotus 72 is a very difficult car to get on the limit. To get the right settings.'

Emerson freely acknowledged Colin Chapman's expertise in this area. 'I always say Colin was a genius,' Fittipaldi said. 'I never worked with anybody who had so much intuition about how a racing car is working. He was the best school a driver could have. Sometimes if my car wasn't working right we went for dinner. I told Colin exactly what it was doing. He'd go back to the garage to think about it and the next day it was better. His solutions to problems always came so quickly.'

Another driver had an experience that convinced him of Chapman's mastery of racing-car development. 'What really impressed me about Chapman's ability to get things done,' said Mario Andretti, 'was the Lotus 64, the four-wheel-drive car he built for Indy in 1969. I tested it at Hanford, California early that year. There just aren't words to describe how bad that car was. The handling was just flat-out spooky. Everything was wrong

and Chapman made a list of more than 80 changes. He didn't bitch about it, just went home and set to work. And the next time I drove it, that car was gorgeous. I guess I've been a believer ever since.'

In lesser categories as well, drivers had a glimpse of the Chapman development expertise. In 1972 Tony Trimmer was signed to drive the Lotus 73 Formula 3 car, very sophisticated for the category. 'He watched the car through a corner,' Trimmer said of Chapman, 'and then I met up later with him in the paddock. I said to him, "What's happening. Colin, is this…" He interrupted and then went through all the problems he saw happening through the corner earlier. He told me how the car would be improved and the changes they were to make to the suspension, wishbones, linkages etc. The man was pure genius. He was like a butterfly, though. He was there with you one moment and gone the next. He would be off to look after the F1 car; the F3 project got left and forgotten.'

Although he was an inveterate tweaker of racing motorcars, Colin Chapman was prepared to acknowledge that sometimes he could go too far. Ironically, Jim Clark's first world championship in 1963 could well have benefited from the extra effort Team Lotus expended to field cars at Indianapolis that year. 'If we hadn't been at Indy,' he said, 'we would probably have been sitting in the garage thinking up

Emerson Fittipaldi – in his Lotus 72 at 1971's US Grand Prix – believed deeply in the value of the extensive private testing that led to his successful 1972 season.

A blur as he passed the line to win the 1972 British GP, Emerson Fittipaldi never ceased being impressed by Chapman's ability to find solutions to racing problems.

improvements on the Lotus 25 and those improvements would probably have got us into trouble!'

By Colin Chapman's final Formula 1 season the interconnection between driver and engineers was electronic via wires and headsets. Engineering Nigel Mansell's Lotus, Steve Hallam 'would plug into Nigel's intercom system, then Chapman would plug into me, Peter Wright would plug into him and we would all be connected by wire. It seems a bit basic, although it had a lot of advantages because it was like having a conversation with four people. There was none of this modern thing where if two people speak at the same time no-one hears anything.'

Between brilliant design from the Chapman draughting board and at least a *soupçon* of reliability the Lotus reputation for high performance was established from the outset. Calling the Mark III of 1951 'astonishing', Bill Boddy in *Motor Sport* said it was 'a scientifically designed, very handsome unblown 750cc road-equipped two-seater which has done a standing quarter-mile in 17

Working with Ronnie Peterson in the 79, Colin Chapman could converse with him and engineer Nigel Bennett through a wired intercom that helped communication.

seconds and 0–50mph in 6.6 seconds.' 'Of course it became an attraction at every meeting,' said Michael Allen, 'because as a result of the enthusiasm with which we had worked on it since the last race, every time it came to the line it was really in a further state of tuning, and it had tremendous entertainment value. People used to come for miles to see the latest performance of the Lotus Austin.'

Curiosity about the attributes that made the Mark III so quick was naturally abundant. 'One chap in particular was sticking to us like glue in spite of all our efforts to make him realise that his presence was a nuisance,' recalled Nigel Allen. 'In the end I said to Colin, "If we do not get rid of this chap soon he will get thumped." "Leave it to me," said Colin. He took the chap on one side and spoke quietly for some time, the guy making notes all the time and he then went away and did not come back. I said to Colin, "Whatever did you tell him to make him go?" "Oh, I just told him that the secret of our success was that we had fitted twin paradiddles on the updraft and he was quite satisfied with that explanation!"'

The distillation of early front-engined know-how into the magnificent Eleven brought the first wave of international success for Lotus, resulting in the award of the Ferodo Trophy for 1956 (see sidebar). Although its main rival, the mid-engined Cooper 'Bobtail', was the concept that would ultimately prevail, the Eleven as the ultimate evolution of the small-capacity sports-racer was

Ferodo Trophy Awarded To Colin Chapman

The Ferodo Gold Trophy has been awarded to Colin Chapman for the most outstanding British contribution to the sport of motor racing in 1956. The citation to the award reads:

'Mr A. C. B. Chapman is responsible for the design and construction of Lotus sports cars and made an important design contribution to the advancement of the design of a British Grand Prix racing car.'

The Trophy was presented on the evening of Wednesday, 13th February, at a ceremony in the Orchid Suite of the Dorchester attended by Mr Hugh Molson, MP, Minister of Works, members of the Trophy Award Panel, Stirling Moss and other racing drivers, the Chairman of the RAC, the President of the Society of Motor Manufacturers and Traders and many other representatives of the motor industry.

During the announcement of the award, heralded by a fanfare from the Ferodo Trumpeters, 10 chequered flags on a simple backcloth dropped in turn to reveal some of the outstanding Lotus racing successes for which Mr Chapman has been responsible.

Mr John Eason Gibson, Vice-Chairman of the Award Panel for 1956, in presenting the Trophy, outlined the reasons for the Panel's choice of Mr Chapman. He said that anyone who sets about manufacturing racing sports cars as a business faces difficulties which would daunt most people. Not only has he to deal with the temperamental driver but at any moment every plan he has may be useless because some other person, or persons, has brought out something with more performance. We all know how difficult the supply of necessary and urgent spares may become. To do all that from a very small works with limited resources is certainly a *tour de force* of the first magnitude. To do it and succeed as Mr Chapman had succeeded is almost a miracle. Yet he had made sports racing cars which carry the British colours magnificently time and again.

In the international and approved events which qualify for the Ferodo Trophy, Mr Chapman's firm has been associated with 30 wins and 38 places without taking into account the five international Class G records established by Stirling Moss and H. Mackay Fraser at Monza in September and October on Lotus cars and all without taking into account the successes of private Lotus entries. Further he had assisted greatly in the evolution of other racing cars and brought that proposition also to well-merited success as one of an engineering team to whom we owe gratitude for success in the face of every obstacle and from whom there will be even more success in the future.

In his reply, Mr Chapman, who is a Director of Lotus Engineering Co Ltd, said that the award would give very great encouragement to all members of the Lotus organisation in their efforts to produce better cars. He emphasised that the Trophy would not have been awarded to him if it had not been for the very many helpers, both within and without his organisation, who had given so much time, work and creative thought to his project. He said that Team Lotus hoped this year to compete seriously in the new major international Formula 2 races as well as sports car races at home and abroad.

Apotheosis of the application of Chapman's front-engined know-how, refined with the vital inputs of de Havilland engineers, was the magnificent Eleven.

The Eleven, in the rear, served as the basis of the Fifteen, suited to bigger engines. The effort to make a smaller successor, the Seventeen in the foreground, misfired.

more than its match. It was the quintessence of the early Chapman years with its structure and aerodynamics courtesy of the de Havilland brigade. It was also a money-spinner unlike its contemporary, the Elite, which however in its own way was as evocative of the Chapman brilliance as any car that ever left the draughting board in his lounge.

The international adoption of Formula Junior in 1959 with its production-based engines was an engraved invitation for Colin Chapman. His mid-engined Eighteen first raced in Formula Junior form in the Brands Hatch Boxing Day meeting at the end of that year. For 1961 he produced the 20, a dedicated Junior. Helped by Keith Duckworth's snappy 105E Ford engines, these were the class of the field. In their Lotus 20s Trevor Taylor won eight races in 1961 and Peter Arundell and Jo Siffert seven apiece.

For 1962 Chapman rolled out the 22, now with disc brakes and an inclined engine to improve induction and lower the rear profile. In a works car Peter Arundell was virtually unbeatable with 18 wins and three second places in 25 races. His team-mate Alan Rees had the misfortune to crash during practice at the Nürburgring. In hospital afterward, under sedation, he was interviewed by German reporters. Rees told them that he thought some Formula Junior competitors were using engines that were larger than the regulation 1,100cc, up to as much as 1,450cc, taking advantage of the fact that engine capacities were seldom physically verified.

The result was an article in the 10 October 1962 issue of Germany's authoritative biweekly *auto motor und sport* by its sports editor Richard von Frankenberg. A former successful driver for Porsche, von Frankenberg was a respected figure in German motor sports. In a detailed two-page article he accused 'the English' of producing these oversized engines and supplying them to drivers including Kurt Ahrens, Jr and Austrian racer Conrado 'Kurt' Bardi-Barry. The implication was clear that the spectacularly successful Team Lotus Juniors were also using such illegal engines.

In his article von Frankenberg suggested that 'Herr

The win by Jim Clark's Eighteen in the Formula Junior race at Goodwood on 19 March 1960 was the first-ever for a Ford-powered single-seater Lotus.

With their reputations on the line Colin Chapman and Peter Arundell were allowed to look serious at the start of a Formula Junior trial at Monza on 1 December 1962.

Chapman' should bring Lotuses with legal engines to Monza, where they were to duplicate the winning speed over 30 laps of 113.47mph at which Arundell had won a race there in June. He also proposed similar exercises at Zandvoort and Goodwood. 'If this doesn't take place in the next four weeks,' he wrote, 'I believe that for an entire season the public, the organisers and all drivers using legal 1,100cc engines will, to put it quite simply, have been betrayed.' The magazine splashed this sensational story with a cover headline: 'Unprecedented Disgrace: Formula Junior Swindle.' prophesying the end of the formula if such major breaches of its rules couldn't be controlled.

When he saw the story Colin Chapman consulted his solicitors, who told him that a suit for heavy damages against *auto motor und sport* could well be successful. Chapman, however, suggested a wager. He accepted the venue of Monza, where engine power would be most decisive and weather had a chance of being decent

Lotus technical manager Mike Costin was present at the 1962 Monza trial, arranged to fight a German assertion that Lotus and its customers were using over-sized engines.

near the end of the year. He proposed the sum of £1,000 be on the table to go to the party proved right in the demonstration. This was accepted by the German side in negotiations between their AvD and Britain's RAC. Italian officials would monitor the event and check the engine's capacity afterwards. The Italian magazine *Auto Italiana* booked Monza for Saturday 1 December for the show-down.

Sunny Italy proved foggy and frosty on the day. The critical Lesmo Bends had to be salted to disperse the ice. By 1:30 pm Arundell was under way in his 22. He easily achieved his goal, improving on his June fastest lap and raising his 30-lap average to 115.16mph. Having completed his assignment he was then timed at a best of 117.14mph in three extra laps. Subsequent verification of the Cosworth-tuned engine showed its dimensions to be 85.0 x 48.15mm for a capacity of 1,092.35cc. The Lotus scaled just three kilograms more than the minimum weight of 400 kilograms.

Von Frankenberg apologised in print and in person and *auto motor und sport* handed over its £1,000 to Chapman on the spot at Monza. The winnings were split between the Lotus chief and Arundell. In the latter's hands the Lotus 22 had done much more than prove its overwhelming superiority during the 1962 season. It had now verified its performance under official supervision while adding materially to the Chapman legend. The episode was one of many during what Mike Warner called 'the core halcyon years' of Lotus in racing.

The Lotus legend was soon burnished in Formula 1. Although Britain was the nation that cavilled most conspicuously at the introduction of the 1½-litre Grand Prix formula in 1961, she came out of it in pole position. It was an era of Britain against Ferrari, the latter winning the world championship in 1961 and '64 and BRM taking the honours in 1962. Cooper, which had starred thanks to Jack Brabham at the end of the 2½-litre formula, was a busted flush.

Once Colin Chapman addressed the 1½-litre formula whole-heartedly he found it playing to his strengths. His skill in extracting the best performance from cars with small engines was tailor-made to the formula's demands. Reclining drivers, inboard front springs and monocoque frames were only his major contributions to the state of the art in these years. The result was two world championships for Jim Clark (1963 and 1965) and two more (1962 and 1964) missed by the narrowest of margins. Of the 47 qualifying Grands Prix Lotus chassis won 22, double the number of runner-up BRM, with 19 of the victories going to the combination of Lotus, Coventry Climax and Jim Clark.

'We thought Graham Hill [BRM] and John Surtees [Ferrari] would cause us the most trouble,' said Chapman of the first Lotus championship year, 1963. 'We were frankly surprised that the Ferrari was not better at the start of the season. It only showed its true form at Monza – as a monocoque, of course. I promised Jim that we were going to win the first five championship races! Unfortunately it took seven races before we got our five victories.' A fast start to each season was important, said later champion Emerson Fittipaldi, 'because then everyone has high hopes. Everybody tries to work that little bit harder – the team, the mechanics, Colin, the tyre people.'

Although it may have looked it, Colin told Gordon Wilkins, Clark's victories weren't all calculated to reduce the races to processions: 'When Jim won a race by a lap it has usually been because he has set a pace which has broken his nearest rivals. Through their retirements he has in effect inherited a lap lead. Jim regards 20 to 25 seconds as a commanding lead and he never deliberately tries to pull out more than that.

'We have a pit signal which is something of a joke in the team,' Chapman continued, 'P1 + 100, which means place one and 100 seconds ahead of the second man. We went to Monza thinking that this was a race we weren't going to win. Discussing signals before the race, Jim jokingly said, "I want P1 + 100 and that's all." Jim had a real fight with three other drivers – Surtees, Graham Hill and Dan Gurney – and when Gurney slowed after the other two had gone, I spotted that Jim was exactly 100 seconds ahead of second man Ginther. You can't imagine what a delight it was to hang out that signal!'

On Monza's icy track with his Lotus 22, Peter Arundell had to equal or better the time with which he'd won a 30-lap Formula Junior race there the previous June.

An ebullient Chapman gave Arundell the thumbs up as a signal displayed his lap timing and how far ahead of its bogey time the Lotus 22 was lapping.

With an Italian official in the foreground, Peter Arundell was besieged by well-wishers at the conclusion of a 30-lap trial that significantly raised his average.

Arundell could be pleased with his 1 December 1962 effort, which put to rest rumours that Lotus was only winning in Formula Junior because its engines were over-sized.

At the end of the 1965 season Colin Chapman analysed the ingredients of his success with Charles Bulmer and Philip Turner. 'It isn't maximum speed that wins motor races,' he told them. 'We have proved this in the last two years. Ironically, the maximum speed of the car is lower now than it's ever been. In 1962 we were faster down the straights than in '65. There have been at least two other makes of Grand Prix car [BRM and Ferrari] which have much better maximum speeds than the Lotus but we have won races because we have had better handling and a better all round envelope.

'We have to put lower and lower gear ratios in each year,' Chapman added, 'because the rolling resistance of these enormous high-hysteresis tyres has gone up out of all proportion. We were 10mph slower in top speed at Spa last year than we were when we started but the lap times keep coming down because of better cornering. During this period engine power went up from about 170 to 204bhp.

'Jimmy won at Clermont Ferrand with the worst old engine you can imagine,' Colin continued, emphasising the need for good roadholding and manoeuvrability. 'The four-valve blew up in practice, the two good two-valvers were back at Coventry Climax so we dragged out an old rusty, dusty thing that had been in the back of the van since the beginning of the season and blew the cobwebs off. It must have been at least 20bhp down. He just made it up because it was so quick through the swoops. In fact it could have been an advantage because there were a lot of sections which he could just take flat, tweaking it from one side to the other, whereas with a bit more power he'd have been off it and on it, off it and on it. It isn't just power that counts on a circuit like that.'

These were the years in which Colin Chapman was stretching his company's capabilities with the production of road cars, first the Elite and then, from 1962 and '63, the Elan and Lotus Cortina. Creating the Elite in the late 1950s was a drain on Chapman's application to racing, thought one of his drivers at the time, Graham Hill. 'I liked his approach to motor racing and I got along with him very well,' said Hill. 'At that time, unfortunately, he was extremely busy with the Lotus Elite and he wasn't spending much time with the motor-racing project at all. Consequently it suffered rather badly and that's why we did so badly, or so I thought.'

By the time Hill returned to Lotus, in 1967, this had changed. 'He is spending much more time with motor racing,' Graham said of Colin. 'In fact he spends most of his time motor racing and lets the commercial side be looked after by commercial men that he has employed.

So the set-up is completely different from the one I remember. It's a much more professional unit.' It took a well-founded organisation to bounce back from the deaths of Clark and Spence in 1967 and win a championship with Hill in '68.

For a man of Colin Chapman's calibre and energy it was a point of pride to be able to cope with both motor racing and road-car development at the same time. He relished the challenge of remembering the key issues in both disciplines and responding to them by setting policy for his teams. Nevertheless his full attention was inevitably diverted from one to the other by exigencies like those described by Graham Hill.

Chapman also taxed himself from time to time with the issue of the value of racing to the sale of his road cars. 'We sometimes get the feeling that because we are so prominent in racing, the general public still feel that Lotuses are really racing cars. In order to expand our market segment we have got to be able to sell cars to professional men – to doctors, dentists, people like that – who do not want a car which they feel has *too* sporting a background. They feel that it wouldn't be a sensible car for their wife to drive, it wouldn't be a sensible car to drive in town and so on.

'We are quite sure that we are putting off a potentially large sector of customers,' Chapman added, 'because they feel that a Lotus is just a racing car that you can drive on the road. I think that there will come a time when we will have to stop racing just to convince people

Supervised by officials from the Italian authorities, the 22's Ford-Cosworth engine was dismantled to check its capacity and Formula Junior conformity.

Joined by Frau von Frankenberg, a vindicated Chapman – happily £1,000 better off after winning the wager – shook hands with his accuser Richard von Frankenberg.

The combination of Lotus, Jim Clark and Coventry Climax brought 19 victories from the 47 championship Grands Prix run during the 1½-litre Formula 1 years.

that we no longer build racing cars.' This never came to pass, of course, during his lifetime. Indeed, he was seen by his associates as choosing drivers with an eye on the markets that they represented. Their prime exhibit was Mario Andretti. The Italian-American, however, was commercially committed to Alfa Romeo and thus not in a position to speak on behalf of Lotus Cars.

'Winning at Indy made no difference to sales in the United States,' said sales chief Graham Arnold, 'although it might have been different if we'd had 4,000 dealers, not 40. I don't think Formula 1 did much to sell Elans. Most were bought by people who had an aesthetic appreciation of the car. Looks attracted them in the first place. Then they went for a drive and discovered how superb the handling was.'

Jim Clark's success in the Lotus 25 – pictured in 1964 – marked a maturing of the Team Lotus racing effort after Chapman had launched his road-car programme.

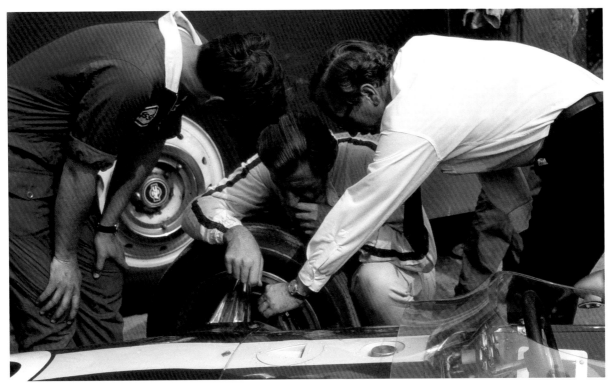

Rejoining Lotus in 1967 to drive the 49-Ford, Graham Hill was gratified to find that Colin Chapman was spending more time with the racing cars and team.

Late in his career Colin Chapman said of racing that 'I do it because it's fun, because racing's also my hobby. I really do enjoy it. I regard my business as running Lotus Cars – that's what I live off, as it were. I don't have to do the other things to continue racing, but if that was all I did then I wouldn't get enough satisfaction. In that case my hobby would become my business and I'd need to get another hobby.' Dipping in and out of racing as he did allowed Chapman to return to it refreshed, eager to advance the state of the art. Only his demoralising and ultimately fruitless struggles with the 'twin-chassis' 88 succeeded in dampening his enthusiasm for racing.

The travails of the 88 were the final straw in Chapman's running battles with racing's rulemakers and organisers. 'There was no-one better than Colin at reading race regulations,' said early colleague Peter Ross, 'and, when it was to his advantage, complying with the letter rather than the spirit. For him a "spare wheel" meant exactly that – without tyre, tube and rim tape. Why carry extra weight when the rules don't require it?'

'I first came to know him,' said Tony Rudd of Chapman, 'when the scrutineers rejected his F2 car at Goodwood as it did not have a fireproof bulkhead. The next day he was back with a cardboard map from the garage wall painted with aluminium paint as his fireproof bulkhead! The scrutineers tried to persuade me, among others, to protest. I told them to do their own dirty work and look at the regulations. The regulations required "that there be some means interposed between the engine and the driving compartment, safe and sufficient in the case of an emergency to prevent the passage of flame."

'Chunky's piece of cardboard might just work.' Rudd continued. 'All it had to do was to keep the flames away from the driver long enough for him to slow the car down to a speed where he could jump out, and this is what it might do. Somehow he heard about this and came and thanked me, saying that not all the racing fraternity would take my attitude with him.' Whether aluminium-look or not, however, a painted-cardboard map as a firewall had to be seen as a gross provocation of the Goodwood officials. Such men had long memories.

More than any other team owner, Colin Chapman was prepared to argue the toss with timekeepers. 'Getting the fastest times during qualifying was important in getting the best positions on the grid,' said Bill Milliken, chief steward for the United States GP at Watkins Glen. 'Timing and scoring for the Grand Prix was handled by Bill and Ginny Close, whose team was so effective that I

In 1967 and '68 Graham Hill drove the Cosworth FVA-powered Type 48 for Team Lotus in Formula 2 but went unrewarded for his efforts.

Deeply dedicated to racing though he was, Chapman expressed concern that his drive upmarket might be derailed by perceptions of his road Lotuses as mere 'racing cars'.

never had to give their work a thought. But the Closes always had problems with Colin Chapman. Colin was timing his own entries and claimed his faster figures were correct, so Bill, a stolid Scotsman, put two clocks on Lotus cars. When electronic timing arrived Chapman had no leg to stand on.'

A major set-to with the race officials was triggered by a disputed finish at Indianapolis in 1966. Lap charting during races was carried out by the RAC's experienced Cyril Audrey and also by Chapman himself. 'His Grand Prix charts could be guaranteed correct right down to last place,' said team manager Andrew Ferguson, while at Indianapolis with its higher speeds and 33-car fields 'Colin's excellent chart-keeping could only be relied on down to 15th place.'

In 1966 the 500-mile race had a chaotic start in which eleven cars were eliminated. After the restart the track gradually became unusually slippery, prompting at least two spins by the STP-sponsored Lotus 38 of Jim Clark with which he managed to cope in his usual calm style – but provoking alarming loudspeaker announcements. Near the finish the main display tower in front of the pits went dark, then came on again with a different race order. Although it showed Graham Hill the leader in a Lola, the Lotus charts showed Clark in the lead. He accordingly headed for the winner's circle only to find Hill there already. 'Without a moment's hesitation Jimmy was out of his car,' said Ferguson, 'congratulating his old friend.'

The Lotus pit was less sanguine about this turn of events. 'Colin was convinced that his chart was right,' Ferguson continued. 'He went completely over the top, shouting and protesting the result and haranguing chief steward Harlan Fengler,' the same man with whom he'd famously tangled in 1963 when Fengler refused to black-flag the Watson-Offy of Parnelli Jones – leading ahead of Clark – which was manifestly leaking oil. In 1966 Chapman was even more vociferous in pressing his case than volatile STP chief Andy Granatelli, 'if that can be believed' said Andy later.

After Vince Granatelli officially protested the result the Indy officials agreed to suspend announcement of the finish order until 10am the next day. That evening Cyril Audrey checked his lap chart against that of his room-mate Jabby Crombac. The latter said that he had done his 'from the press balcony, quite independent of the Lotus pit, and which afforded a much better view of the track. My chart clearly showed that Graham was the winner. Finally it transpired that during the confusion following one of Jimmy's spins Cyril had missed one of Graham's laps. The next day we went to the organisers to tell them that they were right after all.' The difference

COLIN CHAPMAN

in prize money between first and second was $79,305 – well worth arguing over.

Another notable brush with the organisers broke out at Le Mans in 1963. 'That was the best Le Mans ever!' joked Mike Costin afterwards. 'We were disqualified before the race and so we had an easy time!' Team Lotus presented two of its new mid-engined 23s, the type of car that had recently astonished with Clark's performance at the Nürburgring. With engines of 997 and 747cc the cars were potential rivals for the small French racers in classes dear to the home producers. They looked like anything but valid sports-prototypes with glazed panels crudely set into their all-enveloping Perspex windscreens.

As well, acknowledged Jabby Crombac, 'the car was so new that, to be frank, it was just not ready to race.' The scrutineers objected specifically to excessively large turning circles, fuel tanks larger than allowed, insufficient ground clearance and wheels which were not interchangeable front to rear. Supposedly to allow a larger engine to be fitted later, the rear wheels had six studs and the front wheels four. Lotus thought this met the requirement that 'the method of fixation of the wheels must be the same at front and back,' in that the principle was the same, but the official objection was that this made a mockery of the spare, which had to be usable at all four corners.

'We went there with perfectly reasonable cars,' in the view of Mike Costin, 'but the scrutineers were just "bolshie" as only the French can be. We said that we

When presented to scrutineers at Goodwood in 1957, Chapman's Twelve – here with Cliff Allison at Monaco in 1958 – had a firewall of aluminium-painted cardboard.

A dab hand at lap-charting his cars in Grand Prix races, as at the 1965 British GP, Colin Chapman didn't hesitate to challenge official timers and scorers.

would put on whatever wheel studs they wanted and that's all we argued the toss about. We did fly across different stub axles for the rear wheels, but by that time it was too late. Scrutineering had finished and that was it.'

The machining and delivery of new four-stud stub axles surprised the French, who thought they had definitively sidelined the Lotuses, so they fell back on the argument that they expected six studs at all four corners for adequate strength, not four. Finally they declared the cars 'not within the spirit of the regulations'. Both Mike Costin and Colin Chapman, flying over to argue the toss, made vigorous representations but were rebuffed. The two 23s were out.

In a bizarre conclusion to this fiasco a furious Chapman was invited to meet with the chairman of the race organiser, the Automobile Club de l'Ouest, to discuss possible compensation. As related by Jabby Crombac, who interpreted, the chairman said that the club would be prepared to refund to Lotus the cost of the aborted exercise. Chapman noted some figures down and showed them to the chairman, who exclaimed, 'It is too much!' 'In that case,' Chapman

When Lotus scorer Cyril Audrey, in pith helmet, missed one of Graham Hill's laps at Indianapolis in 1966, Chapman thought Jim Clark had won and argued accordingly.

replied, 'we shall never again race at Le Mans.' It was a promise he kept.[3]

'Away from the circuits,' wrote BRM's Louis Stanley, 'Colin could be lively company, irreverent and volatile. Only once did I see him on the defensive.' This was at 1965's Dutch Grand Prix at the seaside circuit of Zandvoort. On a hot day Chapman wore a short-sleeved shirt which left no place to put his armband, so he attached it visibly to his belt as many did. Thinking of something he wanted to say to Clark before the start, he headed for his car.

'Running across the track from the Lotus pit,' said Stanley, Chapman 'was intercepted by a policeman. Arguments followed and Colin was upended over the straw bales. Such indignities would upset anyone, and Colin was already on a short fuse through tension. Tempers erupted, fists flailed and it was the officer's turn to bite the dust. Thoughts of speaking to his driver abandoned, Colin returned to the sanctity of the pit very rapidly. The race ended with a Lotus victory, but the result meant little to the police. No sooner had the chequered flag dropped than the chief of police arrived with several officers at the pit and informed Colin he would be taken to police headquarters to make a statement.

'He refused,' Louis Stanley continued. 'Strong-arm tactics followed. Hazel Chapman intervened and was punched for her trouble. Mechanics waded in. The situation was becoming nasty. Chapman sprinted to the control tower, where race officials tried to calm things down. Eventually Chapman agreed to go provided I would accompany him. At 7.30 pm I collected the Chapman family plus Jim Clark and Mike Spence. Colin and I were taken to the detention wing. After being formally charged, Colin was told the case would be referred to the public prosecutor at Haarlem. As there was no bail, he would be taken to a cell to await trial at the next session in about ten days. Nothing could be done. Dutch legal procedure would take its course.'

So mortified were the race organisers that they cancelled the prizegiving dinner. 'Later that evening,' recorded Jabby Crombac, 'a large party of Team Lotus people, friends and supporters, gathered under the windows of the police station and sang rude English songs to cheer up the inmate who, meanwhile, was using the time to good effect by working on an initial design for his next Formula 3 car, using the back of the writ with which he had just been served!'

---

3 Not long after this, Lotus was approached by Ford as a possible partner in its effort to win at Le Mans after Ford's approach to Ferrari had been rebuffed. This would have required an uncomfortable volte-face by Chapman! Perhaps fortunately Ford decided to ask Lola for help instead.

'Understandably,' related Stanley, 'Colin was upset and apprehensive. Jan van Haaren, the ever-helpful president of the Dutch club, said he could do nothing. For several hours I tried every source to intervene. I called Amsterdam and The Hague, spoke to the Consul, Consul-General, British Ambassador, upset protocol by asking the public prosecutor who was his superior, and finally roused the Queen's Commissioner of the Dutch Government, who was asleep in bed. Maybe because he wanted to get back to sleep, he found a solution. Chapman need not be locked in a cell but could remain in another room until the morning. Uncomfortable but not so humiliating. To satisfy police records, fingerprints were taken plus side- and full-face photographs. He could also appear in court the next morning and return to his hotel pending further enquiries. Some months later, he was fined £25 – so ended a storm in a teacup with the reminder of what can happen in any country if you punch a policeman.'

While the Dutch authorities had every reason to feel kindly towards Chapman, who had chosen their race for the debuts of two of his most significant designs in 1962 and 1967, he had a much more rocky relationship with the Italians. This began in 1961 at Monza when a collision between Jim Clark's Lotus and the Ferrari of Wolfgang von Trips catapulted the latter into a spectator area, killing the driver and fourteen spectators. After the Italian GP Clark's 21 was impounded by the authorities, not to be returned to Lotus for many years.

A similar aftermath clouded Colin Chapman's life after the death of Jochen Rindt during practice for the Italian Grand Prix of 1970. A case was raised against Chapman and Lotus but eventually dismissed on the grounds that Rindt contributed to his own demise by not using the crotch straps that would have kept him from sliding down into the monocoque when he crashed into and under an Armco barrier whose longerons were improperly fixed.

Small wonder, then, that when Ronnie Peterson was hospitalised after his crash at the start of the 1978 Italian GP Chapman arranged to get his damaged 78 out of Italy as soon as possible. He deputed two team members to load it aboard the transporter and make tracks. 'Because of the problems Lotus had had at Monza,' said mechanic Rex Hart, 'with Rindt after Clark and von Trips coming together, when Italian officials confiscated the cars, the two guys were told not to stop until they reached France. They just about had time to wash their hands before they left.'

Earlier that year the Team Lotus mechanics played a key role in the launch of the career of the 79 in the

At Le Mans in 1963 Lotus presented two of its new mid-engined 23s with small engines to compete with the French tiddlers on their home territory.

The 1963 Lotus entries offered the French a chance to exclude them on the grounds of their use of wheel fixings with four studs at the front and six at the rear.

Belgian GP at Zolder. 'The car was tested by Ronnie Peterson in Anderstorp before the Belgian Grand Prix,' Mario Andretti related, 'and the test car was brought to Zolder. I asked Nigel Bennett how the test went. He said, "Oh, really quite well. Ronnie might even want to race the car." I said, "I don't think so. I want to race the car." I told Colin, but he said, "Oh no, no, it will almost certainly break." I went to Bob Dance and said, "The car looks a bit ratty, but can you make it reliable?"'

'That meant a big all-nighter to get it ready,' Glenn Waters remembered, 'so as a carrot Chapman offered us a bonus of £500 for a win. That was five weeks' money in those days. Mario said he would double it and Ronnie's sponsor, Count Guighi Zanon, doubled it again. The Old Man and Mario were good like that; they

gave us a big bonus at the end of the year too, after we'd won the championship.' 'That was the start of a great sequence of events,' said Mario, who qualified the 79 on pole with a margin of four-fifths of a second and led the race from start to finish.

Life for the Lotus mechanics wasn't always so accommodating. 'I remember an incident when we were behind with the preparation of the Lotus 24 spare car,' said Cedric Selzer about the 1962 season. 'It was usual practice for us to clean out the chassis tubes with water, followed by an acid solution. This was no simple process; it really was hours and hours of work. We were too far behind to do this so we left it. It was our hope that they wouldn't need to use the spare car. At Oulton Park we unloaded the car. Colin Chapman came up to me and said, "Did you wash the tubes out?" It was not one of those times when a lie would help. I put my hands up and said, "No." That really irritated Colin. "Get out of my bloody sight," he growled.'

Taking the train back to London, Selzer was on tenterhooks. 'I fully expected to be given my marching orders when they returned. Colin returned but nothing was said. The silence was very eerie! Six weeks went by, when Colin came into the factory and said, "Good morning." I was very relieved.'

In Selzer's day, looking after Jim Clark's cars in his championship years, a Lotus team on the road had four mechanics to attend to three cars. By the end of the

Chapman's difficulties with the Italian authorities began when Jim Clark's Lotus, right, was involved in this accident at Monza in 1961 that killed Wolfgang von Trips.

1960s the total Team Lotus squad numbered 45 people, said Peter Warr. 'We were doing the Tasman Series, Indianapolis, Formula 3 and GT racing with the 47s. The total personnel at a Grand Prix was nine: two drivers, two mechanics on each car and one on the spare, me and Colin. There were the non-championship F1 races too, which Colin usually didn't come to, plus all the testing. No-one who wasn't in F1 in those days can really grasp how hard we worked and how desperately last-minute everything always was.'

Chapman could be contemptuous of the conditions under which his mechanics were prone to work. Calling them 'the pigs-in-shit brigade', he said, 'What do our lads do when they arrive anywhere? First they pour a gallon of oil all over the floor, then they slap their toolboxes in the middle of it and slip and slide for the rest of their stay!'

From his earliest years Colin Chapman had worked with budgets that allowed him to go racing but offered little margin for error. When he went into Formula 1 in 1958, said Bill Gavin, 'Chapman was able to estimate that for a two-car team he would receive about £1,000 starting money per race from the organisers, which would more

Opposite: When Mario Andretti heard that Ronnie Peterson, pictured, might be first to race the 79 in 1978, he pulled rank to score the new model's first victory at Belgium's Zolder.

Above: Though prompted by Lotus's 1963 Indianapolis entry, Russell Brockbank's cartoon accurately foresaw Chapman's pioneering of commercial sponsorship in 1968. [The Brockbank Partnership]

than cover the transportation expenses to races abroad, the driver's fees and so on, while a retainer from Esso contributed towards the cost of building the cars.

'I think it would be true to say that Colin Chapman wouldn't have gone Grand Prix racing,' Gavin continued, 'or certainly not have stuck at it during those early years, if the starting money system hadn't existed. Team Lotus were involved in Grand Prix racing for four years before Innes Ireland won their first world championship event at Watkins Glen in 1961. If they'd had to rely on prize money as they do in the United States, Chapman would certainly have been obliged to abandon Formula 1. Not only were his cars not winning races, they were not even finishing a lot of the time.'

In the system that prevailed in motor racing at the time, since 1956 Esso had been delivering important support to Lotus, not only in providing funds to the team but also in paying retainers to drivers.[4] With an annual stipend of £2,000 Cliff Allison was the first Lotus professional. More than a decade later drivers were doing better. Near the end of his too-short career Jim

Clark's annual income from Esso was £100,000. But in this case as in others, all good things must end. At London's motor show near the end of 1967 Esso announced that it was ceasing its racing support. It had

Prime movers in the implementation of FOCA to represent the Formula 1 teams were Chapman, left, Bernie Ecclestone, right, and McLaren team chief Teddy Mayer.

---

4 These alliances sometimes caused problems, much as tyre-company contracts would later. Innes Ireland was criticised by Esso in 1960 for agreeing to let his works Eighteen be driven by Stirling Moss – a BP driver – in the Italian GP at Monza when Moss had a chance to challenge for the world title. For sportsman Ireland his dressing-down by Esso was 'a sad commentary on the state of motor racing.'

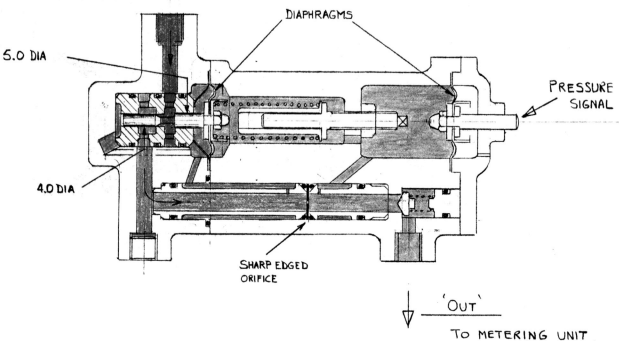

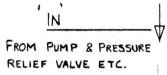

'IN'

FROM PUMP & PRESSURE RELIEF VALVE ETC.

DIAPHRAGMS

5.0 DIA

PRESSURE SIGNAL

4.0 DIA

SHARP EDGED ORIFICE

'OUT'

TO METERING UNIT

When in 1980 Colin Chapman and Keith Duckworth urged the adoption of a limit on fuel flow to F1 engines, Cosworth prepared this design of a suitable control device.

Pictured by Ove Nielsen with Peter Wright, left, and Elio de Angelis in a serious moment, Chapman arranged with Renault to supply turbo V6 engines for 1983.

found the soaring costs of the new 3.0-litre GP formula too rich for its blood.

'Esso have been sponsoring Brabham and ourselves to a very great degree,' Colin Chapman told David Phipps soon afterwards, 'and I think that both Jack and I will find things very difficult if we don't manage to get comparable backing elsewhere.' Shell came aboard for some events, but that still left a significant funding gap. 'We are living in an age when men are about to go to the moon,' Chapman said. 'We have rockets and we have supersonic aeroplanes, so we can't expect racing cars to be produced for the same cost as they were even ten years ago. In order to maintain station in this technological age we need to produce sophisticated machinery. All this costs money.'

New possibilities were opening up, Chapman told Phipps: 'The regulations are being amended to permit some limited form of advertising on racing cars, which does open the door for alternative sponsors to come along. I feel that it would be a very good thing if the scope of advertising on cars could be increased to include non-trade sponsors. This is one way of helping to finance the increasing complexity of race cars and the increasing expense.'

Thanks to a tip from former mechanic Dave Lazenby,

then heading Lotus Components, Andrew Ferguson made contact with cigarette maker John Player, which was interested in the marketing potential of motor sports. The pact made then was to form the foundation of Team Lotus funding well into the future. It became effective on 20 January 1968 in the Lady Wigram Trophy race at Christchurch, New Zealand's Invercargill circuit. Jim Clark won in a Lotus 49T which carried the red and white colours of Gold Leaf Team Lotus for the first time. 'Certainly the cars in their new livery look extremely attractive,' said Philip Turner in *Motor*. 'Perhaps this may be one way to brighten up racing.'

'It is only right and proper that commercial organisations should assist in this way,' said Colin Chapman at the announcement of the new alliance, 'rather than obtaining Government assistance for motor racing with all the ups and downs which are unfortunately associated with any politically based activity.'[5] The new livery's first appearance in Europe was on a single car for Graham Hill at Brands Hatch for the Race of Champions on 17 March.

Although Elio de Angelis often qualified well with the Lotus 93T-Renault, his 1983 season with this and its successor the 94T was blighted by frequent retirements.

Bizarrely at Brands the sailor at the centre of the Gold Leaf logo had to be taped over in deference to the demands of television broadcasters. This was a sign of the growing importance of television as a source of revenue for the sport. That was still in the future in 1964, when the Formula One Constructors Association (FOCA) was officially launched. Colin Chapman was instrumental in its formation as a unifying force among the F1 teams to negotiate more effectively and consistently with the race organisers and other bodies.

The first discussion leading to FOCA's founding was held when Colin, John Cooper, Jack Brabham and BRM's Tony Rudd travelled back from a meeting with the FIA in Paris. Chapman, said Tony Rudd, 'argued that if we all stuck together we could eliminate a lot of the stupidities of the FIA, reduce our costs and increase our earnings. We should invite Ferrari in and we could all contribute towards the cost of a secretary. The first secretary was Lotus's Andrew Ferguson. Ferrari said it was his policy not to join trade associations, but please keep him informed. The first non-founder member was Ken Tyrrell.'

---

5   The thrust of this remark by Chapman is semi-obscure. Certainly the UK government had never shown signs of wanting to support motor racing. It may have been a barb in the direction of Matra and the Tyrrell team, whose activities were supported by Elf, the government-owned French oil company.

Above: *Preceded by a test in 1962 with a 25-Climax, the 1963 Lotus Indianapolis campaign began unprepossessingly with this deceptively innocent-looking 29-Ford prototype.*

Below: *By the month of May 1963 the Lotus-Ford effort seemed more serious with added power from the 'bundle of snakes' exhaust. Chapman, right, checked Gurney's car.*

'I only agreed to a post in the new body as a temporary measure,' Ferguson recalled. 'Initially we kept the arrangement a matter among ourselves, but by the end of 1963 it was decided to "go public". I was given £15 by each team to get the thing off the ground, with the explicit request that it must cover the first year's expenses! In fact I found myself in a post that was to endure for ten long years.'

FOCA, said Rudd, 'really took off when Bernie Ecclestone, having bought Brabham, became their representative. Colin Chapman said he was always cast as the villain, so let someone else have the flak for a change.' Later the Lotus founder tended to assign all the responsibility to Ecclestone. 'In effect,' said Chapman, 'Bernie unionised us. Although the idea of "unions" had always been anathema to me, in this case I quite liked it. We all did.'

In the wake of the controversies over wings and skirts, frustrated by the wilful actions of Jean-Marie Balestre, head of the FIA's sporting arm FISA, the FOCA members essayed a split from the governing body and even staged an outlaw race at Kyalami early in 1981. While barrister Max Mosley wrote the general rules for the World Federation of Motor Sport, the body FOCA hoped to establish to regulate its racing, the technical regulations were the work of Chapman. He explained to Jabby Crombac what he aimed to achieve:

Formula 1 should be the pinnacle of motor racing. It should have the minimum of parameters controlling performance. There are only four parameters which control a racing car: one is the power from the engine; the second is the aerodynamic download it can produce; the third is the amount of grip which can be obtained by the tyres and the fourth is the weight. Then there should be some second category of regulations concerning the passive safety of the cars in the event of an accident. I think this should be controlled by some form of crash test, rather than by myriads of little regulations which, in themselves, very rarely produce the objectives they were set up to achieve.

This was a liberal manifesto to which Chapman was loyal throughout his life. He showed remarkable foresight in suggesting that crash testing for F1 cars be introduced.

While on one hand Colin Chapman relished the challenge of outwitting the rulemakers and his fellow racing-car builders, on the other hand he fought hard on every occasion and in every forum for less restrictive rules. 'I'm not happy with any limits,' he told

With Chapman in the foreground, the offset suspension of Jim Clark's 29 was prominent in this view of the car and driver that stunned Indy's establishment in 1963.

Peter Windsor in 1979. 'My fundamental belief about Formula 1 racing is that the amount of time and the amount of money being spent on racing should have more of an outlet than just a circus. Therefore Formula 1 should be contributing towards the evolution of the motor car and I feel we should have the absolute minimum of restrictions.

'There should be no regulation other than perhaps one parameter governing performance,' Colin continued. 'The rest should be confined to providing maximum safety for the driver. The engineers should be given free rein to develop the best possible projectile to carry man around a race circuit because, somehow or other, eventually advances made on the track will be reflected in the general evolution of the production car. If the cars become too fast for the circuits, then this one performance parameter should be adjusted from time to time to contain the speed.'

This parameter would be controlled by racing's governing body, which should 'follow the recommendations of people who are competent to give them.' Which parameter would Chapman recommend for control? 'The answer is the engine,' he said. 'The power that is being produced. We should be finding some way of restricting the power that the engine can produce – but in no way restricting efficiency. In my

The strategy of every aspect of the Lotus-Ford Indy campaign was scrutinised in depth and detail by Chapman, including a 1963 tyre review with Jim Clark while Stirling Moss looked on.

view the only satisfactory way of doing this is by controlling the amount of fuel that the engine uses. The one controlling parameter should be the rate of fuel consumption.

'Not total quantities of fuel,' Chapman continued. 'Otherwise you'd get cars running out. And you mustn't do it with an air hole, because you shouldn't be rationing something you get for free, such as air.' In these admonitions he dismissed two methods of engine-power control that were being deployed at the time. Limiting air consumption by a regulated aperture was being used in Formula 3. Albeit generously, fuel quantities were controlled by the new Group C rules coming into effect in 1982 as the sole means of limiting engine power. Contrary to Chapman's forecast the cars seldom ran short of fuel precisely because consumption was so closely monitored. Chapman's legendary parsimony with fuel was much more likely to cause his cars to run out.

What a team! Stanley Rosenthall snapped Clark and Gurney starting their Lotus-Fords from the front row in the September 1963 Trenton 200. Not their day, both retired.

On the pit wall during the month of May 1965 Colin Chapman had the full attention of Dave Lazenby as they covered every last detail of their third Indy Speedway campaign.

'There should be some way in which you can ration the rate at which you burn the fuel,' was Colin's recommendation. 'If you did that you would be putting an immediate premium on efficiency, because if the engineer were told he could only have 30cc of fuel per second, or something like that, then he'd be trying hard to find the most efficient way of using that fuel. Also, of course, you could immediately do away with all your equivalence formulas. You could have any engine design you liked so long as it consumed 30cc of fuel per second. With that one simple rule you could do away with all the others.'

In this advocacy Colin Chapman was mirroring a proposal developed in the 1970s by Keith Duckworth. The Cosworth designer had started with a fuel-quantity limit before his thinking turned in 1978 to a device to control fuel flow. As an engine man Duckworth could see what others could not, namely that the turbocharged engines coming into F1 would produce

In the 1965 Indianapolis 500 that he dominated by a two-lap margin, Jim Clark (82) saw A. J. Foyt (1) retire his earlier Lotus-Ford. Both qualified at better than 160mph.

On the right of Clark in the 1965 Indianapolis Winner's Circle Colin Chapman was hidden behind Mike Underwood, who was holding the winner's traditional bottle of milk.

Joe Granatelli led Lazenby and Chapman up the Indy pit lane in 1966, the year in which arch-rivals Lola and Graham Hill won with Clark's STP-Lotus second.

such exorbitant horsepower that those teams not having them would be deeply disadvantaged. With a fuel-flow control the engine's actual design would be free. Keith suggested a maximum flow rate of 27cc per second which he saw as producing around 400bhp. He and his team set to the design of a suitable flow-controlling valve.[6]

Having failed to gain acceptance for this restriction method, Duckworth regrouped in 1981 to recommend the air-entry orifice as the most practical way to constrain power. Although rejected by Formula 1's rulemakers, the use of calibrated inlet apertures to control power became accepted in GT racing. Meanwhile the 1½-litre turbos began rampaging Grand Prix racing with their 1,000-plus horsepower. Chapman joined their ranks with his 93T of 1983, detailed by Martin Ogilvie, the last car to be designed under Colin's direct influence. It had power courtesy of Renault, whose V6 pioneered the breakthrough to turbocharged

engines in Formula 1. Regrettably the Pirelli-tyred 93T was not a success.

The first marriage between Lotus and a turbocharged racing engine took place in 1969 with the creation of the ill-fated four-wheel-drive 64 for Indianapolis with its 2.6-litre Ford V8. With the elaborate cars failing to compete as a result of rear-hub problems, a near-decade of Team Lotus participation at Indianapolis came to an end. Of all the remarkable adventures and achievements of Lotus in racing, its successful invasion of the great Indiana classic rates as a glorious triumph.

When Colin Chapman first visited Indianapolis as the guest of Dan Gurney for the 1962 500-mile race he spotted the sign over its main entrance – 'World Capitol of Auto Racing' – and offered vociferous objection. Seeing the track and race, however, not to mention its legendary prize money, seized his attention. Rodger Ward, winner in 1962, encouraged Chapman to take on the challenge. 'He wasn't embarrassed a bit to get down and look at cars from underneath at a race,' Gurney recalled. 'He was always observing. And he was enthused. It didn't take him too long to say, "Yes, I can do something here."'

---

6   As a vice president at Ford of Europe whose responsibilities included motor sports, the author publicly backed Duckworth's proposal and arranged for a Ford engineer to be delegated to provide him with technical and moral support in meetings with the FISA and others.

Colin Chapman and his sponsor STP persevered at the Speedway in 1967, when Jim Clark and Graham Hill drove Lotuses. Both retired early with engine ailments.

Ridiculing the truck-like creations of the American racers to his Lotus colleagues, Chapman began contemplating the type of car he would build to continue the rear-engined revolution at Indy pioneered by Jack Brabham's Cooper-Climax in 1961 and Mickey Thompson's Buick-powered 1962 racers. Winning the partnership of Ford, which was eager to tout the sporting credentials of its Fairlane V8, Lotus first raced at the Speedway in 1963.

Californian Dan Gurney drove a sister 29 to that of Jim Clark in 1963. Speedway novices Ford and Lotus, he said, were given a wake-up call by the speeds of the veterans. 'Before very long into practice and qualifying they all realised that the so-called dinosaurs of track racing – the Watsons, the Lesovskys and the Kuzmas, the various roadsters with the long, illustrious lineage – were not the pushovers they might have expected.' Nevertheless in spite of an inexperienced pit crew and his unfamiliarity with the manners and mores of racing

Indianapolis in 1968 witnessed the biggest Lotus decals yet, deliberately over-sized to compete with STP's colossal stickers on the Type 56 turbine car.

at Indy, Jim Clark was able to cope with all of them save the pole-setting Watson-Offy of Parnelli Jones.

For Ford, finishing second was anticlimactic after expectations had been raised. 'It had been a lifetime chance,' said Ford's Jacques Passino, 'and I was crushed. First it had been, "If we can just get them qualified," and then when we qualified it was, "Oh, boy," then it was, "If we can only win," and then, toward the end of the race, it was, "We *must* win"…and then it ended the way it did.' Ford was sufficiently hooked, however, to commit to a four-cam 32-valve version of its Fairlane V8 for 1964.

It committed as well to another round with Lotus in spite of a post-race accounting that troubled some in Dearborn. Lotus had done well at Indy, winning $55,000 for second place. 'Ford threw in another $20,000 for qualifying two cars,' wrote Ford racing historian Leo Levine, 'and another $25,000 for finishing second. In addition Ford had paid all expenses. When the company added the entire bill together the feeling in Dearborn was that while Chapman might be a great designer, he was an even better businessman.'

For the 1964 '500' Colin Chapman decided to assess an 'unfair advantage' for his new Type 34 in the shape of Dunlop tyres instead of the Firestones that were standard wear at the Speedway. They gave an advantage in cornering grip at the expense of shorter life, but Chapman – in making the final decision – reckoned that Dunlops were the answer. However during post-qualifying test runs the rear tyres began throwing chunks of rubber. Dunlop agreed to make new batches and send them in time for the race. No better, their failures put both Clark and Gurney out. 'In 1963 we ran Firestone tyres and should have had Dunlops,' said Dave Lazenby, referring to the oily state of the track. 'In 1964 we ran Dunlop when we should have had Firestone.'

Black clouds loomed over Dearborn. Of seven Ford-powered entries – with Lotus the official spearhead – only one had placed in the top ten, Rodger Ward in second with a Watson chassis. Summoned to a meeting at Ford, Andrew Ferguson related, he and Chapman were given a dressing-down by a menacing phalanx of Ford suits:

The inquisitors piled straight in with outright condemnation of Colin's actions during the month of May. I was taken aback at the stream of insinuations that followed, as if addressed to an embarrassed stable boy who was explaining why he had shut the door after the horse had bolted. It was as if Ford had given us their multi-million-dollar ball to play with for a month and we had merely spent the 30 days of May kicking it about with senseless abandon. Then came the bombshell. Ford had come to the opinion that we were incapable of running an efficient ship, and Colin must now hand over the complete team of cars and spares to Ford for them to run.

Braced by a call to Fred Bushell at Hethel during a break in the proceedings, Colin returned to the fray 'absolutely back on song, and he waded in with all guns blazing. The Ford men were aghast, but Colin was adamant that Team Lotus must be allowed to redeem itself at the Milwaukee and Trenton races later that year.' A new agreement was thrashed out that left Team Lotus in charge of its destiny. Redemption came at the one-mile ovals with Parnelli Jones winning both races from pole position in a Team Lotus 34.

'The 1965 Indianapolis "500" provided a good example of how to win a race,' Andrew Ferguson reflected. 'Most of our data collation – full-fuel running, shock-absorber data, fuel-injection tweaking, fuel-consumption calculations – had been completed by the beginning of the second week when several cars, including our number two, had not even ventured on to the track.' In 1965 the choice of rubber for the new 38 was between Firestone and the offerings of Goodyear at the beginning of the tyre wars. Although the newcomer had a speed advantage it also showed signs of chunking so dependable Firestones were chosen.

'Jimmy was fantastic that day,' said girlfriend Sally Stokes, his guest at the 1965 race. 'Right from the start of the race and until he took the chequered flag, he was "on it". His winning margin was some two laps; a great day with a perfect ending. It was a truly remarkable win that would change the face of Indianapolis racing. Colin Chapman and the whole team had taken the race by the scruff of its neck and won. Although I think it smarted at the time, the Americans came to respect the achievement in later years. Jimmy was proud of this victory and I'm sure it ranked among his all-time best.'

Clark's record winning average of 150.686mph was quicker than the four-lap qualifying run of 150.370mph – the first over 150 – set only three years earlier by Parnelli Jones. That was an average pace of less than a minute a lap for 500 miles. Jim was the first foreign driver to win since Dario Resta in 1916. His car was the first rear-engined victor and the first Ford-powered winner, ending a string of wins for the Offy that began in 1947. The winner's prize kitty that year was a welcome $168,500. Placing third was talented rookie of the year Mario Andretti, whose contacts with Clark and Chapman at this race led to his first Lotus drives three years later.

Team Lotus continued at the Speedway for four more years, in harness with flamboyant Andy Granatelli's STP. Clark was second in 1966 and retired in '67. The radical turbine-powered 'wedge' of Joe Leonard took pole in 1968 at a sensational 171.599 mph and was leading at 191 of 200 laps when its fuel-pump drive broke. Nineteen sixty-nine was a disappointing anticlimax with the failure of the elaborate four-wheel-drive 64. 'Bring the cars back to Hethel,' Chapman told Ferguson, 'where I will *personally* hacksaw them in half, *personally* dig a big hole and *personally* bury them.' Mario Andretti jumped from his 64, after it tried to kill him, into a Hawk-Ford which he drove to victory for Andy Granatelli.

Although others had sought to introduce modern mid-engined technology to the hallowed Speedway, only Colin Chapman did so convincingly. His cars were adopted by other leading teams and drivers, notably A. J. Foyt, and virtual replicas such as Dan Gurney's Eagles took to the track. Thus did Chapman more than make up at Indy for his earlier hesitancy in adopting the mid-engined configuration for his sports and racing cars. Only Eric Broadley's Lola made comparable headway at Indianapolis in the 1960s, most annoyingly for Chapman with Graham Hill's 1966 win when Colin's lap chart suggested victory for Clark.

Great days were still ahead for Chapman and Lotus. Concentrating henceforth on Formula 1, Colin would hurl his cap skyward many times. But in the saga of his racing life his exploits at Indianapolis, an alien land far from his comfort zone, stand tall as models of planning, engineering, sponsoring, testing and execution, driven by an unrelenting force of will. Taking on the establishment, in the form of both Ford and Indy – and winning – was a historic achievement that brought him immense satisfaction.

Convincing evidence of Colin Chapman's artistry, the turbine-powered Lotus 56 of 1968 wrote one of the most celebrated pages in the storied history of Indianapolis.

Chapter 12

CODA TO CHAPMAN

Chapman has absolutely been incredibly genial in all the things he has done. I would like to have a tenth of the creativeness that Chapman had. Chapman always looked for an original solution and tried not to copy. This has been his unbelievably great advantage. His was a true genius and – first of all – an impassioned one.

Gianpaolo Dallara

Early in the 21st Century Britain's *Motor Sport* polled a panel of 32 experts on their rating of 'The Most Important People in Formula 1 History'. They were looking for 'those who changed things, made things happen'. They ranked Colin Chapman third of 99 people, behind Enzo Ferrari and top-rated Bernie Ecclestone. Among members of his supporting cast Jim Clark was 9th, Stirling Moss 12th, Keith Duckworth 13th, Walter Hayes 28th, Graham Hill 33rd, Emerson Fittipaldi 37th and Mike Costin 55th. Chapman's great rival Eric Broadley was only 69th.

What about Chapman's cars? In 2003 *Motor Sport* addressed this as well. A 24-man panel 'with a strong sprinkling of engineers' was asked to rate the greatest Formula 1 cars since the world championship was established in 1950. Best, they said, was a car in recent memory, Ferrari's F2002. The next three spots were taken by Lotuses in the order 72, 49 and 79. The 25 was seventh after the Williams FW14B and the Maserati 250F. Strangely the 25's successor the 33 was only 32nd in spite of its major role in Clark's second world championship. The 78 ranked 36th and the Eighteen was 37th. Bringing up the rear were the Sixteen, placed 90th, and the 93rd-placed 80.

Rated near the top of those 'who changed things, made things happen' in Formula 1, Colin Chapman brought creativity, determination and drive to his passion.

Even given the bias likely in a British magazine, these were impressive findings. In his cars and his personal standing Colin Chapman left all rivals in his wake. He wouldn't have minded being below Enzo Ferrari in 'importance'. Chapman always had the greatest respect for Ferrari as a businessman and racer. Indeed, the men had much in common in their ruthless pursuit of excellence. 'Colin Chapman is a fine designer,' avowed Ferrari. 'The Lotus is a complete scientific study.'

The engineer whose Ferraris were pitted most often against Chapman's creations, Mauro Forghieri, said, 'I would be very happy to see a car *completely* made by Chapman. It would be one of the more interesting new cars in the world.' This was a not-so-subtle dig at Lotus, sneered at by the Italians as one of the British 'kit car' builders who relied on Cosworth for engines and Hewland for gearboxes, in contrast to companies like Ferrari and BRM that made Grand Prix cars in their entirety. Forghieri could rightly be proud of having overseen the complete design and manufacture of a successful car like Ferrari's 312T.

Forghieri's hint was not unfair. After he advanced from modified Austins and Fords, Colin Chapman relied chiefly on engines from Coventry Climax and Cosworth to power his racing cars. His own engines were four-cylinder units used more for road cars than racing, the Ford-based Twin-

Above: *Second only to the F2002 Ferrari as the greatest-ever Formula 1 car, experts decided, was the pathbreaking Lotus 72, chock-full as it was of transformative ideas.*

Below: *Only two Formula 1 cars were rated by experts as 'greater' than the Lotus 49-Ford, seen with Chapman and Hill celebrating victory at Monaco in 1969.*

Cam and the versatile 16-valve 907. If one were to nominate an all-Lotus road car that best exemplified the Chapman spirit it would certainly be the Esprit, in which the engineer took a close personal interest. Brilliant in conception albeit mediocre in execution, it exemplified the attributes of Lotus road cars during most of Chapman's tenure. With the launch of its Turbo version in 1980 the Esprit matured magnificently.

Chapman deserved credit for his relentless pursuit of a transmission that would give his cars an unfair advantage. In this he was unique among his *garagiste* contemporaries. His first effort, the 'queerbox', had all the ingredients to be a tremendous success after Keith Duckworth conceived and fitted his push-pull gear selection. It was amazingly versatile, astonishingly compact and sublimely light. It lacked only a smidgen of length to have shifted reliably.

A remarkable might-have-been was the Hobbs Mecha-Matic transmission. Having worked so effectively in the Elite, this box with the potential to be fully automatic could have opened the door early to left-foot braking. Jim Clark would have adapted easily, as did Ronnie Peterson, an enthusiastic advocate of the 77's automatic clutch. But the Hobbs was an initiative too far at the time. Nearer reality, later, was an attempt to revive the 'queerbox' concept for the 78 and 79 with the help of Germany's Getrag. This deserved a better outcome but was swamped by the other urgent needs of these 'wing cars'.

Most successful was Chapman's discovery and

In spite of its structural shortcomings the Lotus 79 was rated fourth greatest of all Formula 1 cars since 1950. It contributed decisively to modern ground effects.

exclusive use of the ZF transaxle, which he spotted when the German company was making parts for the 'queerbox'. Colin's own efforts in the transmission field were blighted by his philosophy of designing for lightness and strengthening when and where failures occurred. While this worked for frames and suspensions he proved it conclusively not to work for transmissions.

So the ingredients for an all-Chapman racing-car design were there. How close did he come to creating a car that would meet Forghieri's criterion? The car that best exemplifies his complete-car creativity is the 49. With Duckworth and Costin designing and building the engine Colin had the help of recent colleagues whom he knew intimately – and vice versa.

For the first time Chapman had a deep personal involvement with the engine of a Grand Prix Lotus. 'After a fairly short discussion with Colin,' Keith Duckworth recalled, 'we decided that although we could probably make a 12-cylinder engine, it was always an advantage to have a small lightweight car. We were both people who subscribed to the view that lightness is next to Godliness and you must be down to weight. Also, I did know something about four-cylinder engines. I felt that if I made a V8 with a common-plane crankshaft I could be fairly sure of it being in the 400bhp category. Colin

Though high 'greatness' ranking was denied the Lotus Eighteen-Climax, for Colin Chapman it was a breakthrough design that led to a wave of innovations.

A paragon of focused simplicity, the Lotus Eighteen was credited by John Surtees as providing him with the greatest advantage over rivals of any car he raced during his career.

always was a "small and light" man so that is really why we decided we would make a V8.'[1]

Working with Maurice Phillippe, Chapman superbly integrated the load-bearing DFV with his pencil-slim monocoque and proven suspension system to create the 49. It was a masterful synthesis of all his ideas on the effectiveness of a light racing car with minimal frontal area. The 49-Ford had a fairy-tale debut with its victory at Zandvoort in the third race of the 11-race 1967 season.

In retrospect it is surprising that Chapman made no objection when Ford told him it would release the DFV to other teams in 1968. The argument that Formula 1 racing would die if more people didn't have the engine was surely exaggerated in the extreme. Having been responsible for the engine's creation, Colin might well have felt at least entitled to the full exclusive season of its use which he was never granted, not to mention one more year.

We can safely take the 49 as the quintessence of the early Colin Chapman as designer of the complete racing car. In four seasons it won a dozen races, a success rate of 29 per cent. It was the last Formula 1 car of Jim Clark, who won five of the ten races he contested in the 49. Colin acknowledged that it was deliberately an evolutionary design, schemed as such to give more time to cope with the new engine's anticipated problems. It didn't speak for the Chapman who was prepared to take big risks in a go-for-broke approach to racing-car design. This attribute was much more evident in the hyper-radical 72, a car bursting with innovation. It was astonishing that such an adventurous car was made race-ready and race-winning so quickly.

Chapman's readiness to bet Team Lotus on a radical new idea was vividly illustrated by his support of the 'wing car' 78 and its successor the 79. This spoke to his unique position as both the conceptual designer and the businessman who wangled special funding for the project from John Player. But with the 80 and then the tragedy of the 88 Colin just as stunningly brought Team Lotus to its knees. By this time he was the big-picture concept man, sidestepping the tedious demands of detailed attention to the engineering of his cars. Always impatient, he left such mundane matters to others to whom he denied the close guidance he'd provided to his earlier colleagues.

Mario Andretti was an intimate observer of these final years. 'If you look historically at Lotus, it had tremendously high peaks but also the deepest valleys.

---

1 'There was also some influence by Ford,' said Duckworth, 'who had always been involved with V8s for a very long time.' This was more true of Ford in America than Ford in Britain, whose biggest engine was a V6. But it was a nice argument for Walter Hayes to use with his bosses in America.

I think it goes back to Colin being the moody genius he was. He would create something and it was good, it was different, a new toy. Then he'd either get bored or just go way over and reach for the stars on his next project. But that was him. That's what made him great. That's what made him special. And that's why he created so many champions.'

'There would be moments of rage' when a new idea failed to mature, said colleague Robin Read, 'but soon he would bounce back and achieve a miracle or two to show us all that he was master of his destiny. The personal charm, the self-confidence and willingness to break rules in the pursuit of his goals had made him a powerful force. Chapman's daring and irreverent approach to established patterns of design showed the way ahead and more than any other single influence shaped the course of modern high-performance car design.'

'Colin was extremely sharp, clever and quick-witted and very charismatic,' said Charles Bulmer, 'but not a really great engineer or designer. He had a few principles which he pursued to great effect, such as light weight and making one component serve more than one purpose, but he never had a really close grasp of fundamental principles. Perhaps he might have had if he had more time to learn. But in his hectic and unscrupulous life it was quicker to rely on other people to whom he gave minimum credit.'

Chapman's inventiveness and the determination with which he exploited his ideas were evident early in his career. After visiting Tottenham Lane in 1955, John Lello 'came away with a feeling of elation that there were still people in this world like Colin Chapman and his collaborators who, despite many difficulties and limited means, have set their sights on the stars and face the future with undaunted enthusiasm.'

In 1955 racer and engineer Russ Kelly road-tested a Lotus Mark IX for *Sports Cars Illustrated*. 'The more time I spent with this,' he said, 'the more I wondered if Colin Chapman, its designer, might not have several heads, all of them busily solving automobile racing problems. The rapid development of this car, its obvious soundness on all engineering points and its general execution would lead one to believe that it was conceived in a large research laboratory staffed by many British boffins. Research on Chapman established that he is a mechanical engineer and has one head, an excellent little factory and a lot of enthusiasm.'

'Chapman began his career as a special builder,' said Robin Read. 'He was certainly still that – albeit at a very elevated level – in 1962. He possessed immense self-confidence rooted in the heady years of the mid-1950s when Lotus carried all before it in small-capacity sports-car racing. So strong was Chapman's innate confidence that even the disastrous experience of the early formula racing cars, the bitter disappointment of the Seventeen and the relentless discouragement of the Elite

Qualifying as an 'all-Chapman' road car the Esprit, with its Lotus-brewed engine, exemplified its creator's dedication to lightness, functionality and agility.

By creating an engine with Cosworth's Keith Duckworth – here chatting with Chris Amon – Chapman could count on a power unit that was sympathetic to his needs.

development programme could not permanently undermine his belief in his own talent and ultimate enduring success.'

Colin Chapman shook off these setbacks to apply himself to the unique challenge of the 1½-litre Formula 1 with sensational success. His experience with the Eleven and the demands of racing cars with small

Not a scintilla bigger than it needed to be, the Lotus 49-Ford exploited the lightness and economy of its Cosworth-built V8 to set new standards in Formula 1.

engines prepared him and his team perfectly to exploit the opportunity these new rules offered. 'Over-praise in the end is said to be the most damaging kind of praise,' wrote Louis Stanley, 'but I will risk it regarding Chapman's achievements in 1963. Clark was only able to surpass the feats of Ascari and Fangio through the engineering skill and ingenuity of Chapman.

'Only a few years ago,' Stanley went on, 'the Lotus chief was dogged by the bogey of unreliability. Nothing went right. Grand Prix racing became an infinite game of poker in which he held only a pair of knaves, expanded by bluff into a full house. Those days are long past. Last year Chapman stood out as the most fertile designing brain in the sport…a crystallised phenomenon of engineering brilliance.'

'I think there are ten solutions to every problem,' Chapman explained, 'and you should never be satisfied with the first one. You work them all out, then find one that has particular merit in terms of simplicity, elegance, cost, refinement. When you've wrung it to death and can say, "That's the essence" – then you build it.' This mantra served the engineer well through much of his career. Towards the end of his life he sought to apply it to pleasure boats and microlight aircraft, in the latter case with exemplary elegance.

Many of those solutions weren't Chapman's to begin with. The preceding chapters illustrate his magpie instincts, his soaking up of knowledge and ideas in any field that interested him. Unlike most people in motor racing, who are inherently conservative and narrowly focused on the sport, Colin Chapman saw the advantage of technology transfer from other disciplines. Reading widely, open to new experiences and ideas, he cherry-picked advances in designs, materials and applications that he could use in his designs.

Not only as a magpie for ideas but also as a chameleon to his people, Colin Chapman knew how to motivate those around him. 'Chapman really was a chameleon figure,' said Mike Warner, 'because he was in lots of ways all things to all people. He was the team leader in Team Lotus, very much so, hands on working all through the night, a brilliant designer and a brilliant innovator. He just got involved in everything.'

'He has the rare ability to inspire every man in his team from the drawing office through every stage until the Lotus takes the chequered flag,' wrote Louis Stanley in 1968. 'It is a priceless quality that differentiates him from his rivals. In that sense Colin Chapman is on his own.'

Stanley's assessment may not have been entirely fair. Bruce McLaren was another team leader who earned the undying loyalty of his colleagues by his modest yet

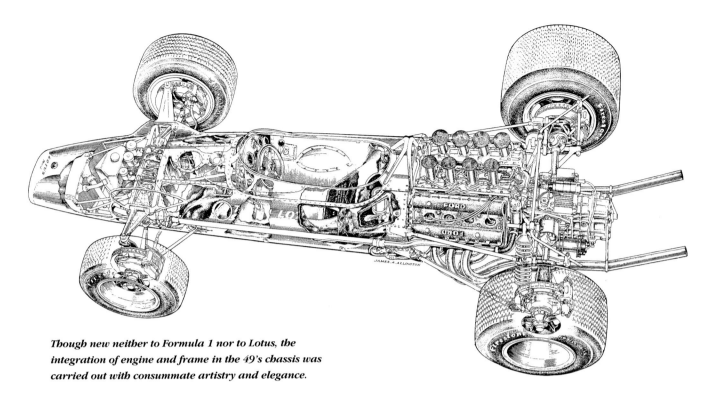

Though new neither to Formula 1 nor to Lotus, the integration of engine and frame in the 49's chassis was carried out with consummate artistry and elegance.

inspiring demeanour. Enzo Ferrari couldn't have achieved so much without deserving the fidelity of his key employees. Ken Tyrrell could always gather a strong team to build and race his cars, as could Frank Williams. Among them, however, Chapman stood out for his chameleon-like ability to present to each person the demeanour and argument that would inspire them to help him achieve his goals.

'He was tremendously industrious,' wrote Leonard Setright, 'prepared to work all the hours that God sends; he had an exceptionally strong sense of the rightness of design, which he sought with a passionate logic, scorning the shabby compromises of other engineers and designers in the industry; as a shrewd businessman, wholly committed to the deadly serious pursuit of his own goals, he was prepared almost remorselessly to exploit every opportunity available to him, either material or human, driving other people as hard as he drove himself.' The result was a ruthlessness of which even his most faithful co-workers were well aware.

In the words of former colleague Graham Arnold, Chapman was 'an incredible bloke who could do *anything* better than the next man. If he'd been in charge of the Royal Shakespeare Company, within a year he'd have produced the definitive *Macbeth*, the most controversial *Macbeth* or even the most controversially definitive *Macbeth*. Colin, who loved bending rules, was the most innovative engineer since Brunel. Concorde would have been *far* better if he'd been in charge of the design team. But deep down he was a motor trader, so that enormous genius was totally wasted.'

Apart from their impact on his design and engineering decisions, issues surrounding Colin Chapman's behaviour in business are beyond the scope of this book. Nevertheless it must be said that his ruthlessness, bordering on arrogance, about rules that he felt applied more to others than to himself, sometimes spilled over into actions that were ultimately neither in his own best interests or those of others.

'I quite liked the man,' recalled Stirling Moss. 'I wouldn't say we were particularly close because Colin wasn't the sort of person that one would normally get close to. But it is very difficult to look down a corkscrew straight – he had devious ways. If I were going to do something with Colin I would write and confirm it. There are people like Bernie Ecclestone and John Webb who were very tough, difficult people. If they said something on the phone I would take it as fixed but with Colin I don't think I would have done that. He could be quite devious – he could think round ahead of you.'

Sales colleague Robin Read was unsparing in his assessment of his former chief's approach to production cars. 'Chapman was not interested to create a lasting memorial to his talent by the design and production of durable works of art,' wrote Read. 'The "bomb-site" salesman lurking within propelled him to ever-newer, equally unenduring cars which have spawned an industry providing replacement parts to recreate the flimsy or rusted structures that issued from the Lotus Works. Close examination of the survivors from the Fifties and early Sixties confirms that Chapman designed and created for the moment rather than for all time.'

In the Lotus 49's debut season of 1967 the powerhouse duo of Jim Clark and Graham Hill easily led from pole in every race entered but suffered frequent retirements.

To the frustration of those involved, the interest of *Le Patron* in his road cars fluctuated wildly. That he saw them in the beginning as a way to finance his racing is undeniable. With this in mind he moved quickly from the unprofitable Elite to the profitable Europa and Elan. That Lotus was a maker of road cars as well as successful racers gave both the company and its chief the greater gravitas that was appealing to sources of funding such as the Stock Market and American Express.

By the end of the 1970s, however, the soaring cost of racing reduced the annual contribution of Lotus Cars to a drop in the bucket. Writing of this period, Tony Rudd referred to Chapman's 'waning interest in the car company. I know that the various construction regulations infuriated him. Half the cost of developing a new car went into making it meet bureaucratic regulations, not in making it faster or more economical. EEC regulations were the last straw.'

With his Europa and Elan Chapman set the pattern for all his road cars. These were sports cars of high dynamic standards tested and produced with a certain contempt for the end customer. 'The package that results,' opined Leonard Setright, 'may not appeal to those conditioned to judge a car by the shut of the door, the depth of the upholstery or the weight of the paint; but to those whose sensual and cerebral appreciations of motoring offer more relevant criteria, the Lotus is as much a machine for driving as a house by Le Corbusier is a machine for living.'

Chapman's passion for lightness, the diminution of dead weight, was at the heart of some of the shortcomings of his road cars. Their lightness was at one and the same time the source of their outrageous performance, for their engine size, and their ephemeral existences. This mattered little in a racing car, which traditionally is built to disintegrate after it crosses the finish line – in the lead. It was a less acceptable attribute in a road car.

Of all Colin Chapman's imperatives in the design of automobiles his ruthlessness showed most strikingly in his antipathy for weight. Lightness was paramount; all other parameters were secondary. In this there is great merit. Chapman's grounding in the design and driving of small-engined competition cars taught him that every aspect of a car's performance benefits from lightness.

In the 3-litre Formula 1, thought to favour 12-cylinder engines, the Lotus 49's V8 seemed inadequate. A Chapman-Duckworth inspiration, it was destined for greatness.

That so many of his contemporaries failed to grasp the importance of this – judging by their creations – boggles the mind. But it was his speed secret to the last.

Crucially, however, Chapman's loathing of dead weight undermined some of his racing endeavours. Although a master of structural visualisation, he failed in such cases as the Twelve and 79 – bookending his single-seater career – to ensure that cars were strong enough. He would get arguments from his designers. 'Most of the time I was at Lotus,' said Len Terry, 'Chapman and I worked well together. We had our differences, often on the weight/strength theme, but usually we found a successful compromise.' Usually – but not always, as in the case of the 30, from which Terry kept a barge-pole distance after judging it unlikely to succeed.

Among Colin Chapman's many projects one was conspicuous for its apparent disregard of the importance of lightness. This was the Grand Prix 63. Chapman promised a design from scratch for four-wheel drive, not a rear-drive car warmed over. He and Maurice Phillippe produced such a car, but one that astonished by failing to exploit the DFV's stress-bearing capability to reduce weight. The only way to ascertain the inherent advantages of four-wheel drive was to build a car as close in weight as possible to its rear-drive counterpart.[2] This they materially failed to achieve.

---

2   Another way to carry out an assessment would be to ballast the two-wheel-drive car to match the weight of its four-wheel-drive sister. There's no indication that this was ever done.

Exemplified by the Lotus 25 driven by Pedro Rodriguez at Silverstone in 1965, Colin Chapman's ability to reduce to the max was tailor-made for the 1½-litre Formula 1.

Chapman's parsimony with weight often fatally impaired his racing through his insistence on fuel tanks filled to the bare minimum. This led to game-playing among the designer, his mechanics and his drivers that ultimately frustrated all of them and wasted crucial preparation time and energy. He was right; less weight translated directly into faster lap times. But it helped little if a driver failed to finish or had to make an unplanned pit stop.

Some of his drivers were frustrated by Colin Chapman in other ways. Those of the first rank were able to form close relationships with the Guv'nor. If a driver proved responsive to the Chapman tuition, he was welcomed into the inner circle of racing know-how accumulated at first hand by a man who was no mean racer himself. Jim Clark, Graham Hill, Emerson Fittipaldi, Mario Andretti and Nigel Mansell were those on the most intimate terms with the Master. All proved through their world championships the merit that Chapman discerned in them.

Those not in the anointed echelon were able enough – or they wouldn't be on the team – but seldom enjoyed full access to Chapman's advice and guidance. He judged it more productive to concentrate his attention on the driver he saw as the most able, a ruthlessly

Thanks to a team that included such talented and experienced designers as Maurice Phillippe, Colin Chapman was able to realise advanced racing cars like 1970's 72.

The enthusiastic Chapman, urging on Jim Clark's comeback drive in the 1967 Italian Grand Prix, knew exactly how best to motivate every man on his team.

rational approach to racing success. Only rarely did he have driver pairings with strength in depth such as Clark/Surtees, Clark/Hill, Fittipaldi/Peterson and Andretti/Peterson. These inevitably led to tensions that were sometimes unproductive.

Although Chapman was demonstrably shy in many of his driver contacts, he went down in history as a first-class spotter of prime talent. In this he was materially aided by the feeder categories in which his cars competed in the days of Formula Junior and Formula 2 on the way to Formula 1. For drivers coming up through these classes a Lotus was often the car to have, giving Chapman an intimate look at their abilities. Later the sheer lustre of Lotus success was enough to attract talent. But when Team Lotus fortunes declined, so did the class of drivers it attracted. That Andretti and Chapman formed an alliance at the low point of their F1 fortunes was astonishing. That it led to spectacular success was undeniable.

Andretti was aboard in two eras when overreaching by an ambitious Colin Chapman brought technologies to a sudden conclusion. The first was his use of high-mounted wings. He didn't introduce them but he was quick to exploit their most effective form. The towering wings were accepted by racing's ruling body until excessively large airfoils on the Lotus 49 collapsed, causing serious crashes that brought that technology to an immediate halt. Though not the only team to have structural troubles with its wings, Lotus was by far the worst offender.

Then with his 80 in 1979 Chapman brought his own revolution, that of the venturi-generated downforce, to a screeching halt. Both Lotus and Arrows thought it possible to take a further step towards a wingless car with complete underbody contouring; neither was successful. While other teams capitalised on the new know-how by building structurally robust Lotus 79s, Chapman raced down the blind alley of the 88. Outlet though it was for his creativity, the 'twin-chassis' concept had flaws that were technical as well as legal. Its failure slammed doors shut on Chapman's commitment to Formula 1 racing.

'He has had his failures,' said colleague Len Terry, 'as have all of us, but his successful cars have been far more numerous. I think that on several occasions the failures have been due to trying too hard to prove a particular point.' He was referring clearly to such cars as the 30, hamstrung by its creation as part of a multi-model programme, and both the 80 and the 88, brave conceptions which failed because they were based on ideas that were insufficiently understood at the time.

Among Chapman's engineering disciplines one of the most perplexing is his attitude to aerodynamics. He

approached this mysterious science in fits and starts. In the early years he accepted Frank Costin as a member of his de Havilland team and adopted his approach of reduced form drag at the expense of frontal area. Then he reverted to his fundamental affection for minimal frontal area, first with the Twelve and later with the ultra-reclined seating of his cars for the 1½-litre Formula 1. Grafted on to cars designed to this criterion were the high rear wings of 1968 and '69, arrived at largely by trial and error.

In spite of having wind-tunnel-tested his cars for Indianapolis, Colin Chapman was surprised when instrumentation on one of them showed aerodynamic lift under all conditions. This led to his famous and much-copied 'wedge' designs, which were effective in cancelling lift but at the price of high drag. The 72's successors lost their way aerodynamically, only to be rescued by the 'wing car' concept advanced by wind-tunnel testing that had been paid for by arch-rival BRM. Now under the tunnel's spell, Chapman committed major resources to the intractable 80. Aerodynamics, which he had treated more as a dilettante than with dedication, were ultimately his downfall.

Tweaking of their aerodynamics figured in the long years of success of both the 49 and 72. The stories of these cars, not to mention the evolution of the 25 and 29, give the lie to the oft-heard criticism of Chapman that he was uninterested in the nitty-gritty of development, preferring instead the big leap forward. To be sure, some of this development was necessary

On 15 August 1982 Elio de Angelis beat Keke Rosberg by five hundredths of a second on the Österreichring to give Chapman his final Formula 1 victory.[1]

because the next big leap wasn't ready on time. But he often proved that he could graft the detail of a racing car as effectively as the next man. Only in his later years, about which many have testified, was Colin in the grip of an innovative compulsion that seemed unstoppable.

A legacy of Colin Chapman was an analytical approach to racing-car design that had hitherto been rare in Britain. 'He was the first to adopt what I call the semi-scientific approach,' said Len Terry, 'the drawing board first and then the workshop. In this respect he could be said to have founded a new school of philosophy, since the majority of later designers, having adopted the same approach, can be regarded as Chapman's disciples.' Chapman did his level best to understand the forces working on a racing car and design his Lotuses accordingly. If, as Charles Bulmer said, 'he never had a really close grasp of fundamental principles,' he came closer to grasping them than his rivals, which was all he needed to do to prevail over them.

Another lasting legacy was Colin Chapman's transformation of racing in Formula 1, sports cars and Indianapolis. In Grand Prix racing such innovations as

---

1   This was also the 150th victory for the Ford-Cosworth DFV. To celebrate this the author arranged for Keith Duckworth to have 'DFV 150' for the registration of his Ford Granada. Typically he spurned it.

At the end of the 1982 season Chapman posed at Ketteringham Hall with the 91 that took victory in Austria. He was looking forward to Renault turbo power in 1983.

the monocoque frame, side-mounted radiators and venturi downforce generation have prevailed. None was his exclusive creation but his successful implementation carried the day for all of them. The deep venturis of Chapman's day are gone but they linger at the extreme rear of Formula 1 cars to powerful effect.

In sports cars the Chapman contribution was less profound but still important. With his Nineteen and 23 he created a new idiom that inspired many. When Jim Hall and Hap Sharp built their first mid-engined Chaparrals they used Lotus wheels and front and rear suspensions in their entirety, introducing them to the New World. With the failure of his 30 and its 40 successor, however, Colin Chapman withdrew from the world of big sports-racers. Thus we were denied the innovative solutions he might have used under the liberal rules of the Group 7 category used for Can-Am racing.

At Indianapolis, Chapman's impact was profound. Others had raced mid-engined cars before, Brabham a Cooper in 1961 and Gurney a Mickey Thompson creation in 1962.[3] Brabham waited until 1964 to return

with an Offy-powered car while Thompson failed to follow up with a natural evolution, preferring a Chapman-like radical reach. Thus it was left to Chapman, with convincingly fast cars that finally won in their third attempt, to show incontrovertibly the advantage of the mid-engined 'funny car'. His later introduction of the 'wedge' configuration at Indy had its impact as well.

Not since Ernest Henri's 16-valve twin-cam Peugeot fours won both at Indy and in major road races before World War I had the work of a single designer had such a broad influence on the designs of racing cars the world over. This was Colin Chapman's phenomenal achievement, unmatched since. Does this qualify him to be considered a genius? A good case can be made that it does.

Some argue to the contrary. 'Chapman is not a genius except in his infinite capacity for taking pains,' said Leonard Setright. 'He is not really an artist, although there is a mathematical beauty in many of his structures; nor is he a tyrant, though he has left a wake of broken and despairing men. History has proved him to be one of the most intelligent, purposeful and creative designers of high-performance cars, one whose work has been emulated more than that of almost any other.'

Tony Rudd had a similar view. 'Several people have suggested he was a genius,' wrote Rudd, 'but I do not think he ever set out to be. He always told me not to invent anything new and, whatever I did, do not try to break the laws of physics. I believe a genius is someone who manages

---

3   The first mid-engined car to qualify and race at the fabled Speedway was Harry Miller's Gulf-sponsored four-wheel-drive creation of 1939. It retired that year. Two such cars qualified in 1941, one destroyed in a pre-race garage fire and the other retiring. One of the cars qualified to compete in 1946 and 1947, retiring both times. In 1949 the mid-Offy-engined Rounds Rocket appeared but didn't qualify, a fate it duplicated in its last appearance in 1950.

to do that and get away with it. I am not quite convinced he was a genius – within my definition – but he was most certainly one of the most brilliant engineers the racing and motor-car industry has ever known.'

Rudd's remark about breaking the laws of physics recalls the achievements in another sphere of Frank Lloyd Wright, acknowledged a genius as an architect. In his uses of materials and conceptions of structures Wright pushed the state of the art far more than his contemporaries, often to the despair of his clients. Wright once said that if a building didn't leak, its design wasn't pushing the envelope. His customers remained loyal to him, however, beguiled by the sheer beauty of his buildings.

'It was in Wright's nature,' said his biographer Brendan Gill, 'to invent emergencies when they failed to develop of their own accord. Wright's hypnotic powers were invariably heightened by adversity.' 'He was a hustler,' said architectural critic Paul Goldberger of Wright. 'He was a wild self-promoter, he exaggerated his life story, inventing all kinds of details – but he was no less an artistic genius for having done that.' Here were strong echoes of many comments about Colin Chapman.

'A famous mathematician, Mark Kae, once divided geniuses into two classes,' wrote Gino Segré. 'He said there are the ordinary ones whose achievements might be emulated by intelligent people through enormous hard work and a good dose of luck. Then come the magicians, whose inventions are so astounding, so counter to all the intuitions of their colleagues, that it is hard to see how any human being could have imagined them.'

Colin Chapman neatly bridged these two definitions. He worked harder than others with the enthusiastic support of his family, friends and colleagues. He had the luck to be born into an era for motor sports that desperately needed his brand of innovation and inspiration, equipped with the right tools to win under the Grand Prix rules that applied when he was in his early prime. And he astonished his rivals and the world time and time again with brilliant designs that made giant leaps in the state of the art. That adds up to genius by anyone's standards.

Though genial when it suited him, Colin Chapman could be ruthless with men and machinery. This helped him transform the shape of racing cars the world over.

BIBLIOGRAPHY

Barker, Ronald and Harding, Anthony, *Automobile Design: Great Designers and Their Work*, Colin Chapman chapter by Philip Turner, Robert Bentley, Cambridge, 1970.

Blunsden, John, *The Power to Win*, Motor Racing Publications, London, 1983.

Bryant, Peter, *Can-Am Challenger*, David Bull Publishing, Phoenix, 2007.

Clark, Jim, *Jim Clark at the Wheel*, Arthur Barker, London, 1964.

Costin, Michael and Phipps, David, *Racing and Sports Car Chassis Design*, Robert Bentley, Cambridge, 1961.

Crombac, Gerard 'Jabby', *Colin Chapman – The Man and His Cars*, Patrick Stephens, Wellingborough, 1986.

_____, *Turbine Grand Prix*, Automobilia, Milan, 1989.

Ferguson, Andrew, *Team Lotus – The Indianapolis Years*, Patrick Stephens, Sparkford, 1994.

Fittipaldi, Emerson with Hayward, Elizabeth, *Flying on the Ground*, William Kimber, London, 1973.

Gavin, Bill, *The Jim Clark Story*, Leslie Frewin, London, 1967.

Gauld, Graham, *From the Fells to Ferrari – The Official Biography of Cliff Allison*, Veloce Publishing, Dorchester, 2008.

Hammill, Des, *Coventry Climax Racing Engines*, Veloce Publishing, Dorchester, 2004.

Haskell, Hugh, *Colin Chapman – Lotus Engineering*, Osprey Automotive, London, 1993.

Hassan, Walter with Robson, Graham, *Climax in Coventry*, Motor Racing Publications, Croydon, 1975.

Hayes, Walter et al, *Lotus Ford – The Story of a Partnership*, Ford of Britain, Dagenham, 1963.

Henry, Alan, *The 4-Wheel Drives – Racing's Formula for Failure?* Macmillan, London, 1975.

Herrmann, Hans with Völker, Bernhard, *Ein Leben Für den Rennsport*, Motorbuch Verlag, Stuttgart, 1998.

Hill, Graham, *Life at the Limit*, William Kimber, London, 1969.

Ireland, Innes, *All Arms and Elbows*, Pelham Books, London, 1967.

Jenkinson, Denis and Posthumus, Cyril, *Vanwall – The story of Tony Vandervell and his racing cars*, Patrick Stephens, Cambridge, 1975.

Lawrence, Mike, *Colin Chapman – Wayward Genius*, Breedon Books, Derby, 2002.

Levine, Leo, *Ford: The Dust and the Glory – A Racing History*, Macmillan, New York, 1968.

Ludvigsen, Karl, *Dan Gurney – The Ultimate Racer*, Haynes Publishing, Sparkford, 2000.

_____, *Emerson Fittipaldi – Heart of a Racer*, Haynes Publishing, Sparkford, 2002.

Mansell, Nigel OBE with Allen, James, *Nigel Mansell – My Autobiography*, CollinsWillow, London, 1995.

Morgan, David, *Seven Fifty Motor Club*, Haynes Publishing, Sparkford, 2009.

Moss, Stirling with Nye, Doug, *Stirling Moss – My Cars, My Career*, Patrick Stephens, Wellingborough, 1987.

Nye, Doug, *BRM – The Saga of British Racing Motors, Volume 1*, Motor Racing Publications, Croydon, 1994.

_____, *The Autocourse History of the Grand Prix Car – 1945-65*, Hazleton, Richmond, 1993.

_____, *The Story of Lotus – 1961-1971: Growth of a Legend*, Motor Racing Publications, London, 1972.

_____, *Theme Lotus*, Motor Racing Publications, London, 1978.

O'Hara, Sarah, *Moonraker & JCL Marine Ltd – Colin Chapman's Boat Industry*, Nighthawk Publishing, Halesworth, 2005.

Oliver, Michael, *Lotus 49 – The Story of a Legend*, Veloce Publishing, Dorchester, 1999.

_____, *Lotus 72 – Formula One Icon*, Coterie Press, London, 2003.

Ortenburger, Dennis, *Flying on Four Wheels – Frank Costin and his car designs*, Patrick Stephens, Wellingborough, 1986.

_____, *The Original Lotus Elite – Racing Car For the Road*, The Newport Press, Newport Beach, 1977.

Pitt, Colin, *The Lotus Book – Type 1 to 72*, CP Press, Hockley, 2005.

Pritchard, Anthony, *Lotus – All the Cars*, Aston Publications, Bourne End, 1992.

_____, *Lotus – The Competition Cars*, Haynes Publishing, Sparkford, 2006.

Read, Robin, *Colin Chapman's Lotus*, GT Foulis, Sparkford, 1989.

Robson, Graham, *Cosworth – The Search for Power*, Patrick Stephens, Wellingborough, 1990.

Roebuck, Nigel with Andretti, Mario, *Mario Andretti World Champion*, Hamlyn, London, 1979.

Ross, Peter, *Lotus – The Early Years*, Coterie Press, Luton, 2004.

Rudd, Tony, *It Was Fun! – My fifty years of high performance*, Patrick Stephens, Sparkford, 1993.

Salvadori, Roy and Pritchard, Anthony, *Roy Salvadori – Racing Driver*, Patrick Stephens, Wellingborough, 1985.

Setright, L. J. K., *The Designers – Great automobiles and the men who made them*, Follett Publishing, Chicago, 1976.

Sheldon, Paul with Rabagliati, Duncan, *A Record of Grand Prix and Voiturette Racing*, Volume 5 1950-1953, Volume 6 1954-1959, Volume 7 1960-1964 and Volume 8 1965-1969, St Leonards, Bradford, 1988, 1987, 1991 and 1994.

Simon, Ted, *Grand Prix Year*, Coward, McCann and Geoghegan, New York, 1972.

Small, Steve, *Grand Prix Who's Who*, 3rd Edition, Travel Publishing, Reading, 2000.

Smith, Ian H., *The Story of Lotus – 1947-1960 Birth of a Legend*, Motor Racing Publications, London, 1972.

Stanley, Louis, *Grand Prix – The Legendary Years*, Queen Anne Press, Harpenden, 1994.

Surtees, John with Henry, Alan, *John Surtees – World Champion*, Hazleton, Richmond, 1991.

Terry, Len and Baker, Alan, *Racing Car Design and Development*, Robert Bentley, Cambridge, 1973.

Tipler, John, *Lotus 78 and 79 – The Ground-Effect Cars*, Crowood Press, Marlborough, 2003.

Walton, Jeremy, *Lotus Esprit – The Official Story*, Coterie Press, Luton, 2006.

Charles Nichol's drawing captures the dynamism of Colin Chapman

Wimpffen, János L., *Time and Two Seats – Five Decades of Long Distance Racing*, Motorsport Research Group, Redmond, 1999.

Wood, Jonathan, *Alec Issigonis – The Man Who Made the Mini*, Breedon Books, Derby, 2005.

Wright, Peter, *Formula 1 Technology*, Society of Automotive Engineers, Warrendale, 2001.

Many contemporary periodicals were consulted in the Ludvigsen Library during the research; where relevant they and the respective authors are referenced in the text. Of particular value to the work were, *The Autocar, Automobile Engineer, Automobile Quarterly, Automobil Revue* catalogue issues, *Autosport, BusinessF1, Car, Car and Driver, Cars Illustrated, Classic & Sportscar, Classic Cars, F1 Racing, Forza, Historic Lotus, Lotus, The Motor, Motor Racing, Motor Sport, Road & Track, Sporting Motorist, Sports Cars Illustrated, Vintage Motorsport* and *Vintage Racecar Journal*. The annuals *Autocourse* and *Automobile Year* have also been of value, as have websites including Atlas F1, Autosport and Forix.

INDEX

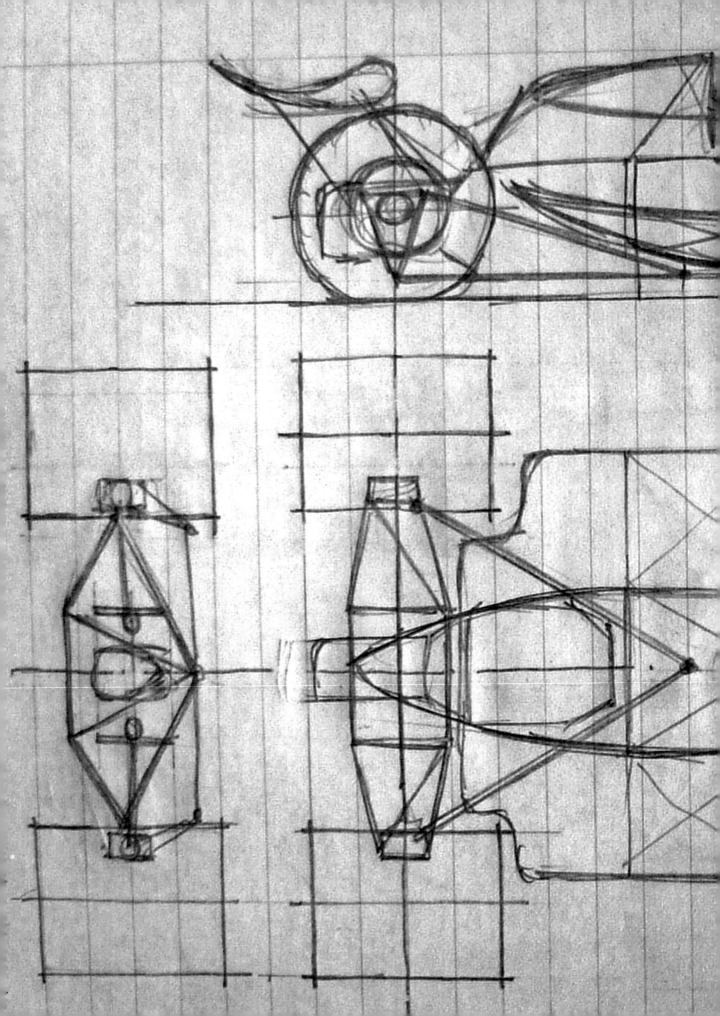